DIGITAL MEDIA DISTRIBUTION

CW00740830

CRITICAL CULTURAL COMMUNICATION

General Editors: Jonathan Gray, Aswin Punathambekar, Adrienne Shaw
Founding Editors: Sarah Banet-Weiser and Kent A. Ono

Digital Media Distribution

Portals, Platforms, Pipelines

Edited by
Paul McDonald,
Courtney Brannon Donoghue, *and*
Timothy Havens

NEW YORK UNIVERSITY PRESS
New York

NEW YORK UNIVERSITY PRESS
New York
www.nyupress.org

© 2021 by New York University
All rights reserved

References to Internet websites (URLs) were accurate at the time of writing. Neither the author nor New York University Press is responsible for URLs that may have expired or changed since the manuscript was prepared.

Library of Congress Cataloging-in-Publication Data
Names: McDonald, Paul, 1963–   editor. | Brannon Donoghue, Courtney, editor. | Havens, Timothy, editor.
Title: Digital media distribution : portals, platforms, pipelines / edited by Paul McDonald, Courtney Brannon Donoghue and Timothy Havens.
Description: New York : New York University Press, [2021] | Series: Critical cultural communication | Includes bibliographical references and index.
Identifiers: LCCN 2021001824 | ISBN 9781479806775 (hardback) | ISBN 9781479806782 (paperback) | ISBN 9781479806805 (ebook) | ISBN 9781479806812 (ebook other)
Subjects: LCSH: Mass media—Management. | Digital media—Management. | Multimedia systems—Management. | Information resources management.
Classification: LCC P96.M34 D54 2021 | DDC 302.23/068—dc23
LC record available at https://lccn.loc.gov/2021001824

New York University Press books are printed on acid-free paper, and their binding materials are chosen for strength and durability. We strive to use environmentally responsible suppliers and materials to the greatest extent possible in publishing our books.

Manufactured in the United States of America

10 9 8 7 6 5 4 3 2 1

Also available as an ebook

CONTENTS

FIGURES

Introduction

Media Distribution Today

COURTNEY BRANNON DONOGHUE, TIMOTHY HAVENS, AND
PAUL MCDONALD

Media distribution in the digital era is undergoing changes so profound that they can be difficult to trace, both empirically and theoretically. Those of us who study media distribution have long known that distribution is much more than a purely functional practice—the middle ground between the far more interesting practices of media "production" and "consumption." Rather, distribution acts as a shaping force in the industrialized practices of cultural dissemination. Distribution does more than just "move," "relay," or "transmit" content. For critical studies of media industries, distribution holds dual significance, inviting interrogation of the systemized processes by which the media industries supply cultural content between parties (i.e., how are media distributed?), but also the time and space over which that content is spread and made available (i.e., when, where, and to whom are media distributed?). By managing "the movement of media through time and space" (Lobato 2007, 114), distribution holds importance for how it "organizes information in space and time, accelerating or delaying its delivery" (Cubitt 2005, 194), thereby "acting as a gatekeeper, separating producers from potential audiences" (Crisp 2015, 3), and so "determining what we as audiences get to see" (Knight and Thomas 2008, 354). Distribution is never a transparent or frictionless task; it enacts mediation, determining what forms of culture are made available or withheld.

The purpose of the book is to capture the ongoing moment of digital disruption, reevaluation, and transition across the various sectors of the media industries, from book publishing to streaming music. We have brought together experts from around the world and across the media industries to analyze *both* continuities and changes between analog and digital methods of media distribution. What practices of distribution have changed in each industry, and which have remained the same? What are the consequences of these changes for media workers, texts, consumers, and researchers? These are the fundamental questions with which each of the chapters in the anthology wrestles.

Digitization, Digitalization, and "Disruption"

Speaking of *digital* media distribution immediately grants technology a privileged place in the discussion. Frequently, attention to the transformative impacts of digital technologies in the media industries is embedded in the discourse of "digital disruption," a phrase that positions the digital as a central force for sweeping changes in industry structures and operations. Indeed, this collection is exactly predicated on assessing how implementation of digital technologies facilitates numerous changes in the distributive practices of the book publishing, recorded music, film, television, social media, and electronic games industries.

Signs of change have materialized in several ways:

- structural reorganization of media distribution chains (e.g., satellite relay of films and events to cinemas; bypassing broadcast networks to deliver television programming via over-the-top services)
- transformations in the commodity forms of media products (e.g., e-books) or services (e.g., aggregating and delivering music, film, television, and games through portals and platforms)
- introduction of new business models (e.g., subscriber, transactional, premium, advertising-supported, and free forms of video-on-demand) and service features (e.g., algorithmically driven recommendations)
- reconfiguring the landscape of media with new categories of corporate entities, most significantly through the closer interactions formed between media, communication, and computer technology (e.g., content aggregators, content delivery networks)
- emergent categories of media labor (e.g., community managers, interactive title producers), particularly as digital distribution necessitates media work integrating roles hitherto confined to the tech sector (e.g., analytics engineers, database administrators)

- modernizing regulatory and legal instruments to meet the new digital environment (e.g., including "safe harbor" provisions in intellectual property laws to protect internet service providers from liability for copyright infringements committed by their users)
- generating new sources of value (e.g., capturing and commercializing user data, or re-versioning archival content for additional digital formats)

These changes are so multiple and now established that the impacts of digitization on media distribution are unavoidable. At the same time, however, if we are to evade reductive technological determinist accounts, it is necessary to see separations between the *digitization* of media (i.e., the technological effect of converting continuous analog information into discrete units of digital data represented in the form of numerical values) and the *digitalization* of the media industries (i.e., the organizational effect of restructuring business practices through the application of digital technologies and data). Making a cognitive break between digitization and digitalization offers a first step toward productively avoiding conclusions that technological change *causes* industry change. This separation is crucial for critical studies of media industries, as it ensures industry processes and actions become viewed in their own terms rather than as just the epiphenomenal aftereffects of technological innovation. Digitalization of media distribution therefore represents an instance where it becomes necessary to interrogate without simplifying the fundamental copresence of continuity and change in the media industries.

Conceptually, rather than causality, it is more helpful to think of digitization facilitating but never determining digitalization. Empirically, the history of digital media evidences multiple disconnections between technological and industrial change. Digitization of entertainment media products did not inexorably bring about the digitalization of distribution practices. CDs, DVDs, VCDs, and even the "born digital" market of console and computer games digitized the commodity form of entertainment storage media while preserving the distributive model of analog media, with multiple physical copies reproduced from a master version for storage in warehouses before transportation and eventual sale in brick-and-mortar retail outlets. Online, electronic commerce digitalized media retailing for a whole mix of physical print, audio, and video products that—as the enduring popularity of the book testifies—in many cases might remain in analog form. In the history of media distribution, commercialized music downloading and streaming therefore attains significance by employing digital data throughout arrangements for the storage, delivery, management, marketing, and payment of entertainment. With similar arrangements routinely evident in book, film, television, and games markets, media distribution has certainly seen a large-scale digital makeover. Still, to avoid universalizing accounts of technological and industrial change, claims for "disruption" must be contextualized. This collection therefore brings together contributors to provide a number of context-specific studies that cumulatively examine digital transformation of media distribution as a process variously negotiated between media industries and/or geocultural contexts. Contextualizing digital transformations in media distribution offers a way toward forming a nuanced assessment sensitive to the many differences, disjunctions, divergences, and asymmetries in how "digital disruption" has materialized in the distributive landscape.

Understanding Distribution

By enabling or inhibiting end user access to cultural forms, distribution contributes to the formation of mediated publics, communities, and identities. Limiting when and where media are available, distribution defines the temporal and spatial conditions in which media exist. "Releasing," "windowing," "scheduling," and "on-demand" strategies organize the times of media availability. Delaying or denying access to media acquires broad significance if the results are perceived as a measure of whether a community or nation is cut off from the vanguard of modernity, appearing instead to be culturally "backward" or "out-of-date" (Wilk 1994, 96). Equally, by mapping availability across multiple spatial levels—e.g., local, national, regional, and global markets, or domestic vs. public spheres—distribution creates, rather than simply occupies, space. In media industries, distribution encompasses flows of products or "content" but also of money and information (Cubitt 2005, 202). "Pushing" content while also administering financial "returns," distribution forms the conduit through which media industries capture economic value. Commercial success for distributors is contingent on knowing the markets they address, yet as messy social realities, media markets cannot be easily comprehended for they are fluid and constantly in flux. Part of the work of distribution therefore involves generating and disseminating representations of markets in the abstract and disciplined form of "data," whereby information in itself becomes an asset and source of value. As institutional and industrial discourse, this "market intelligence" imagines perceived or potential target audiences, impacting not only the distribution process but also what is produced and who is (and is not) considered a valuable audience. Functionally separating distribution from production or consumption is therefore misleading, ignoring how distribution operates as a site of cultural production. Distribution "makes" culture, for in commercial culture at least, generating and feeding back knowledge about what sells will shape creative decisions, while organizing the means of cultural dissemination, with one of the key effects being to facilitate the conditions in which consumption becomes possible.

In the business landscape of the media industries, distribution always represents a locus of corporate power. Control of distribution not only differentiates which companies will hold the most influence but also, more fundamentally, creates barriers to who gets to participate in an industry. To foreground the power of distribution, critical analysis may cite constellations of monopolistic or oligopolistic concentration represented in the form of collective market shares held by the leading distributors. While foregrounding concentrations of distributive power, such insights distort understanding of corporate workings if it is then presumed such influence is exercised as if it were a monolithic tool. Whatever power a distributor holds arises from the coordination of multiple subsidiary actions. For example, according to a 2017 account, located in Burbank, California, the home office handling film distribution in the North American domestic market for Hollywood studio Warner Bros. was divided into departments dealing with

- *distribution services*—ordering and distributing physical media to theaters
- *exhibitor services*—creating and providing promotional materials and information for theatrical exhibition
- *nontheatrical*—licensing films to airlines, cruise ships, and military bases
- *legal affairs*—handling all legal matters relating to film distribution,

including contracts, violations of business agreements, exhibitor complaints, and bankruptcy proceedings

- *financing*—accounting and financial reporting for corporate management
- *financial administration and operations*—collecting revenues and monitoring the financial status of customers
- *systems and sales operations*—producing distribution plans for films, monitoring sales negotiations, and billing for film rentals, while also monitoring
the release schedules and box office performance of competitors
- *administration*—coordinating business with branch offices in the United
States while undertaking other administrative tasks including negotiating contracts with vendors and checking box office receipts (adapted and
abbreviated from Fellman 2017, 372)

"Doing" media distribution actually necessitates a specialized division
of labor combining inputs from multiple categories of creative, craft,
administrative, and managerial workers.

Reading distribution power through the market power of monopolies or oligopolies suspends analysis at the level of a macro top-down
account, so that any single "distributor" is implicitly understood as a
unitary corporate entity. Such a view obscures the micro-level bottom-
up workings of media industries, particularly how the role of distributor actually comprises multiple instances of individual agency. Looking
beyond the horizon of the market to the many individuals involved in
making distribution happen is vital to seeing distribution as work, and
so as an arena of cultural labor. Acknowledging that many people contribute to the work of distribution, and so might be considered "distributors," does not divert from an interest in distribution as a site of control,
but rather encourages a more nuanced understanding of distributive
power attentive to the microsocial practices of individuals working in
teams or departments among whom control is devolved, divided, and
differentiated, that is to say, distributed. When conducting their work,
media distribution professionals undertake their own routines and rituals, guided by systems of meaning, belief, and value through which they
reflexively make sense of what they do, not only to themselves and their
colleagues but also to the readers, listeners, viewers, or players they seek
to reach. By routinely reflecting on their work through the talk, behaviors, and artifacts they generate, media professionals subject distribution

to "industrial self-theorizing" (Caldwell 2008). Insights obtained from interviews or statements made by media professionals may therefore be "conceptually rich, theoretically suggestive, and culturally revealing," yet critical media researchers commonly acknowledge these "are almost always offered from some perspective of self-interest, promotion and spin" (Caldwell 2008, 14). Maybe this note of caution rings doubly true when approaching a field like distribution where at least certain tasks are expressly dedicated to generating spin.

While academic commentators could at one point fairly note how media scholarship frequently overlooked distribution in favor of attention to the processes of production or the activities of audiences (e.g., Cubitt 2005; Knight and Thomas 2008; Miller, Schiwy, and Salván 2011), distribution has now achieved critical importance in the research agenda. In part, the previous paucity of distribution-focused research might be attributed to some understandable uncertainty over what actually represents distribution or how research in certain areas (e.g., marketing, infrastructures, archiving, piracy) held implications for the study of distribution but without being explicitly declared distribution research (Perren 2013, 171). More recently, however, a range of studies have foregrounded matters of media distribution (identifying just a few—Braun 2015; Crisp 2015; Cunningham and Craig 2019; Curtin, Holt, and Sanson 2014; Johnson 2019; Kerr 2017; Knight and Thomas 2011; Lobato 2012; Lotz 2017; Spilker 2017; and Tryon 2013). Given this growth, it could be tempting to propose "distribution studies" as an emergent subfield of enquiry, yet such labeling would limit the significance of this work. Rather than fence in such interventions, it seems more important that questions of distribution achieve broader currency, becoming integral to all studies of media. Therefore, this collection should be approached not only as a study of media distribution but also as presenting a range of insights to enable our thinking through what distribution means for the study of media.

For the reasons so far given, distribution is always important to the media industries, but one possible explanation for the recent growth in distribution-focused research is how the uses of digital technologies in distributive processes are catalyzing key transformations in the ways these industries are organizationally structured and practically operate and the means by which they generate value. Moreover, outside the media industries themselves, the means of media distribution have achieved a new level of visibility in public consciousness. Where previously the workings of distribution might have remained invisible or of very little concern to readers, listeners or viewers, or players, the popularization of various online platforms has increased the profile of distribution, intensifying awareness of how we get the media we do get. This is most obvious in how references to branded entities like Amazon, iQIYI, NetEase, Netflix, Spotify, Steam, Taobao, Tencent, TikTok, and YouTube routinely feature in everyday talk. Articulated in this new visibility is how participants in media distribution have become not only known but significant to people.

Conceptualizing Digital Transformations

As digitalization has transformed every aspect of contemporary media, including distribution, the question arises whether "distribution," as a concept, retains relevance for contemporary media corporations, particularly for born-digital platforms and portals that operate through informal sharing of media content and large-scale surveillance of consumers and content. The contributors to this book take various positions on the concept of distribution, with some arguing that distribution, as conventionally understood in legacy media industries, still works in largely the same way in a digital era, while others insist it is time to jettison the concept all together.

The editors of this volume have no particular investment in whether distribution continues as a concept in critical media studies, but we recognize it has been a productive metaphor for critical media scholars to think with, particularly in the twenty-first century. Whether we call it "circulation," "valuation," or "consumer intelligence," the practices of evaluating potential markets for media products, setting production and intellectual property rights costs, ensuring that targeted consumers know about and have access to the products, and evaluating their success are necessary for all contemporary media corporations, regardless of what we might call these practices. At the same time, the contributions to this volume make it clear that digitalization has revolutionized distribution practices, organizations, and technologies.

The studies presented here not only address a variety of media industries but also draw on a wide range of methodologies and theoretical questions. Those chapters exploring distribution in legacy media industries, not surprisingly, find quite a bit more continuity between the past and present, while those exploring born-digital industries find quite substantial breaks. Similarly, scholars who broadly come from a background in critical political economy tend to see a great deal of similarity in distribution over time, while scholars working from more sociological or humanistic approaches tend to emphasize fundamental disruptions in their analyses. Rather than understand the transitions taking place in the distribution industries as an inevitable march from older practice to newer ones, we prefer to see the old and the new as structured through a set of dialectical opposites, which remain consistently in tension and provide a good deal of the dynamism inherent in contemporary media distribution.

While each author in this volume draws their own conclusions about whether contemporary distribution practices in the industry under analysis fall on the "traditional" or "disruptive" side of the overall dialectic, we can draw out a number of comparative dialectics that run through all of the media distribution industries today. These include (1) entrepreneurialism versus corporate consolidation, (2) competition versus cooperation, (3) the dematerialization versus the rematerialization of the physical aspects of media distribution, and (4) the global versus the local. Because the dialectic between the local and the global is among the most obvious and theoretically explored of the four dialectics, we treat it in a separate section below.

Digital storage and delivery of media content are among the major revolutionizing forces in present-day media distribution and provide good sites for exploring how the dialectical tensions in distribution identified above play out in specific instances. Content delivery networks (CDN) offer an example of how digital distribution exhibits the dialectic tension between entrepreneurialism, or the multiplication of independent competitors, and ownership consolidation in the same niche industries. CDNs optimize the delivery of internet content by providing proxy servers close to consumers for popular web-based applications; they essentially provide a technical delivery layer between content providers and ISPs to help eliminate bottlenecks that can slow digital content. Until 2012, Netflix used third-party CDNs, in particular Akamai Technologies and Level 3 Communications, before developing its own CDN, Netflix Open Connect. Netflix Open Connect competes with Amazon CloudFront and Google Cloud CDN, but also with independent upstarts, including Akamai Technologies, Limelight Networks, and G-Core Labs in Luxembourg. Because CDNs sit between most popular internet sites and local ISPs, the CDN market is relatively unconsolidated.

The presence of conglomerates and independents in the CDN market is akin to the presence of both competition and cooperation among digital distributors, the second dialectical tension that characterizes contemporary distribution. If we turn our attention to the computer servers that store media content for delivery over streaming services, we find a high degree of cooperation among otherwise competitors. Take the example of Netflix and Amazon, two streaming giants that are competing among themselves to try to dominate many of the most lucrative streaming markets in the world. Despite their cutthroat competition in Latin America, Europe, South Asia, and East Asia, Netflix relies on Amazon Web Services (AWS) to provide cloud computing solutions for its content servers.

Finally, streaming media servers offer a good case study for the dialectical tension between dematerialization and rematerialization of the physical aspects of distribution. As Jeremy Wade Morris (2015, 14) notes regarding the dematerialization and rematerialization of digital music, "The digital music commodity is not as intangible as it is sometimes presented. . . . Users may not be flipping through album covers or poring over album liners, but they are still touching, looking and sorting. . . . Rather than dematerialization, digital music is a *rematerialized* commodity." Indeed, among the human sciences, media distribution studies has perhaps been the most materialist field of study and thus is best poised to contribute to the growing reexamination of materialism known as "new materialisms" (Bennett et al. 2010). Given the emphasis on the "dematerialization" of media objects in some circles (Burkart and Leijonhufvud 2019), it is important to recognize that the physical aspects of distribution rarely disappear but rather reappear in other places and other guises.

The dialectic of disappearance/reappearance undergirds the most immaterial of media distribution objects, streaming media products. While once embodied in things like films reels, videotape, and vinyl albums, today's film, television, and music are stored in immaterial digital files on computer servers. The servers themselves, however, are quite material. Google, for instance, runs more than 2.5 million servers around the world that store data, network with other computers, and run software to ensure the smooth operations of their services. These servers require a large amount of energy to run, especially to maintain proper temperature and humidity controls. Tech firms have sought to minimize their carbon footprints by powering the servers with solar energy and locating them in cold climates, such as the Facebook server farm in Luleå in northern Sweden, which threatens the indigenous Sami practices of reindeer husbandry (Bickford, Krans, and Bickford 2016).

As stated, the dialectics of entrepreneurialism versus corporate consolidation, competition versus cooperation, dematerialization versus rematerialization and global versus local are not the product of an incomplete transition from analog to digital media distribution. Instead, we view these tensions as more permanent features of a digital distribution ecology, where some of the basic realities of distribution remain the same, while other dimensions are transformed by digitalization.

Always Global: A Comparative Approach

The complex interplay between local and global forces emerges as a significant dialectic alongside digitalization. Recent media studies debates increasingly work to locate and identify the stark tension between utopian promises and detrimental impacts against the rapidly changing digital distribution landscape. Optimistic projection from some industry circles and scholarly conversations, on the one hand, has imagined digital disruption bringing democratic expansion for media industries worldwide—consumer choice! democratic, unfiltered access! a new era of global cinephilia! (Anderson 2006; Iordanova 2012). A critical perspective on distribution platforms and pipelines, on the other hand, traces how industrial logic around scalability and territorial expansion increasingly drives globalized content distribution and localized consumer access.

In this twenty-first-century transformative moment, digital sectors appear as rapidly expanding media and entertainment industries—whether expanding physical infrastructure locally or diversity of available content globally. We once again find what David Morley and Kevin Robins observed nearly three decades ago: "Our senses of space and place are all being significantly reconfigured" (1995, 1). Two foundational global media studies debates appear to revisit familiar territory—*media imperialism* tracing the one-way flow from the West to the rest and the *contraflow* of players, platforms, and content originating from the Global South. In the case of media imperialism, the political-economic critique points to the oppressive cultural and political economic reach of Hollywood around the world. Key issues include concentration of ownership, free-market deregulation, established distribution channels, cultural homogenization, and the omnipresence of American media products worldwide.

Disney, one of the most examined case studies from classroom discussions to scholarly critiques, is often vilified as the symbol of American cultural imperialism. From Ariel Dorfman and Armand Mattelart's (1975) groundbreaking polemical Marxist analysis *How to Read Donald Duck* to Janet Wasko's (2001) *Understanding Disney: The Manufacture of Fantasy*, this scholarly tradition argues the Mouse House circulates family-friendly media worldwide that are rooted in Western capitalist ideologies. In an industrial moment driven by lucrative intellectual property feeding an ever-expanding and -diversifying distribution pipeline, Disney again raised concerns after a buying spree, with the parent company purchasing Lucasfilm, Marvel Studios, and 21st Century Fox in the span of a decade. By 2019, Disney represented one of the biggest media conglomerates in the world, boasting close to a 40 percent share of the U.S. theatrical market, record-breaking earnings of $10 billion in global theatrical revenue, and an aggressively growing digital business (Hughes 2019; Rubin 2019). Building on a successful international multimedia business, Disney began to expand its newest platform, Disney+, globally in 2020.

An overcrowded digital market also brings challenges for even established brands working to stay relevant and become a digital player. New York–based Criterion Collection launched in 1984 by distributing high-quality LaserDisc versions of classic Hollywood and global art films before transitioning to DVD sales in the 1990s. The distribution company matured into a specialty brand beloved by cinephiles for restored prints and difficult-to-find titles. Criterion transitioned into streaming its film library by 2009 after negotiating a video-on-demand (VOD) licensing deal with MUBI, the subscription-based streamer of global art cinema.

By 2011, Criterion moved platforms to Hulu and then again in 2016 to be housed by Time Warner's short-lived service FilmStruck. After AT&T purchased Time Warner in 2018, the new parent company unexpectedly shuttered the niche streamer that exclusively featured Turner Classic Movies and Criterion titles. In response, Criterion developed its own specialty streaming service that launched the following year. A rocky road to the Criterion Collection as a standalone streamer reveals how ownership changes, shifting technological infrastructure and ancillary markets, and exclusive licensing deals with control of entire media libraries offer challenges within a rapidly changing digital landscape (Kendrick 2001; Smits and Nikdel 2019; Hayes 2019; Littleton and Low 2019). Despite the consistent creeping growth of legacy media conglomerates like Disney and AT&T as well as the emergence of big tech companies moving from distribution into content creation, notably Apple, Amazon, and Netflix, the editors of this collection caution against reproducing older media imperialism debates. Considering a gleeful outlook for a diversified global market characterized by increased circulation and unprecedented access, it is a mistake to frame international media hubs—South Korea, India, China, Nigeria, Brazil, Mexico—as emerging markets. Emerging according to whose perspective and compared to what market? Industries in the Global South already have emerged and have long operated as globally centered media capitals (Curtin 2003; Keane 2006). As opposed to viewing these global distribution channels as one-way pipelines from the United States, or the larger Global North, to Asia-Pacific, Africa, and Latin America, contraflow or reverse flow emerged as an alternative framework to map how media moves in both directions from industry hubs in the Global South (Thussu 2019). However, new frameworks are necessary to understand the current distribution climate where the local, national, regional, and global may coexist, compete, clash, or combine simultaneously. The increased global circulation of Brazilian telenovelas, K-pop music, Nollywood dramas, and Bollywood blockbusters available alongside Disney animation or Warner Bros.' latest superhero franchise represents the complexities of the multilayered content climate at the start of the 2020s.

As a division of the media conglomerate Grupo Globo, the powerful Brazilian television network Globo serves as a much-cited case study of reverse flow as the fourth largest global broadcaster. Globo expanded internationally early by licensing its telenovelas during the 1970s in territories worldwide and later launching the international pay television channel TV Globo Internacional in the late 1990s (Sinclair and Straubhaar 2013). With the emergence of streaming platforms came an increasingly crowded marketplace, particularly Netflix's expansion in Latin America in 2011 alongside local services. The traditional free-to-air network developed a digital strategy to sustain domestic audiences and continue to expand international ones. In 2015, the Brazilian broadcaster launched a local VOD service featuring older programming as well as new exclusive digital content. The "freemium" model offered a range of options from basic free content to premium paid subscriptions. Against a 2010s context when U.S. streamers, namely Netflix, Amazon, HBO, and Disney+, raced each other to expand internationally, Globo launched its over-the-top service Globoplay. Featuring exclusive original series available in international markets, including the United States, in early 2020, the Brazilian media giant hopes to compete with the expanding presence of SVOD turned studios like Netflix. As Netflix rapidly acquires and coproduces original film and television series worldwide, Portuguese-language originals 3% (2016–), *O Mecanismo / The Mechanism* (2018–), and *Coisa Mais Linda / Girl from Ipanema* (2019–) are increasingly developed not only for Brazil—one of the streamer's biggest international markets—but also for global audiences (Littleton 2016; Hopewell 2020).

A central concern is to offer a path that distribution studies may follow in the future, particularly one that is not solely located in Hollywood practices, Anglophone content, or Western institutions. We need to contextualize Hollywood's century-long dominant global presence in a way that does not reproduce the West-versus-the-rest dynamic. If considering industry debates at the end of the decade, it would be easy to center Netflix's vast global expansion in the streaming wars discourse. On the one hand, Netflix offers a near total global coverage, operating in 190 countries by 2020. As the platform has expanded, on the other hand, localization efforts include coproducing with local players, dubbing and subtitling, and investing in a handful of state-supported funding schemes. Whether through a lens of imperialist dominance, flexible localization, or international cooperation/competition, Netflix highlights the complexities and contradictions of the contemporary global media landscape. While Netflix may be an essential case, it is merely one example in a rapidly growing digital market. When compared to the vast array of media systems, cultures, and practices around the world, Netflix (much like Hollywood) is the exception, not the rule. As such, media scholars should take care that examples like Netflix and its competitors should not be allowed to "colonize" studies of digital distribution.

As the second largest online video market in the world, China's digital ecosystem has evolved within a state-controlled media system from distinct regulatory policies and protectionisms, notably the highly restrictive measures creating the so-called Great Firewall. The powerful rise of the BAT trio (Baidu, Beijing-based biggest search engine; Alibaba, Hangzhou-based e-commerce giant; Tencent, Shenzhen-based video game and social media company) largely represent a Chinese model of soft power and global competitiveness through platformization (Keane and Wu 2018). Often compared to Silicon Valley's FAANG (Facebook, Amazon, Apple, Netflix, Google), BAT own and control China's biggest video platforms—iQIYI (Baidu), Youku Tudou (Alibaba), and Tencent Video (Tencent). With the emergence of a fourth power player, Byte-Dance, the digital landscape continued to shift with the launch of their Chinese news platform Toutiao in 2012 and globally popular video-sharing app Douyin/TikTok in 2016 (Bhushan 2019). Chinese video platforms face what Elaine Jing Zhao (2018, 108) points to as unique "territorial challenges" when expanding distribution and windowing strategies across the diverse Asia-Pacific marketplace alongside competing players and their priorities. In contrast to major regional markets like Japan and South Korea, Netflix cannot operate in the Chinese local market. Even with iQIYI partnering to deliver Netflix content to Chinese audiences in 2017, industry alliances that are built with Hollywood players result in a unique global/local power dynamic requiring specific theorizations, categories, and contexts beyond traditional Western-centric approaches to distribution studies (Wang and Lobato 2019).

What this collection highlights is neither a completely open pipeline for content to circulate freely worldwide nor a situation of complete domination. Instead, a series of case studies span national borders, geolinguistic markets, corporate or state ownership, and medium specificity. What are the different uses of the international as a site of enquiry, where does it get us theoretically, and how will this perspective open up new questions and avenues? We consider digital distribution as a mediated site to understand the complexities around competition and cooperation that challenge contemporary understandings of space and place, borders and boundaries, and movement and flow. In contrast with industrial discourse around saturation, abundance, and overflow, how can mapping the global distribution landscape along spatial lines open up questions about obstructed access and restricted pipelines, uneven infrastructure, and friction and tension across authorized/unauthorized channels and formal/informal markets (Appadurai 1990; Lobato 2019; Elkins 2019; Plantin and Punathambekar 2019)? What can delayed or accelerated strategies for releasing old and new movies, television series, music albums, video games, social media apps, books, and so on tell us about shifting temporal logic that increasingly privileges simultaneity and immediacy? Finally, how do global issues of contingency, scalability, and sustainability play out differently across a vast array of local political, economic, industrial, technological, and sociocultural conditions and contexts?

Therefore, as we assembled the collection to feature prominent and emerging international scholars covering an array of distribution case studies, two central objectives developed—comparative and locally specific approaches. A transnational framework is just as important as a locally grounded approach. In other words, the macro should not be sacrificed for the micro, and vice versa. For distribution studies to truly offer a global scope, we argue, the field must internationalize in ways that are meaningful, complex, and layered.

* * *

The chapters in section 1 offer perspectives on the general conceptualization of media distribution and how the impacts of digitalization demand new theorizations of distribution. Rather than seeking to conclusively define distribution, authors productively problematize our understandings of the term. Avoiding offering overly broad definitions, whereby distribution becomes synonymous with mediation, Joshua Braun proposes a number of properties common to, yet varying between, media distribution systems: distinctive economies of scale, how distribution systems become tied to physical places or virtual platforms, and tendencies toward the formation of monopolistic structures. It is through these properties that media distribution achieves social importance by facilitating or denying access to culture, with implications for the formation of publics, individual identity, and patterns of social exclusion, inequality, or discrimination.

Amanda Lotz also interrogates definitional complexities, challenging the conventional tripartite production-distribution-consumption supply chain. Focusing on the context of U.S. television, Lotz sees the singular label "distribution" as masking how networks, channels, stations, and multichannel cable and satellite services have all variously operated models for delivering programming, with internet-distributed television now adding further density to this landscape. Recognizing the limitations of "distribution" and "distributor" as operative labels, Lotz proposes that "circulation" necessarily provides a more expansive descriptor for understanding the multiple actions and actors now involved with disseminating television content.

Alisa Perren makes three proposals for enriching the field of media distribution studies: contextualizing contemporary digital transformations through explorations of how media distribution systems have historically structured space to form local, regional, national, or transnational geographies; looking beyond high-profile players to see how digital distribution creates an arena of opportunity for other corporate entities, including talent agencies and medium-sized financier-distributors; and recognizing how the impacts of digital distribution exceed the familiar examples of popular music, long-form television serials, or feature films, to "outlier" cases such as sports, news, comic books, and theater.

Distribution is an area of critical importance to media industries research for it crucially raises questions concerning the conditions and controls through which media content becomes publicly accessible. To conceptualize those controls, Virginia Crisp anchors her study in the tradition of gatekeeping theory. She presents a macro-level model of gatekeeping power in which distribution or publishing processes are one control point or node among others: hardware manufacturing, funding, production practices, marketing, retail, regulatory systems, curation, archiving, and the ownership of intellectual property (IP).

Adopting a production logics approach, Aphra Kerr emphasizes how digital gaming contains multiple moments at which economic value can be extracted. Arguing "distribution" may connote only one-way flow, Kerr proposes thinking more broadly about the (echoing Lotz) "circulation" of content within the overall gaming ecosystem. These circulations, she argues, influence the culture of gaming in multiple ways, including the use of implicit user data for content production, the ways community managers support online gaming communities, and the phenomenon of livestreaming game play.

Taking music streaming service Spotify as his point of departure, Patrick Vonderau argues the many forms of data transmission conducted through acts of digital dissemination require a fundamental shift in how we think of distribution. Whereas physical distribution always necessitated actual movement or transportation of goods through a "channel," in the case of streaming data don't move but rather proliferate. Accessing any individual song on Spotify triggers multiple exchanges of data beyond the track's audio, so that any single instance becomes a moment of value creation for parties from multiple industries. Instead of accepting distribution as a function or activity that is bounded, self-evident, and settled, these chapters valuably interrogate our foundational understandings of the organizational, technological, and commercial arrangements whereby media forms enter social and cultural life.

On a global scale, digitalization is rapidly transforming not only how media products circulate but also how entire distribution ecosystems and cultures operate. Collectively, the essays in section 2 trace the cultural and industrial specificity of the interaction between global and local forces in digital distribution industries and the differential cultural impact of these interactions. While digital distribution has created opportunities for more complex local, regional, and international media markets to emerge, it has also multiplied the variety of sites where global conglomerates seek to control distribution, cultural circulation, and media capital. Competition between legacy media and new players reflects tension between regional and national languages, legacy and streaming television platforms, transnational and local commercial organizations, and various kinds of content production and infrastructure industries. The authors in this section tackle how a myriad of factors—value, accessibility, inclusivity, ownership, convergence, algorithms, personalization, rituals—are shaping and being shaped by digital media systems worldwide.

Stuart Cunningham and David Craig open the section with a comparative approach for examining social media ecologies in the United States and China. Google/YouTube and Facebook/Instagram successfully created platforms driven by user-generated content, or what the authors categorize as social media entertainment (SME), yet failed to incorporate professionally generated content to compete with Netflix and Hulu. In contrast, the development of SME has played out differently for Chinese tech companies Baidu, Alibaba, and Tencent. By integrating professionally generated content alongside "wanghong" amateur content creators, the authors argue that Chinese companies successfully converge SME with IP, overcoming the platform/portal distinction that is prevalent in the West.

Working from an understanding that digital platforms are inherently regional, Aswin Punathambekar and Sriram Mohan show how the Tamil-language YouTube channel Put Chutney exhibits a tendency to map media, advertising, and marketing regions onto linguistic differences in India. While digital distribution and media regions scale well in relation to language, they argue, digital media regions continue to be shaped by earlier forms of media geography as well. Their chapter makes a compelling case for applying the insights of critical geography to the study of media distribution.

In the next chapter, Evan Elkins explores public-facing anti-geoblocking discourse in North American and European media markets. Push back against geoblocking—distribution mechanisms that limit users in IP-specific locations from accessing an online platform or content—ranges from Hulu, YouTube, and Spotify displaying "not available in your country" messages, to the European Union implementing a Digital Single Market. Elkins demonstrates how potentially different private and public stakeholders all utilize similar discourse that fails to see beyond the internet as an open/closed model.

Moving to the business culture of global television trade, Joonseok Choi analyzes the different industrial discourses surrounding streaming television among participants in the global content markets, MIPTV and MIPFormats. He argues that the distribution model of streaming media among companies such as Netflix and Amazon disrupts the traditional value chain of commercial TV through industrial discourses that surround, make sense of, and deploy that technology in particular ways. What we are seeing in industry debates about streaming TV, he maintains, is a struggle for the very future of how global television distribution works, with significant implications for the future of television content as well.

Naomi Sakr and Jeanette Steemers compare the state of children's media distribution in Europe and the Middle East in their contribution to explain the continuing dominance of global producer-distributors such as Disney and Nickelodeon. Through a careful analysis of cable and streaming television channels, they show how the major global players in children's television have locked down rights sales and distribution revenues, thereby dampening children's television production in both Europe and the Middle East. At the same time, they note how traditional political-economic considerations, including the size of geolinguistic regions and investment in public service media, lead to important differences in the amount of children's television that both regions are able to produce.

Next, Juan Piñón and Ezequiel Rivero take a media infrastructure approach to analyzing the state of subscription video-on-demand services across Latin America. Global corporations control not only a large amount of streaming content but also important sectors of the streaming infrastructure. Nations in the region that do maintain a strong presence in the distribution chain are largely restricted to the broadcasting and cable sectors, and few have any significant toehold in telecommunications or computing. The consequences of this infrastructural arrangement limit the kinds of content and audiences regional streaming services can assemble.

From a broad analytical frame, Jade Miller focuses on the threat that streaming distribution poses to informal, hard-copy distribution practices in sub-Saharan Africa, particularly Nollywood videofilms. She identifies a number of organizational, economic, and audience reception practices that undergird traditional distribution practices in the Nigerian media market. In the case of Nollywood, she argues, existing cultural and economic realities guarantee that streaming distribution will remain a minor sector of the distribution industry for the foreseeable future.

Examining an area of media industry studies that is often marginalized in discussions of shifting distribution practices, Peter Alilunas traces how the emergence of tube sites and rise of the vertically integrated corporate giant MindGeek have come to dominate digital distribution for adult media. MindGeek's online empire, characterized by data-driven decision making, advertising, and ancillary markets, has radically upended conventional business models. Alilunas highlights how the new "King of Porn" resembles the ecosystem of big tech companies and is increasingly raising questions about data privacy and security.

Julian Thomas explores the transformation of the electronic book industry where competing formats, geoblocking, digital rights management tools, and e-book platforms have led to problems with access and circulation. In this climate, Amazon has evolved into a powerful "rule-setting and market-making" platform relying on a complex automated recommendation system. Item-based algorithms depend upon scale and speed to quickly recommend "related items" to purchase based on user-generated data. Thomas raises important questions about public interest and the larger ethical impact of every interaction becoming a recommendation.

By distinguishing between media content goods and media systems, Ramon Lobato's chapter offers a striking conceptual contribution for media studies to consider the flexibility and elasticity of pricing models. The chapter highlights the importance of considering how pricing varies in specific moments and across entire periods of time from the windowing of feature films to pricing structures for streaming services. Lobato questions how the increased integration of price experimentations and algorithmic price personalization from bundled services to online retailers transforms access and availability across a variety of industrial and geographical markets.

In the final chapter in this section, Daniel Herbert and Derek Johnson emphasize the importance of studying retail spaces to understand the commodified and ritualized nature of consumer-facing media circulation. Combined with analyzing printed advertisements, Herbert and Johnson contribute a rich on-the-ground approach by visiting multiple Target, Walmart, and Best Buy locations on the shopping holiday Black Friday. Their detailed description of retail spaces demonstrates ways in which "media overflow" of products strategically spills across each store and shapes an ever-expanding retail holiday into a media event.

The initial idea for the collection grew from the editors' shared curiosity in mapping the tensions between continuity and change at the foundation of digital distribution. While it was impossible to fully cover the scope and scale of the current industrial moment within these pages, the following chapters pose a wide array of conceptual queries, methods, and perspectives for examining the multifaceted distribution landscape in a moment of transformation. As a whole, the chapters here provide a vast array of critical approaches and illustrative case studies for understanding how a multitude of factors impact the way media travel and move throughout our digital lives. As a result, *Digital Media Distribution: Portals, Platforms, Pipelines* offers a new path for media industry studies to locate, uncover, and access the digital turn in distribution in new and surprising ways.

BIBLIOGRAPHY

Anderson, Chris. 2006. *The Long Tail: Why the Future of Business Is Selling Less of More*. New York: Hachette Books.

Appadurai, Arjun. 1990. "Disjuncture and Difference in the Global Cultural Economy." *Public Culture* 2 (2): 1–24.

Bennett, Jane, Pheng Cheah, Melissa A. Orlie, and Elizabeth Grosz. 2010. *New Materialisms: Ontology, Agency, and Politics*. Durham, NC: Duke University Press.

Bhushan, Nyay. 2019. "U.S. VOD Services to Dominate Asian Market Outside China in 2019: Study." *Hollywood Reporter*, September 17. www.hollywoodreporter.com.

Bickford, Sonja H., Jon-Eric Krans, and Nate Bickford. 2016. "Social and Environmental Impacts of Development on Rural Traditional Arctic Communities: Focus on Northern Sweden and the Sami." *Journal EU Research in Business* 2016: 1–11.

Braun, Joshua A. 2015. *This Program Is Brought to You By . . . : Distributing Television News Online*. New Haven, CT: Yale University Press.

Burkart, Patrick, and Susanna Leijonhufvud. 2019. "The Spotification of Public Service Media." *Information Society* 35 (4): 173–83.

Caldwell, John T. 2008. *Production Culture: Industrial Reflexivity and Critical Practice in Film and Television*. Durham, NC: Duke University Press.

Chadwick, Jonathan. 2020. "Epic Games Delays the Release of Fortnite's New Season Until Early June." *Daily Mail*, April 15. www.dailymail.co.uk.

Cimpanu, Catalin. 2020. "Audible to Provide Free Audiobooks for Children & Teens during COVID-19 Pandemic." *ZDNet*, March 19. www.zdnet.com.

Crisp, Virginia. 2015. *Film Distribution in the Digital Age: Pirates and Practitioners*. New York: Palgrave Macmillan.

Cubitt, Sean. 2005. "Distribution and Media Flows." *Cultural Politics* 1 (2): 193–214.

Cunningham, Stuart, and David Craig. 2019. *Social Media Entertainment: The New Intersection of Hollywood and Silicon Valley*. New York: New York University Press.

Curtin, Michael. 2003. "Media Capital: Towards the Study of Spatial Flows." *International Journal of Cultural Studies* 6 (2): 202–28.

Curtin, Michael, Jennifer Holt, and Kevin Sanson, eds. 2014. *Distribution Revolution: Conversations about the Digital Future of Film and Television*. Berkeley: University of California Press.

Dorfman, Ariel, and Armand Mattelart. 1975. *How to Read Donald Duck*. New York: International General.

Elkins, Evan. 2019. *Locked Out: Regional Restrictions in Digital Entertainment Culture*. New York: New York University Press.

Fellman, Daniel R. 2017. "Studio Distribution." In *The Movie Business Book*, 4th ed., edited by Jason E. Squire, 371–82. New York: Routledge.

Hayes, Dade. 2019. "Criterion Channel Gives Classic Films New Streaming Life after FilmStruck Demise." *Deadline*, April 8. https://deadline.com.

Johnson, Catherine. 2019. *Online TV*. Abingdon: Routledge.

Hopewell, John. 2020. "Brazil's Globo Set to Launch Streamer Globoplay in the U.S." *Variety*, January 17. https://variety.com.

Hughes, Mark. 2019. "Disney Tops $5.7+ Billion in Global Box Office in First Half of 2019." *Forbes*, July 6. www.forbes.com.

Iordanova, Dina. 2012. "Digital Disruption: Technological Innovation and Global Film Circulation." In *Digital Disruption: Cinema Moves On-Line*, edited by Dina Iordanova and Stuart Cunningham, 1–31. St. Andrews: St. Andrews Film Studies.

Keane, Michael. 2006. "Once Were Peripheral: Creating Media Capacity in East Asia." *Media, Culture & Society* 28 (6): 835–55.

Keane, Michael, and Huan Wu. 2018. "Lofty Ambitions, New Territories, and Turf Battles: China's Platforms 'Go Out.'" *Media Industries Journal* 5 (1): 51–68.

Kendrick, James. 2001. "What Is the Criterion? The Criterion Collection as an Archive of Film as Culture." *Journal of Film and Video* 53 (2/3): 124–39.

Kerr, Aphra. 2017. *Global Games: Production, Circulation and Policy in the Networked Era*. New York: Routledge.

Knight, Julia, and Peter Thomas. 2008. "Distribution and the Question of Diversity: A Case Study of Cinenova." *Screen* 49 (3): 354–65.

———. 2011. *Reaching Audiences: Distribution and Promotion of Alternative Moving Image*. Bristol: Intellect.

Littleton, Cynthia. 2016. "Latin American TV Sees Long-Term Growth with Deregulation, New Affluence." *Variety*, December 14. https://variety.com.

Littleton, Cynthia, and Elaine Low. 2019. "Adapt or Die: Why 2020 Will Be All about Entertainment's New Streaming Battleground." *Variety*, December 17. https://variety.com.

Lobato, Ramon. 2007. "Subcinema: Theorizing Marginal Film Distribution." *Limina* 13: 113–20.

———. 2012. *Shadow Economies of Cinema*. London: British Film Institute.

———. 2019. *Netflix Nations: The Geography of Digital Distribution*. New York: New York University Press.

Lotz, Amanda. 2017. *Portals: A Treatise on Internet-Distributed Television*. Ann Arbor, MI: Maize Books.

Lovely, Stephen. 2020. "How COVID-19 Is Affecting Streaming Launches Around the World." *Motley Fool*, April 4. www.fool.com.

Miller, Toby, Freya Schiwy, and Marta Hernández Salván. 2011. "Distribution, the Forgotten Element in Transnational Cinema." *Transnational Cinemas* 2 (2): 197–215.

Morley, David, and Kevin Robins. 1995. *Spaces of Identity: Global Media, Electronic Landscapes and Cultural Boundaries*. Abingdon: Routledge.

Morris, Jeremy W. 2015. *Selling Digital Music, Formatting Culture*. Berkeley: University of California Press.

Nieborg, David B., and Thomas Poell. 2018. "The Platformization of Cultural Production: Theorizing the Contingent Cultural Commodity." *New Media & Society* 20 (11): 4275–92.

Perren, Alisa. 2013. "Rethinking Distribution for the Future of Media Industry Studies." *Cinema Journal* 52 (3): 165–71.

Plantin, Jean-Christophe, and Aswin Punathambekar. 2019. "Digital Media Infrastructures: Pipes, Platforms, and Politics." *Media, Culture & Society* 41 (2): 163–74.

Rubin, Rebecca. 2019. "Disney Crushes Own Global Box Office Record with Historic $10 Billion." *Variety*, December 8. https://variety.com.

Sinclair, John, and Joseph D. Straubhaar. 2013. *Latin American Television Industries*. London: British Film Institute Press.

Smits, Roderik, and E. W. Nikdel. 2019. "Beyond Netflix and Amazon: MUBI and the Curation of On-Demand Film." *Studies in European Cinema* 16 (1): 22–37.

Spilker, Hendrik S. 2017. *Digital Music Distribution: The Sociology of Online Music Streams*. Abingdon: Routledge.

Thussu, Daya Kishan. 2019. *International Communication: Continuity and Change*. 3rd ed. London: Bloomsbury.

Tryon, Chuck. 2013. *On-Demand Culture: Digital Delivery and the Future of Movies*. New Brunswick, NJ: Rutgers University Press.

Wang, Wilfred Yang, and Ramon Lobato. 2019. "Chinese Video Streaming Services in the Context of Global Platform Studies." *Chinese Journal of Communication* 12 (3): 356–71.

Wasko, Janet. 2001. *Understanding Disney: The Manufacture of Fantasy*. Cambridge: Polity.

Wilk, Richard R. 1994. "Colonial Time and TV Time: Television and Temporality in Belize." *Visual Anthropology Review* 10 (1): 94–102.

Zhao, Elaine Jing. 2018. "Negotiating State and Copyright Territorialities in Overseas Expansion: The Case of China's Online Video Streaming Platforms." *Media Industries Journal* 5 (1): 106–21.

Conceptualizing Distribution and Circulation

1

Points of Origin

Asking Questions in Distribution Research

JOSHUA A. BRAUN

This essay offers a number of "ways in" to the study of media distribution by outlining several key issues scholars of media circulation will invariably need to address in their work. In particular I put forward—and provide conceptual scaffolding for grappling with—three foundational questions: (1) How do we define distribution as an object of study? (2) Are there particular properties that are common to distribution systems? And (3) what is the social importance of distribution systems? I close by considering how the ideas delineated in the previous sections might provide guidance regarding methodological best practices for scholars of distribution, with particular attention to the study of emerging forms of digital media distribution.

Defining Distribution

Any field of study requires careful definitions of its subject matter, and research on media distribution is no exception. While I argue against policing a single scholarly definition of distribution, useful definitions will tend to share several characteristics: they will (1) avoid uncritical adoption of definitions and other actor categories dictated by industry; (2) be flexible enough to account for variance across different sorts of distribution systems (for example, point-to-point versus one-to-many); and (3) be constrained enough to avoid deploying distribution as a synonym for expansive field-level topics, such as the nature of mediation.

Avoiding Actor Categories

The need for researchers to offer their own definitions of distribution is more than a matter of scholarly precision. It is also a means of safeguarding their independence and establishing critical distance from the subject matter. To wit, media industries and regulators often have their own definitions of distribution, enshrined in organizational bureaucracies and maintained through professional gatekeeping practices. For example, in the film industry "distribution" has often been shorthand specifically for those practices falling to specialized "marketing and distribution" divisions within studios, which traditionally focused on theatrical releases and the publicity associated with them. Industry executives and regulators can be correspondingly quick to engage in boundary work regarding what practices and infrastructures should and should not fall under the rubric of distribution.

While scholars must certainly understand and be able to describe the impact of these actor categories, it is typically counterproductive for researchers to be beholden to the definitions used by their sources to the extent that they cannot step outside them. Industry distribution practices—and understandings of what distribution entails—change over time, as well as across national and market contexts. They differ across industries (e.g., journalism versus film versus games). And, perhaps most salient to the present volume, formerly stable boundaries separating traditional actor categories—distribution, marketing, and exhibition, for instance—are rapidly collapsing and being reconfigured as legacy media industries are upended and adapt themselves to a digital future (Curtin, Holt, and Sanson 2014). In such an environment, media executives' definitions of distribution demand to be explored, but also to be examined at a critical distance—for instance, they may represent attempts at boundary work aimed at preserving categories that best serve legacy business models or preferred regulatory frameworks, rather than shifting on-the-ground realities.

Moreover, while industry definitions of distribution are potentially limiting to researchers, scholarly definitions should be helpful. As Alisa Perren (2013) has noted, within media scholarship, distribution as a focus area has the potential to generatively tie together threads from a range of theoretical traditions. She argues that distribution, in the past, has not so much been understudied as folded into other topics of study, such as work on media infrastructures, technology studies, or business history. In the early twenty-first century, as the challenges and opportunities wrought by digital delivery have become a unifying theme in our understanding of many seismic shifts in the media industries, Perren argues that centering distribution as an object of study has great potential. Making good on the promise of such work, however, will require careful synthesis and definitional work on the part of scholars weaving together threads from the various disciplines into which media distribution has typically been folded in the past.

For all the above reasons, scholars pursuing questions about distribution would be well advised to explicitly lay out their own analytical definitions of the topic. In my own work, I have defined distribution as the "movement of content from the time it is produced to the time it reaches the consumer" (Braun 2015, 46). Correspondingly, I describe distribution scholarship as "that which focuses on the actors, processes, strategic considerations, and infrastructures that shape this movement" (Braun 2019). In offering up this definition, it is my intention not to police it as a singular description of the field but rather to demonstrate the space created by divorcing analytical demarcations of distribution from ones offered by industry. The conceptual framework I have offered not only ties together the delivery of content to a device or exhibition space and its subsequent showing, which are less divisible in the age of streaming than in the heyday of theatrical distribution, but also opens to scrutiny the movement of content within media organizations. For instance, in examining television news distribution, I included discussions of the work developers did to create infrastructures for repurposing editorial content across different web properties, the work video editors and web producers did to recut television programs for sharing online, and the pitching practices web producers engaged in when they wanted to convince editors of the MSNBC.com home page to feature a clip from a news program that might otherwise "live" solely on a different website (Braun 2015).

In other words, as an analytic category, distribution captured a constellation of interlocking cases, practices, and infrastructures that were important to the study at hand but may not have been connected under traditional industry definitions. Scholarly definitions of distribution may vary but should always be deployed to serve the analysis at hand rather than the industry under scrutiny. Ultimately, understanding the dynamics of media distribution promises to yield a complementary, if not more comprehensive, understanding of the workings of essential cultural industries compared to isolated studies of production, media texts, or audience reception. Moreover, as I have written elsewhere, research on distribution fits squarely within the remit of communication research as a social science interested in the intersection of culture and power—"perhaps even more directly than questions of production or content, the study of distribution cuts straight to the heart of who has access to culture and on what terms" (Braun 2014, 127).

Point-to-Point and One-to-Many Networks

Adopting broader analytical definitions of distribution can, in many ways, serve the comparative purposes of scholarship—across industries, time periods, markets, national contexts, and related sets of practices. At the same time, analytical definitions must have boundaries as well in order to be of use. Momentarily, I will turn to examples of things that should probably *not* be included in analytical definitions of distribution if the category is to be prevented from becoming overly broad. First, however, I consider a gray area that such categories might more reasonably encompass. Much of the discussion surrounding "convergence" in the late 1990s and early 2000s can be read as troubling previously commonsense distinctions between media distribution on the one hand and telecommunications on the other (e.g., Winseck 1997; Blackman 1998). Attention to historical detail, however, suggests such distinctions were always somewhat blurry.

Telecommunications networks—and physical point-to-point communication systems like postal services before them—have long underpinned media distribution. The birth of wire services meant news stories were circulated along telegraph lines to the offices of local papers, increasing the pace at which information traveled (John 2010).[1] And in the era of radio, broadcast affiliates received much of their programming through the telephone system (Douglas 2004, 63).

Moreover, as the internet has come to underpin the circulation of new and legacy media products, distribution via point-to-point telecommunications networks has become the norm. Such a situation invites us to not only loosen distinctions between distribution and telecommunications going forward but also reevaluate conceptual divisions we may have applied to historical examples. As I will subsequently argue, network structures certainly matter to the dynamics of distribution systems, but an initial way of (re)thinking through the issue is that while different network structures—e.g., point-to-point versus one-to-many, centralized versus rhizomatic—impose distinct affordances and constraints on message delivery, so will disparities in structural power and other asymmetries of resources (Couldry 2008). In other words, if we regard distribution as a sociotechnical exercise, there are plenty of factors beyond technology or network structure that can help to determine the size of the prospective audience for a given message. To give one example, the early U.S. postal network—while we might think about it as a point-to-point delivery system for letters—became a massive circulation mechanism for newspapers in the nineteenth century because of an act of Congress that dramatically subsidized the delivery of newspapers through the mail. So successful was it that entrepreneurs began printing other media genres—novels, for example—on newsprint to take advantage of the same favorable rates (John 1995).

Definitional Limits

If scholarship turns to broader analytical definitions of distribution to avoid becoming captive to narrower actor categories, this movement will also require thinking about the limits of a useful definition of distribution. Broad accounts describing, say, the "movement of information" may be generative in helping researchers to explore more closely and critically the relationship between mass media and telecommunications or industrial and informal modes of media circulation (e.g., Lobato 2012). But the need to avoid casting too wide a definitional net also seems clear. For instance, while distribution clearly implies a focus on things standing between senders and receivers, any useful conception of distribution should not be a synonym for "mediation." This would create a slippery slope toward conflating the study of distribution with the whole of communication research. To my mind, distribution is concerned with the actors and infrastructures whose decisions impact to whom media messages go. It is about access to cultural products rather than, for example, the relative richness of social cues available to individuals communicating through different channels like audio, video, or text chat. And while distribution can be formal (e.g., a Hollywood studio arranging the circulation of a film) or informal (e.g., digital piracy), it involves a set of practices aimed at ensuring the movement of messages to particular imagined audiences. It is not reducible to the study of media technologies—physical geography and social forces ranging from cultural norms to business strategies, systems of patent rights, and other political and regulatory factors will always be part of the conversation to an equal or greater extent.

Between the need to avoid too-provincial or actor-driven conceptions of distribution on the one hand and overly cosmic definitions on the other, there will obviously be room for plenty of reasonable and potentially generative disagreements as to what an analytical category of distribution might include. To name a few examples, it's easy to see how scholarly discourses on the circulation of affect (Ahmed 2004) or the circulation of currency (Swartz 2013, 2020) are differentiable from the study of media distribution. But it's also intriguing and potentially rewarding to think about how these other forms of circulation might be connected to media distribution, or about definitions of media distribution richly informed, through analogy or otherwise, by these other conversations. For instance, Swartz (2020) goes beyond the broad observation that communication networks have often been created to serve the market, showing that the technologies and practices around the circulation of currency have closely tracked the technologies and practices of media distribution in ways that make arguments about one domain suitable and clever conceptual interventions in speaking about the other.

Properties of Distribution Systems

Insofar as any area of scholarship thrives on discussions and arguments over ideal types and categories, it's worth asking whether there are particular features or properties commonly associated with distribution systems. This section identifies a number of candidates for such properties. For the sake of space, I focus here on telecommunications networks, utilizing examples from Richard John's extensive historical work on

American networks as illustrative cases. However, my intent is not to create an exhaustive or definitive catalog. I set out a number of features as objects for discussion and contestation, rather than as cardinal truths about distribution networks. While I refer here to telecommunication networks, an argument could be made that much of the following discussion about electronic telecommunications is applicable to physical point-to-point networks like the postal service as well.

Distinctive Economies of Scale

Telecommunications networks are subject to distinctive economies of scale. To see how, it is instructive to compare the ways in which costs evolve in a telecommunications firm as opposed to a different sort of business, like manufacturing. As you grow a company that makes ice cream, for example, your costs will shift in a fairly intuitive fashion. As you sell more pints, you can buy in larger quantities from your suppliers, allowing you to negotiate lower prices on ingredients like cream, sugar, and strawberries. Because you're still selling the finished product to consumers at the same price, your profit on the sale of each carton of ice cream climbs as you grow your business.

However, as John (2010) illustrates, when you're connecting customers in a point-to-point communications network, something quite different happens. He takes as his subject matter the Bell telephone system. While this was not a media distribution network per se, the historical challenges he highlights pertain (mutatis mutandis) to running any of a variety of past and contemporary point-to-point systems, from a telegraph company to internet infrastructure and online services. Imagine the simplest way of connecting two telephone customers—stringing a wire between their homes with no switchboard in between. Connecting two customers requires one line. Connecting three customers directly to one another in this way means three lines. Once your network has four customers, you'll need six lines; five customers require ten. At the point the hundredth user joins your burgeoning phone network, you'll need 4,900 wires to link all your customers using direct connections. In other words, by default the costs to point-to-point network providers go up exponentially as they add customers—quite the opposite of what we see with many other sorts of businesses, like manufacturing.

A logical answer to this problem on the part of telecom companies is to route customers' connections through a centralized switchboard, replacing permanent connections with transient ones (momentarily connecting a pair of phones when a call is placed or two servers when an email is sent). However, while this strategy may partially mitigate the problem of geometrically scaling infrastructure costs, managing this eternally protean network of connections is labor-intensive and expensive in its own right. This has often led telecommunications companies to turn to heavy automation, or—when this proves difficult or otherwise disadvantageous—the cheapest available labor forces, from "hello girls" (Martin 1991) to telegraph messenger boys (Downey 2002).[2] As I wrote in an earlier essay, "This quickly leads to questions about whether such solutions, which often focus on marginalized groups, are exploitative. Scholars like Martin (1991), for instance, describe deplorable conditions for female operators in the early Bell System. At the same time, historians will point out that such working environments were in many cases comparable—or even favorable—to other employment options available to the same individuals during the period in question (Richard John, personal communication, February 1, 2018)" (Braun, 2019).[3] In speaking of historical examples, it is also possible to name point-to-point delivery networks with well-protected working conditions. For example, throughout the nineteenth century, many jobs in the U.S. postal network were highly sought as prestigious and well-compensated employment. In some cases, they were even viewed as sinecures to be exchanged for political patronage (John 1995).

Again, while the telephone network to which I've repeatedly pointed as an exemplar in this section is arguably not in itself a media distribution network, the economic logics I have described here pertain to a broad array of telecommunications networks, from the telegraph to the internet. They also apply, in some respects, to physical point-to-point networks, such as the network of postal roads maintained by the nineteenth-century U.S. government. Even "virtual" point-to-point networks, like social media services, experience geometric growth in the connections they make between users as they grow, and these connections must be cashed out somewhere in the form of vast relational databases that require physical infrastructures like massive data centers to maintain (Holt 2014). Different point-to-point system providers working with different media may approach distribution's distinctive economies of scale in different ways, but the existence of a shared underlying dynamic is sufficiently clear to offer researchers a baseline from which to ask questions about variations between systems, particularly when it comes to their approaches to automation and the labor practices in which they engage. Meanwhile, though one-to-many distribution networks such as broadcasting also have their own distinctive cost structures, from an infrastructure perspective they often enjoy more traditional economies of scale. The extensive connective infrastructure built out by telecommunications providers is most comparable to that laid by gas, power, water, and sewage companies, which also connect customers across large geographic areas. Broadcasters, on the other hand, may rely on a single well-placed tower to reach a sizable community. As noted long ago by FCC chief economist H. H. Goldin (1954, 223), "From an economic standpoint, the typical broadcast station is basically unlike the typical public utility. . . . Investment in fixed plant and equipment is very small by public utility standards."

Complications of Place and Platform

Another distinctive feature of physical distribution networks is that they are tied to particular places in ways other enterprises aren't necessarily. If your ice cream factory is in Philadelphia and Massachusetts offers you a set of tax incentives to move production to Framingham, you're largely free to up and leave—or use your new leverage to negotiate an even more favorable deal from the powers that be in Philly. If your business is distributing the local newspaper, you obviously don't have the same mobility. Physical infrastructure is also typically firmly tied to geographic location. If you're a cable company or internet service provider, your enterprise relies on a network of cables beneath city streets that's not portable. The special permissions, or "rights of way," necessary to lay those cables or to use airwaves for wireless delivery are all things that must be obtained from the local (or, in some cases, national) government. Officials are highly cognizant of both distributors' lack of mobility and their dependence on government-issued rights of way. With this knowledge in hand, they have at times driven exceedingly hard bargains with telecommunications companies and small broadcasters, all of which can raise the costs to distributors still further. Moreover, the historical record is rife with examples of negotiations over rights of way extending into outright extortion and logrolling. While such corruption brings to mind old-timey political machines like nineteenth-century Chicago, it's not some relic of a bygone era. For instance, 2019 saw the end of court proceedings surrounding $330 million in bribes apparently paid by telecommunications firm Telia to the family of Uzbek officials for rights to operate in the country. Even in above-board regulatory environments, telecom providers have argued in recent years that the cost of establishing rights of way as much as doubled the expense of laying infrastructure (Szóka, Henke, and Starr 2013)—though, as I discuss later, incumbent distributors often amass political power in ways that enable them to turn the tables on the government.

In the realm of "virtual" distribution networks, platforms often play a role akin to municipalities in the physical world. For example, a news organization that depends on Apple News or Facebook to place its content in front of users cannot simply leave the platform without abandoning the audience they have built there. As a consequence, they may have to live with the platform's uncomfortable revenue splits or dictates about what sorts of content will be most readily promoted into users' news feeds (Bell and Owen 2017). Of course, issues of platform dependency are not necessarily new—Western Union, for example, exerted considerable political and editorial influence over the output of the New York Associated Press, as the latter depended on its relationship with the telegraph monopoly to get its stories to readers at the various newspapers across the country that carried wire stories (John 2010).

The Question of Monopoly

John (2010) describes at great length how early attempts to regulate the telegraph industry in the United States notably backfired. A strong antimonopoly movement, concerned with the rapid growth of Western Union, offered government incentives for entrepreneurs to start new telegraph companies to compete with the giant incumbent, hoping to bring it in check by injecting competition into the market. What happened instead is instructive. As the would-be regulators had hoped, people did create telegraph start-ups to compete with Western Union but tended to do so without appreciating the distinctive economies of scale described above. These companies failed as the exponential costs of growth overtook their initial revenues, leaving behind a series of moribund medium-sized telegraph networks. The coup de grâce came when Western Union subsequently bought and incorporated these networks, growing from a giant into a still larger behemoth and leaving regulators shaken at the development. Following such failed experiments at introducing competition into the telecom industry in particular, U.S. regulators developed a preference for treating telegraph and telephone companies (and later other networks like cable providers) as "natural monopolies," arguing that the better strategy was to regulate one, or a small handful, of companies carefully.

In short, there are a variety of material and economic forces that tend to compound the operating expenses of telecommunications firms and other distribution enterprises in ways that favor deep-pocketed monopolies and large incumbencies. Certainly, market competition can exist, but it will often depend on policy approaches developed with a nuanced understanding of forces that might otherwise favor industry consolidation. Alternatively, these issues with economies of scale and the necessity of close relationships between system operators and government authorities can lead to situations where it makes sense to simply put the government in charge rather than contend with market forces (as was the case with the early U.S. Postal Service). Even non-point-to-point distributors like broadcasters must deal with municipal governments over rights of way, which creates expenses and logistical hurdles that can limit traditional competition in the market.

Of course, once network providers have reached colossal size, nuanced regulatory oversight is easier said than done. If certain distribution networks, by their nature or the political economy in which they operate, come to employ vast numbers of people and command extensive material infrastructures and resources, they become politically powerful. The revolving door between top posts at American distribution companies like Comcast and their regulatory counterpart, the Federal Communications Commission, for example, is one symptom of an environment in which industry has turned the tables on government with respect to political leverage, creating, for example, rules that limit the ability of municipal authorities to extract concessions from network providers in negotiations over rights of way. Network providers have long projected an image of neutrality, framing themselves as impartial conduits for information. But if indeed they tend naturally toward monopoly, scale, and lobbying clout, we might instead regard them as inherently political in nature.

While I have focused largely on point-to-point distribution networks for the sake of space, the broader point is this: the material realities of moving messages set up challenges and dynamics that, while not necessarily universal, are at least highly common across distribution systems. Scholars of distribution would do well to pay attention to such characteristics, as they promise to be helpful in highlighting aspects of various systems that *are* distinctive by casting attention on how different system builders and network structures provide unique responses to common challenges. Similarly, identifying differences and similarities along these lines can also help to explain variance in the relationships media producers have with their distributors—for instance, whether producers operate their own means of circulation, whether doing so necessitates special subsidies or permissions, or whether producers find it necessary to engage outside vendors to reach audiences.

Social Importance

Michael Warner (2002, 90), in laying out his concept of reflexive circulation, articulated well the social importance of distribution when he wrote, "Not texts themselves create publics, but the concatenation of texts through time. Only when a previously existing discourse can be supposed, and when a responding discourse can be postulated, can a text address a public." In other words, reliable distribution networks create a central conceit of democratic life—that, through our media, we are speaking to the same assembled audience day in and day out. When, at least in principle, today's broadcast or letter to the editor reaches the same audience as yesterday's, it enables us to conceive of that public as a single, inclusive body that deliberates collectively. Put simply, in a highly mediated society distribution networks are what allow us to conceive of ourselves as existing within a common public.

A corollary of this, of course, is that it is essential to the democratic project to study whom distribution networks are, in actuality, including and leaving out—and what other networks of circulation exist to fill these gaps or provide alternatives. This is true on several levels. First, of course, patterns of discrimination and social inequality are frequently reflected in (and often compounded by) inequities in access to media (Baker 2002). Distribution strategies and infrastructures are central to such concerns. For example, in the United States in the nineteenth century, women were discouraged from visiting the post offices where communities received, read, and discussed newspapers (John 1995). In the twentieth century, discount subscription offers for magazines and other publications were often mailed to wealthy, predominantly white neighborhoods whose demographics were deemed desirable to advertisers rather than poorer neighborhoods and those with larger nonwhite populations (Baker 2002). In the late 2000s and early 2010s, despite the fact that smartphone adoption was still its infancy, media organizations like MSNBC.com pivoted their mobile web development strategies from broad support for mobile phones toward the creation of apps and websites optimized for the iPhone and iPad, as owners of these devices were identified as having more expendable income and therefore being more desirable to advertisers (Braun 2015).

Moreover, distribution systems can serve as—and at times facilitate the creation of—markers of social identity. This can be true in an empowering sense, as when, for example, the presence of underground papers in local shops made the existence of the counterculture seem a concrete thing with which prospective readers could identify (McMillian 2011). But distribution infrastructures can also serve as systems of stigmatization and surveillance. Lisa Parks (2012), for example, has described how far-right politician Geert Wilders antagonized immigrants to the Netherlands from Muslim countries who oriented satellite dishes to receive television signals from their countries of origin. The visible infrastructure of distribution was used in a highly problematic and discriminatory way as a proxy for social identity. Brian Larkin's 2008 *Signal and Noise* also provides examples of how distribution intersects with the prejudice. As I've summarized elsewhere, his work demonstrates how the distribution of BBC services and other foreign radio broadcasts in northern Nigeria by the British introduced new markers of class (for instance, those who could afford a radio versus those who could listen only by congregating at public listening stations), education (such as a

British-educated middle class that spoke English and so could understand the new broadcasts versus those who could not), and culture (for instance, groups who understood the station's Arabic-language programming versus the majority who spoke the regional Hausa dialect) (Braun 2015, 22).

Unsurprisingly, the suppression of social and political identities often involves interfering with the distribution of these groups' media. Upon its formation, party officials in the Soviet Union "cleansed" libraries to prevent the circulation of politically objectionable materials, while at the same time creating new distribution networks to ensure the wide availability of publications favorable to their interests (Dobrenko 1997; Parthé 2004). In the twenty-first century, the National Intelligence and Security Service in Sudan has confiscated print runs of newspapers featuring content critical of Sudanese authorities, while in Kenya authorities disassembled the transmitters of four television stations to prevent them from airing acts of political protest by opposition candidate Raila Odinga following irregularities in the country's presidential election.

If distribution practices and infrastructures can serve to facilitate shared conceptions of a public, they can also cut across social boundaries to great effect. During the American civil rights movement of the 1960s, for example, African American activists strategically relied on national media coverage in no small part because they understood the national distribution infrastructure of the major television networks would carry images of racial injustice and violence beyond their local contexts to other regions of the country where these acts would be viewed more harshly. National reach would subject the discrimination and violence perpetrated in local communities to the "conscience of the nation," as Martin Luther King Jr. (1998) put it.

Distribution, in other words, is powerful in its ability to recontextualize media messages—and also, at times, to decontextualize them. Communication infrastructure theory holds that groups who share a common distribution infrastructure—a broadcast footprint or newspaper circulation area, for example—are more likely to think of themselves as members of a common public with shared civic responsibilities (Kim and Ball-Rokeach 2006). But Zeynep Tufekci (2018) argues that today's digital platforms are severely disrupting this phenomenon. In particular, she suggests that continually shifting and highly personalized algorithmic decisions about which content to place in front of individual users have replaced the stable and continuous (if inequitable) concatenation of texts into a public discourse that previous distribution systems afforded: "Online speech is no longer public in any traditional sense. Sure, Facebook and Twitter sometimes feel like places where masses of people experience things together simultaneously. But in reality, posts are targeted and delivered privately, screen by screen by screen. Today's phantom public sphere has been fragmented and submerged into billions of individual capillaries. Yes, mass discourse has become far easier for everyone to participate in—but it has simultaneously become a set of private conversations happening behind your back. Behind everyone's backs." The impact of these automated systems—what Gillespie (2014) has called "public relevance algorithms"—is twofold. First, as Tufekci notes, they deliver information more selectively and mercurially than the broadcast mechanisms of years past, such that today's op-ed and tomorrow's response end up in different news feeds. Publics are now "networked," to use danah boyd's (2007) term, or "calculated," to use Gillespie's (2014). Second, as Tufekci argues, this mode of delivery may further widen the gap between the conceit of a common mediated public and the underlying reality, in which the visibility of media to different groups and individuals is not only highly uneven, but now constantly in flux. The caveat, of course, is that the gap has long been greater than was generally appreciated, as minority communities of all types have always made and circulated media in distribution communities that were radically different from the dominant.

Methodological Practice in Tracing Distribution

As I have conveyed in this essay, distribution touches on a host of problems of interest to social scientists and critical media scholars at various levels of analysis. As such, it invites a wide variety of methodological approaches, many of which will be suggested by the motivating concerns to which a particular study is most closely tied, ranging from media policy discourses to sociological analyses of economic inequality and structural racism. While, as I've argued above, distribution systems are invariably sociotechnical systems that demand attention to material concerns alongside social ones, there is no one "right" way to study distribution, and the scholars I have cited throughout this piece have used a variety of tools, ranging from historiographic archival research to ethnographic work to interviews and content analysis of corporate documents. Rather than inviting a religious debate about the correct way to study distribution systems, then, I close here by suggesting a helpful mechanism for mapping distribution ecosystems that I have elsewhere called "tracing" (Braun 2015).

Tracing draws theoretical inspiration from John Law's (1987) study of the *volta do mar*, an ocean trade route developed by the Portuguese in the late fifteenth century. By examining the various components of the route and how it unfolded, Law's study unpacks the contributions of (and, at times, the limitations imposed by) the myriad actors, processes, natural forces, and material artifacts vis-à-vis the route traversed by Portuguese sailing vessels and trade goods. Analogously, I have found it highly useful from a methodological standpoint to trace out the route taken by media products as they make their way from the producer to the consumer, (re)exploring the system from the vantage point of each of the various individuals and intermediaries who handle the content along the way. For example, in my 2015 book on television news distribution, I examined the individuals, infrastructures, and services that handled video clips from MSNBC on their way to audiences. These included editorial staff on two coasts, white-label infrastructures produced by Newsvine (an MSNBC.com subsidiary), and an array of third-party firms, including one defense intelligence contractor. In short, a whole ecosystem of services and companies existed for bringing MSNBC video to consumers, enabling and constraining its commercial possibilities and the audiences it reached. And many of these intermediaries would have gone largely unnoticed in production-focused accounts and without tracing as methodological strategy.

Tracing distribution paths in this fashion is useful for a variety of reasons. First, as evidenced above, distribution networks involve many intermediaries—circulation outsource firms, logistics services providers, content delivery networks, white-label video platforms, and so on—whose job it is to provide seamless delivery for branded content providers while themselves remaining invisible to consumers (Braun 2014). There are, in other words, a host of sociologically interesting actors to be studied who have a dramatic impact on the media ecosystem and the public's access to culture, whose work is easy to overlook. This is due not simply to the frequent tendency among researchers to ignore infrastructure, but because the firms involved make their living by remaining unseen. Carefully tracing the path of media products as they make their way to audiences allows scholars to uncover the influence of these actors and better understand networks of relationships between firms that shape the media ecosystem. These "transparent intermediaries" are not neutral actors within the media sphere. They are aggressive companies acting with their own interests and preferred vision of the market and regulatory environment in mind. Even when it comes to more commonly studied media organizations like film studios and newsrooms, scholars can develop a fuller and more nuanced picture of what makes them tick by exploring these spaces from the perspective of the groups within them responsible for getting content to audiences.

Of course, tracing as a methodological approach involves choices and contains limitations that should be clearly understood. First, tracing a distribution path will typically involve making a choice about what aspect of the route the researcher wishes to understand. One scholar tracing a distribution path might decide to focus on the individuals and software platforms involved in repackaging content as it moves from the producer to the consumer. Another might focus on the physical infrastructures—wide-area networks, data centers, internet backbones, cable landings, and so on—that underpin that journey. Second, because tracing often uncovers long chains of custody involving numerous actors, firms, and infrastructures standing between the media producer and the audience, it can easily emphasize breadth over depth. For example, it's far easier to reach a satisfying sample size for an interview-driven study when participants all hold comparable jobs or work at the same firm than when faced with the task of understanding five firms in a lengthy supply chain. As such, tracing as a method may tend to favor pilot studies on the one hand, where saturation is not the objective, and extended monographs on the other, wherein lengthier research processes are more feasible. Alternatively—and perhaps most productively—tracing may serve to ground a more selective analysis rooted in a different primary method. For example, a scholar might develop a list of intermediaries handling content on its path to the consumer, not as a prelude to studying every link in the chain but as a first step in selecting two or three of the most telling locations for a multisite ethnography. In other words, tracing is not a standalone technique but a tool for contextually grounding the rich array of ethnographic, historiographic, and other methods with which social scientists and critical media scholars explore their subject matter.

Finally, in this role, tracing is also advantageous for the way in which it requires scholars to confront, in a systematic way, the core questions I outlined above. It involves making a clear decision about what types of actors and infrastructures to trace, which forces the researcher to articulate a definition of distribution and distributors. It creates a map of a distribution network that can be compared to others, which opens up space for thinking about common and distinctive features of distribution systems. And tracing achieves critical significance by uncovering the sites and mechanisms through which distribution choices come to have social consequences.

NOTES

1 While the telegraph and subsequent electronic communications were, of course, faster than the postal system that preceded them in ways that would come to be meaningful, John (1995, 11) has argued at length against the notion that the telegraph broke the conceptual link between transportation and communication. Rather, in looking at the discourse of the time, he argued, "Indeed, it would be hard to isolate a single bit of figurative language that commentators used to describe the electric telegraph in the period following its commercialization in 1844 that had not already been deployed to describe the postal system."

2 To give an example where automation was seen as disadvantageous, the Bell System resisted automated call switching for quite some time because it owned lucrative patents on the intricate switchboards used by its human operators and viewed its patent monopoly as an overwhelming competitive advantage.

3 It is also worth noting here that, as Mary L. Gray and Siddharth Suri (2019) highlight in their scholarship on "ghost work," in many cases automation not only replaces cheap labor but also displaces it, creating increasingly marginalized workforces who provide uncredited labor that supports the work of algorithms and machines.

BIBLIOGRAPHY

Ahmed, Sara. 2004. "Affective Economies." *Social Text* 22 (2): 117–39.

Baker, C. Edwin. 2002. *Media, Markets, and Democracy*. Cambridge: Cambridge University Press.

Bell, Emily, and Taylor Owen. 2017. *The Platform Press*. New York: Tow Center for Digital Journalism.

Blackman, Colin R. 1998. "Convergence between Telecommunications and Other Media." *Telecommunications Policy* 22 (3): 163–70.

boyd, danah. 2007. "Why Youth (Heart) Social Network Sites." In *Youth, Identity, and Digital Media*, edited by David Buckingham, 119–42. Cambridge, MA: MIT Press.

Braun, Joshua A. 2014. "Transparent Intermediaries." In *Connected Viewing*, edited by Jennifer Holt and Kevin Sanson, 124–43. New York: Routledge.

———. 2015. *This Program Is Brought to You By . . . : Distributing Television News Online*. New Haven, CT: Yale University Press.

———. 2019. "News Distribution." In *The Oxford Research Encyclopedia of Communication*, edited by Jon F. Nussbaum. New York: Oxford University Press. https://oxfordre.com/communication.

Couldry, Nick. 2008. "Actor Network Theory and Media." In *Connectivity, Networks and Flows*, edited by Andreas Hepp, Friedrich Krotz, Shaun Moores, and Carsten Winter, 93–109. Cresskill, NJ: Hampton Press.

Curtin, Michael, Jennifer Holt, and Kevin Sanson, eds. 2014. "Introduction." In *Distribution Revolution*, 1–17. Oakland: University of California Press.

Dobrenko, Evgeny. 1997. *The Making of the State Reader*. Stanford, CA: Stanford University Press.

Douglas, Susan J. 2004. *Listening In*. Minneapolis: University of Minnesota Press.

Downey, Gregory J. 2002. *Telegraph Messenger Boys*. New York: Routledge.

Gillespie, Tarleton. 2014. "The Relevance of Algorithms." In *Media Technologies*, edited by Tarleton Gillespie, Pablo J. Boczkowski, and Kirsten A. Foot, 167–94. Cambridge, MA: MIT Press.

Goldin, Hyman H. 1954. "Economic and Regulatory Problems in the Broadcast Field." *Land Economics* 30 (3): 223–33.

Gray, Mary L., and Siddharth Suri. 2019. *Ghost Work*. New York: Houghton Mifflin Harcourt.

Holt, Jennifer. 2014. "Regulating Connected Viewing." In *Connected Viewing*, edited by Jennifer Holt and Kevin Sanson, 19–39. New York: Routledge.

John, Richard R. 1995. *Spreading the News*. Cambridge, MA: Harvard University Press.

———. 2010. *Network Nation*. Cambridge, MA: Harvard University Press.

Kim, Yong-Chan, and Sandra Ball-Rokeach. 2006. "Civic Engagement from a Communication Infrastructure Perspective." *Communication Theory* 16 (2): 173–97.

King, Martin Luther, Jr. 1998. *The Autobiography of Martin Luther King, Jr.* Edited by Clayborne Carson. New York: Warner Books.

Larkin, Brian. 2008. *Signal and Noise*. Durham, NC: Duke University Press.

Law, John. 1987. "Technology and Heterogeneous Engineering." In *The Social Construction of Technological Systems*, edited by Wiebe E. Bijker, Thomas Parke Hughes, and Trevor Pinch, 111–34. Cambridge, MA: MIT Press.

Lobato, Ramon. 2012. *Shadow Economies of Cinema*. London: British Film Institute.

Martin, Michèle. 1991. *Hello, Central?* Montreal: McGill-Queen's University Press.

McMillian, John. 2011. *Smoking Typewriters*. New York: Oxford University Press.

Parks, Lisa. 2012. "Technostruggles and the Satellite Dish." In *Cultural Technologies*, edited by Göran Bolin, 64–84. New York: Routledge.

Parthé, Kathleen. 2004. *Russia's Dangerous Texts*. New Haven, CT: Yale University Press.

Perren, Alisa. 2013. "Rethinking Distribution for the Future of Media Industry Studies." *Cinema Journal* 52 (3): 165–71.

Swartz, Lana. 2013. "Goodbye, Wallet! Towards a Transactional Geography of Mobile Payment." *Media Fields Journal* 6. http://mediafieldsjournal.squarespace.com.

———. 2020. *New Money: How Payment Became Social Media*. New Haven, CT: Yale University Press.

Szóka, Erin, Jon Henke, and Matthew Starr. 2013. "Don't Blame Big Cable: It's Local Governments That Choke Broadband Competition." *Wired*, July 16. www.wired.com.

Tufekci, Zeynep. 2018. "It's the (Democracy-Poisoning) Golden Age of Free Speech." *Wired*, January 16. www.wired.com.

Warner, Michael. 2002. *Publics and Counterpublics*. New York: Zone Books.

Winseck, Dwayne. 1997. "Canadian Telecommunications." *Canadian Journal of Communication* 22 (2). www.cjc-online.ca.

2

Media Circulation

Reconceptualizing Television Distribution and Exhibition

AMANDA D. LOTZ

Media industries scholarship has primarily focused on building theoretical frameworks for understanding production practices—the making of media—to the neglect of the industrial practices that follow after production, the processes involved in completed media reaching audiences, often categorized as "distribution." Distribution tasks are multifaceted, varied, and often hidden from view; as Perren describes, "Distribution can be seen as taking place when 'fan subbers' (i.e., amateur translators of movies and television series who operate outside sanctioned industrial channels) upload content to torrents, when truck drivers transport comic books from warehouses to retail stores, and when tablet devices are shipped from online retailers to individual residences" (Perren 2013, 170). The maturation of media industry studies and scholars' fascination with the arrival of internet distribution technologies have begun to rectify this oversight.

Too often, understandings of distribution have been left to pithy claims debating whether content or distribution was "king," but each obviously requires the other both industrially and culturally. The considerable variation in distributors and distribution practices across media industries has made deep insight into its cultural implications difficult to discern because "distributors" perform many tasks in a range of contexts. As Perren argues, distribution research has tended toward macro-level accounts of global rights exploitation or case-level study of practices of distribution workers. Research at both of these scales is valuable, but middle-range theory (Cunningham and Jacka 1996) and meso-level accounts that identify industry-scale patterns or attempt to more broadly conceptualize and theorize power negotiations within this varied distribution sector remain lacking. Though some scholarship explains the tasks and activities of distribution practices with as much detail as many afford production (Havens 2006; McDonald 2007; Cunningham and Silver 2013; Braun 2015; Crisp 2015; Lobato 2012, 2019), broader conceptual frameworks of the varied tasks, relative power, and consequence of distributor behavior lagged so significantly that a comprehensive body of pre-internet knowledge of distribution was often not available for comparing new developments initiated by internet distribution.

Rather than attempt the scale of conceptualizing distribution across multiple media industries, this chapter focuses on the scope of tasks involved in disseminating television texts to audiences. The distinctions of distribution and exhibition have been one of the most common frameworks for categorizing these tasks, distinctions willed by film studies to other media, but these categories never mapped elegantly onto television. The term "distributor" can be applied to many different entities; networks, channels, stations, and multichannel cable and satellite services count only the major entities of television distribution.[1] The television industry has always been better understood as composed of sectors of distributors rather than bifurcated among distributors and exhibitors, and the arrival of internet distribution has only added new sectors and complexity. But it is difficult to build theory about distribution when its dynamics vary both among and within multiple industrial sectors. Many entities that can be described as "distributors" share little in common; "distribution" also encompasses tasks such as marketing, dubbing/subtitling, technical formatting, and much else. Such differentiation amid television distribution thwarts efforts to commonly conceptualize their agency and cultural power. To focus this brief chapter, I attend only to the sector of distribution tasked with transmitting content, which, as revealed below, is quite multifaceted on its own.

This chapter proposes "circulation" as a concept that encompasses all the practices involved in completed television texts reaching audiences. It eschews the traditional tripartite categorization of production, distribution, and exhibition of audiovisual media and instead organizes the industrial processes of television into two stages: production and circulation. The analysis concentrates on how theory can be built from focusing on the *tasks* of circulation, the *strategies* used to negotiate among circulation tasks, and the *factors* that enhance agency and allow leverage among circulators. Rather than a loosely bifurcated realm of distribution and exhibition, media circulation encompasses many tasks, and the dynamics of those tasks can be analyzed, compared, and theorized. Thus, such an approach does not merely trade circulation for distribution but dislodges thinking bound by concepts of commensurate distributors. Critical theory can then be generated to explain how those tasks are enabled and constrained and with what consequences. A task-based framework of media circulation identifies the many entities that may engage in both distribution (select, coordinate) and exhibition (offer) functions in order to probe the nuances of the different tasks these entities perform in search of identifiable conditions and patterns with broader applicability. Building such theory requires more precise understandings of circulation activities and establishing sophisticated conceptual fields with internal consistency. Although questions raised by the arrival of internet-distributed media have drawn attention to distribution through the significant changes it has introduced to industrial practices and established industrial "logics" (Thompson 2012), the limitations of how television distribution has been conceptualized predate these technologies.

It is necessary to ground this examination in a specific context in order to build its argument about the inadequacy of conceptual frames that do not distinguish among the different tasks within the ecosystem we've called distributors. The chapter uses the context of the United States to build this argument, but, to be clear, the networks, channels, production companies, and so on cited here are merely for grounded illustration. The dynamics in other contexts might vary in extent of multichannel take-up, the standard industrial arrangement between channels and multichannel services, or whether broadcasters rely on networks of affiliated stations, but the underlying point is of the complexity and multifaceted nature of television "distributors," which has wider relevance than the context illustrated here.

Moving Beyond the Tripartite

In pioneering scholarship that tied film form and style to its mode of production, film scholars David Bordwell, Janet Staiger, and Kristin Thompson organized the activities of the classic Hollywood film industry into stages of production, distribution, and exhibition (Bordwell,

Staiger, and Thompson 1985), a conceptualization drawn from the work of Douglas Gomery (1986).[2] Although their widely taught and cited text focuses on production, it valuably called attention to distribution and exhibition in the context of linking textual outcomes with industrial practices. Janet Wasko's (1994, 146–57) scholarship on the expanding complexity of film circulation in the 1990s also relies on these categories of distribution and exhibition and adds refinement with categories such as retail and wholesale distribution.

Bordwell, Staiger, and Thompson's analysis was one of multiple strands of production and media industry research that developed in the mid-1980s. The role of distribution also drew attention from those who identified with research traditions such as political economy of communication, sociology of media, and cultural studies research. Nicholas Garnham (1990, 183) argued forcefully for the considerable cultural power in distribution, going so far as to attribute the status of the "majors" (film studios) to distribution. As the study of audiovisual media branched beyond film to seriously consider television as a cultural form, the stages of distribution and exhibition became more difficult to apply. They even became awkward for film after the classical Hollywood period and once film consumption expanded beyond theatrical screening. The expansion in sites for engaging film outside the theater decreased the explanatory power of exhibition as a category and added layers of complexity to film distribution.

Another key work in establishing the industrial category of distribution is Joseph Turow's *Media Systems in Society*, first published in 1992. Turow's path-charting text encouraged greater complexity in the conceptualization of industrial practices by enumerating thirteen different "power roles" that structure the operation of media in society, including the roles of both distributors and exhibitors. Turow distinguishes distributors as those who "select and coordinate dispersal of material to the point of exhibition," and exhibitors as those who "offer material for public viewing or purchase" (26). This delineation of specific tasks is helpful, as is his subsequent discussion of key distributors. Turow identifies a complex web of relationships among producers, distributors, and exhibitors who seek to exert leverage over the others in negotiations aimed at business goals, but that also have corresponding cultural significance. Such negotiations play a significant cultural role because of their implications in determining "the amount and kind of mass media materials producers make" (40).

Turow's distinction between distribution and exhibition largely conceives of distribution as a business-to-business (B2B) activity, while exhibitors are audience/consumer facing (B2C). This is a valuable distinction and useful for some industries and contexts—particularly media sold by transaction. Turow's text aimed to speak of media in general though, and this distributor/exhibitor distinction does not hold up well in the practices of television industries, nor does it account for the increasing variety of ways viewers access movies.

The complicated functions and range of tasks required in transmitting completed media products to viewers can be illustrated by rudimentary circulation supply chains. Several factors create considerable complexity, such as vertical integration among circulation tasks and with content producers, or variations arising from the technologies used by viewers to receive television. Thus, multiple chains are presented to illustrate this variation. In the case of a broadcast network received over the air, a producer makes programming at the behest of the network, which funds a significant amount of the production budget and organizes its availability as part of a schedule. In the language of distribution, the broadcast network is a distributor, but so too are the stations that are responsible for the actual transmission of the program to the viewers.

Entities: Production co. → Broadcast network → Station →   Viewer
Tasks: *Create*   *Fund/organize*   *Organize/deliver*

Of course, this merely captures network-generated content. U.S. broadcasting also can be organized with a supply chain in which a station creates programming—perhaps a local newscast—and transmits via broadcast signal such that the station creates, funds, organizes, and delivers to form a much simpler supply chain. In this case, stations effectively encompass all the tasks of production, distribution, and exhibition.

Station →   Viewer

But it is also the case that since the late 1980s, most U.S. television viewers have received even their "broadcast" stations by multichannel service providers—typically cable or satellite companies—that are the consumer-facing entities that also participate in tasks of organization and selection of the range of channels available.[3] A cable subscriber living next door to someone with only over-the-air reception (for whom the first two supply chains might apply) would have the following supply chain within the same national system:

Production co. → Broadcast network → Station → Multichannel → Viewer

Create *Fund/organize* *Organize* *Organize/deliver*

The supply chain for cable channels resembles that of broadcast networks but diminishes the number of organizing nodes:

Production co. → Cable channel → Multichannel → Viewer

Create *Fund/organize* *Organize/deliver*

These supply chains indicate the complexity of actual practice and why a distinction between distributors and exhibitors is unhelpful to conceptualizing television circulation. Many entities do perform tasks characteristic of distributors as Turow defines them; they select and coordinate, but the nature of those tasks varies significantly. Moreover, in the realm of television, some who *select* and *coordinate* also *offer*. The fact that "distributors" fulfill such a multiplicity of tasks—and must work with and are constrained by other "distributors"—makes only the most general claims of distributors possible. Their tasks, nevertheless, are vital and in need of greater understanding.

Notably, any geographic market may have multiple circulation supply chains, which makes it difficult—if not impossible—to speak in multinational terms, let alone account for distribution beyond the first window. Jean Chalaby argues that the complexity of U.S. supply chains was the exception until the late 1980s. To that point, broadcasters elsewhere were "fully integrated operations" (Chalaby 2016, 38). But multichannel services, and more recently internet-distributed television, have added complexity in these contexts as well.

Reconceptualizing media circulation in terms of task and investigating the conditions that moderate how an entity performs those tasks is also helpful for integrating internet-distributed television into established frameworks of industrial operation. The basic supply chain for internet-distributed television can be modeled as:

Production co. → Portal →   ISP   ← Viewer
Create   *Fund/organize*   *Deliver*

In this case, a portal such as Netflix funds content—either by licensing existing or by developing original content—and organizes a library of content that is delivered by internet service providers (ISPs) to viewers. The nonlinearity of portals warrants the reversal of the arrows to acknowledge that portals do not "push" their library so much as a viewer requests access to particular programs.[4] This case also illustrates the limits of conceiving of exhibitors as having a common role in "delivering" content. Here the service that interacts with the viewer is the ISP, but unlike many other entities that directly engage viewers, the ISP performs no selection of material or organizational function.[5] Even multichannel services organize the channels and engage in a curation process by making deals that determine what channels are available. The fact that many American households contract with a single company for both multichannel and internet services adds further complexity to this situation. A company such as Comcast might own, organize, and deliver broadcast stations and cable channels for some subscribers, but merely deliver portals for others.[6]

In sum, all the entities to the right of production companies in these supply chains "select" and "coordinate" media in Turow's terms—though these tasks are described here as fund or organize. Organization happens in varied units and might include the development of shows into schedules or libraries, or organizing channels into a linear package. Entirely new patterns of organization develop through the home screen interface design of portals such as Netflix or the home screen of devices such as Amazon Fire TV Stick or the Apple TV app that channel viewers' selection of services and programs (Hesmondhalgh and Lotz 2020).

Even before the adjustments introduced by internet-distributed television, discussing the circulation of media in terms of distribution and exhibition obscured significant nuances about the processes and relationships involved in programming reaching viewers. The supply chains presented here illustrate the many layers of distributors that can operate in the transmission of television and prevent conducting an adequately sophisticated analysis of their circulation power. The next section continues to offer evidence against common conceptualization of distribution by illustrating how even within a single distribution sector, factors such as vertical integration and other attributes of ownership can significantly vary the agency of those tasked with delivering programming and their leverage relative to adjacent entities. As this analysis illustrates, more robust media circulation theory can be built around the economic and cultural power of tasks, and the conditions that aid and constrain them, than can be asserted of categorical classifications such as distributor or exhibitor.

Power Relations within Circulation before the Internet

Although supply chains provide an illustrative tool for teasing apart the interconnected sectors of distributors, they are unable to capture the considerable variation in agency and leverage that exists within each sector. Channels, networks, and multichannel services all perform similar circulation functions, but they possess very different power in the field of cultural circulation and in their intersection with cultural production. To first outline key players:

SECTORS AND TASKS

Broadcast networks (NBC, ABC, Fox)—fund programs, organize schedule[7]

Cable channels (ESPN, TNT, Discovery)—fund programs, organize schedule

Stations (holders of broadcast license, can be independent or affiliated with a network; of those affiliated, a few are also network owned)—organize schedule, fund programs (other than those offered by network), deliver to over-the-air viewers, contract with multichannel services for carriage

Portals (Netflix, Disney+)—fund programs, organize library, can transact directly with viewers (billing), but ISPs deliver

Multichannel services (Comcast, DirecTV)—organize channels/stations, deliver to subscribers

ISPs (Comcast, AT&T)—provide internet access to viewer, thus deliver internet-distributed media

Conglomerates (Disney, Comcast)—own some mix of broadcast networks, cable channels, production companies, broadcast stations, portals, and ISPs, participate in nearly every task of production and circulation

These key circulation entities—networks, channels, multichannel services—exert economic power in transactions between companies based in a competitive, commercial marketplace in which they vie to be most profitable. That pursuit of profit simultaneously enacts cultural power through the selection, scheduling, and differential promotion of programing consumed as common popular culture. This section illustrates the complicated negotiations that occur between different nodes of the circulation supply chain and the strategies that have been successful in creating leverage by considering the cases of relationships between television stations and networks, the vertical integration of program production within the companies that organize and circulate those series, and conglomerates' use of must-have channels in negotiations with multichannel service providers. These examples further illustrate the complexity and variability even within a single sector of video circulation.

In the United States, broadcast networks were arguably the dominant circulation force until the twenty-first century. Their key cultural power resided in their status as gatekeepers: few suppliers of television existed, and among those that did, programming capacity was constrained by the twenty-four-hour schedule. Networks had considerable power over the production companies from which they licensed programs—enacted by the affiliated stations that actually delivered their programming to viewers—and of course over the viewers, in establishing the gamut of programming available. In the network era, the broadcast networks' oligopsony status as buyers allowed them considerable leverage over studios in setting licensing conditions—until that power was checked by regulation (Holt 2011). Even though the networks licensed only a first run from production companies, they had extensive gatekeeping power over what would be available in the second run and later markets as well because so little original programming—particularly scripted series— could be afforded by independent stations or cable channels.

Beyond the cultural power of determining what programming would be made, the economic power of the broadcast networks was constrained by the fact that the networks had limited direct access to viewers, which required their relationship with affiliated stations. Regulations designed to encourage a "marketplace of ideas" and localism (Napoli 2001) limited the number of stations the network could own, so the station sector was bifurcated among stations that are either owned and operated (O&O) or simply affiliated.[8] O&O stations were, and continue to be, the economic lifeblood of the network, for they return more profit than the "network" business because the cost of prime-time programming is so great that it largely offsets the national commercial revenue. But networks located their O&O stations in the largest markets in the country (New York City, Los Angeles) and earn considerable revenue from local advertising in these areas. The O&O stations also can be relied upon to operate in the interest of the network.

The power dynamics among affiliated stations and networks have shifted considerably over time, particularly as cable services emerged as an alternative distribution technology, and additional broadcast networks and cable channels fragmented the marketplace. Affiliate stations also transitioned from being locally owned, often family businesses, to being held in large station ownership groups such as by Sinclair and Nexstar. These shifting competitive conditions and owner interests adjusted the priorities and relative leverage of local stations. Affiliated stations were initially compensated by the networks and also benefited because the programming the network provided attracted far more viewers than the station was likely to draw if it remained independent. (Affiliated stations give up most advertising slots in network-provided programming, but maintain a few minutes per hour for local spots for which they keep the revenue.) As competition for audiences intensified, compensation stopped and affiliated stations began "compensating" the network by splitting the revenue earned from retransmission fees from multichannel services in 2007. Affiliated stations have long had a right to refuse programming from the network, though this rarely occurs. Stations need the network programming to achieve audience scale but also are incentivized by regulatory structures to prioritize the station's interest rather than that of the network. Although the networks have economic power over the stations, the stations derive political power through appealing to regulators who prioritize the supposed localism they offer as a top policy priority. Throughout much of the twentieth century, the collective organization of local stations in the National Association of Broadcasters (NAB) enabled stations considerable political power that delayed competition from cable distribution.

The different priorities of O&O and affiliate stations illustrate that even in a particular circulation sector (stations), ownership can meaningfully adjust behavior, leverage, and priorities. Or, more bluntly, stations do not consistently wield circulation power. Moreover, by the late 1990s, the network-era power dynamics among circulators changed considerably. Although many might presume this adjustment owed to the widespread adoption of multichannel services, in fact it resulted from a series of mergers and acquisitions that restructured the industry. The ownership and regulatory changes allowed networks and channels that perform circulation tasks such as funding and organizing programming to be commonly owned by the companies that also owned the production companies (media conglomerates). The consolidation of once separate broadcast, cable, and film businesses into conglomerated media companies and the elimination of the rules that prevented the networks from owning much of their programming—the Financial Interest and Syndication Rules that were in place from the early 1970s through the mid-1990s—shored up the power of those that fund and organize over those that deliver (Holt 2011).

The distinctions between producers and circulators consequentially grew blurry in practice. Previously adversarial relations between networks and production companies became more symbiotic once they were co-owned, though network negotiations with production companies making shows for networks/channels without shared ownership became more precarious. Here, even categorization by task is inadequate to understanding the power dynamics. One set of relations governed norms for series with vertically integrated production and circulation—a show produced by ABC Studios for ABC network—and another for those that split these tasks between companies (a Warner Bros. show produced for NBC).

By the late 1990s, conglomerates also owned both broadcast networks/stations and cable channels. This ownership structure likewise diminished the value of analysis by sector, for example broadcast versus cable. Once conglomerates owned the majority of cable channels as well as broadcast networks, a broadcast versus cable channel horse race became an artificial and meaningless frame for understanding industrial dynamics. Conglomerates aimed to attract audiences to both broadcast and cable offerings and strategically used both to support the series they produced.

More relevant to informing the factors that yield leverage between different circulators was how important conglomerate ownership was for negotiating with multichannel services. The conglomerates that own entities that fund, organize, and—in some cases—deliver content achieved considerable leverage over the multichannel services that had become the dominant deliverers of programming. By amassing broad portfolios encompassing broadcast networks and cable channels, the conglomerates were able to use their most desired content and channels to ensure preferred status for content and channels that lacked significant demand. The ability of a channel to gain carriage on a multichannel service and negotiate carriage fees was largely divorced from market forces and determined by conglomerate power: a conglomerate such as Disney could secure access for many of its cable channels because multichannel services were desperate to have its ESPN channel. Thus, the power of channels varied greatly. Channels owned by a conglomerate had an exceptional advantage—so long as the conglomerate had at least one channel the multichannel services perceived they must have—while it became nearly impossible to launch a channel from outside a conglomerate. But this also illustrates limitations to claims of "distribution" power, as this instance indicates leverage resulting from content ownership.

This outlining and review of the shifting relations within the field of U.S. television circulation is meant to illustrate how difficult it is to theorize the power role of circulation by sector (network, channel). This is due to differentiated leverage available to various circulation roles and the reality that power accessible to circulators with the same role can vary based on other factors such as the underlying political economy or more specific conditions such as corporate ownership and regulatory policies governing delivery technologies. Though obviously cursory, it identifies the multiple forces that have allowed strategic leverage within the field of circulation in the context of broadcast and multichannel television. This context valuably frames efforts to explain the emerging dynamics of internet distribution that have added further complexity to circulation.

Television Circulation and Internet Distribution

The general argument of this chapter is that the tasks attributed to the role of "distributors" are too broad and varied to lead to useful theory building. This is further emphasized by the increasing range of distributors now active in the context of internet-distributed video who cumulatively add further complexity to the field. As noted earlier, the fact that a single entity such as Comcast or AT&T functions both as internet and multichannel service provider adds to the confusion, as the companies' different but simultaneous roles as multichannel video and internet service providers allow them to exert different leverage in each of these capacities. This discrepancy results in part from the precedent of regulating video "by technology" in the United States (Napoli 2001) as opposed to acknowledging the interconnected ecosystem across audiovisual services. It also derives from the still somewhat "early" stage of internet-distributed video and slow identification of governing regulatory regimes, at least in the United States.

TASKS OF DIFFERENT CATEGORIES OF INTERNET-
    DISTRIBUTED VIDEO BUSINESSES
ISPs (Comcast, AT&T)—deliver internet-distributed content
Video app marketplaces (Amazon Channels, Apple TV app)—make available, organize (recommend), sell portals
Streaming video devices (Amazon Fire TV Stick, Apple TV, Xbox, PlayStation, set-top boxes, smart TVs)—connect televisions to the internet (and often video app marketplaces), facilitate app access, organize, recommend programming and portals

The technological capacity of internet-distributed television introduces at least two additional sectors of distributors: the portals that replicate the role of channels in organizing and developing a library of programming and home and mobile ISPs that transmit the video files.[9] ISPs play multiple possible circulation roles in delivering video, which makes depicting ISPs in the video supply chain complicated. Their role is to deliver, but they do not precisely mirror the duties and tasks of multichannel services, nor is their power and leverage the same.

Video accessed by a home may go through a single combined multi-channel and internet service provider, but varied supply chains undergird the industrial practices of multichannel services and ISPs. The task and leverage of a service provider such as Comcast vary depending on the originator of the video: multichannel service providers remunerate channels and stations, while ISPs transmit (i.e., move the digital packets containing video encoding) video without underlying contracts, agreements, or remuneration.

Production co.→ Broadcast network→ Station→   Comcast as MVPD→ Viewer

Production co.→ Portal→   Comcast as ISP ←Viewer

Thus, it is impossible to even make universal claims about "Comcast's" role in video circulation because the company's role differs depending on whether video is being delivered by "cable" or internet due to established industrial practices and regulatory structures.

ISPs are becoming a crucial part of the video supply chain and potentially powerful video circulators. In an environment governed by net neutrality, however, their tasks are clearly circumscribed, and thus their power to provide preference to content circulators is limited: the role of ISPs is delivery—they do not organize, they cannot prioritize. However, without net neutrality policy, paid prioritization is an available industrial practice that enables the ISP to take on gatekeeping or "access" power (Rahman 2018) that is largely unchecked in the many markets in which no competition among ISPs exists.

ISPs lobbied for the elimination of net neutrality in the United States so that they might institute paid prioritization—fees levied on internet-distributed services for preferential distribution treatment—in order to expand their power over circulation and, of course, to increase profits. In response to their experience as multichannel services, in which their access power was rendered impotent by content-owning conglomerates (Disney, Time Warner) that were able to leverage must-have programming to extort high carriage fees and demand conditions for channels such as inclusion on basic tiers, ISPs sought to shift the balance of power in their favor. It is already the case that ISPs do not remunerate content services in the way multichannel services do, but with paid prioritization, ISPs seek to reverse the industrial practice of multichannel services and require payment *from* content creators or others in the circulation supply chain.

These political and economic structures hint at supply chain relationships for portals that are still developing. Although a sizable service such as Netflix can be reasonably depicted as in the supply chain above, many other start-up services are dependent on other circulation entities that might exert meaningful leverage. For example, many portals do not have the capacity to develop direct-to-consumer infrastructure and rely on "marketplaces" (app stores or preloading of apps) maintained by companies such as Amazon, Apple, and Google in order to reach viewers. Adding complexity, portals can be available direct to consumer (the Netflix website) *as well as* offered and serviced through marketplaces (Amazon Channels, Apple TV/App Store), multichannel service providers, streaming video devices (Apple TV, Roku, Fire TV Stick), and smart TVs and gaming systems. Marketplaces organize portals and sometimes perform tasks such as billing that are fulfilled by multichannel services in the case of cable/satellite (and some multichannel services are also creating such portal services).[10] These marketplaces are often tied to the technologies used for viewing or connecting sets (Amazon Fire TV Stick, Apple TV, Roku, smart TV manufacturers, gaming devices) (Hesmondhalgh and Lobato 2019). These streaming media devices also perform circulation tasks such as organization. They develop the interfaces through which viewers access and choose programs—often based on proprietary search and recommendation functions that simultaneously help users manage the increasing abundance of programming options while also powerfully channeling viewer attention toward particular programs and services. These entities—the marketplace managers and streaming technologies—are now also potentially powerful nodes in video circulation.

Acknowledging the role of these circulators in terms of the supply chains modeled above is challenging. There is considerable variation, at the moment, in viewer practices and devices used. This variation has created the appearance that no entity has outsized influence, but much about the industrial practices—such as details of the transaction that led to Netflix buttons on device remotes or for Amazon Prime to appear in the top row of preloaded apps on the Apple TV home screen—remain private. Of course, the business-to-business terms behind Disney's negotiation of carriage for its channels on Comcast were also not publicly disclosed, though if a failed negotiation led to a service-wide channel blackout, journalists, and sometimes regulators, paid attention. The interplay among those involved in the circulation of internet-distributed television is quite opaque, and it is difficult for a viewer to know whether a Netflix video streams poorly because of a problem with Netflix or one with the ISP, because the ISP is throttling Netflix, or if it is just a glitch with a home Wi-Fi router.

Many of the industrial practices between portals and marketplaces, or between marketplaces and device technologies, remain unknown and likely are only in their earliest stages. Recognizing comparable circulation relations for existing video distribution technologies helps flesh out how leverage can be used and abused and can lead to consideration of how abuses could be mitigated before they develop. ISPs obviously deliver far more than video content—they are also conduits for email, social media, and access to all forms of websites and apps—and those uses may encourage certain approaches to regulatory policy distinct from the concerns of video distribution. It is also the case that in delivering video, ISPs reproduce the tasks of entities such as broadcast stations and multichannel services that are often governed by specific regulatory and industrial precedent. Complicated questions thus emerge about whether rules that apply to broadcasters and multichannel providers should also apply to internet-distributed video.

It is early in the adoption of viewing technologies and video app marketplaces, but some version of these tasks will continue to be crucial to video circulation going forward. Abuses of market power are not yet clear, but we should expect commercially driven companies to seek advantages in dealing with creators and other circulators in the same way the networks once leveraged their power over studios. Further, these companies are incentivized to decrease competition so they can enhance their own leverage, and thus they will engage in practices aimed to winnow the field. Competitive conditions may not perfectly replicate the oligopsony conditions of the network era, but they are also not radically different. To some degree, instead of a field dominated by NBC, ABC, and CBS, U.S. television circulation—and perhaps television more broadly—faces reconfiguration at the hands of Apple, Amazon, and Netflix: Apple and Amazon through their endeavors to control the technological pathways of apps and devices and gather data about use, and by selling, recommending, and providing users' primary interface; and Netflix as a programming service with unprecedented scale that might translate into unconstrained leverage. But crucially, great power remains in the hands of the ISPs who operate outside of market conditions as often monopolistic, high-speed providers that, particularly without net neutrality protections, have extraordinary power over all companies reliant on internet-based customer interaction.

Conclusion

Although the emergence of internet-distributed video services—and their blend of similarity to and difference from broadcast, cable, and satellite—has drawn increased attention to video distribution in recent years, it is important not only to conceptualize internet video distribution but also to develop frameworks that include the variety of technologies still widely in use. To that end, this chapter has argued for theory building about video circulation that distinguishes among tasks involved and identifies mechanisms of power that can be used in performance of those tasks as a productive route to more sophisticated understandings of the dynamics that affect how video—and what video—reaches viewers. The examples used may seem very specific to the U.S. industry; indeed, they are, as circulation practices are highly contextual. Similar critical investigations of such circulation power dynamics in other contexts are needed to identify broader patterns.

The supply chain diagrams illustrate the multiple and complicated array of "distributors" involved in transmitting video to viewers' homes. When we subcategorize the established field of distributors into discrete sectors (broadcast station, network, multichannel) we see that even within a sector such as broadcast stations, differentiated access to leverage derives from a station's independence or affiliation with a network and whether it is owned by the network. Theorizing circulation requires focused examination of particular tasks and identification of the industrial features that enable and inhibit leverage among those performing the task.

Notably, this effort to acknowledge the complexity of television circulation and advocate for frameworks more sophisticated than lumping practices into those of distributors or exhibitors merely scratches the surface of many of the cultural functions of media circulators in its focus on the entities that transmit video. Many circulators play important roles in marketing and promotion that significantly contribute to the scope and nature of the audience achieved, and theorizing circulators must also account for these activities. Likewise, circulators have borne responsibility for tasks such as re-editing series (such as when commercial breaks need to be added or extracted) and in adding dubbing and subtitling that are also important to reshaping the text in ways that have cultural implications. Such practices are also being restructured as the norms of international television trade change amid the adoption of services such as Netflix and Amazon Prime Video that are capable of multinational reach and manage multiple circulation tasks internally.

NOTES

1 Some may query whether some of these are exhibitors—I get to that later.

2 Although Gomery published a year later, Staiger was a student of Gomery and recalls his teaching as informing the tripartite construction of her coauthored work.

3 Since the elimination of the Financial Interest and Syndication Rules, networks have purchased most of their prime-time offerings from studios owned by a common conglomerate. This may suggest a need to conceptualize studios/networks as a common firm in such cases.

4 Some portals do feature both a linear feed and on-demand access, which might warrant a "push" rather than "pull" directional arrow, and of course in pulling, viewers do not have endless choice and perceive their choice through the lens of personalization algorithms that do encourage certain choices, but this encouragement still warrants differentiation from the preselection of the linear schedule.

5 Some multichannel services / ISPs have begun to function as intermediaries (as when Comcast and Netflix establish terms through which Comcast offers Netflix to its subscribers). Such arrangements add complexity, but it remains the case that customers can contract directly with portals as well.

6 One last facet of confusion relates to the conflation of tasks of ISPs that technologically deliver the service but may or may not provide customer service for portals. For example, I can subscribe to Netflix and directly pay Netflix, or I can pay Netflix through my multichannel service provider.

7 Fund is meant to indicate payment for acquisition of both licensed and original programs.

8 Of course another subsector of independent stations exists, but given their small percentage of the marketplace, they are not examined here.

9 A more technologically nuanced examination would also note the role of content delivery networks (CDNs; e.g., Akamai, CloudFront [Amazon Web Services]),

the infrastructure of servers paid by portals to transmit the files, and who in turn pays ISPs to host their servers. This layer of distribution infrastructure is certainly important but is not engaged in detail due to the brevity of this chapter.

10 It is difficult to discern when Comcast is acting as a multichannel service or as an ISP. One route may be to distinguish those activities available to consumers who do not receive cable service as characteristic of an ISP activity, though this is still complicated.

BIBLIOGRAPHY

Bordwell, David, Janet Staiger, and Kristin Thompson. 1985. *The Classical Hollywood Cinema: Film Style and Mode of Production to 1960*. New York: Columbia University Press.

Braun, Joshua A. 2015. *This Program Is Brought to You By . . . : Distributing Television News Online*. New Haven, CT: Yale University Press.

Chalaby, Jean. 2016. "Television and Globalization: The TV Content Global Value Chain." *Journal of Communication* 66 (1): 35–59.

Crisp, Virginia. 2015. *Film Distribution in the Digital Age: Pirates and Professionals*. London: Palgrave Macmillan.

Cunningham, Stuart, and Elizabeth Jacka. 1996. *Australian Television and International Mediascapes*. Cambridge: Cambridge University Press.

Cunningham, Stuart, and Jon Silver. 2013. *Screen Distribution and the New King Kongs of the Online World*. New York: Palgrave Macmillan.

Garnham, Nicholas. 1990. *Capitalism and Communication: Global Culture and the Economics of Information*. London: Sage.

Gomery, Douglas. 1986. *The Hollywood Studio System*. London: British Film Institute.

Havens, Timothy. 2006. *Global Television Marketplace*. London: British Film Institute.

Hesmondhalgh, David, and Ramon Lobato. 2019. "Television Device Ecologies, Prominence and Datafication: The Neglected Importance of the Set-Top Box." *Media, Culture & Society* 41 (7): 958–74.

Hesmondhalgh, David, and Amanda D. Lotz. 2020. "Video Screen Interfaces as New Sites of Circulation Power." *International Journal of Communication* 14: 386–409.

Holt, Jennifer. 2011. *Empires of Entertainment: Media Industries and the Politics of Deregulation, 1980–1996*. New Brunswick, NJ: Rutgers University Press.

Lobato, Ramon. 2012. *Shadow Economies of Cinema: Mapping Informal Film Distribution*. London: British Film Institute.

———. 2019. *Netflix Nations: The Geography of Digital Distribution*. New York: New York University Press.

Lotz, Amanda D. 2019. "Teasing Apart Television Industry Disruption: Consequences of Meso-level Financing Practices Before and After the US Multiplatform Era." *Media, Culture & Society* 41 (7): 923–38.

McDonald, Paul. 2007. *Video and DVD Industries*. London: British Film Institute.

Napoli, Philip M. 2001. *Foundations of Communications Policy: Principles and Process in the Regulation of Electronic Media*. Cresskill, NJ: Hampton Press.

Perren, Alisa. 2013. "Rethinking Distribution for the Future of Media Industry Studies." *Cinema Journal* 52 (3): 165–71.

Rahman, K. Sabeel. 2018. "The New Octopus." *Logic* 4. https://logicmag.io.

Thompson, John B. 2012. *Merchants of Culture: The Publishing Business in the Twenty-First Century*. London: Penguin.

Turow, Joseph. 1992. *Media Systems in Society*. White Plains, NY: Longman.

Wasko, Janet. 1994. *Hollywood in the Information Age: Beyond the Silver Screen*. Austin: University of Texas Press.

3

Reassessing the "Space in Between"

Distribution Studies in Transition

ALISA PERREN

In 2013, I argued for the development of a scholarly subfield of "distribution studies" within media industry studies to facilitate a more focused, cross-disciplinary dialogue about the "space in between" production and consumption (Perren 2013). Such a subfield appeared warranted to make sense of the dramatic, ongoing industrial transformations resulting from digitization, globalization, and consolidation. Although substantial work on the topic of distribution already had occurred across a wide range of fields (e.g., television studies, film history, political economy of communication, moving-image archiving, and global media studies), I hoped that the general mantle of "distribution studies" would elicit more dedicated interdisciplinary conversation.

In the ensuing years, media and communication studies scholars have taken up calls like mine in ways beyond what I then could have anticipated. Special issues of journals, as well as a growing number of conference panels, produced increasingly nuanced ways of researching, theorizing, and writing about distribution ("Media Distribution" 2015; "Digital Distribution" 2015; "Distribution Matters: Media Circulation in Civic Life and Popular Culture" 2017; "Distribution" 2019). Much of this scholarship has been undertaken by the contributors and editors of this collection; such work has discussed the industrial, cultural, and material dimensions of contemporary media distribution in the digital age in increasingly nuanced ways.[1] Concurrently, of course, organizational structures, business models, and cultural practices have continued to evolve in ways that challenge scholars to continually revise their assumptions, update their analytical frameworks, and adjust their research methods.

The following are among the most notable developments in media distribution since the early 2010s:

- the continued decline in the distribution of physical media (e.g., DVDs) and the concurrent proliferation of digital distribution services
- legacy media companies' (e.g., Disney, WarnerMedia) ongoing shift away from maximizing revenue by licensing content to individual markets (space-based distribution) and staggering release windows (time-based distribution) in favor of reclaiming global control over rights (intellectual property [IP] ownership) for as many markets and windows as possible
- growing efforts by these same legacy companies, along with Silicon Valley–based technology companies, to gain exclusive access to original content in the interest of attracting consumers to new subscription video-on-demand (SVOD) or advertising video-on-demand (AVOD), direct-to-consumer (DTC) streaming services (e.g., Disney+, Peacock, and Apple TV+)
- the intensification of industry consolidation (e.g., Comcast's acquisition of Sky; Disney's acquisition of Fox) as media conglomerates aim to attract more subscribers to proprietary digital delivery services

This list, albeit largely focused on U.S. entertainment media, points to some of the most significant changes in the distribution landscape—changes that have impacted industry economics, institutional relationships, cultural assumptions, and access to content. Many of the developments above certainly are applicable to other national and regional contexts as well as to other industry sectors such as games, music, journalism, and books. Importantly, the *variations and divergences* across industry sector, medium, and locale are often equally—if not more—revealing than the *similarities and convergences* taking place in terms of contemporary distribution practices. As I previously argued, through processes of comparison—as well as by attending to the cultural and material dimensions of distribution—we can better make sense of the complexity of the current industrial landscape in general and the transformations in distribution practices more specifically (Perren 2013, 168).

During the past decade, numerous scholars initiated studies of the cultural and material dimensions of media distribution. Yet comparative analyses remain more limited in number.[2] Through processes of comparison, however, we are often able to challenge dominant cultural, industrial, and (increasingly) scholarly narratives and taken-for-granted assumptions. As I illustrate below, such comparative studies might include, first, drawing connections between the historical analog and contemporary digital-era distribution contexts; second, looking beyond the more visible—and widely covered—stakeholders involved in distributing content; and, third, analyzing formats and genres traditionally viewed as "outliers" (e.g., sports, theater, comic books) by many film and media scholars.

Historical Legacies

Much distribution-oriented scholarship has evaluated the continuities and changes driven by the shift from analog *to* digital technologies. Topics including the redefinition of markets, the collapse of release windows, the expansion and layering of physical and technological infrastructures, and the revaluation of library content have all been explored in this context (Doyle 2016; Hoyt 2014). Of course, as media historians regularly remind us, in making assertions about continuity and/or change in the digital age, we are often drawing from uneven and incomplete knowledge of the past (Gitelman 2006; Sterne 2012). This can lead to assertions about the "newness" or distinctiveness of contemporary practices that don't necessarily fully hold up upon greater scrutiny.

It is understandable that digital technologies have been foregrounded in recent scholarship due to the striking pace of present-day industry change, our own personal investments as researchers, and our own lived experiences engaging with these services. Nonetheless, it is worth indicating some of the ways that more historically oriented projects might not only enrich contemporary work on distribution but also point to fresh ways of thinking about the past. While historical film distribution practices have been examined extensively for decades, different topics continue to be explored and new methods used, fueled in part by the digitization of online source materials by the Media History Digital Library, the Internet Archive, the Entertainment Industry Magazine Archive, and the Texas Archive of the Moving Image, among others. What's more, in just the past few years, several scholars—including Govil (2015), in surveying the long history of film exchange between India and the

United States, and Sandvig (2015), in tracing how those involved in the development of early internet infrastructures in the 1960s envisioned it as "anti-television"—have further revealed ways that historical practices can inform contemporary understandings and shape current research.

Yet still more can be done. Scholars such as Morgan-Parmett (2006), Parks (2007), and Russo (2010) already have provided grounded examples of how distribution technologies, policies, and practices evolved in diverse localized historical contexts. Additional historical research on how local spaces and places have been assimilated into national distribution systems—or, at times, struggled to do so—can further inform our contemporary scholarship on digital distribution in several ways. First, such historical studies can push us to consider, with a greater level of precision, which earlier distribution technologies and industry stakeholders have remained active into the present and how they were able to remain viable.[3] New layers of distribution infrastructures and intermediaries obviously have developed in relation to—and often in tension with—legacy infrastructures and intermediaries, impacting both what we access and how we do so in complicated ways.

Second, projects by scholars such as Morgan-Parmett, Parks, and Russo further contribute to ongoing discussions about what we mean when we employ terms such as local, regional, national, and transnational. At times "local" is either used imprecisely or conflated with the national, thereby disassociating the concept from grounded, place-based analysis. While a vital, growing body of current scholarship is focusing on the international flows of media content—or the forces constraining such international flows—this scope can lead us to lose sight of how distribution functions in much more geographically specific, place-based situations. Already, at least in terms of the United States, the federal government largely has abandoned its efforts to regulate media in the interest of localism (Ali 2017; Kirkpatrick 2007). Within this context, there is particular political value in attending to the specificities of space and place, and considering the precise means by which distribution infrastructures—and the content disseminated through them—function within and in relation to local communities. As much as media distribution practices can structure spaces and places, spaces and places also can structure distribution practices. A historically grounded place-based orientation offers a means of connecting the fraught status of legacy infrastructures in specific locales (e.g., cable system operators, local broadcast stations) with the unequal access to new technologies (e.g., broadband, wireless) faced by many of these and other, often rural, frequently economically disadvantaged communities.

Even as we continue to develop new modes of studying historical distribution practices and stakeholders—and drawing linkages between such historical cases and present-day conditions—there is another way in which we might engage with the past: by tracing how historical content is presently being stored, digitized, preserved, catalogued, and circulated by a blend of for-profit, nonprofit, and governmental institutions for a variety of different reasons. Complementing the range of companies invested in finding new ways of generating revenue from old and new content alike via emergent digital delivery services is a wider ecosystem of institutions, including museums, archives (public and private, regional and national), universities, heritage organizations, professional associations, service providers, and libraries that are invested in making media accessible to the public for diverse reasons. While such (often nonprofit) institutions can be driven by educational, informational, and/or political goals, they also often either service or collaborate with corporations in the interest of generating revenue and entertaining audiences. Even if such stakeholders are often motivated primarily by realizing public interest objectives, as opposed to achieving commercial goals, the scope of their activities is often enabled or constrained by the activities of for-profit media corporations. For instance, an archive might license stock footage for a documentary that appears on Netflix, a museum might arrange a special exhibit and related screening series (and accompanying program for public television) that promotes a particular group of filmmakers, and an association might organize conference sessions or webinars that communicate the latest tools, standards, or professional practices.

As Frick (2009) argues, these stakeholders frequently don't operate in opposition to or even in parallel to media industries; rather they compose *a part of* the larger industry ecology. Fusing work by Frick and others based in moving-image archiving, information science, and media history, doctoral student Kate Cronin in the Department of Radio-Television-Film at the University of Texas at Austin represents an example of an emerging scholar pointing to new directions in the study of distribution by looking to the past. Cronin (2021) examines the underlying economic and political rationales of how nascent U.S. television broadcast news organizations of the 1940s and 1950s sought to acquire, organize, and monetize early newsfilm content.[4] She illustrates how libraries and archives within news organizations such as CBS and NBC not only helped to shape cultural history but also functioned as important, underexamined actors in the life cycle of media content. Work involving assistant editors logging who is on camera or when a segment was shot typically has been interpreted by industry practitioners primarily as production labor. Yet when this content is later licensed for use by other outlets—whether as stock footage for a movie or as a segment in another channel's nightly news broadcast—it becomes part of the distribution process.

Crucially, much of the content that we currently access through different digital platforms—whether YouTube or Netflix or PBS Living—is available because of choices made by different historical and contemporary stakeholders about what was worth saving, what costs are involved with restoring and/or preserving content, how something might be catalogued, and who could potentially monetize it and in what ways. Such choices, of course, are fueled by the financial and cultural resources as well as the political power available to varied stakeholders. Importantly, somewhat different assessments of value have been and continue to be made in terms of preserving and circulating news, sports, advertising, and educational content (among other forms) than have been and are being made for much entertainment content.

Content Matters

How and why does content matter when we talk about contemporary distribution? Certainly numerous scholars and journalists have addressed how the new distribution platforms—whether cable channels or streaming services—have successfully released content that was financially unsustainable via traditional linear television outlets or through theatrical exhibition (Tryon 2013; Christian 2018). Yet scholarship on emergent delivery services, and the content that they distribute, has remained circumscribed in several identifiable ways. Thus far, in the U.S. context, for example, a disproportionate amount of attention has been paid to analyzing the most high-profile services, whether linear channels such as HBO and AMC or over-the-top services such as Netflix and Amazon. These outlets' prioritization of entertainment content—including both scripted fictional material and unscripted reality fare—along with the tendency of film and media studies scholars to gravitate toward studying such content, has meant less attention has gone to other thriving, distinctive forms of media, including sports and news. The conditions within which these other types of content are licensed, distributed, and consumed are often substantively different from the conditions within which entertainment-oriented content circulates, and as such, merit heightened attention for how they might complicate larger industrial claims and cultural assumptions.

The emphasis on the most *visible* players in the streaming ecosystem, like the Big Three of Netflix, Hulu, and Amazon, has been complemented by a dynamic body of work examining the role of what Braun (2013) labels "transparent" or "invisible" intermediaries, which include infrastructure providers such as Nexidia and YuMe. As scholars like Braun and Vonderau have demonstrated, the study of these digital intermediaries is important for a range of reasons. These intermediaries rightfully have been examined for their role in automating the functions of traditional (human) gatekeepers such as talent agents, managers, and media buyers; contesting national regulatory regimes via largely unregulated data centers located around the globe; enabling the seamless transmission of data and the smooth functioning of digital networks; and reshaping retail chains and distribution channels through their role as content aggregators (Vonderau 2015).

Other, less visible stakeholders that have emerged or evolved concurrently have generated less scrutiny from scholars thus far but have played important roles in financing, developing, producing, and distributing varied types of media content. Examples here include talent agencies-cum-media corporations (e.g., WME, CAA, UTA), midrange producer-distributors (e.g., MRC, STX, Lionsgate), and specialty SVOD and AVOD services (e.g., Cheddar, FuboTV, Pluto TV). Examinations of other stakeholders like these can shed light on the evolving distribution landscape and the different types of content produced within it in somewhat different ways. First, take talent agencies. During the past couple of decades, the major talent agencies increasingly have diversified their activities, shifting from primarily representing talent and corporations to becoming multinational media conglomerates in their own right. For example, following a merger of the William Morris and Endeavor talent agencies in 2009, the rebranded WME (under the auspices of holding company Endeavor) proceeded to acquire the Ultimate Fighting Championship (UFC), Miss Universe Organization, sports, fashion, and entertainment management company IMG, and arts event company Frieze. In addition, WME gained ownership stakes in a variety of different types of companies, including e-sports gaming league ELEAGUE (ELEAGUE n.d.; Endeavor n.d.). What's more, as Fleming (2017) notes, WME evolved from its role in the 1990s as a key force in the indie film world—where, as William Morris Independent, it primarily packaged indie films and procured financing and distribution deals for such titles as *Monster's Ball* (2001), *Half Nelson* (2006), and *Frozen River* (2008)—to its current status as WME Global Finance and Distribution Group, where it procures financing and assembles packages for a full spectrum of film and television projects globally (e.g., *The Night Manager* [2016], *The Young Pope* [2016]).

Even as WME Global Finance and Distribution maintains its previous activities, it also raises private equity, serves as a sales agent for more varied media properties, cultivates partnerships with advertisers, and so on. At the same time, this more expansive role is complemented by WME's launch of "affiliated studios" in the form of IMG Original Content (*Gleason* [2016]; *Battle of the Network Stars* [2017]) and Endeavor Content (*Killing Eve* [2018–], *The First* [2018]), along with the launch of its own streaming platform, Endeavor Streaming (Chmielewski 2019). To support these expansion efforts, WME has turned to outside investment firms for financial support, with technology-oriented company Silver Lake Partners now holding a majority stake in the company (de-Waard 2020).

A variety of technological, economic, and industrial forces have contributed to the move by the major talent agencies into diverse distribution activities including building their own libraries, serving as financiers, arranging licensing deals, and launching streaming services. Certainly, the proliferation of new content buyers on a global basis—for both linear outlets as well as internet-based services—has been a driving force in their growth. Significantly, the largest talent agencies have been important participants in spurring the growth of a *different* stakeholder—midrange studios. As deWaard (2020) shows in his important work on the financialization of the film, television, and music industries, the infusion of private equity funds during the 2000s led corporations such as WME and CAA to become vertically and horizontally integrated behemoths—behemoths whose full influence over global content production has only just begun to be reckoned with by either the industry or the press. These agencies, in turn, have an ownership stake in *separate* investment subsidiaries (e.g., Raine for Endeavor). As if that isn't complicated enough, these investment arms, in turn, have a stake in companies involved in the financing, production, and distribution of film, TV, and digital content (WME with Media Rights Capital, CAA with STX Productions). Companies like MRC and STX have become providers of premier content for services such as Netflix (MRC's *House of Cards* [2013–18] and *Ozark* [2017–]) and Starz (MRC's *Counterpart* [2017–19]). As Sun and Handel (2018) have observed, talent represented by these agency-cum-media conglomerates figures prominently in many of these studios' projects (potential conflicts of interest be damned). MRC, STX, and other midrange studios benefit from an industrial context in which legacy media companies such as Disney and WarnerMedia increasingly have reclaimed rights to their most popular titles in the interest of exploiting them exclusively on their own nascent streaming services.

MRC and STX are notable for more than just their affiliations to major talent agencies. They represent a small contingent of a new generation of midrange film and TV financier-distributors—along with Annapurna and Lionsgate—that have grown in prominence since the mid-2000s. To an extent, these companies filled the gap left when many specialty operations (e.g., Warner Independent, and Paramount Vantage) closed and others (e.g., Fox Searchlight, Focus Features) diminished their output and otherwise altered their production and distribution strategies. Despite a theatrical exhibition context ever more hostile to all but the most high-concept event films and low-budget genre pictures, these latest "mini-majors" have focused to varying degrees on supporting genres such as romances (*Second Act* [2018]), crime dramas (*Molly's Game* [2017]), and comedies (*I Feel Pretty* [2018]) that have been all but abandoned by the major studio-distributors. Concurrently, such genres, along with others (e.g., teen romances like *To All the Boys I've Loved Before* [2018]; Westerns like *The Ballad of Buster Scruggs* [2018]), have found an increasingly hospitable environment on streaming services like Netflix, which are focused on pursuing such projects in the interest of appealing to as wide a range of taste cultures as possible (Adalian 2018).

The long-term viability of these midrange companies remains in question for a variety of economic, legal, and industrial reasons.[5] Nonetheless, this discussion calls attention to how two additional stakeholders, agency-conglomerates and midrange financier-distributors, are structuring the contemporary distribution landscape. These stakeholders are variably competing, collaborating with, benefiting from, and adversely affecting other stakeholders in this complicated ecosystem. In accounting for these companies' involvement with financing, licensing, acquiring, owning, and circulating content, I have made a point to highlight examples of particular film and TV projects with which they have been involved. I did so in part as a means of encouraging us to keep in mind a fundamental issue that has occupied film and media studies scholars for decades—and, I would argue, has gotten less attention in some of the work on distribution in recent years: namely, how might we remain attentive to the relationship between shifting structural conditions and *media content*?

There are a couple of different ways this question might be addressed. One way pertains to how we might assess both the representational and formal-aesthetic dimensions of content in relation to changes in distribution. A key issue here involves the extent to which new delivery services and shifting market imperatives can enable or constrain the production and monetization of different kinds of content—a point alluded to in the discussion above about the ebbs and flows of certain genres across different platforms over time. Distribution shifts have fueled changes in some ways more than others. As scholars such as Christian (2018), Saha (2018), and Henderson (2019) note, despite heightened public scrutiny and limited corporate diversification efforts of late, institutional racism continues to limit opportunities for people of color, women, people with disabilities, and LGBTQ talent both in the creative and in the executive ranks.

The second issue involves how much specific types of content can help *drive* the success—and shape the scope of activities—of different distribution services. Recent scholarship on both media libraries and content aggregation leads to some skepticism here. Building on Hoyt's argument that contemporary SVOD services rely primarily on "revolving collections of licensing agreements" (2014, 200), Vonderau (2015) argues that such services and their strategies of aggregation have contributed to the *devaluation* of content. This is the case despite the fact that such services have heightened their emphasis on exclusive content as a means of luring and sustaining subscribers. Executives may hope that particular flagship titles—*Game of Thrones* (2011–19) on HBO, *Stranger Things* (2016–) on Netflix, or *The Handmaid's Tale* (2017–) on Hulu—will increase the value proposition of these services for many subscribers. Yet as Vonderau notes, the "wider techno-social ensemble that constitutes today's digital media infrastructures" contributes to transforming films and TV series from (potentially) valued artifacts, which they were perceived as being at least for a period of time, to ephemera. Most of this ephemera, he adds, amounts to little more than "waste that is deeply buried in storage" (2015, 729).

Brand names, whether of star creatives (e.g., Shonda Rhimes, Ryan Murphy) or select IP (*Star Wars, Star Trek*), can counter these ephemeral tendencies to an extent. Even so, there are signs that this process of content devaluation is likely to accelerate. Disney's acquisition of Fox, its reclamation of the rights for many of its licensed properties (at a tremendous financial loss, at least in the short term), and its launch of its new streaming service, Disney+, are all moves designed to counter the growing dominance of Netflix. All are also part of a new wave of consolidation. So is AT&T's purchase of Time Warner, its launch of the HBO Max service, and its closure of several of its niche services, including FilmStruck and DramaFever. In this context, the viability of standalone subscription-based niche-oriented streaming services is ever more precarious (Ball 2019). The shift toward a volume business—with most library content available only exclusively via one SVOD service—is likely to lead to even more corporate content being deeply buried on a site (if it is even there at all).

The diminishing availability of physical media forms, financial disincentives to invest in preservation and digitization, ongoing copyright claims, and algorithmic manipulation are just some of the ways that access to much of film and television media of the last century will be further constrained. It is worth reinforcing at this point that the discussion above has focused mainly on relatively high-end, commercial entertainment content. As noted at the start of this section, if we look to other types of content, such as sports and news, distinct issues—and different approaches—often come to the fore.

Attending to Outliers

It has become increasingly common for the wide range of media forms passing through pipelines to be considered "just content" (or even "just data"). On one level, this is true: oftentimes executives involved in licensing content for channels or platforms prioritize access (e.g., it's part of their library holdings) or cost (e.g., they can afford to license it) when they decide what shows to make available to audiences. What that content *is* matters less than that it is readily available; it then gets packaged to suit an individual channel or platform's brand identity as necessary. On a policy level, as well, discriminating on the basis of content attributes can be fraught to say the least, as the net neutrality battles indicate.

The particularities of content might seem to be of less and less significance to many industry practitioners as well as to some of those researching distribution. But as addressed above, we should not lose sight of when, how, and why content matters, in part because of the affective dimensions of such content to audiences and in part because we must continue to counter the mythology of the celestial (or digital) jukebox and interrogate the terms by which we do or don't have access to certain types of content in distinct geographical contexts. Even beyond these reasons, specific types of content have played a disproportionate role in shaping distribution networks and practices, both past and present. This is evident by looking at what might be called "outlier" cases—cultural forms that have been less regularly discussed as part of the distribution ecosystem for a variety of reasons. Comic books, theater, news, and sports all might be categorized as such "outlier" cases—less consistently examined at least in part due to disciplinary boundaries, research priorities, and definitional inconsistencies. Such cases might be of less interest to many film and media scholars, to entertainment-oriented journalists, and to the major SVOD services such as Netflix and Amazon. Yet a closer examination of outlier cases such as these leads us to see a far more complex landscape for both historical and contemporary media distribution.

The case of sports is instructive here. As Jhally observed in 1989, "Most people do the vast majority of sports spectating via the media (largely through television) so that the cultural experience of sports is largely mediated." He continued, "From a financial point of view, professional, and increasingly college, sports are dependent on media money for their very survival and organizational structure" (77–78). What Jhally initially conceptualized as the "sports/media complex" later became described by Rowe (1999) as the "media sports cultural complex," consisting of "all the media and sports organizations, processes, personnel, services, products and texts which combine in the creation of the broad, dynamic field of contemporary sports culture" (174). Whether sports are considered part of the media and cultural industries or not—a point about which there is not agreement and that is beyond the scope of what can be examined here—at the very least, sports industries and media industries are and long have been codependent, a point that media studies scholars including Whannel (1992) and Johnson (2009) have shown.

Historically, sports programming has been instrumental in driving the development and expansion of distribution networks across a range of media technologies. For example, HBO relied on the *Thrilla in Manila* (1975) boxing match between Muhammad Ali and Joe Frazier as the mechanism by which it initiated satellite broadcasting. Ted Turner's purchase of the Atlanta Braves baseball team and the Atlanta Hawks basketball team in 1976 enabled him to transform his local television station, WTBS, into a superstation carried across U.S. cable systems. Or think about Rupert Murdoch's 1993 acquisition of rights to NFL games— "stolen" from CBS after it had held those rights since 1956. This move not only provided Fox Broadcasting with greater legitimacy and enabled it to shift from being a "weblet" to a true competitor with ABC, CBS, and NBC, but it also helped Fox strengthen its affiliate relations and attract new affiliates as well (Curtin 2018).

Sports have remained as valuable, if not more so, in shaping distribution practices in the digital age. As Secular (2018) notes, since the 1990s, due to their need for "live and spontaneous content" that can be customizable based on geography, sports leagues have taken the lead in driving the development of streaming intermediaries. For example, in 2000, MLB formed BAMTech (Baseball Advanced Media), initially as a way of constructing "team-building websites and developing internet distribution in-house" (Secular 2018). Disney subsequently leased the platform for its ESPN+ streaming service, before purchasing a majority stake in BAMTech in 2017 for use in powering its Disney+ service.

Significantly, even as sports programming regularly has been exploited to grow new distribution technologies and reach affluent early adopters, it also has been one of the primary means by which legacy broadcasters and cable companies have sustained viewers. As BTIG media analyst Rich Greenfield states, "Sports is holding up the whole ecosystem . . . I call it the Jenga game. Pull out the sports block and the entire system collapses" (quoted in Winkler 2019). Importantly, when Murdoch sold off much of 21st Century Fox to Disney in 2018, he held on to most of his sports and news assets, including Fox Sports, Fox Deportes, and Fox Sports Digital Media. Fox Broadcasting—aka "the New Fox"—shifted to focusing more heavily on broadcasting sports programming, including airing two nights of NFL programming and one night of WWE content. Meanwhile, in its bid to remain competitive in the post-network era, in 2019 Sinclair Broadcast Group acquired the twenty-one former regional sports networks previously owned by Fox; with this acquisition, Sinclair gained exclusive rights to air forty-two different professional teams across baseball, basketball, and hockey (Darcy 2019). Different parts of the United States had access to different teams.

Conclusion

As these examples indicate, in contrast to certain types of entertainment-oriented content favored by mass-market SVOD services such as Netflix and Amazon, sports-related content has been and continues to be valued by media companies in a variety of ways. The time-sensitive, space-bound nature of sport programming leads to it being valued differently by varied industry stakeholders. These different modes of valuation of sports, in turn, complicate arguments about media distribution in the digital age that emerge when focusing primarily on the most high-profile stakeholders and most visible SVOD services. By analyzing points of variation and divergence—along with points of similarity and convergence—we can gain a more nuanced, complex understanding of the contemporary digital distribution landscape.

Indeed, the above discussion of the evolving historical relationship between sports, media, and technology companies reinforces how film and media scholars aiming to better understand distribution might further benefit from studies that attend to analog-era historical legacies, address the linkages between content attributes and distribution practices, and compare "outlier" media cases (e.g., theater, comic books) with more widely analyzed examples.[6] Sinclair's decision to focus on growing its regional sports networks, for example, can push us to nuance our theorizations of the relationship of the local, the national, and the global. Disney's acquisition of BAMTech points to how sports-related companies and the content they have prioritized disseminating have impacted the formation and diffusion of particular technological infrastructures. Meanwhile, Fox's ongoing reliance on live sports programming, whether football in the past or wrestling more recently, points to the continuing sociocultural, political, and economic importance of sporting content in different historical contexts. In addition, it reminds us of the longevity of legacy business models and distribution practices. Further, as the earlier discussion of WME's ownership of the UFC and IMG suggests, sports talent and teams have been and continue to be packaged along with other types of talent and media properties. What's more, as scholars such as Vogan (2010) and Piper (2018) have shown, the value of "old" sports content continues to be exploited through a wide range of delivery services—whether via documentaries, clip shows, unscripted programming, or feature films.

In my 2013 *Cinema Journal* essay, I highlighted the breadth of work that might be labeled as distribution studies with the goal of encouraging interdisciplinary openness, scholarly dialogue, and methodological innovation. Such objectives have been and continue to be realized. Without question distribution studies is now a vibrant subfield of media industry studies. As we chart new routes for this rich area of study, we stand to gain a great deal by looking beyond those stakeholders, objects, and sites that attract the most media coverage, generate the largest subscriber numbers, or wield the greatest cultural cachet.

NOTES

1 Compelling examples of how scholars have discussed distribution-related topics just since I published "Rethinking Distribution" in 2013 include (1) shifting spatial geographies of distribution and the forces constraining free flows of content (e.g., Herbert 2014; Lobato and Thomas 2016); (2) the cultural dimensions of distribution and the roles played by diverse stakeholders such as acquisitions executives, festival programmers, television syndicators, and policy makers (e.g., Brannon Donoghue 2017; Havens 2013); (3) the rise of new types of distribution intermediary technologies in the form of portals, platforms, content delivery networks (CDNs), and more (e.g., Vonderau 2016; van Dijck, Nieborg, and Poell 2019); (4) the dynamic relationship between formal and informal modes of circulation (e.g., Crisp 2015; Miller 2016); (5) the challenges—and growing necessity—of regulating internet infrastructures to spur competition and contain bad actors (e.g., Kimball 2015; Holt 2013); (6) the ways that cultural policy at the national and regional levels has sought to control distribution and structure markets (e.g., Harris 2018; Kokas 2018); (7) the opportunities and challenges faced by independent practitioners, fan communities, media activists, and small-scale operations in exploiting online platforms such as YouTube and iTunes (e.g., Arditi 2014; Hondros 2016); and (8) the consistent struggles by industry players of varied sizes and scopes to develop viable business models as value is reconstituted in the digital realm (e.g., Curtin, Holt, and Sanson 2014; McIntosh 2016).

2 Herbert, Lotz, and Marshall (2018) are a notable recent exception.

3 At my own institution, Radio-Television-Film doctoral student Selena Dickey (2019) is building on the historical studies noted here to explore the "multilayered, multiscalar, and multi-sited ways distribution infrastructures developed" in more marginal geographic sites. Drawing from a range of audiovisual and paper collections in the Mountain West, Pacific, and Southern United States, Dickey exposes the complex array of corporate, governmental, and community efforts to expand the reach of the national distribution networks via advancements in transmission technologies from the 1940s into the 1970s.

4 Cooper et al. (2018) is another useful example.

5 Space limitations prevent addressing the particularities of each of their business models and distribution strategies at length here.

6 For example, Felschow (2019) offers a helpful discussion of the distribution of live theater, and Perren and Steirer (2021) examine the distinctiveness of comics distribution.

BIBLIOGRAPHY

Adalian, Josef. 2018. "Inside the Binge Factory." *Vulture*, June 11. www.vulture.com.

Ali, Christopher. 2017. *Media Localism: The Politics of Place*. Urbana: University of Illinois Press.

Arditi, David. 2014. "iTunes: Breaking Barriers and Building Walls." *Popular Music and Society* 37 (4): 408–24.

Ball, Matthew. 2019. "The Streaming Wars: Its Models, Surprises, and Remaining Opportunities." *REDEF*, July 12. https://redef.com.

Brannon Donoghue, Courtney. 2017. *Localising Hollywood*. London: British Film Institute.

Braun, Joshua. 2013. "Transparent Intermediaries: Building the Infrastructures of Connected Viewing." In *Connected Viewing: Sharing, Streaming, & Selling Media in the Digital Age*, edited by Jennifer Holt and Kevin Sanson, 124–43. New York: Routledge.

Chmielewski, Dawn C. 2019. "Endeavor Forms Streaming Company, Combining NeuLion with Other Assets." *Deadline*, January 14. https://deadline.com.

Christian, Aymar Jean. 2018. *Open TV: Innovation beyond Hollywood and the Rise of Web Television*. New York: New York University Press.

Cooper, Mark Garrett, Sarah Beth Levavy, Ross Melnick, and Mark Williams, eds. 2018. *Rediscovering U.S. Newsfilm: Cinema, Television, and the Archive*. New York: Routledge.

Crisp, Virginia. 2015. *Film Distribution in the Digital Age: Pirates and Practitioners*. New York: Palgrave Macmillan.

Cronin, Kate. 2021. "Yesterday's News: Film Libraries and the Commercial Afterlife of Early Television News." Paper presented at the Society for Cinema and Media Studies Conference, March.

Curtin, Bryan. 2018. "The Great NFL Heist." *The Ringer*, December 13. www.theringer.com.

Curtin, Michael, Jennifer Holt, and Kevin Sanson, eds. 2014. *Distribution Revolution: Conversations about the Digital Future of Film and Television*. Berkeley: University of California Press.

Darcy, Oliver. 2019. "Sinclair to Purchase 21 Regional Sports Networks from Disney." *CNN*, May 3. www.cnn.com.

deWaard, Andrew. 2020. "Financialized Hollywood: Institutional Investment, Venture Capital, and Private Equity in the Film and Television Industries." *Journal of Cinema and Media Studies* 59 (4): 54–84.

Dickey, Selena A. 2019. "Complicating Television Distribution History: VHF Boosters and the Fight for National Television." Paper presented at the Society for Cinema and Media Studies Conference, Seattle, March.

"Digital Distribution." 2015. *Media Fields Journal* 10. http://mediafieldsjournal.org.

"Distribution." 2019. *On_Culture* 8 (Winter). www.on-culture.org.

"Distribution Matters: Media Circulation in Civic Life and Popular Culture." 2017. International Communication Association Preconference, San Diego, May 25. https://distributionmatters.net.

Doyle, Gillian. 2016. "Digitization and Changing Windowing Strategies in the Television Industry: Negotiating New Windows on the World." *Television & New Media* 17 (7): 629–45.

ELEAGUE. n.d. "About Us." www.eleague.com.

Endeavor. n.d. "Our Story." www.endeavorco.com.

Felschow, Laura E. 2019. "Broadway Is a Two-Way Street: Integrating Hollywood Distribution and Exhibition." *Media Industries* 6 (1): 21–42.

Fleming, Mike, Jr. 2017. "How Agencies Became So Vital to the Indie Film Ecosystem." *Deadline*, May 18. https://deadline.com.

Frick, Caroline. 2009. "Manufacturing Heritage: The Moving Image Archive and Media Industry Studies." In *Media Industries: History, Theory, and Method*, edited by Jennifer Holt and Alisa Perren, 34–44. Malden, MA: Wiley-Blackwell.

Gitelman, Lisa. 2006. *Always Already New: Media, History, and the Data of Culture.* Cambridge, MA: MIT Press.

Govil, Nitin. 2015. *Orienting Hollywood: A Century of Film Culture Between Los Angeles and Bombay.* New York: New York University Press.

Harris, Lauren Carroll. 2018. "Film Distribution as Policy: Current Standards and Alternatives." *International Journal of Cultural Policy* 24 (2): 236–55.

Havens, Timothy. 2013. *Black Television Travels: African American Media Around the Globe.* New York: New York University Press.

Henderson, Felicia. 2019. "Felicia D. Henderson—Nov 11, 2019." *Media Industry Conversations*, November 11. https://rtf.utexas.edu.

Herbert, Daniel. 2014. *Videoland: Movie Culture at the American Video Store.* Berkeley: University of California Press.

Herbert, Daniel, Amanda Lotz, and Lee Marshall. 2018. "Approaching the Media Industries Comparatively: A Case Study of Streaming." *International Journal of Cultural Studies* 22 (3): 349–66.

Holt, Jennifer. 2013. "Regulating Connected Viewing: Media Pipelines and Cloud Policy." In *Connected Viewing: Sharing, Streaming, & Selling Media in the Digital Age*, edited by Jennifer Holt and Kevin Sanson, 19–39. New York: Routledge.

Hondros, John J. 2016. "Problematizing the Internet as Video Distribution Technology: An Assemblage Theory Analysis." *Information, Communication & Society* 19 (2): 221–33.

Hoyt, Eric. 2014. *Hollywood Vault: Film Libraries before Home Video.* Berkeley: University of California Press.

Jhally, Sut. 1989. "Cultural Studies and the Sports/Media Complex." In *Media, Sports & Society*, edited by Lawrence Wenner, 70–93. Newbury Park, CA: Sage.

Johnson, Victoria E. 2009. "Everything Old Is New Again: Sport Television, Innovation, and Tradition for a Multi-platform Era." In *Beyond Prime Time: Television Programming in the Post-network Era*, edited by Amanda D. Lotz, 114–37. New York: Routledge.

Kimball, Danny. 2015. "Sponsored Data and Net Neutrality: Exemption and Discrimination in the Mobile Broadband Industry." *Media Industries* 2 (1): 38–59. https://quod.lib.umich.edu.

Kirkpatrick, Bill. 2007. "Localism in American Media Policy, 1920–34: Reconsidering a Bedrock Concept." *Radio Journal* 4 (1–3): 87–110.

Kokas, Aynne. 2018. "Predicting Volatility between China and Hollywood: Using Network Management to Understand Sino-US Film Collaboration." *Global Media and Communication* 14 (3): 233–48.

Lobato, Ramon, and Julian Thomas, eds. 2016. *Geoblocking and Global Video Culture*. Amsterdam: Institute of Network Cultures.

McIntosh, Heather. 2016. "Vevo and the Business of Online Music Distribution." *Popular Music and Society* 39 (5): 487–500.

"Media Distribution." 2015. *The Velvet Light Trap* 75.

Miller, Jade. 2016. *Nollywood Central: The Nigerian Videofilm Industry*. London: Palgrave Macmillan.

Morgan-Parmett, Helen. 2016. "KVOS in the Local, Public Interest: Early Broadcasting and the Constitution of the Local." *Journal of Radio and Audio Media* 23 (1): 95–106.

Parks, Lisa. 2007. "Where the Cable Ends: Television in Fringe Areas." In *Cable Visions: Television Beyond Broadcasting*, edited by Sarah Banet-Weiser, Cynthia Chris, and Anthony Freitas, 103–26. New York: New York University Press.

Perren, Alisa. 2013. "Rethinking Distribution for the Future of Media Industry Studies." *Cinema Journal* 52 (3): 165–71.

Perren, Alisa, and Greg Steirer. 2021. *The American Comic Book Industry and Hollywood*. London: British Film Institute/Bloomsbury.

Piper, Timothy J. 2018. "Where 'Post-Race' Happens: National Basketball Association Branding and the Recontextualization of Archival Sports Footage." *The Moving Image* 18 (1): 1–24.

Rowe, David. 1999. *Sport, Culture, and Media*. Buckingham: Open University Press.

Russo, Alexander. 2010. *Points on the Dial: Golden Age Radio Beyond the Networks*. Durham, NC: Duke University Press.

Saha, Anamik. 2018. *Race and the Cultural Industries*. Medford, MA: Polity.

Sandvig, Christian. 2015. "The Internet as Anti-television: Distribution Infrastructure as Culture and Power." In *Signal Traffic: Critical Studies of Media Infrastructures*, edited by Lisa Parks and Nicole Starosielski, 225–45. Champaign: University of Illinois Press.

Secular, Steven. 2018. "Games without Frontiers: Streaming Sports and the Evolution of Digital Intermediaries." *Media Industries* 5 (2): 143–57. https://quod.lib.umich.edu.

Sterne, Jonathan. 2012. *MP3: The Meaning of a Format*. Durham, NC: Duke University Press.

Sun, Rebecca, and Jonathan Handel. 2018. "As Talent Agencies Push to Own Content, Some Creators Cry Foul." *Hollywood Reporter*, September 12. www.hollywoodreporter.com.

Tryon, Chuck. 2013. *On-Demand Culture and Digital Delivery*. New Brunswick, NJ: Routledge.

van Dijck, José, David Nieborg, and Thomas Poell. 2019. "Reframing Platform Power." *Internet Policy Review* 8 (2). https://policyreview.info.

Vogan, Travis. 2010. "Football's Wine Cellar: The NFL Films Archive." *The Moving Image* 10 (2): 1–29.

Vonderau, Patrick. 2015. "The Politics of Content Aggregation." *Television & New Media* 16 (8): 717–33.

———. 2016. "The Video Bubble: Multichannel Networks and the Transformation of YouTube." *Convergence* 22 (4): 361–75.

Whannel, Garry. 1992. *Fields in Vision: Television Sport and Cultural Transformation.* New York: Routledge.

Winkler, Elizabeth. 2019. "Why the Clock Is Running Out on Big Media Companies." *Wall Street Journal,* April 26. www.wsj.com.

4

Disingenuous Intermediaries

The Gatekeeping Power of Distributors and Publishers

VIRGINIA CRISP

This chapter provides a macro-level analysis of formal gatekeeping power across multiple creative industries (film, TV, games, book publishing, and music), where gatekeeping power is defined as the capacity for specific actors (individuals or companies) to influence the creation and circulation of cultural products. In doing so, it proposes key nodes where the most potential for gatekeeping power lies but also makes the central claim that any player's power at one single node may have only limited influence on the broader circulation of cultural products unless that player also enjoys control over multiple nodes within the broader system.

A model is proposed to illustrate the nodes where gatekeeping power might be found (distribution/publishing, marketing, intellectual property [IP] ownership, funding, hardware manufacture, production, retail, curation, regulation, and archiving) as well as the players that tend to have more control over those nodes (book publishers, record companies, film distributors, TV broadcasters, game publishers, and tech companies). In doing so, the model illustrates the following central arguments. First, control over any one node does not in and of itself increase gatekeeping power over the whole system. Second, new platforms (e.g., Google, Amazon, Facebook) either already occupy or are maneuvering toward a very similar gatekeeping position to their "old media" counterparts. As such, while they might be changing the balance of power between specific companies, they are not fundamentally disrupting the power dynamics within the system as a whole. Finally, whereas the exact companies might change across industries, the nodes of gatekeeping power are largely the same. So although Nintendo is a significant player in the games industry and Netflix is a global name in film and television, these particular companies do not overlap in terms of their parent companies or industry focus. Nonetheless, they share similar positions in terms of the gatekeeping power they might potentially wield over their respective industries and the manner in which that power is accrued shares key similarities, as will be examined in more detail later.

This chapter approaches gatekeeping from a political economy approach. While acknowledging the limitations of any macro-level analysis, including political economy, that scholars like Lotz (2009) have argued has dominated media industry studies, this chapter contends that such a conceptual framework is nonetheless a useful tool through which to holistically examine gatekeeping power across multiple industries (film, TV, games, book publishing, and music). This is partly because of the emphasis such an approach puts on how *power* operates (Cunningham, Flew, and Swift 2015, 41), thus providing a useful tool to interrogate where potential gatekeeping control or influence is located within the media industries. The examination presented here interrogates the gatekeeping power that conglomeration provides while also stressing the continued power of incumbent monopolies even in the face of competition from what Hesmondhalgh has referred to as the "GAFAM oligopoly" (Google, Amazon, Facebook, Apple, Microsoft) (2019, 218).

Gatekeeping Theory

Broadly speaking, research on gatekeeping within the media industries concerns itself with the power of various actors to dictate the extent and ease with which audiences can access varying forms of symbolic content. The gatekeeper metaphor is employed to capture the potential power of these actors to control the circulation of cultural goods and experiences. In the words of Smits, gatekeepers "decide which creative works are let through the gates as they move from the early stage of development, to production, to distribution and ultimately to consumption; how those products pass through those gates; and what is barred" (2019, 83).

Gatekeeping theory has a long tradition within media and communications research, most notably within news and journalism studies. This tradition is often seen to begin with the seminal studies of David Manning White (1950) and Walter Gieber (1964), who demonstrated that the process of "expert" selection (or not) of media for publication or dissemination is subject to vagaries of personal subjectivity (Manning White 1950) or to bureaucratic routine (Gieber 1964). Shoemaker and Vos's *Gatekeeping Theory* (2009) then extrapolates how media groups and individuals (both professional and amateur) filter and mediate information for public consumption.

Within studies of the media industries more generally, the term has been used repeatedly within various micro-level studies of industry practice (e.g., Smits 2019; Curran 1999), but this research is not recognized as a unified corpus of work (as it is within journalism studies). Alongside the aforementioned rather narrow focus on specific gatekeepers and the operation of their gates, Keith Negus suggests the "gatekeeper concept is limited by the assumption that cultural items simply appear at the 'gates' of the media or culture producing corporation where they are either admitted or excluded" (2002, 510). This chapter seeks to address such concerns by focusing not on the operation of the gates in isolation, but on the system that surrounds the individual gates/gatekeepers and thus shapes their operation. In doing so, I also argue that studies of specific gatekeeping processes should also always be mindful of the broader systems of production, distribution, and consumption within which each gate resides.

It is significant to note that gatekeeping research is often closely aligned with the wider study of cultural intermediaries, but these categorizations are marked by an important distinction—while gatekeepers may well be cultural intermediaries (i.e., professionals who operate in the spaces between production and consumption, and who contribute to the creation of symbolic value), they do not necessarily have much influence over what cultural products are created, promoted, and packaged for widespread consumption. As Smits summarizes, "While the concept of cultural intermediaries is often employed in a variety of contexts, the more specific concept of gatekeepers is often employed to describe powerful occupations and professions with decision-making authority over the creation and circulation of creative works. . . . Their ability to control cultural flows separates them from other types of cultural intermediaries in conceptual terms" (2019, 83). More recent examinations of gatekeeping have claimed that the metaphor has become outdated in the face of various technological developments. Bro and Wallberg, for instance, suggest, perhaps a little prematurely, that the kind of "last" or "final" gatekeeper that White and Gieber referred to (i.e., the editors who had the final say on what content actually went into newspapers) no longer exists and "instead, the last gatekeeper has increasingly become a friend, a member of the family or someone else with whom they are familiar in their private and professional life" (2014, 448–49). If such an argument is to be believed, the average person's news consumption is no longer shaped by the editorial decisions of professionals in charge of newspapers, magazines, and television programs; instead, the news one consumes is made up of a disconnected mishmash of recommendations from friends, family, and algorithms brought to us through tweets, private messages, and social media feeds. Arguably, the concept of a last gatekeeper always somewhat overemphasizes the control that one might have over an individual's news consumption—indeed, while some people might read newspapers front to back not missing a single article, the existence of themed sections (e.g., Sport, Finance) and attention-grabbing headlines would suggest that the medium is designed for readers to select from the whole what most interests them. Furthermore, the romanticized figure of the last editor has certainly not been entirely replaced because news engagement precipitated through social media recommendations exists alongside more traditional practices of reading the Sunday paper or watching the evening news.

That being said, the same proliferation of options for consumers to sidestep the gatekeeping actions of TV schedulers, cinema programmers, and radio DJs exists in other fields (albeit, I would stress, alongside rather than replacing traditional viewing and listening practices). Indeed, we can choose what to watch on Netflix and we curate our Spotify playlist as well as downloading what we want to read or play from the vast libraries of Kindle or Steam. Indeed, Smith Maguire and Matthews (2012) have posited the provocation "are we all intermediaries now?" in response to their claim that technological developments have enabled so many more nonprofessionals to have a broader and further reaching role in promotion, distribution, and other forms of "adding value" to creative content through "sharing," "liking," "commenting," "tagging," and various other activities. However, such a provocation (while undoubtedly deliberately bombastic) erroneously suggests a context where nonprofessional "gatekeeping" has no historical precedents and also attributes a greater degree of agency to "ordinary" citizens than they necessarily possess.

First, while our actions on social media might potentially afford us a greater reach than in the past, friends, family, and acquaintances have no doubt long shaped the media consumption of those around them through, for instance, the newsagent selecting which papers and magazines to stock, the local bar subscribing to particular cable channels, or parents sharing TV recommendations at the school gates. All of these might be understood to be "intermediary" practices akin to the web 2.0 activities that Smith Maguire and Matthews describe.

Second, and more significantly for this particular chapter, just having access to technologies of circulation does not in and of itself provide a notable increase in gatekeeping power. Indeed, even if we enjoy more choice from seemingly vast libraries of content, there are multiple factors dictating what makes it into those libraries in the first place. The power to dictate what is funded, produced, and formally distributed is still incredibly important, even in an era of seemingly endless opportunities for peer recommendation, review, and sharing. As such, even though the media landscape is in constant flux and the absolute power of the "final" editors of the newsroom may no longer exist (or may have never existed), this chapter maintains that the metaphor of gatekeeping is still useful as it foregrounds the power of certain key players within content creation and circulation.

A Model of Gatekeeping Power

This chapter proposes a model (figure 4.1) that highlights ten key nodes of gatekeeping power (hardware manufacture, funding, production, distribution/publishing, marketing, retail, regulation, curation, archiving, IP ownership—indicated by rectangles) while also indicating which actors (e.g., conglomerates, platforms, audiences, creators—represented as circles/ellipsis) are likely to have more gatekeeping influence over each node. In looking at gatekeeping power across five creative industries, it is possible to identify the actors whose power multiplies as they have the *potential* to exert more influence at numerous points within the system. Thus, the more influential actors (i.e., platforms and conglomerates) in

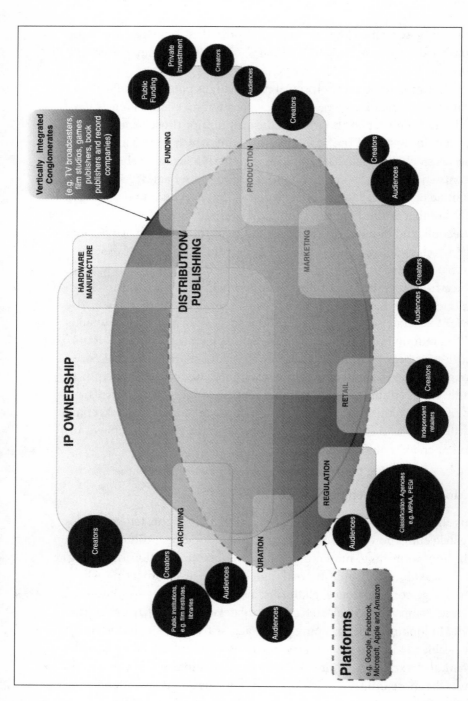

Figure 4.1. A Model of Gatekeeping Power across Five Creative Industries (Film, TV, Digital Games, Books, and Music)

fact dominate the model, occupying a central position where they intersect with all of the nodes simultaneously. The relative shape and size of
each actor (circle) as well as the extent to which it overlaps with any one
node (rectangle) illustrate the influence that each actor has over each
node. Less influential actors (e.g., creators and audiences—who may
have gatekeeping power over multiple nodes but whose power is distributed unevenly across those nodes) are represented by separate circles at
each node (rather than as a singular category intersecting with multiple
nodes simultaneously) to demonstrate the fragmented nature of their
gatekeeping power across the entire ecosystem. The nodes (represented
as rectangles in the diagram) are presented so the size of each node
indicates its relative significance within the ecosystem. The nodes also
sometimes overlap to acknowledge that the boundaries between certain nodes are markedly porous. For instance, the fact that distributors/
publishers frequently exert influence across many of the other nodes is
illustrated by their dominance of the diagram and the way they overlap with so many of the other nodes depicted. Similarly, the significant
role of IP ownership is illustrated through its size in the diagram and
the frequency with which it overlaps with other nodes to depict how
IP ownership may be divided in complex ways across those who fund,
produce, curate, distribute, and archive cultural products.

The model demonstrates ten key nodes where gatekeeping power
potentially resides, but despite this disaggregation of a complex system
into discrete nodes, the model also demonstrates that concentration of
ownership within conglomerates and platforms, and thus influence over
multiple nodes at once, is the most significant factor in dictating gatekeeping power across the ecosystem. In other words, increased opportunities to affect any one node in isolation, such as funding or distribution,
might result in an increase of gatekeeping power at that juncture, but it
does not in and of itself mean that the actor has a significant amount
of gatekeeping power when looking at the ecosystem as a whole. For
instance, audiences might be able to influence the likelihood of a sequel to their favorite film being made if they contribute to a crowdfund-
ing campaign, but, even if made, this does not mean that the film will
reach audiences through cinemas, major retailers, or popular video-on-
demand (VOD) services as these nodes are largely controlled by a set of
elite actors, that is, vertically integrated conglomerates and platforms.

While there are undoubtedly some variations between industries, the model seeks to illustrate how conglomerates, in the form of book publishers, TV studios/broadcasters, film studios, record labels, games publishers, and, more latterly, the GAFAM oligopoly and associated "disruptive innovators" (e.g., Netflix), accrue gatekeeping power precisely because they extend their reach across multiple nodes simultaneously (vertical integration). In particular, conglomerates then extend their power over the media ecosystem more broadly by owning book publishers, TV studios/broadcasters, film studios, record labels, games publishers (horizontal integration). The following subsections outline in more detail why each node has been identified as an important juncture where gatekeeping power might be accrued.

Distribution/Publishing

Given the focus of this entire collection, it is perhaps unsurprising that the relative size of the distribution/publishing node within the diagram highlights its prominence within the ecosystem. As Harold Vogel so eloquently states, "Ownership of entertainment distribution capability is like ownership of a toll road or bridge. No matter how good or bad the software product (i.e., movie, record, book, magazine, TV show, or whatever) is, it must pass over or cross through a distribution pipeline in order to reach the consumer. And like at any toll road or bridge that cannot be circumvented, the distributor is a local monopolist who can extract a relatively high fee for the use of his facility" (cited in Balio 2013, 11). However, despite their undisputable power, reference to "disingenuous intermediaries" in the title of this chapter points to the rather unassuming and potentially misleading nature of the moniker "distributor" and to a certain extent "publisher." Such titles do little to hint at the multiple responsibilities that come under the aegis of these powerful gatekeepers. To take the book publishing industry as one example, publishers are responsible for "content acquisition . . . content development, . . . book design, . . . management of the production cycle, . . . pre-press, printing, paper binding (PPB), or the preparation of an ebook, . . . marketing, . . . sales, . . . fulfilment, . . . customer service, . . . [and] other revenue streams" (Greco, Miliot, and Wharton 2014, 6). The situation is similar in the film industry, where distributors "can influence script and title changes, casting decisions, final edits, marketing strategies and financing" (Wasko 2003, 84) as well as overseeing the more logistical aspects of distribution, such as organizing exhibition and licensing agreements.

With such an extensive list of activities potentially under their purview, it is perhaps unsurprising that I argue the distribution/publishing node is one of the key sources of gatekeeping power within the broader model of gatekeeping power proposed. As the list above attests, publishers will often have the power to decide which content will be acquired/ developed (and thus produced) as well as what the content will look like and how it will be marketed. In this respect, distribution/publishing is more significant than the other nodes, because it also represents a significant proportion of the entire system. Indeed, it is true that multiple nodes often fall within the purview of large publishing and distribution companies. However, as this is not necessarily the case, responsibilities such as marketing and funding as well as significant nodes of gatekeeping power such as IP ownership have been disaggregated in the paragraphs that follow (and the model they describe) so they might be discussed in their own right as significant nodes while still acknowledging the significant gatekeeping power frequently enjoyed by large distribution/publishing organizations in these areas.

Marketing

The marketing node, that is, bringing content to the attention of audiences and persuading engagement with that content, is one of the aforementioned disaggregated elements that is frequently intertwined with distribution/publishing. Furthermore, in some ways we might look at marketing as a matter of influence rather than gatekeeping, and so including marketing as a separate node might seem either unnecessary or unwarranted. However, because the marketing of a creative product is invariably a consideration during early development stages rather than as a post hoc addition to the creative process, marketing is identified as a key gatekeeping node because of how marketing considerations ultimately feed into production, funding, and distribution decisions.

Furthermore, in an era of tentpole blockbuster films and AAA games, it is marketing budgets that are contributing to the increasing gulf between small and large media productions. This is in evidence in the games industry, where "to an extent, the size of an organization's promotion budget represents its ability to affect consumer expenditures. . . . Promotional budgets within the industry are carried by publishers and console owners. . . . Clearly this portion of the industry is heavily promotionally orientated where typically 50 percent of revenues are ploughed back into promoting business in one aspect or another" (Zackariasson and Wilson 2012, 65). On the other end of the spectrum, and particularly in the music industry, promotional activities (e.g., managing social media presence through posting and fan engagement activities) are also "increasingly being done by the creative practitioners themselves or those working immediately with them" (Davies and Sigthorsson 2013, 162). In some ways this could be viewed as creators having more control over the ways their creative endeavors are promoted; on the other hand, this could be seen as a situation where more of the risk and expense of creative production is being pushed back onto artists.

IP Ownership

The significance of IP ownership across the whole of the proposed gate-keeping ecosystem cannot be overstated because of the influence this node has across so many of the others. In short, intellectual property gatekeepers can dictate what can be made, funded, distributed, marketed, exhibited, and archived and the nature and duration of such arrangements. For one, IP ownership can influence what products can be developed in the first place: for instance, whoever owns IP for certain characters, films, music, and so on can significantly influence the construction of future cultural products (e.g., through the music or characters that are licensed to be in certain films and TV shows). One notable example is Sony Pictures' control of the rights to the Spider-Man character since 1999; only after considerable negotiation was Disney able to come to an arrangement with Sony that allowed the character to feature in the later Avengers films (Graser and Lang 2015).[1] In a similar vein, the acquisition of Fox allowed Disney to reintegrate the X-men franchise into the larger Marvel Cinematic Universe (MCU). The length of this chapter prevents any in-depth examination of the true significance of this node across the whole ecosystem, and so the relative size of the node within the diagram attempts to at least highlight (if not comprehensively examine) the significance of the gatekeeping power that ownership of IP provides.

Funding

As with IP ownership, control over funding (i.e., the financial assistance provided to enable the initial and/or continued creation, marketing, and circulation of creative content) can obviously play a significant role in dictating whether creative products are even produced in the first place, let alone reach their intended audiences. Of course, the medium can have significant influence here. It is possible to imagine an aspiring author or musician writing a book or an album without the need for significant funding—the key resources being items they may well have ready access to, for example, a computer with word processing software or music-making equipment/instruments and basic recording software/hardware. Indeed, even films, TV programs, and games can be made on micro budgets. However, while it might be *possible* for micro-budget projects to go into production, this is not the norm, and arguably funding for the creation of the work is only part of the story. Having financial support for the marketing, reproduction, and distribution of the work is often a much more significant issue.

Indeed, cultural production is a risky business because of the inescapably unpredictable nature of consumption—audience appreciation can never be guaranteed—and so even the most modest cultural product typically requires the input of a third party to fund creation and distribution. Indeed, while costs vary across different media and industries and "a variety of approaches can be used to try and mitigate the risks inherent in making media content, the fact remains that production is an expensive process" (Doyle 2013, 111). This then brings us again to the influence of distribution/publishing across the other nodes because it is invariably the case that third party funding can be found in established distribution/publishing companies. As Zackariasson and Wilson note about the games industry, "Because game developers tend to lack financial capabilities to fund and promote their games, publishers are essential participants in bringing games to consumers" (2012, 3).

Production

As with funding, some creative endeavors are complex enough that they require not just upfront funding but large teams of people to enable production in the first place. Even ostensibly "single-author" works like novels will involve the contributions of (among others) editors, copy editors, typesetters, cover designers, and printers to transform an author's text into the final book. Even a cursory glance at the credits that follow any film, TV program, or game reveals that many cultural products require the input of hundreds or even thousands of people. Furthermore, even if an individual artist writes a song or an author produces a manuscript, numerous people are involved in the transformation of that song or manuscript into a cultural product. Therefore, as not all manuscripts can be turned into books and not all scripts can be transformed into fully fledged TV dramas without significant support from numerous individuals, institutions, and companies, a certain degree of gatekeeping is inherent within all processes that turn ideas into products because the actions, interests, concerns, and finances of so many parties are involved.

This, of course, does not designate all contributors to any creative process as gatekeepers, for they do not all have the power to influence what products do and do not get developed, marketed, and distributed and ultimately find their way to audiences. Indeed, within my own previous work I have noted that within both professional companies and informal distribution mechanisms, there are usually only a few key individuals who have the power to dictate what films are disseminated within formal and informal distribution networks (see Crisp 2015 and 2017). So while we must acknowledge that cultural production is invariably a collective endeavor, it does not follow that all contributors enjoy equal amounts of gatekeeping power.

Hardware Manufacture

It is important to acknowledge that control over the manufacture of the hardware that enables our consumption of many cultural goods (smartphones, smart TVs, tablets, e-readers, mp3 players, consoles, etc.), while represented in the diagram as somewhat less significant than some of the other nodes, does hold an extremely significant role in dictating what content is widely and easily available for consumers. Such influence might often go unnoticed because during everyday consumption we do not overly concern ourselves with considerations of how particular hardware might shape our media consumption. The exception to this comes when new technologies enable shifts in media consumption, such as home video formats allowing us to watch films out of the cinema, the Sony Walkman enabling us to listen to music on the move, or smartphones empowering us to watch TV anywhere. However, even during such schisms in our day-to-day media consumption practices, there is still little examination of the gatekeeping potential of such hardware and the associated interfaces despite the fact that certain markets (e.g., games) are largely under the control of hardware manufacturers who also own the major publishers (Nichols 2014, 80).

Indeed, it is important to highlight that the significance of control over hardware manufacture as a gatekeeping node is perhaps the most variable between industries. Indeed, in the games industry hardware is strongly linked to the development and publishing arms of the industry as well as their associated technologies. Due to the nature of the industry, a game must be developed for particular hardware (e.g., consoles, PCs) and operating systems. While some games (particularly older titles) can often be emulated on PCs or otherwise might be played via a "retro mini console," historically games have been tied to particular consoles/platforms. While this landscape is potentially changing (e.g., with *Pokémon Go* as an example of a game based on Nintendo IP available on non-Nintendo platforms, i.e., smartphones), in other industries, such as book publishing, a printed book is infinitely available and transferrable between people and over time. While books published on Kindle / Google Books / Apple Books might bring these proprietary and technological ties into the book publishing world somewhat, it is still safe to say that the gatekeeping significance of hardware manufacture may vary considerably across industries.

Retail

Although the term "retail" might mean different things in varying contexts, in this model media retail is interpreted broadly to include all activities that involve selling of content access direct to consumers. As such, retailers in this context might mean independent book shops, cinemas, game retailers, and record stores as well as large cinema chains, supermarkets, transactional on-demand services (iTunes, Steam), app stores (Google Play, Apple App Store), and online retail giants (Amazon, eBay, Alibaba). The power of retailers within such a context is often overlooked as though retailers transparently provide the means to purchase any and all products without providing their own filtering of availability through processes such as their stock acquisition decisions or store and/or interface design.

Chris Anderson's (2009) concept of the long tail proposed that because online retailers are not subject to the same restrictions of shelf space or stock room size encountered by physical brick-and-mortar high street retailers; potentially, their inventories of products for sale could be infinite. In this view, new channels for digital sales afford retailers opportunities to provide consumers with limitless choice. Such an argument would seem to add credence to any assumption that retailers simply respond to audience demand and thus will supply anything an audience wishes in an era of infinite virtual shelf space. However, Anderson's concept has come under considerable scrutiny as it has been argued that his prediction of "an environment in which a much greater array of content would be provided to audiences . . . has failed to materialize" (Napoli 2016, 342).

However, retailers must obviously make their own decisions about what to sell to consumers based on monetary, legal, and physical constraints as well as the retail brand or image they wish to present through the items stocked. One example along these lines is almost inadvertently pointed out in the documentary *This Film Is Not Yet Rated* (Kirby Dick, 2006). Examining the power of the Motion Picture Association of America's (MPAA) film classification processes, the documentary noted films classified NC-17 (i.e., "No one 17 and under admitted"; MPA n.d.) were automatically not stocked for sale by the U.S. retail chain Walmart.[2] By not stocking films in a particular classification category, one of the largest U.S. retailers could therefore act as a gatekeeper by dramatically reducing opportunities for films to reach consumers. So, far from being transparent conduits allowing consumers to purchase whatever products they might wish to, retailers also have the potential to wield considerable gatekeeping power according to their own interests and concerns.

Regulation

An area that typically straddles a line between governmental and corporate control is content regulation (e.g., censorship, classification, broadcasting standards, etc.). Books, music, and to a certain extent TV programs are largely exempt from compulsory age ratings in many Western countries, but films and games typically have to be passed and age rated by classification bodies (e.g., British Board of Film Classification, Pan European Game Information, MPA) in order to be legally sold within particular territories. While there are numerous noncompulsory methods of regulation (e.g., parental advisory stickers, Netflix's bespoke age ratings) that are designed to inform and shape purchasing decisions, they do not ultimately dictate whether the content is formally available or not. In contrast, those with formal classification powers also have the potential for significant gatekeeping power within the broader structure, dictating what content is legally allocated for formal distribution.

Curation

In a similar way to regulation, curation (a word I use here as an umbrella term to describe multiple practices involved with organizing and/or scheduling content, e.g., film programming, TV and radio scheduling) might seem at first to be more about influencing consumer behavior than clearly demarcating what content is available and what is not. When online libraries appear vast, curation of content (increasingly by computational means) is of vast importance to enable people to negotiate the complex array of media options at their disposal. Such curation might therefore seem advantageous to the consumer, and in many ways it may well be. However, those with curation power over what content is included within these libraries, rather than those mechanisms that simply assist us to negotiate these preconstituted catalogues, also represent a significant node of gatekeeping power. In this way, those in charge of devising television schedules, VOD service catalogues, and music subscription libraries have another level of control over what content is available for consumers to choose from (albeit ultimately also restricted by the gatekeeping practices enacted by others across the other nodes).

So while the choice of content across many media services may seem endless, this is an illusion that again obscures the many gatekeeping decisions that may influence the final roster of entertainment choices that reach audiences.

Archiving

Archiving is identified as another significant node of gatekeeping power because we must consider the availability of content beyond the immediate moment and thus, the power of those who have the means and motivation to keep, maintain, catalogue, and preserve content for future consumption. Attention to archiving therefore adds a long-term temporal dimension to gatekeeping power. This is a particular issue in an era of seemingly limitless access to historical media content through numerous online "libraries" (e.g., Google Books, Spotify, Netflix, Microsoft Game Pass), first because of the limited and unstable nature of these catalogues/portals and, second, because of the illusion of ubiquity and perpetuity that many of these online portals present.

It is important to note that while presenting an illusion of abundance, online libraries can be transient and incomplete. There are a number of services that offer subscription-based services to TV and film (Netflix, Hulu, Amazon Prime Video) or catch-up services (U.K. examples include BBC iPlayer, itvHub, and All4). In the case of subscription VOD services, their catalogues change based upon the terms of licensing agreements, while for catch-up services, the availability of much content is dependent upon traditional scheduling decisions as well as licensing agreements. While such services offer many of us considerably more opportunities to access film and TV programs than a few decades ago, the items within their catalogues, and indeed the services themselves, cannot be guaranteed in perpetuity.

The VOD market is far from stable, as illustrated by the closure of services like FilmStruck (Brody 2018) and the repatriation of previously platform-agnostic content under the aegis of new distributor-specific VOD platforms from the likes of the Criterion Collection and Disney. The same is true of subscription services like Microsoft Game Pass, Apple Music, and Amazon Prime Music, where access to the library is available only as long as subscriptions are current and available content can change without notice. In some cases, the fact that content will soon disappear from a catalogue is used as a badge of exclusivity or an incentive to engage with the content, as with the "limited time on Prime" category from Amazon Prime Video. Such practices should, however, be read as tactical ways for reframing catalogue limitations as "limited time offers" rather than acknowledge the temporary nature of the service's license agreements or the tendency of such platforms to create "artificial scarcity" within their own catalogues.

Furthermore, access to full catalogues may be restricted for consumers using advertising-supported subscription services (Spotify) or hybrid subscription/transactional on-demand services (Amazon Music, Amazon Prime Video, iTunes). Deliberately showing by default the content that basic/free subscribers cannot access within their current subscriptions is clearly designed to prompt consumers to upgrade their subscriptions while also reminding us that online streaming services are not universal and that the attractions of ubiquity and perpetuity they promise are illusions.

Conclusion

Overall, the model of gatekeeping power outlined here foregrounds a range of foundational concerns. First, as gatekeeping processes and practices are multiple, we must examine them in relation to their position within an overall ecosystem of gates. Second, within that ecosystem, gatekeeping power does not fit into a straightforward linear model, for power is concentrated at certain points within the overall system. Third, control over particular nodes affords increased gatekeeping power across the whole structure. Finally, while new platforms may make for a more complex ecosystem, they do not fundamentally disrupt the power dynamics within the system.

These conclusions highlight that control over any one node does not increase gatekeeping power over the whole ecosystem. In this respect, democratization of distribution or marketing technologies does not increase the gatekeeping powers of audiences and/or creators per se. While in theory anyone can host their own videos on YouTube or circulate their music via Soundcloud, the opportunities these afford are not as extensive as those offered by well-financed vertically integrated companies who have the networks and market knowledge to most advantageously position their products in the market.

Furthermore, companies like Google, Amazon, and Microsoft occupy a similar space to the vertically integrated conglomerates of the past; in other words, they are not just disrupting a single point in the value chain (e.g., through distribution of Google Books) but are infiltrating at all points by producing, distributing, and marketing their own content, devising their own classification systems, creating their own libraries, owning their own intellectual property, and, often, creating the hardware that is required to access the media content they produce.

In addition, it must be acknowledged that while the model has been designed to be applied across the creative industries, the significance of gatekeeping power at any one node may be differentially distributed between media industries. On the one hand, due to permeability between industries, any consideration of gatekeeping power across any one industry must take into account the wider media or creative sector. This is particularly the case where gatekeeping decisions are made based on judging the marketability and profitability of products across media. For instance, publishers are not only looking for the next best seller but also looking for, say, the next *Harry Potter*—a multimedia phenomenon where rights can be sold for film adaptations, spin-off TV shows, graphic novels, merchandising, theme parks, and so on. On the other hand, industries vary over how much proprietorial control companies can hold over the means of accessing content. For instance, while variations certainly exist, e-books are likely to be available in formats compatible with multiple devices, and the brand of television or CD player someone uses does not restrict the library of content that she or he can access. Games, in contrast, are commonly platform specific, and so in this particular sphere hardware holds much more significant influence than in other media industries.

As mentioned, this chapter is about mapping the potential for gatekeeping power, and I am not making claims here about how that power may or may not be enacted. Indeed, there is not an issue per se with the incumbent media conglomerates or the new tech giants providing everything from dishwasher salt to VOD services, but we need to examine "when and how the powers of ownership are mobilized" (Hesmondhalgh 2019, 207). Unlike Hesmondhalgh, however, I am concerned not about the "quality" of the cultural products on offer (as this is a highly subjective judgement) but about *access* to them, whether that be controlled by the dominance of circulation mechanisms or by opportunities to dictate which cultural products are produced in the first place.

NOTES

1 Although Spider-Man was not a member of the "original" Avengers team from the 1960s Marvel comics, the character has featured numerous times in Avengers story lines since then, and Disney was very keen to buy back the rights to Spider-Man from Sony so the character could figure more prominently in the Marvel Cinematic Universe (MCU) franchise.

2 In a move explicitly communicating the association's global reach, in September 2019 the MPAA officially changed its name to the Motion Picture Association (MPA), a title previously reserved only for the association's international operations.

BIBLIOGRAPHY

Anderson, Chris. 2009. *The Longer Long Tail: How Endless Choice Is Creating Unlimited Demand.* New York: Random House.

Balio, Tino. 2013. *Hollywood in the New Millennium.* London: British Film Institute.

Bro, Peter, and Filip Wallberg. 2014. "Digital Gatekeeping." *Digital Journalism* 2 (3): 446–54. https://doi.org/10.1080/21670811.2014.895507.

Brody, Richard. 2018. "The Shutting Down of FilmStruck and the False Promise of Streaming Classics." *New Yorker,* October 27. www.newyorker.com.

Crisp, Virginia. 2015. *Film Distribution in the Digital Age.* London: Palgrave Macmillan.

———. 2017. "Release Groups and the Scene: Re-intermediation and Competitive Gatekeepers Online." *Cinéma and Cie* 17 (29): 67–80.

———. Forthcoming. "Shifting Gatekeepers: Power and Influence in Informal Online Film Distribution." In *World Cinema on Demand: Global Film Cultures in the Era of Online Distribution,* edited by Stefano Baschiera and Alexander Fisher. London: Bloomsbury.

Cunningham, Stuart, Terry Flew, and Adam Swift. 2015. *Media Economics.* London: Palgrave Macmillan.

Curran, James. 1999. "Literary Editors, Social Networks and Cultural Tradition." In *Media Organisations in Society,* edited by James Curran, 215–39. London: Hodder Arnold.

Davies, Rosamund, and Gauti Sigthorsson. 2013. *The Creative Industries from Theory to Practice.* London: Sage.

Doyle, Gillian. 2013. *Understanding Media Economics.* 2nd ed. London: Sage

Gieber, Walter. 1964. "News Is What Newspapermen Make It." In *People, Society, and Mass Communication,* edited by Lewis A. Dexter and David Manning White, 171–80. London: The Free Press of Glencoe.

Graser, Marc, and Brent Lang. 2015. "Spider-Man: How Sony, Marvel Will Benefit from Unique Deal." *Variety*, February 10. https://variety.com.

Greco, Albert, Jim Miliot, and Robert Wharton. 2014. *The Book Publishing Industry*. 3rd ed. London: Routledge.

Hearn, Greg, Simon Roodhouse, and Julie Blakey. 2007. "From Value Chain to Value Creating Ecology." *International Journal of Cultural Policy* 13 (4): 419–36. https://doi.org/10.1080/10286630701683367.

Hesmondhalgh, David. 2019. *The Cultural Industries*. 4th ed. London: Sage.

Lotz, Amanda. 2009. "Industry-Level Studies and the Contributions of Gitlin's Inside Prime Time." In *Production Studies: Cultural Studies of Media Industries*, edited by Vicki Mayer, Miranda J. Banks, and John T. Caldwell, 25–38. New York: Routledge.

MPA. n.d. "The Film Rating System." www.filmratings.com.

Napoli, Philip. M. 2016. "Requiem for the Long Tail: Towards a Political Economy of Content Aggregation and Fragmentation." *International Journal of Media and Politics* 12 (3): 341–56. https://doi.org/10.1386/macp.12.3.341_1.

Negus, Keith. 2002. "The Work of Cultural Intermediaries and the Enduring Distance between Production and Consumption." *Cultural Studies* 16 (4): 501–15. https://doi.org/10.1080/09502380210139089.

Nichols, Randy. 2014. *The Video Game Business*. London: Palgrave Macmillan.

Shoemaker, Pamela J., and Timothy Vos. 2009. *Gatekeeping Theory*. London: Routledge.

Smith Maguire, Jennifer, and Julian Matthews. 2012. "Are We All Cultural Intermediaries Now? An Introduction to Cultural Intermediaries in Context." *European Journal of Cultural Studies* 15 (5): 551–62. https://doi.org/10.1177/1367549412445762.

Smits, Roderik. 2019. *Gatekeeping in the Evolving Business of Independent Film Distribution*. London: Palgrave Macmillan.

Wasko, Janet. 2003. *How Hollywood Works*. London: Sage.

White, David Manning. 1950. "The 'Gate Keeper': A Case Study in the Selection of News." *Journalism Quarterly* 27 (4): 383–90.

Zackariasson, Peter, and Timothy J. Wilson. 2012. *The Video Game Industry: Formation, Present State, and Future*. London: Routledge.

5

The Circulation Game

Shifting Production Logics and Circulation Moments in the Digital Games Industry

APHRA KERR

Over the past two decades digital game companies have had to compete against internet companies, grapple with online distribution, and rethink games as a "free to play" (F2P) service. Change came incrementally. In the early 2000s, the PlayStation 2 (PS2, 2000) and the Xbox (2001) consoles shipped with internet capabilities, while a few years later the Xbox 360 (2005), the PlayStation 3 (PS3, 2006) and the Nintendo Wii (2006) were Wi-Fi enabled. Digital game consoles moved from being "walled gardens" for playing games on physical artifacts to networked environments where players could both access and create a range of content and communication services. PC games have long been networked to some extent, but during the 2000s online digital distribution stores like Steam were launched. These were followed shortly after by the Apple and Android mobile application stores. By 2012 industry data in North America revealed that revenues from digital distribution had surpassed sales of games on physical artifacts (ESA 2013). The revenues of successful mobile start-up game companies quickly surpassed the annual revenues of well-established game companies. Internet and communication giants like Google, Facebook, Apple, and Tencent began to report significant revenues from distributing mobile and social networking games. Indeed, these companies are now regularly among the top ten publicly listed game companies by revenue (Kerr 2017).

From the current vantage point we see evidence of significant change but also adaptations and resistance. Slowly many of the successful new game developers have been acquired by legacy game publishers, and some of those legacy publishers have launched their own online retail stores. Consumers in certain markets have resisted "online only" game consoles and attempts to suppress secondhand markets in physical game artifacts. Some countries have introduced new regulations restricting the spread of transnational game services. These countertrends are what media historian Brian Winston (1998, 11–13) referred to as brakes, or the "suppression of radical potential." This chapter takes the view that technological change is part of a broader process of innovation, which is punctuated by choices and the push and pull of various factors. As such, we need to empirically examine how individuals, organizations, and existing institutions and cultures shape, adapt to, and resist technological change.

Understanding contemporary cultural production structures also requires us to evaluate our existing conceptual frameworks. In the 1980s, the "production logics" approach emerged within the cultural industries tradition. Initially according to this approach, each media industry had a single dominant production logic based around the institutionalization of a particular sociotechnical system. Use of a production logics approach has recently been applied in studies of television (Lotz 2017), music (Meier 2019), and digital games (Kerr 2017). A key strength of the approach is that we can begin to identify similarities and differences across the cultural industries. It prompts us to identify the key brokers who capture most of the economic value in the cultural production circuit and the crucial creative personnel who produce it. Also, it distinguishes the major market characteristics underpinning particular industries and attends to innovative processes and products.

This chapter uses a production logics approach to examine the digital games industry over the past decade, proposing that the concept of "circulation" is more useful than distribution in understanding recent innovations within the characteristics of the relevant logics. Circulation and distribution are not used synonymously. Circulation was a core concept for Karl Marx, who used it to describe when value was realized from the sale of commodities. Additionally, circulation was also a distinctive moment for Stuart Hall (1973) in his encoding/decoding model. The production logics approach draws upon these critical theoretical traditions but updates these to examine where both economic and cultural value is created in contemporary two-way interactive online services, including the activities of consumers and amateur producers (Bødker 2016). In emerging production logics, we can identify moments in the economic chain when exchange value becomes use value, but also where use value becomes exchange value. Circulation as a concept is used to describe the two-way nature of both implicit (data) and explicit (communication and content) flows where there is a clear exchange of value and influence on professional content generation. Changes in circulation are evident in both existing and new production logics.

In this chapter I first briefly outline the production logics approach and then introduce the key production logics in the digital games industry, including adaptations and new logics. The final section focuses on three moments of circulation in contemporary production logics: the influence of implicit user data on professional content production, the role of community managers in supporting online communities, and finally the development of live performance forms of user-generated content. The chapter is informed by two decades of projects examining the circuits of production in the digital games industry in Europe.

Production Logics in the Cultural Industries

Production logics identify the core industrial, market, and social characteristics of production processes in the cultural industries. These logics have been defined as the "dominant institutional forms and relationships assumed by the commodification and industrialisation of culture at a given historical moment" (Lacroix and Tremblay 1997, 53). For Lacroix and Tremblay, each production logic identifies the major institutional forms that define the "field of constraints and possibilities" (1997, 53). Every logic is based on five characteristics: the economic value chain, the dominant power brokers, the creative professions, the revenue stream, and the overall market structure. While production logics are dependent on the state of technology at a given moment, the approach does not list technology as a defining characteristic.

Miège (1987) identified five logics across the cultural industries: editorial, written press, flow, live entertainment, and electronic information. He noted three dominant logics: publishing, written press, and flow (1989, 12). Book publishing and the early music industry best exemplified the publishing logic, in which users directly purchased physical media products from specialist retail outlets, and with artists compensated through a royalty system. Publishers were the key brokers and captured much of the economic value in the system. The relationship between publishers/editors and creators was a key aspect of production, but knowledge of and engagement with consumers were relatively limited. Retailers played an important role in mediating the relationship with consumers and capturing value. For publishers, uncertain demand was offset by the development of a catalogue of content, the use of intellectual property licenses, and the cultivation of "stars." The press logic refers to the mass production of highly ephemeral products such as newspapers and magazines. In these industries companies employed a large salaried workforce of content producers and worked with hundreds of organizations to distribute a physical commodity as widely as possible, and the consumer's role was restricted to the regular purchase of the physical good from a retail outlet. Direct sales and advertising were the main revenue sources.

Flow was characterized by traditional broadcast radio and television, with programs centrally broadcast and received by dispersed reception devices. The flow logic was characterized by the uninterrupted output of content, and for broadcasters—the key broker in the value chain—the main challenges involved creating a programming schedule while maintaining ratings that delivered audiences to advertisers. Consumers in some countries directly paid for programmed content via license fees or otherwise indirectly through generating the ratings that attracted advertising income.

Across these logics the distribution of cultural commodities to audiences was mostly a one-way process, involving physical devices, networks, and retail outlets. Table 5.1 summarizes the three dominant production logics as outlined by Miège and others. When Miège was first writing, the publishing logic was dominant, with professional cultural workers directly employed in the creation of content and other workers employed in the reproduction and distribution of that content. New media such as videotext and cable television were mentioned by Miège and placed within the flow logic. While these three logics were dominant, Miège also referred to two more in passing—computer programming and live performance. The computer programming logic included home computer games (1989, 141–43 and 150), and Miège distinguished computer games from other types of software. At this time, digital games were mostly sold on cassettes through retail outlets, and Miège stated that early "videogame inventors" were often salaried workers and dependent on royalties, and so for him the digital games industry operated according to the publishing logic. For years the flow and catalogue concepts provided a useful shorthand for understanding production in the cultural industries. In these logics, the challenges were to produce, program, and distribute content to mass audiences, manage a mixture of revenue sources—including sales, subscriptions, advertising, and in some cases license fees—and keep attuned to audience and consumer trends (Garnham 2000, 52).

TABLE 5.1. Principal Logics Underlying the Production of Culture and Information

Characteristics	Publishing (e.g., books, records)	Press (e.g., newspapers)	Flow (e.g., radio, TV)
General	One-off commodities	Regularly purchased commodities	Continuous flow of content
Central broker	Publisher	Editor	Programmer/broadcaster
Economic chain	Project-by-project production by small companies, payment via royalties and copyright, irregular employment, physical distribution network, retail outlets	Mostly waged writers and journalists, physical distribution network, retail outlets	Quasi-industrial organization, wage labor but some royalties and copyright, purchasing of catalogues and formats, physical distribution network, reception devices
Creative professions	Authors, composers, directors, artists, and specialized technicians	Journalists and specialized technicians	Authors, journalists, hosts, performing artists, directors, and specialized technicians
Sales revenues	Direct revenues from the sale of individual products	Revenues from subscriptions and indirect revenues from advertising	Indirect revenues from license fees and advertising, ratings important
Market characteristics	Segmented mass market	Segmented mass market	Undifferentiated and indirect mass market

Source: Author's summary of Miège (1989, 146–47).

An early attempt to extend the production logics approach to take account of distribution innovations was made by Lacroix and Tremblay (1997). While acknowledging that the publishing logic was the "classic mode of commodification and industrialisation," and that the flow logic still existed (1997, 60), they proposed a new "club logic" had developed, which shifted power toward the distributor and reflected increasingly interactive communications technologies. This new logic created a "hegemonic position for distributors" (1997, 64), which they argued would only advance with the development of broadband networks. The club logic attempted to capture the ways in which some companies harnessed telecommunications to make available a vast catalogue of content to their subscribers (or club members), thus combining the individualized commodity form of the publishing logic and the continuous programming of the flow logic. In this logic, content access is seen as "metered" with users regularly billed, although a variety of financing models were possible. Consumers connected to a computerized server, from which they could select their content. For Lacroix and Tremblay, the club logic did not replace the other two logics, but instead competed with them.

By the early 2000s, Bustamante (2004) noted a tendency for companies to "hybridise" elements of the publishing and flow logics and to offer both direct and indirect payment options. Miège (2011, 64) has argued that while publishing and flow logics persist, new logics such as neo-club, online portals, and brokerage have emerged. He argues that to really establish themselves, these new logics need to leave a mark on content conception. Lotz (2017) suggests that internet-distributed television introduces a new portal logic characterized by a subscription model of payment, whereby users access a curated catalogue of programming over the internet at a time of their own choosing. Netflix is a key example for her, and of course the company has moved into original content development. Meier (2019) also draws upon the production logics approach in her analysis of the contemporary music industry and notes that while publishing and flow still exist in that industry, they are now joined by club and live logics. Finally, Miège (2019, 77) identifies six contemporary production logics: print news, online documentary products, a club logic, brokerage, online specialist portals, and online social networks/platforms. The characteristics of these logics are poorly delineated, and work remains to be done on how these logics are defined in different cultural industries.

Contemporary studies of the cultural industries therefore suggest there is a persistence and hybridization of some production logics as well as the emergence of new logics and decline of others. While the publishing and flow logics continue to exist in many cultural industries, new production logics like neo-club, portal, and social network/platform have emerged. Some logics have declined (press) and others have had a resurgence (live performance). What is clear is that today we can identify more than one production logic in each cultural industry and there are similarities and differences across the industries. What is also clear is that in this literature we rarely see detailed analysis of the digital games industry.

Production Logics in the Digital Games Industry: Adaptation and Innovation

The digital games industry emerged as a commercial home entertainment industry in the early 1970s in North America and Europe. Originally games were distributed on cartridges, disks, and CDs and sold via both specialist and generalist retail outlets. They required a home console, a personal computer, or a handheld device to play. By the mid-2000s, the latest home and handheld console devices came with built-in network capabilities, and while initially these connections were used for downloading game updates, quickly more interactive possibilities emerged (Nieborg 2014). Physical distribution of games still exists, but digital distribution revenues now supersede physical revenues in many markets. Digital distribution can range from players downloading game updates to downloading full games and accessing online multiplayer games. Digital distribution is dominant on mobile devices but is common in the PC and console markets also. Boxed content is important in sustaining secondhand and developing markets. Attempts by the industry to launch "online only" game play via consoles have been resisted by consumers, and most consoles still allow a hybrid of offline and online forms of game play and distribution. However, these facts about digital distribution get us only so far. To understand the wider impact of these changes, we now turn to examining production logics in the digital games industry.

We can identify at least five production logics in the digital games industry, four of which are familiar from other cultural industries and one of which is influenced by social media and the internet industries. In the early 2000s the production of console and personal computer games largely conformed to the publishing logic. When interviewed, game developers spoke of pitching ideas to publishers, securing a publishing deal, and receiving royalties after launch (Kerr 2006). There were virtual stars, like Lara Croft, and significant licensing of intellectual properties from real-world sports and music. The most successful publishers often acquired the most successful game development studios, while the key hardware owners—Nintendo, Sony, and Microsoft—became fully integrated into development, publishing, and distribution. The console market had an oligopolistic structure, and the dominant companies used hardware as a "loss leader." Exclusive game titles for these proprietary game systems were used to drive sales and profits. While developers might hope to capture five dollars from each game sold for fifty-five, publishers might take thirty, with ten dollars each for the retailer and the distributor. Some large game companies established their own distribution divisions, but specialist retail shops, like Game in the United Kingdom, had a lot of power to negotiate the shelf life of a game (Williams 2003).

Commercial online games first emerged in the 1990s on personal computers. Massively multiplayer online games (MMOGs) like *Ultima Online* (Origin, 1997) became a successful game genre and demonstrated that subscription-based online games could be a successful business. These games had to be purchased as "boxed products" in retail shops, but to play them one needed a monthly subscription (often fifteen dollars), a personal computer, and a good internet connection. These computers were expensive, internet connections were often slow, and the technical know-how required to play them meant this segment of the market remained small. Countries with high-speed internet connections, like South Korea, were pioneers in MMOGs and online games (Jin and Chee 2008). Yet MMOGs had flow-like characteristics: MMOGs were persistent, with games continuing after individual players logged out, content updates were scheduled regularly, and companies maintained large bodies of salaried development staff. MMOGs attracted millions of subscribers, supporting hundreds of simultaneous players through a transnational internet-based infrastructure, giving rise to rich online and offline cultures (Taylor 2006), and creating significant governance challenges for the game companies that drove the development of community management processes. These early genres of networked games

combined physical and digital distribution and pioneered the sociotechnical and occupational innovations evident in today's services.

One decade later fully digital "games as a service" have emerged (Kerr
2017). Games as a service provide more predictable revenues for game
companies and enable them to bypass the revenue cut demanded by
retailers. During the early 2000s Microsoft and Sony developed their
own digital distribution and multiplayer networks: Xbox Live and the
PlayStation Network (PSN). A core strategic goal was that these services
would turn game consoles into networked entertainment devices for
games, video, and music content. In 2003, Valve developed a specialist
online retail and distribution service for computer games called Steam.
This service emerged initially to distribute game updates for Valve's
own games, but over the next decade Steam developed into distributing
games and related services across multiple devices for other companies.
Steam takes a 30 percent revenue split, and some reports claim the service is responsible for 70 percent of digital game sales (Statt 2019). These
reports are hard to verify, but the evidence points to significant market dominance (Joseph 2018). Steam is both consumer and developer/
publisher facing, supporting content, communication, and business services. Steam had few competitors until the Epic Games Store launched
at the end of 2018, proposing to take a significantly lower 12 percent cut
in revenues.

Games as a service are enabled by digital distribution but constitute
a much broader set of organizational and sociotechnical innovations.
These digital services offer a catalogue of games for sale but in many
cases are crucial to the player accessing the multiplayer version of the
game. They also provide players with a range of communication, match-
making, ranking, and streaming tools. Crucially, they enable publishers
to take advantage of digital rights management technology to tackle piracy, monitor IP violations, and manage player behavior in their games.
Finally, they have developed into services to curate and distribute independent and amateur-created game modifications and content. Until
2016, for example, Steam offered the Steam Greenlight, which allowed
subscribers to vote on which new games should be published. Steam
Workshop allows players to upload game modifications, and Community Market is where players can buy and sell virtual items. The same
company also offers a range of services to developers. Alongside offering

security services for digital rights management and monitoring player behavior, *Steamworks* also offers real-time data analytics, payment, and language support.

The production logics concept provides one way to evaluate these changes and to highlight where digital game services converge and diverge from other cultural industries. By 2012, while a publishing logic still existed, there were also a significant number of subscription-based MMOGs conforming more to the flow logic. In addition, more club or portal services that emerged were slow to take off in many markets due to the bandwidth demands of multiplayer games. New entrants to games, Google and Apple respectively launched Play Pass and Arcade as their cloud-based game subscription services during 2019.

While these three production logics (i.e., publishing, flow, club) seem to conform to established production logics in other cultural industries, the emergence of e-sports and livestreaming by amateur and professional gamers sees the reemergence of a live performance logic. E-sports is growing rapidly in some countries with new central brokers emerging and a range of new creative professionals. Games are designed so that teams can compete online as part of tournaments, which borrow heavily from North American sports leagues with the development of professional player contracts, team franchises, broadcasting collaborations, and university scholarships. They are also designed to work as spectacles to be viewed in sports stadiums. *League of Legends* (Riot, 2009) and *Overwatch* (Activision Blizzard, 2016) have major leagues in many countries and full-time professional players competing for significant prize money (Taylor 2012). Semiprofessional and amateur players are also engaging in online performances and monetization of their game play on YouTube Gaming and Twitch. Here, the key brokers vary, but legacy game developer/publishers play a key role through their ownership of the underlying intellectual property rights. E-sports follow a performance logic but one where professional and amateur players are playing a crucial role in value generation and circulation.

Finally, the past decade has seen the emergence of a new production logic based around F2P games on social, mobile, and online platforms. The launches of the iPhone App Store (2008) and Android Market (2008) standardized the digital distribution process for mobile game developers, replacing the hundreds of competing phone handsets and channels that posed significant cost barriers to mobile game developers in the 1990s and 2000s. In Asia, Chinese internet technology companies like Tencent and NetEase now offer similar services. This emerging logic positions internet companies as key brokers. Most take a 30 percent cut on the cover price or in-game purchases. Crucially this production logic has encouraged the reimagining of games, adopting the form of shorter, more casual types of games that require less technical or gaming knowledge from players and are designed specifically for the affordances of social and mobile technologies (Leaver and Willson 2016).

An important characteristic of this new production logic has been the focus on indirect revenues and a shift away from premium up-front payments toward freemium. F2P's freemium business model has come to dominate the production and circulation of games on social media, mobile technologies, and to some degree on PC. In this model, content is made available for free to a player and at various points in the game players are prompted by the game to engage in micro transactions. F2P games make money through a combination of behavioral data-driven advertising, in-game purchases of content, cosmetic items or extra powers, and in some cases extra downloadable content (Nieborg 2015, 2016). Crucially, freemium value chains are characterized by ongoing dataveillance of players and core game play "mechanics" designed to monetize game play. Many legacy game developers and publishers resisted the development of freemium, as they viewed the business model as having a negative impact on the game play experience (Whitson 2012). Over the past decade, however, more legacy game companies have launched F2P games.

We can trace F2P games back to browser-based MMOGs, including *Runescape* (Jagex, 2001). This logic really started to develop, however, when F2P became available on mobile devices, integrating real-time advertising networks and exploiting the preexisting online social networks of players. In 2006, Facebook introduced its Facebook Development Platform and became a more programmable social platform for third-party companies (Helmond 2015). Companies like Zynga made significant revenues with games like *Farmville* (Zynga, 2009) by designing their games to optimize Facebook users' social media friend networks and infrastructure. Other successful F2P mobile games were *Clash of Clans* (Supercell, 2012) and *Angry Birds* (Rovio, 2009). The release of *Pokémon Go* (Niantic, 2016) combined a much-loved preexisting intellectual property with the F2P model to become a huge market success. More recently, Epic Games' F2P online game *Fortnite Battle Royale* (2018) dominated charts across multiple devices, and *Fortnite* is now developing an e-sports infrastructure.

Over time a set of characteristics have emerged and stabilized, with the establishment of internet companies as key brokers, the dominance of data-driven indirect revenue sources, and a large number of small companies developing highly tailored games for particular social media and mobile platforms. In this logic, the list of core creative professionals has expanded beyond design and programmers to include data scientists and community managers. While players are core to any interactive game play experience, their role in this logic has expanded beyond play to involve content generation and the activities of rating, reviewing, commenting, and sharing. Arguably, players should now be thought of as core creatives. This logic can be called a platform production logic (Kerr 2017), which may conform to Miège's online social networks/platform logic (2019).

To recap, multiple production logics coexist in the digital games industry (Kerr 2017, 77–78). A *publishing* logic continues to exist and develop. New games take a significant time to come to market, and large development teams are usually contracted by game publishers to develop a game. The key brokers are a small number of vertically integrated game publishers and computer companies like Microsoft. The *flow* logic is epitomized by subscription-based MMOGs. For example, *World of Warcraft* (*WoW*; Blizzard, 2004) has millions of subscribers and a vast human and technical infrastructure supporting ongoing game play. It is significant that *WoW* has been in development continuously for over a decade, with salaried or contracted full-time developers scheduling content updates to keep top-level players engaged. In a persistent MMOG, the role of the community manager has become professionalized, both driving player engagement and responding to player harassment (see below). The production of MMOGs has much in common with traditional broadcasting services, but in most cases players have to buy the game and then pay an additional monthly subscription in order to play. We see some games mix elements of both these logics, but the core characteristics remain.

Since 2012, *performance* and *platform* logics have become institutionalized, with a strong influence on content development. In these logics, we can identify new central brokers from outside of the digital games industry, distinct revenue models, and the extension of creative roles to include players. Apple, Facebook, Google, and Tencent have become central brokers as they intermediate between content creators, advertisers, and players. Valve's Steam is also significant here. In addition, a range of new professional occupational roles have been developing, ranging from technical roles in network operation centers to data scientists and community managers. New technologies support the F2P model by gathering data, serving advertisements, offering personalized rewards, and governing unacceptable player behavior. These processes have had a significant impact on the design and life cycle of games, on the generation of revenues, and on the relationship between game developers/publishers and their players. The next section examines the creation and exchange of value in three different circulation moments.

Circulation Moments in Contemporary Production Logics

Circulation as a concept has a long history in studies of capitalism and cultural production: Karl Marx (1995) described the circulation of commodities moving from the production to the consumption spheres and from surplus to use value; Stuart Hall distinguished between production/circulation and consumption/circulation in television production (Hall 1973). Certainly, the development of online participatory practices has focused attention on the productive roles of media consumers. Some scholars note that informational capitalism exploits both the immaterial and affective labor of digital media users to create economic value (Jarrett 2016). Most recently the literature on surveillance capitalism has detailed the extraction of value from "behavioral surplus" (Zuboff 2019). This section focuses on aspects of emerging value chains and creative work where distinctions between production and consumption spheres are blurred, and where economic and social values are created, exchanged, and circulated. In what remains we reflect on three significant "moments" that shape circulation in the emerging platform logic: the use of player data to continually adapt the design of digital games, the professionalization of community management as a new occupational role, and the commodification of game play as live performance.

In the platform logic, gathering data on player behavior is crucial to indirect revenue generation and has an important impact on content development. Gathering and analyzing aggregate and targeted data relating to consumer activity is hardly unique to digital games, but it is core to the F2P model. The platform production logic relies on a variety of technologies to capture the creative and communicative activity of players during game play. Internet intermediaries like Facebook, Steam, and the app stores mediate access to player data and advertising networks. They also extract significant value, usually 30 percent of sales revenues. Interviews conducted with representatives from game companies identified the increasing use of player data to inform ongoing content development. In addition, an increasing number of data analytics job ads are appearing on game industry websites (Kerr 2017).

Designing F2P games requires different skills and tools from those used in older production logics. As F2P online games can be frequently updated, developers may run real-time experiments on design options (Leaver and Willson 2016). Data analytics is viewed by game companies as a tool for reducing risk. Interviewees noted that aggregate player data can be used to identify which game avatars were the most popular (Kerr 2017). If avatars are based on licensed intellectual properties, companies can save money by removing unpopular avatars. On the other hand, play data can be used to reduce game difficulty in areas that are proving difficult for players. As in other cultural industries, we are only beginning to understand how data analytics and metrics are being used to inform, direct, and adapt content generation and mediate the circuit of value generation between professional game developers and their players. Much of the data gathered by professional developers goes unnoticed by the game player.

Community management is a second important example of a new role at work in contemporary circulation and provides an important insight into the exchange of value between game developers and game players. Previously, community management was performed voluntarily by experienced game players who responded to questions from other players. In the past two decades, however, the growth of online multiplayer games with transnational communities has meant the role has been professionalized, undertaken in-house or externally subcontracted to specialist agencies in near-to-market locations. Today community managers play an important intermediary role between game developers and game players, driving user engagement and acting as advocates for game players. Community managers communicate directly with players, answering queries and informing them of major service updates. They also communicate to game publishers or developers if players have grievances. This new category of professional performs a crucial role in maintaining the social value of the community for game players and thus sustaining the revenues of game companies.

While the role is clearly important in terms of understanding online games, the work of community managers is mostly hidden from view. Interviews with community managers located in Ireland, together with analysis of job advertisements, found that employees were hired for their passion for games and their linguistic and cultural knowledge (Kerr and Kelleher 2015). Community managers are often game players themselves and thus have translated their game playing expertise into an employment opportunity. Hundreds of community managers moved from around Europe to Ireland in order to support European players of North American or Asian online games. Ireland's community management center for the *WoW* European market, for example, had up to eight hundred employees. They operated in a multilingual environment and were called upon to mediate complex social situations between game players. This type of work seems crucial to the economic success of online games but is poorly paid, and community managers in our sample felt they often had little opportunity to advocate on behalf of gamers and indeed often became the target of online harassment, homophobia, and sexism.

A final example of a circulation moment in the new platform logic is how the digital games industry and its consumers create value from player-generated content. The industry has a relatively long history of making available tools to modify professional game content to game players, who engage in forms of creativity colloquially called modifications or "mods." *Doom* was one of the first games to embrace player modifications, and some of the earliest modders went on to work in the games industry, turning their modding knowledge into jobs. Modding may occur at the level of the hardware, software, code, interface, or graphics, and game companies may exert considerable control over the creations of modders through the tools they make available and restrictions imposed in legal contracts (Nieborg and van der Graaf 2008; Kerr 2011). While some game companies explicitly rule out remunerating players for their modifications, other companies provide ways for game players to monetize their work.

So far, these examples seem very similar to fan creations in other cultural industries. However, recently game players have started recording and streaming videos of themselves playing digital games and sharing them on services tailored to games, including Twitch, which launched in 2011, and YouTube's Gaming channel. Today Twitch has over two million player broadcasters and about fifteen million daily viewers. Most of these gamers are livestreaming themselves playing a small number of games daily from their PC or console while also chatting or commentating on their play. They can be seen playing popular games such as *WoW*, *Fortnite*, and *League of Legends*. By performing their expertise online, the most successful game streamers can earn sufficient revenues from advertising, sponsorship, subscriptions, and donations to become full-time professionals. Some become courted by game publishers and other brands for their market influence. Many of the most viewed streamers are current or former professional e-sports players. As this new form of player-generated content becomes professionalized, we can identify a moment of circulation where the meaning and economic value of cultural productions are negotiated.

Datafication, community management, and player content generation illustrate important moments in the interaction between developers and gamers where explicit player activity (making content, commenting on or reacting to content) and implicit player activity (game play tracked though datafication) are used to shape content. They also offer a spectrum of player agency, from passive tracking to active content generation. These moments or roles expand both the value chain and list of creative workers involved in contemporary production logics and prompt us to rethink the role of circulation. Professional community managers and data scientists are rarely examined in relation to contemporary cultural production. Equally, the monetization of game streamers challenges our conceptualization of user-generated content and shifts the consumer gamer more explicitly into the role of producer gamer. Indeed, in the current social media platform logic, popular gamers on Twitch with millions of followers become a key moment in the circuit of cultural production, capturing economic value for themselves while generating revenues for the professional developers of the game and for the hosting platform. While game streamers are far from key brokers, this chapter suggests that identifying and paying attention to innovative circulation moments within different production logics is crucial to understanding continuity and change in contemporary cultural production.

BIBLIOGRAPHY

Bødker, Henrik. 2016. "Stuart Hall's Encoding/Decoding Model and the Circulation of Journalism in the Digital Landscape." *Critical Studies in Media Communication* 33 (5): 409–23. https://doi.org/10.1080/15295036.2016.1227862.

Bustamante, Enrique. 2004. "Cultural Industries in a Digital Age: Some Provisional Conclusions." *Media, Culture & Society* 26 (6): 803–20.

ESA. 2013. *2013 Sales, Demographic and Usage Data: Essential Facts about the Computer and Video Game Industry.* Washington, DC: Entertainment Software Association.

Garnham, Nicholas. 2000. *Emancipation, the Media and Modernity. Arguments about the Media and Social Theory.* New York: Oxford University Press.

Hall, Stuart. 1973. *Encoding and Decoding in the Television Discourse.* Birmingham: Centre for Contemporary Cultural Studies, University of Birmingham.

Helmond, Anne. 2015. "The Platformization of the Web: Making Web Data Platform Ready." *Social Media + Society* 1 (2). https://doi.org/10.1177/2056305115603080.

Jarrett, Kylie. 2016. *Feminism, and Digital Media: The Digital Housewife.* London: Routledge.

Jenkins, Henry, Sam Ford, and Joshua Green. 2013. *Spreadable Media.* New York: New York University Press.

Jin, Dal Yong, and Florence Chee. 2008. "Age of New Media Empires: A Critical Interpretation of the Korean Online Game Industry." *Games and Culture* 3 (1): 38–58. https://doi.org/10.1177/1555412007309528.

Joseph, Daniel James. 2018. "The Discourse of Digital Dispossession: Paid Modifications and Community Crisis on Steam." *Games and Culture* 13 (7): 690–707. https://doi.org/10.1177/1555412018756488.

Kerr, Aphra. 2006. *The Business and Culture of Digital Games: Gamework/Gameplay.* London: Sage.

———. 2011. "Player Production and Innovation in Online Games: Time for New Rules?" In *Online Gaming in Context: The Social and Cultural Significance of Online Games,* edited by Garry Crawford, Victoria Gosling, and Ben Light, 25–39. Oxon: Routledge.

———. 2017. *Global Games: Production, Circulation and Policy in the Networked Age.* New York: Routledge.

Kerr, Aphra, and John D. Kelleher. 2015. "The Recruitment of Passion and Community in the Service of Capital: Community Managers in the Digital Games Industry." *Critical Studies in Media Communication* 32 (3): 177–92. https://doi.org/10.1080/1529 5036.2015.1045005.

Lacroix, J.-G., and Gaetan Tremblay. 1997. "The Institutionalization of Cultural Commodification: Logics and Strategies." *Current Sociology* 45 (4): 39–69. https://doi.org/10.1177/001139297045004004.

Leaver, Tama, and Michele Willson, eds. 2016. *Social, Casual and Mobile Games: The Changing Gaming Landscape*. New York: Bloomsbury.

Lotz, Amanda D. 2017. *Portals: A Treatise on Internet-Distributed Television*. Ann Arbor, MI: Maize Books.

Marx, Karl. 1995. *Capital: A New Abridgement*. Edited by David McLellan. Oxford: Oxford University Press.

Meier, Leslie M. 2019. "Popular Music, Streaming, and Promotional Media: Enduring and Emerging Industrial Logics." In *Making Media: Production, Practices and Professions*, edited by Mark Deuze and Mirjam Prenger, 321–34. Amsterdam: Amsterdam University Press.

Miège, Bernard. 1987. "The Logics at Work in the New Cultural Industries." *Media, Culture & Society* 9 (3): 273–89. https://doi.org/10.1177/016344387009003002.

———. 1989. *The Capitalisation of Cultural Production*. New York: International General.

———. 2011. "Principal Ongoing Mutations of Cultural and Informational Industries." In *The Political Economies of Media*, edited by Dwayne Winseck and Dal Yong Jin, 51–65. London: Bloomsbury.

———. 2019. "Cultural and Creative Industries and the Political Economy of Communication." In *Making Media: Production, Practices and Professions*, edited by Mark Deuze and Mirjam Prenger, 73–83. Amsterdam: Amsterdam University Press.

Nieborg, David B. 2014. "Prolonging the Magic: The Political Economy of the 7th Generation Console Game." *Eludamos. Journal for Computer Game Culture* 8 (1): 47–63.

———. 2015. "Crushing Candy: The Free-to-Play Game in Its Connective Commodity Form." *Social Media + Society* 1 (2). https://doi.org/10.1177/2056305115621932.

———. 2016. "From Premium to Freemium. The Political Economy of the App." In *Social, Casual and Mobile Games: The Changing Gaming Landscape*, edited by Tama Leaver and Michelle Willson, 225–37. New York: Bloomsbury.

Nieborg, David B., and Shenja van der Graaf. 2008. "The Mod Industries? The Industrial Logic of Non-market Game Production." *European Journal of Cultural Studies* 11 (2): 177–95.

Statt, Nick. 2019. "Epic vs Steam: The Console War Reimagined on the PC." *The Verge*, April 16. www.theverge.com.

Taylor, T. L. 2006. *Play between Worlds: Exploring Online Game Culture*. Cambridge, MA: MIT Press.

———. 2012. *Raising the Stakes: E-sports and the Professionalization of Computer Gaming*. Cambridge, MA: MIT Press.

Whitson, Jennifer. 2012. "Game Design by Numbers: Instrumental Play and the Quantitative Shift in the Digital Game Industry." PhD dissertation, Carleton University.

Williams, Dmitri. 2003. "The Video Game Lightning Rod: Constructions of a New Technology 1970–2000." *Information, Communication & Society* 6 (4): 523–50.

Winston, Brian. 1998. *Media, Technology and Society. A History: From the Telegraph to the Internet*. London: Routledge.

Zuboff, Shoshana. 2019. *The Age of Surveillance Capitalism: The Fight for a Human Future at the New Frontier of Power*. London: Profile Books.

6

Questioning the Content Supply Model

A Provocation

PATRICK VONDERAU

In June 2016, a major consumer outburst erupted on several online forums concerned with Swedish music streaming service Spotify. Users were beginning to notice that their Spotify client was running amok and had suddenly started to record large amounts of junk data on their drives, which could potentially slow down—if not destroy—their storage capacities. As the news spread, reports of ever-larger examples of trash generation began to roll in. Journalists at the tech website *Ars Technica* ran a test and found that their Spotify clients were unwittingly writing five to ten gigabytes of data per hour on their computers—even when the clients were put in idle mode (Goodin 2016). In cases where the program had been running for months, users reported having terabytes of junk dumped on their hard drives (Hampton 2016). Blog outlets were calling the debacle an "assault on user's storage devices," a case of excessive "data gobbling," and an issue that was "quietly killing" the lifespan of hard drives (Brown 2016). It quickly became clear that Spotify had unwantedly turned the computers of thousands of users into garbage dumps. Instead of momentarily diffusing music, the program was spitting out digital trash.

While Spotify's data trash incident has remained a singular event in the service's history, it challenges us to rethink conventional accounts of digital distribution in two ways. As in other instances of technical failure, the glitch reveals the propensities of a system designed to hide its own complexity. The unexpected break within the flow of technology reminded users that Spotify defines access to music in a particular way. Companies like Spotify obtain existing copyrighted content from sources they do not directly control, aggregate this content, and produce customer data based on the interest the content generates. Spotify's Terms and Conditions of Use organize this arrangement by granting users a "limited, non-exclusive, revocable permission to make personal, non-commercial use of the Content" (Spotify USA 2019). At the same time, users have to grant Spotify a "non-exclusive, transferable, sublicensable, royalty-free, perpetual, irrevocable, fully paid, worldwide license to use, reproduce, make available to the public (e.g., perform or display), publish, translate, modify, create derivative works from, and distribute any of your User Content in connection with the Service through any medium." Users also are required to allow the service to use the processor, bandwidth, and storage hardware on their devices, to "provide advertising and other information," and "to allow our business partners to do the same" (Spotify USA 2019). To those who noted it, the glitch demonstrated the comparatively formal, restrictive, and imbalanced nature of this arrangement.

Second, and on a more general level, the glitch also illustrates the difficulty of comparing traditional models of physical distribution to the ways in which songs, movies, or news are now made accessible. There is no historical equivalent in media distribution to a hard drive being fed with vast amounts of useless data without knowledge of its owner. To stick to our example, streaming differs in several ways from the physical transportation of things through a singular, linear chain of supply between a producer and consumer (Johansson 2013). Economically, streaming music is a model that approaches recorded music by creating revenue streams from the *usage*, or consumption of music, not on the distribution of cassette tapes, LP records, compact discs, or à la carte downloads. What is more, data are not technically *transported*—as in being moved from one location to the next—when information is streamed. Instead, data are copied and multiplied. For instance, in its early days, Spotify operated more like a progressive downloading service, based on peer-to-peer networks, enabling users to download (or copy) data to their devices. Thus, the question of how streamed data "move" is not only a matter of tracing changed data locations but an issue of tracking how data proliferate. Finally, streamed music does not simply concern the replication of *audio* data. Many other types of data transmission occur every time content is streamed, including data related to user behavior, preferences, or advertising. While it is certainly possible to single out and isolate specific audio content in such floods of data traffic, it makes little sense to do so, since streaming is inevitably bound up in larger computational processes.

The streaming of music, then, is not simply about the "movement of content from the time it is produced to the time it reaches the consumer" (Braun 2015, 46). As in digital distribution more generally, streaming music via Spotify or other services means complex data traffic that involves connections between a broad variety of actors, networks, and infrastructures dispersed around the globe. This includes musicians and their fans as much as servers and clients, content providers and aggregators, advertisers, and ad exchanges, music intelligence companies such as the Echo Nest, and social media platforms such as Facebook. Consequently, media distribution research has recently been challenged to move beyond its traditional focus on major brands, entertainment content, and the "last-mile interface between distributors' products and consumers" (Herbert and Johnson 2020, 3). Despite such calls, however, most of this research remains conceptually locked into a more traditional understanding of media distribution.

This chapter takes a closer look at what this understanding implies and how it could be complemented by an approach that fully acknowledges the shift from analog supply channels to today's platformized digital markets. The main proposition is to move from an interest centered on *how, to whom, and by whom media content is physically distributed*, toward questions of *how, why, and by whom value is attributed to content*. The aim here is neither to provide an exhaustive survey of relevant works in the field nor to devise a general theory of distribution. Using streamed music, specifically Spotify, to elaborate on its proposition, the chapter first and foremost invites rethinking of the usual canon of cases on which the building of such theories tends to be founded. In doing so, I am drawing both from earlier collaborative efforts to trace streamed content (Eriksson et al. 2019; Vonderau 2014, 2017) and from an ongoing project on the nonauthorized digital cultural production of engagement, or what is commonly referred to as "fake likes" or "fake followers." The intent of bringing these two different strands of research together is to underline that what we routinely describe as distribution is a rather complex, even contradictory phenomenon composed of various markets embedded in or stacked on top of each other.

Distribution—A Standard Definition

As a concept and practice, "distribution" is rooted in nineteenth-century thought and the Industrial Revolution. It is difficult to overlook its deep connection to the mechanical age—to steam power, increased speeds and volumes of material processing, the social division of labor, acceleration and alienation. It's a term that evokes a "control crisis" brought about by massively heightened production outputs as much as new forms of information processing to regain control, including telecommunications and bureaucracy (Beniger 1986). The term is inextricably linked to the economies of scale and scope inherent in volume distribution and to managerial capitalism as societal form (Chandler 1990). Given how large factories had started to integrate forward into distribution and backward into purchasing, contemporaries such as Karl Marx and John Stuart Mill chose to ground political economy on the evident relation of production to distribution and consumption. Alongside the industrial processing of energy, matter, and information evolved the modern mass media as well as large technical systems, such as electricity, and the idea of the network began to take hold in various cultural contexts, including transportation and signal transmission (Hughes 1983). What also survives from these times is an etymological remnant conveying a double sense of distribution as both a dispersal of commodities among consumers and, at the same time, the (unequal) division of the aggregate produce of the industry of a society among its individual members.

Despite some obvious analogies, it would be a bit of a stretch to tie the etymology of the word to today's practices of media distribution and the service monopolies of Spotify or Amazon. In fact, it took only a few decades until scholars started to notice that the concept of distribution and the conceptual trinity (production-distribution-consumption) it had come to form part of were not particularly useful when getting to terms with cultural industries. In his monumental 1902 study, *Psychologie économique* (Economic Psychology), sociologist Gabriel Tarde aimed to develop an alternative to the conventional division of political economy into three branches. Tarde attempted to give greater consideration to the spread of ideas and desires, books, music, art, or fashion on the one hand, and of wealth on the other. His book was a call to "change the label on the bag whose content is no longer the same and which is destined to be modified further," as conventional political economy with its "scholastic abstraction" and "contempt for living reality" seemed unhelpful to understanding the "new genre of riches" now being produced (Tarde 2007, 617 and 627). Evoking the moment of artistic creation in an art academy, for instance, Tarde suggested distinguishing between the actual gestation of an idea and the subsequent process of (industrial) reproduction and opposition, noting that ideas and desires are not mechanically handed down a preexisting value chain but undergo an often conflicted process of imitative repetition and destruction. In noting the ambiguity inherent in the term "distribution," Tarde also proposed to confine political economy entirely to production, in order "to develop as a bloc, in a single chapter and without any artificial discontinuity, everything that concerns the reproduction and distribution of riches."

Tarde's provocative ideas have later been taken up in sociology and partly in media studies (e.g., Latour and Lépinay 2008; Couldry 2014), and they also contributed to one of two broader tendencies that shape distribution research overall. On the one hand, Tarde as well as Marx and others insist on understanding distribution, production, or consumption only as part of a larger totality, as "distinctions within a unity" (Marx 1973, 99) or relational terms whose analytical value precisely lies in studying the interlinkage between various phases of production. A second tendency, on the other hand, taking hold in the late 1910s, built on separating distribution from the other phases in order to develop knowledge that could be operationalized within the industries themselves. Paradoxically, it is within this body of applied work that the now predominant critical understanding of media distribution appears to be rooted. As the concept is used in today's media research, it owes a lot to early marketing theory's notion of "channels of distribution" to describe types and functions of various intermediaries (e.g., Clark 1922). In this narrower view, distribution equals a supply channel that acts as the main artery in a business system through which the flow of goods and services is regulated. While there are differing schools in marketing theory, most of them are less invested in theories than in managerial implications. "Distribution," in this context, is just an "older term" for commercial practices of marketing-management (Slater 2011, 25).

Such a managerial understanding has been formative to the field of distribution research within media and communication studies, as demonstrated by the resemblance between today's standard definition of media distribution as a "movement of content from the time it is produced to the time it reaches the consumer" (Braun 2015, 46), to supply chain management theory in particular, where distribution, likewise, is conceptualized as a "movement" of "usually finished goods" from manufacturer to consumer (e.g., Ross 2015, 46; Noam 2018, 344). A narrower focus on content supply over broader theories or interlinkages may have advantages, but it also obscures, rather than clarifies, key aspects of (digital) distribution.

To be fair, the standard definition has been used in many productive ways. It allows us to conceptualize online distribution as a meeting place between traditional media industries and various new digital media services, enabling discussion of the politics of access to cultural content alongside economic models and business strategies, and how these relate to ongoing processes of media transformation. Spotify, in this view, is an online on-demand service that provides "greater choice and convenience" as compared to previous or competing music providers, alongside novel "navigational techniques" such as playlists (Herbert, Marshall, and Lotz 2019, 354–55). Relations can thus be drawn both backward and sideways, linking music streaming to the history of the recording industry or physical retail sales as much as to platforms, their affordances, infrastructures, and regulatory conundrums. The advantage of this approach is to provide a conceptual framework that may be applied to various media and to all kinds of issues that cannot be subsumed under the categories of production and consumption, including artists' royalties, music libraries, industry structures, piracy, and other user practices that go beyond listening (e.g., Spilker 2018; Wikström and DeFillipi 2016). It also enables comparisons to be made between "platforms" and "portals" such as Spotify and Netflix, for instance, much in line with communication studies' long-standing predilection to sort, classify, and rank global media systems (Lotz 2017; Lobato 2019).

At the same time, the focus remains on content and distribution as the supply channel through which the flow of content is regulated. This risks confining distribution studies to a set agenda derived from analyses of television and film, and to an implicitly managerial take on distribution that undermines the critical intent of this research. While there is no need to insist on the "ontological distinctiveness" of digital media (Gerlitz and Helmond 2013, 1349), moving the agenda beyond the media and communication textbook may help to develop a more comprehensive view of the field. In the case of streamed music, for instance, media scholars might easily object to the often-heard, explicitly managerial argument that Spotify successfully converted digital piracy into a business model by adapting its value creation and value capture activities (e.g., Aversa, Hervas-Drane, and Evenou 2019). Historically, Spotify is known to have infiltrated and literally incorporated the Swedish file-sharing community, building on a peer-to-peer (P2P) network and unlicensed music, of which a large portion was downloaded from illicit services such as the Pirate Bay (Eriksson et al. 2019, 33). Still, it may be more controversial to question what is implicit to the managerial view: the idea, for instance, that Spotify is "decidedly" a tech company that, in "replacing" the earlier "retail chain," would merely provide an "intermediary" service (Hesmondhalgh 2019, 298) or that the key function of the "internet" could be something else than being a "distribution channel" for "content" (Lobato 2019, 6).

Yet such questioning of the content supply model is exactly what may be required, given its limited explanatory potential in regard to streamed music and other instances of digital distribution. To replace "distribution" with "circulation," in this context, remains cosmetical as long as such change of terminology doesn't go along with a conceptual clarification of what this ecological metaphor in turn implies, not least regarding its origins in early twentieth-century evolutionist political philosophy.[1] If anything, streaming appears more like a layering of various "supply chains," each with its own system and object of commodification, than the transportation of a stable unit of commodified content such as prerecorded music or film. Audiences, music preferences, and music metadata can, among other things, all be turned into tradeable goods in the process of streaming music via a service such as Spotify. Clicking play on Spotify's free desktop application may start a recording of a song while also setting in motion the placing of a banner ad, both in a few milliseconds and involving entirely separate chains of actions that mobilize actors in separate industries, such as music and "ad tech" (advertising technology). What is more, the interaction between user, song, and ad may itself prompt a provision of data on another level, as in the case of an information broker collecting user data to be sold to third parties, a practice Spotify is currently being investigated for (Datainspektionen 2019). Still another aspect of such streaming is the entertainment metadata necessary to make a film or song accessible to users, involving, in Spotify's case, a specialized company called TiVo (formerly Rovi), for instance. The song itself, data about the song, user or "target"-related datapoints, and data on user behavior or preference are all, in their different contexts, economically exploitable and indeed exploited by actors who do not even need to interact with each other. How do we acknowledge the complexity of this situation without overstating the new at the expense of the old?

From Content Supply to Valuation Practice

A first step is, I argue, to accept that the notion of distribution cannot be detached from the basic economic properties of what is distributed and from the practices through which it attains economic value. Noted long ago by Marshall McLuhan, "To measure the transfer of content as if it were some pellet moving from point to point" seems like "a futile effort" (1960, 14). The problem is that "content" has become a placeholder often used interchangeably with terms such as information, message, product, or text, but without further specifying if, how, and for whom data are made valuable or indeed commodified. Here, the "system of provisions" approach developed by economist Ben Fine may be a useful remedy to start with. Responding to the lack of consideration given to material culture and its relation to markets in consumption studies, Fine advocates being more "sensitive to the difference between commodities, not so much as items of consumption alone, but in terms of the economic and social processes and structures by which they become such" (2002, 82). A system of provision, in this respect, is an "inclusive chain of activity" that attaches consumption to the production that makes it possible (79), differing from that of other commodity types. In other words, Fine's idea, not unlike Tarde's, is to abandon the horizontal tracing of distribution paths in favor of a vertical approach anchored in the material and cultural specifics of a given commodity and the real-world practices from which it originates (cf. Innis 1950). Not unlike Marx, Fine also defines distribution relationally rather than essentially.

Economists have taken up Fine's approach with regard to film, for instance, in order to explain how this "commodity-type" and its system of provision differ from others because of certain inherent material properties of the film strip and also immaterial properties in the way film is consumed, including the infinitely reproducible but excludable nature of the photographic image, or the uniqueness and short life cycles of film as a product (Pokorny and Sedgwick 2004, 10–15). Although distribution analyses of music and other cultural goods benefit from reflecting on such properties (e.g., Towse 2017), the Spotify example demonstrates that this will not suffice, given that music is only one "commodity" made valuable via Spotify (alongside audiences, metadata, private data, etc.), and also because media scholars, unlike economists, might need to qualify the commodification of cultural goods beyond the scope of any economic model. How does the process of commodification actually work? In digital environments, how does commodification play out on the levels of data, information, content, and IP? Are digital media commodities stable? What are the distributive practices, devices, and agencies involved in generating and maintaining commodity value? To replace the notion of distribution channel with that of a "system of provision arrangement" (Fine 2002, 11) still leaves us with the fact that videos or songs, unlike cars or soap, differ in terms of their openness to audience feedback, for instance, the way such information is fed back into production, and the more general propensity of the social web to regulate access to entertainment content via users' online engagement with said content.

Such deliberations have been a recurring topic in recent research on digital platforms such as Google or Facebook. In integrating business studies, political economy, and software studies, some of this research has highlighted the role of platforms in shaping markets for news or entertainment and what such "platformization of cultural production" entails for the commodities that are its result (e.g., Nieborg and Poell 2018). In this view, "cultural content" becomes increasingly "contingent," in the double sense of being dependent on platforms to reach an audience, and also in being more "malleable, modular in design, and informed by datafied user feedback, open to constant revision and recirculation" (2). While such malleability is confined to neither digital production nor online consumption, but rather is a recurring feature of all songs or films, the suggestion of a process perspective on these "goods" and their "market" is useful in connecting distribution studies to market theories and new work on the practices of valuation and engagement.[2] Contingency is the precise reason why distribution remains a "key locus of power and profit" (Garnham 1990, 162). This is because markets are always constituted by practice, and "to distribute" is but one such practice interlinked with other forms of marketization. Hence my second suggestion: to update political economy on insights from economic sociology (e.g., Araujo, Finch, and Kjellberg 2010) in order to explicate, and retheorize, some of distribution research's managerial undercurrents.

A basic sociological distinction here is the one between goods and products. In this view, a product is a process, "whereas the good corresponds to a state, to a result or, more precisely, to a moment in that never-ending process," stabilized via property rights and qualities attributed to it during qualification trials (Callon, Méadel, and Rabeharisoa 2011, 197). In other words, a product is a good in the context of its ongoing qualification. The web offers countless possibilities to observe how cultural content is "productified" in this sense, while not necessarily being fully commodified. One might argue that the web largely operates like a service economy in which the qualification of goods is a central and constant concern (cf. Miller et al. 2005, 137). Distribution here means a trajectory of innovation, reproduction, and reuse in a setting where traditional property rights or one-size-fits-all qualities have ceased to be the default for defining value. In order to be reproduced and reused, cultural content needs to be perceived as valuable, and what counts as valuable in cultural industries also tends to be subject to our perception of the choices made by others (Potts et al. 2008). The "sharp distinction" sometimes drawn between traditional "content industries" and "social media entertainment" precisely rests on the idea of the latter being subject to "IP dynamics" that result from platforms not taking on an intellectual property ownership position, allowing a "Darwinian-like economic selection" to shape the "SME content universe" (Cunningham and Craig 2019, 15, 149).

Similar to other media companies engaging the social web, Spotify initially offered its users both the uploading and streaming of songs, thus enabling in principle even unknown artists to grow a community. While platforms such as YouTube employed open viewer metrics to organize access to content according to displayed popularity, Spotify gradually replaced its user- and community-centric navigation by one geared more toward top-down recommendations, in order to establish itself as a service not so much for selling music but for "personalized music experiences" (Eriksson et al. 2019, 39–42). This strategy also allowed the company to intensify the valuation of works provided by large repertoire owners, such as the major record labels Universal, Sony, and Warner, which license their music directly to the service and own major stakes in Spotify. In other words, the company changed over time from what initially was a generic "media distribution platform" building on peer contributions into a highly specialized "producer" of both music experiences and user data, while becoming increasingly dependent on risk capital and music licenses (42). Spotify's history thus documents once more that it is not only the "cultural commodity" that is "contingent," but the service or platform itself.

If the web can be described as a calculative space for those who seek to value goods and services, platforms such as Google are nothing more than the proverbial tip of the iceberg when it comes to how, why, and by whom such value is attributed. Markets, arguably the most politically significant institution of valuation in the world (Reinecke 2015, 211), extend well beyond the area of influence occupied by Facebook or Spotify. To understand the politics of today's media markets, we need to attend to the broader cultural scenarios of capitalization that play out on and off the internet. My third and final proposal is to follow not only the money but the mundane practices of valuation preceding it, wherever they may lead.

Similar proposals of course have been made by other researchers who, on the one hand, have suggested to define "media" more generally as "a wide range of historically distinct, but now connected, consumer markets in communication, information, and entertainment" (Lobato and Thomas 2015, 5), and, on the other, as a key site to study value and valuation practices (e.g., Gerlitz 2016). These research strands have never been fully integrated, however: studying media as markets usually means to focus on the "products of media industries," that is, goods disseminated by film, television, music, and other sectors (Havens and Lotz 2012, viii), while studies of value and valuation have been focused on social media platforms. What here appears to be needed is a clearer definition of media and communication, in line with a general turn taken in communication studies over the past decades, away from a transmission model of communication and toward a constitutive model that acknowledges that "elements of communication, rather than being fixed in advance, are reflexively constituted within the act of communication itself" (Craig 2001, 125). If "content" is not a pellet or banana, then marketing and consumption obviously can't be reduced to issues of packaging or price.

In consequence, and for the purpose of this argument, we may define media not so much as the aggregate of economic sectors specializing in the production of cultural texts but as sociotechnical systems that enable and constrain exchange. Given their capacity to transmit, store, and process data, media "produce and enable inscriptions of individual and collective actions," including forms of market exchange (Venturini, Bounegru, and Gray 2018, 4196). Without papyrus, the telegraph, or the computer, today's abstracted notion of the market as a space detached from personal relations would hardly be conceivable. Rather than a pipeline for transmitting messages, the internet provides a material infrastructure for web applications that create countless spaces for market (and of course also nonmarket) exchange, from consumer-facing branded services such as eBay, Spotify, and YouTube, to closed online forums. A key issue here is perhaps not so much if some of these activities are informal in the sense of being unmeasured by a given nation-state's tax bureaucracy, but how normative claims or institutionalized social rules are built into the machines that enable or constrain exchange. This includes rules or affordances that directly affect the relationship between people, particularly the relationship of equal status, as illustrated earlier by Spotify's Terms of Use.

Conclusion

In April 2018, researchers at the Norwegian University of Science and Technology discovered that music streaming service Tidal had manipulated streaming numbers, inflating album streams for Beyoncé's *Lemonade* and Kanye West's *The Life of Pablo* by using more than one million accounts to lift the play counts, in order to increase payouts (Johnsen and Franke 2018). That same year, a Bulgarian playlist maker scammed the Spotify payout system. Using about 1,200 paid-for premium accounts that "listened" to two playlists, the Bulgarian received an estimated $1 million from Spotify's revenue pool (Ingham 2018). Today, hundreds of online shops such as Wendy's Magic Shop offer "more plays, followers and monthly listeners on your Spotify account," and correctly state that "it's easy to do with us" (wendysmagicshop.com). A user buying at Wendy's connects to a song or playlist on Spotify, to PayPal or other epayment providers, and probably first found the shop and service via Google. Wendy's, in turn, connects to a so-called panel, similar to a retailer ordering at a wholesaler, with the panel then linking up to Spotify accounts, involving an avalanche of subsequent logistic service providers that may include services offering IP addresses and proxies, hosting, phone verification, botnets, or authentically "grown" user accounts, as well as software for automation, scripts for setting up panels, and so on. At one major Russian retailer selling Spotify payouts, an investment of $690 will lead to a guaranteed net revenue of $3,680 without risk of legal prosecution.[3]

Given that cultural content needs to be reproduced and reused, or "shared," to count as valuable online, it may not be a surprise that on top of the social web and its markets, a network of meta-markets, or what I call the "engagement industry" (cf. Abidin 2018; Gerlitz and Helmond 2013), has materialized, entirely geared toward creating reputation and status to help push videos, songs, and other content toward users. Not unlike the junk data incident with which this chapter began, the Tidal discovery or "fake listeners" are easily scandalized and then forgotten. An alternative is to explore such "mishaps in valuation" for what they tell us about valuation practices (Helgesson and Woolgar 2018), especially in regard to the disruptive organizing of today's service economies. Instead of invoking the notion of fake or false representation, that is, a critique of capital where some kind of value is real and some other kind is not, we may see such events, actors, and networks not as outside or opposed to distribution, but as part and parcel of distributive practices. This is of course not to say that Spotify and other platforms are involved in systemic fraud. Rather, it means that it is productive (as once noted by Marx and others) to study distribution as part of a larger totality, and also to rethink how we weigh "central" against "marginal" cases in building theories. Long-lasting research fields develop not because we recenter attention from one timely case to another, but because all cases are put in a conversation that allows us to develop an adequate conceptual terminology on top.

This chapter has proposed to complement a horizontal view on distribution in current research with a vertical view on how content relates to material culture and markets. It also suggested to specify how such "content" gains (or loses) its economic properties in a social process that brings together various devices and practices of conducting, representing, and normalizing a specific form of exchange (Kjellberg and Helgesson 2007). While mass media, large technical systems, networks, and the industrial processing of information all have been around for more than a century, current distribution practices call for approaches and concepts that are more adequate than the traditional content supply model. This necessitates not abandoning the model but rather realizing that distribution often has been "studied in the ways that fishermen study fish rather than as marine biologists study them" (Tucker 1974, 30). Instead of constantly catching and unhooking yet another species, research may benefit from taking a joint look at the full biodiversity before its eyes.

NOTES

1 To replace "distribution" with "circulation" seems often more motivated by taste or a political distancing from one's industrial object of study than because of the metaphor's actual theoretical productivity. Sometimes, this may lead to conceptual absurdities (e.g., "linear circulation"; Hesmondhalgh and Lotz 2020, 390), and the term's economic implications, rooting back to the genesis of the very notion of neoliberalism (Stiegler 2019), certainly deserve more than a casual treatment.

2 Hennion (1989), for instance, in a famous article, describes the sociology of intermediation between popular music and its market as a "full production-consumption cycle" that includes how producers at work in the studio constantly translate audience feedback into the emergent form of the song. Examples from film and other industries abound. More recently, Caldwell (2016) has provided an ethnographically rich description of how the conceptualization process in film production has increasingly gained prominence, leading to more anticipatory "spec work" and a distribution-linked opening up of the once more "stable program master."

3 The retailer is a key informant in a current research project, "Shadow Economies of the Internet: An Ethnography of Click Farming" (2018–2020), co-led by Johan Lindquist (Department of Social Anthropology, Stockholm University) and myself. The financial support of the Swedish Research Council/Vetenskapsrådet (D0731050o) is gratefully acknowledged.

BIBLIOGRAPHY

Abidin, Crystal. 2018. *Internet Celebrity: Understanding Fame Online*. Bingley: Emerald.

Araujo, Luis, John Finch, and Hans Kjellberg. 2010. *Reconnecting Marketing to Markets*. Oxford: Oxford University Press.

Aversa, Paolo, Andres Hervas-Drane, and Morgane Evenou. 2019. "Business Model Responses to Digital Piracy." *California Management Review* 61 (2): 30–58.

Beniger, James R. 1986. *The Control Revolution: Technological and Economic Origins of the Information Society*. Cambridge, MA: Harvard University Press.

Braun, Joshua A. 2015. *This Program Is Brought to You By . . . : Distributing Television News Online*. New Haven, CT: Yale University Press.

Brown, Aaron. 2016. "Spotify Could Be Damaging Your Computer Behind Your Back, and This Is Why." *Express*, November 15. www.express.co.uk.

Caldwell, John T. 2016. "Spec World, Craft World, Brand World." In *Precarious Creativity: Global Media, Local Labor*, edited by Michael Curtin and Kevin Sanson, 33–48. Oakland: University of California Press.

Callon, Michel, Cécile Méadel, and Vololona Rabeharisoa. 2011. "The Economy of Qualities." *Economy and Society* 31 (2): 194–217.

Chandler, Alfred D. 1990. *Scale and Scope: The Dynamics of Industrial Capitalism*. Cambridge, MA: Harvard University Press.

Clark, Fred W. 1922. *Principles of Marketing*. New York: Macmillan.

Couldry, Nick. 2014. "Inaugural: A Necessary Disenchantment—Myth, Agency and Injustice in a Digital World." *Sociological Review* 62 (4): 880–97.

Craig, Robert. 2001. "Communication." In *Encyclopedia of Rhetoric*, edited by Thomas O. Sloane, 125–37. Oxford: Oxford University Press.

Cunningham, Stuart, and David Craig. 2019. *Social Media Entertainment: The New Intersection of Hollywood and Silicon Valley*. New York: New York University Press.

Datainspektionen. 2019. Letter to Spotify, June 11.

Eriksson, Maria, Rasmus Fleischer, Anna Johansson, Pelle Snickars, and Patrick Vonderau. 2019. *Spotify Teardown: Inside the Black Box of Streaming Music*. Cambridge, MA: MIT Press.

Fine, Ben. 2002. *The World of Consumption: The Material and Cultural Revisited*. London: Routledge.

Garnham, Nicholas. 1990. *Capitalism and Communication: Global Culture and the Economics of Information*. London: Sage.

Gerlitz, Carolin. 2016. "What Counts? Reflections on the Multivalence of Social Media Data." *Digital Culture & Society* 2 (2): 19–38.

Gerlitz, Carolin, and Anne Helmond. 2013. "The Like Economy—Social Buttons and the Data Intensive Web." *New Media & Society* 15 (8): 1348–65.

Goodin, Dan. 2016. "Spotify Is Writing Massive Amounts of Junk Data to Storage Drives." *Ars Technica*, November 10. https://arstechnica.com.

Hampton, Chris. 2016. "Spotify Is Killing Your Computer's Storage with Junk Data." *Chart Attack*, November 17. www.chartattack.com.

Havens, Timothy, and Amanda D. Lotz. 2012. *Understanding the Media Industries*. New York: Oxford University Press.

Helgesson, Claes F., and Steve Woolgar. 2018. "Research Note: Valuation Mishaps and the Choreography of Repair." *Valuation Studies* 5 (2): 154–62.

Hennion, Antoine. 1989. "An Intermediary between Production and Consumption: The Producer of Popular Music." *Science, Technology & Human Values* 14 (4): 400–424.

Herbert, Daniel, and Derek Johnson. 2020. "Introduction: Media Studies in the Retail Apocalypse." In *Point of Sale: Analyzing Media Retail*, edited by Daniel Herbert and Derek Johnson, 2–20. New Brunswick, NJ: Rutgers University Press.

Herbert, Daniel, Lee Marshall, and Amanda D. Lotz. 2019. "Approaching Media Industries Comparatively: A Case Study of Streaming." *International Journal of Cultural Studies* 22 (3): 349–66.

Hesmondhalgh, David. 2019. *The Cultural Industries*. 4th ed. London: Sage.

Hesmondhalgh, David, and Amanda D. Lotz. 2020. "Video Screen Interfaces as New Sites of Media Circulation Power." *International Journal of Communication* 14:386–409.

Hughes, Thomas P. 1983. *Networks of Power: Electrification in Western Society, 1880–1930*. Baltimore: Johns Hopkins University Press.

Ingham, Tim. 2018. "The Great Big Spotify Scam: Did a Bulgarian Playlister Swindle Their Way to a Fortune on Streaming Service?" *Music Business Worldwide*, February 20. www.musicbusinessworldwide.com.

Innis, Harold. 1950. *Empire and Communications*. Oxford: Clarendon.

Johansson, Daniel. 2013. "From Products to Consumption: Changes on the Swedish Music Market as a Result of Streaming Technologies." Working paper, Linnaeus University. http://docplayer.net.

Johnsen, Jan William, and Katrin Franke. 2018. *Digital Forensics Report*. Trondheim: Norwegian University of Science and Technology.

Kjellberg, Hans, and Claes-Fredrik Helgesson. 2007. "On the Nature of Markets and Their Practices." *Marketing Theory* 7 (2): 137–62.

Latour, Bruno, and Vincent Lépinay. 2008. *L'Économie science des intérêts passionnés*. Paris: La Découverte.

Lobato, Ramon. 2019. *Netflix Nations: The Geography of Digital Distribution*. New York: New York University Press.

Lobato, Ramon, and Julian Thomas. 2015. *The Informal Media Economy*. Cambridge: Polity.

Lotz, Amanda D. 2017. *Portals: A Treatise on Internet-Distributed Television*. Ann Arbor, MI: Maize Books.

Marx, Karl. 1973. *Grundrisse: Foundations of the Critique of Political Economy*. New York: Penguin.

McLuhan, Marshall. 1960. *Report on Project in Understanding New Media*. Washington, DC: National Association of Educational Broadcasters.

Miller, Toby, Nitin Govil, John McMurria, Richard Maxwell, and Ting Wang. 2005. *Global Hollywood 2*. London: British Film Institute.

Nieborg, David, and Thomas Poell. 2018. "The Platformization of Cultural Production: Theorizing the Contingent Cultural Commodity." *New Media & Society* 20 (11): 4275–92.

Noam, Eli M. 2018. *Media and Digital Management*. New York: Palgrave.

Pokorny, Michael, and John Sedgwick. 2004. *An Economic History of Film*. London: Routledge.

Potts, Jason, Stuart Cunningham, John Hartley, and Paul Ormerod. 2008. "Social Network Markets: A New Definition of the Creative Industries." *Journal of Cultural Economics* 32 (3): 167–85.

Reinecke, Juliane. 2015. "The Politics of Values." In *Making Things Valuable*, edited by Martin Kornberger, Lise Justesen, Anders Koed Madsen, and Jan Mouritsen, 209–31. Oxford: Oxford University Press.

Ross, David Fredrick. 2015. *Distribution Planning and Control*. 3rd ed. New York: Springer.

Slater, Don. 2011. "Marketing as a Monstrosity: The Impossible Place between Culture and Economy." In *Inside Marketing: Practices, Ideologies, Devices*, edited by Detlev Zwick and Julien Cayla, 23–41. Oxford: Oxford University Press.

Spilker, Hendrik. 2018. *Digital Music Distribution: The Sociology of Online Music Streams*. New York: Routledge.

Spotify USA. 2019. "Spotify Terms and Conditions of Use." www.spotify.com.

Stiegler, Barbara. 2019. *"Il faut s'adapter": Sur un nouvel impératif politique*. Paris: Gallimard.

Tarde, Gabriel. 1902. *Psychologie économique*. Paris: F. Alcan.

———. 2007. "Economic Psychology. Translation by Alberto Toscana." *Economy and Society* 36 (4): 614–43.

Thomas, Julian, and Ramon Lobato. 2015. *The Informal Media Economy*. Cambridge: Polity Press.

Towse, Ruth. 2017. "Economics of Music Publishing: Copyright and the Market." *Journal of Cultural Economics* 41 (4): 403–20.

Tucker, Fred W. 1974. "Future Directions in Marketing Theory: A Provocative Look at Conflicting Pressures on Marketing Theory and Suggestions for Its Future Orientation." *Journal of Marketing Theory* 38 (2): 30–35.

Venturini, Tommaso, Liliana Bounegru, and Jonathan Gray. 2018. "A Reality Check(List) for Digital Methods." *New Media & Society* 20 (11): 4195–217.

Vonderau, Patrick. 2014. "The Politics of Content Aggregation." *Television & New Media* 16 (8): 717–33.

———. 2017. "The Spotify Effect: Digital Distribution and Financial Growth." *Television & New Media* 20 (1): 3–19.

Wikström, Patrik, and Robert DeFillipi. 2016. *Business Innovation and Disruption in the Music Industry*. Cheltenham: Elgar.

Distribution Ecosystems and Cultures

7

"Tech-Tonic" Shifts

The U.S. and China Models of Online Screen Distribution

STUART CUNNINGHAM AND DAVID CRAIG

The battle over online distribution of entertainment intellectual property (IP) is multilateral and multiplying. For the past decade, commentary has focused on the impact of new tech platforms and global streaming services (most notably Amazon, Hulu, and Netflix) dubbed "King Kongs" by Cunningham and Silver (2013, 4): "If content is *king*, then distribution is *King Kong*. The power and profitability in screen industries have always resided in distribution." In 2019, these firms are facing increasing competition from all corners. The launch of Apple TV+ signals that company's move from hardware, and content services and platforms, to its first pure-media play for online distribution. The Hollywood majors are poised to return serve against the tech rebels, infused with capital from acquisition by telecoms and through mergers. Disney, WarnerMedia, and Comcast have announced the launch of their own subscription platforms, heralded as walled gardens designed to extract full vertically integrated value from their studio-owned IP. Disney+ will provide long tail exploitation of their evergreen library that includes the expensive acquisitions of Pixar, Lucas, and Marvel. Subscription video-on-demand (SVOD) platforms are proliferating globally, like India's Hotstar, supported by local telecoms. Even Africa has joined the fray, launching a suite of "homegrown Netflixes" (DTVE Reporter 2016; see Miller, this volume). As noted by a Hollywood executive, "the Great Streaming War is upon us" (de Moraes 2019).

Yet the rise of online video distribution is not new, dating as it does to the early years of the internet. As Cunningham and Silver's (2013) history shows, the first of three waves of attempts to develop online video distribution started in the mid-1990s. These waves saw undercapitalized firms like Atom Films met by a raft of experimental joint ventures by studios like Movielink, before Netflix, Amazon, and Hulu emerged as market leaders.

In addition, social media platforms like Google/YouTube and Facebook/Instagram have failed to compete with their tech competitors (as our profiles of YouTube Premium, Facebook Watch, and IGTV will show). What these platforms have accomplished, however, is to have facilitated "social media entertainment" (SME) (Cunningham and Craig 2019). We argue that SME is an emerging, distinct industry based on previously amateur creators professionalizing and monetizing their content across multiple social media platforms to build global fan communities and incubate their own media brands. SME comprises an industry ecology of platforms, creators, intermediary firms, and fan communities operating interdependently, and disruptively, alongside legacy media industries as well as VOD portals, down the middle of Madison Avenue (the advertising industry), and across global media cultures.

These platforms include first-generation platforms like YouTube, Twitter, and Facebook competing against—sometimes acquiring—later-generation platforms like Twitch, Instagram, and TikTok. SME creators range from the more prominent—game players like Ninja, Markiplier, and PewDiePie; lifestyle and beauty vloggers like Huda Beauty and Michelle Phan; personality vloggers Jake and Logan Paul and the Vlogbrothers; unboxers EvanTube and Ryan ToysReview—to midlevel creators and early career aspirationals. SME intermediaries, or, as YouTube refers to them, "creative services" firms, include acquired divisions of media corporations (Disney's Maker Studios, RTL's Yohobo and Stylehaul), multichannel networks (BroadbandTV, Brave Bison), influencer advertising and talent management agencies (ViralNation, Fullscreen), and data providers (Tubefilter, SocialBlade).

But our study of how user-generated content (UGC) became SME also revealed the degree to which platforms such as YouTube have attempted to attract professionally generated content (PGC) producers and distributors from Hollywood as well as convert their native UGC creators into Hollywood-like talent. Both strategies have been largely unsuccessful.

This U.S.-originated model of separate streaming video and social media platforms has advanced globally, with one notable exception.

Facilitated by state-based protection and intervention, China has fostered a model of online screen distribution that integrates UGC and PGC and aligns the interests of competing screen industries more effectively. While a few first-generation Chinese platforms predate their Western counterparts, most were launched subsequently to emulate them. But Chinese platforms have advanced to eclipse the Western innovations of both streaming video and social media platforms. The Chinese SME industry has emerged across hundreds of more diverse platforms, including over one hundred livestreaming platforms. Unlike their Western counterparts, these platforms also host PGC, at the same time integrating e-commerce and online payment systems. In other words, China's platform ecology has overcome the Western PGC-SME divide (exemplified in the radically different content that typifies Netflix on the one hand, and YouTube on the other), while integrating Amazon's ecommerce, PayPal's online payment, and Twitch's livestreaming features.

What caused the delay in the rise of SVOD competitors? Why have social media platforms struggled to compete? And how has China outpaced the West in online video distribution, converging SME alongside traditional entertainment IP? This chapter maps the evolution of online media distribution, which has been marked by a series of "tech-tonic" shifts between Western portals and platforms as well as Chinese platform innovation, informed by their distinctive sociocultural and political-economic conditions (Cunningham, Craig, and Lv 2019). These shifts have evolved rapidly from twentieth-century methods of media distribution (theatrical, broadcast, satellite, and cable) toward video streaming and social media platform ecologies. In SME (seen on YouTube, Instagram, Twitch, Facebook) and PGC streaming services (for example, Netflix, Amazon Prime Video, Hulu), the Western system has produced two quite separate online screen distribution industries, while China's distinctive platform ecology comprised twinned cultural industries designed to advance their digital economy, furthering the rise of the "Chinese Internet" (Yang 2014). While challenging recent claims around U.S.-originated platform imperialism (Jin 2013), these competing Western and Chinese media platform ecologies presage new complexities and contests over cultural and economic influence.

Platformization and Portalization

These developments are framed conceptually by the distinctions between platforms and portals and, in turn, the processes of platformization and portalization. The definition of platforms has evolved from any kind of physical structure to, more precisely, online content hosting services. Beyond computational services, platforms provide an array of intermediary services that facilitate the means for communication and media, engagement and economic activity. As Gillespie notes, "'Platforms' are 'platforms' not necessarily because they allow code to be written or run, but because they afford an opportunity to communicate, interact, or sell" (2010, 351). Platforms provide for media to be circulated, communities to socialize, and users to generate various forms of value.

In time, platforms have come to dominate the internet, which has been explained by the concept of platformization (Nieborg and Poell 2018; see also Bucher and Helmond 2018), a process whereby the relatively open online domain has been colonized by proprietary interests. More specifically for our purposes, platformization describes "how the political economy of the cultural industries changes through platformization: the penetration of economic and infrastructural extensions of online platforms into the web, affecting the production, distribution, and circulation of cultural content" (Nieborg and Poell 2018, 4275).

Platforms are not all equal, especially regarding the distinction between PGC and UGC. Lotz has established the critical distinction between platforms and "portals" (2017; see also 2018). Major "internet-distributed television" (IDTV) portals such as Hulu, Netflix, Amazon Prime Video, and Apple's iTunes should be differentiated from platforms (Google/YouTube, Facebook), she argues, stressing the continuity of portals' content with television and PGC as traditionally understood. Portals are those sites that feature internet-based protocols "to distinguish the crucial intermediary services that collect, curate, and distribute television programming by Internet distribution" (2017, 8). Portals typically operate as subscription video-on-demand (SVOD) distribution services (e.g., Netflix, Amazon Prime Video), but can also use transactional video-on-demand (TVOD) (e.g., iTunes), while SME typically operates in an advertising video-on-demand (AVOD) environment (e.g., YouTube).

Like platformization, the process that can readily be dubbed "portal-ization" describes the migration of professionalized entertainment IP to online portals. The process of portalization may have reached a significant moment in its disruption of the structure and organization of traditional screen distribution. The shift to over-the-top television portals may spell acceleration in the decline of the cable industry, much as it already has ended the home video industry.

Lotz further distinguishes portals from social media platforms that provide a distribution medium for amateur content or UGC, which she describes as an "emerging Internet-distributed television industry that utilizes the dynamics of social media and is based on personalities that cultivate a community of followers . . . but distinct enough to require its own focus" (2017, 10). In drawing these distinction, Lotz anticipates what we call SME—at once platformized communication and social media phenomena as well as a media industry. While coevolving and at times overlapping the industrial logics of legacy media and SVOD platforms, SME is distinguished by the ability of creators to monetize their socialization practices across platforms rather than through either IP exploitation or distribution control.

The rest of the chapter traces the efforts by Western and Chinese social media platforms to overcome the portal-platform divide. The U.S. system has produced two screen distribution industries—SME and IDTV. Despite many efforts to synergize the systems, they work in contrast to and contradistinction from each other. The Chinese system has blurred these distinctions and arguably synergized them.

The Western Portal-Platform Divide

Over more than ten years, Silicon Valley platforms have engaged in strategies that directly compete with established media and telecoms' distribution and content strategies. These strategies signal the complicated, often contradictory, efforts by platforms to expand their commercial ecosystems. These moves may also be attributed to Silicon Valley philosophy, as espoused by Facebook's Mark Zuckerberg, to "move fast and break things" (cf. Taplin 2017). These also affirm the shifting "cultural economic logics" (Lobato 2016) of platforms and the iterative, experimental, "permanent beta"–driven nature of tech and platform management. More often, these strategies have also proved to be expensive failures.

Since the platform was launched, YouTube has aspired to compete against Hollywood control of media distribution and content. The platform has introduced numerous initiatives, features, platforms, and policies designed to integrate PGC entertainment IP alongside UGC generated by their native creators. Examples of YouTube's PGC efforts include the multimillion-dollar original channel initiatives launched in 2010 and 2011, when established media producers and news organizations, along with YouTube creators and intermediaries, were selected to produce professional content. By 2013, the initiative was scrapped and "YouTube removed their affiliation with all those 185 YouTube channels and redirected the original channels initiative to a 404 error page" (Chandra 2017).

A year later, YouTube shifted to a distribution and content strategy with the launch and multiple relaunches of YouTube's subscription platform. In 2014 YouTube announced Music Key, an ad-free site for music streaming and videos. These moves were touted as a "game changer" (Popper 2015), designed to assuage the concerns by musicians and industry professionals about lost revenue and industrial disruption.

One year later, Music Key was relaunched as YouTube Red, a subscription site that allowed access to YouTube video content ad-free. Included was a content play: the launch of YouTube-financed and -produced originals, including scripted web series, films, reality programs, stage shows, animation, game shows, and more (Mitroff and Martin 2017). With the hire of Susanne Daniels, a former MTV and WB programming chief, YouTube appeared to be poised to compete with SVOD platforms. Meanwhile, YouTube simultaneously launched a separate app for streaming music and music videos as direct competition for platforms like Spotify. Combined, these moves signaled YouTube and its parent company Alphabet/Google were implementing a multilateral, multiplatform strategy aimed at responding to threats to their platform primacy.

YouTube Red generated only a few buzzworthy programs, including the *Karate Kid* franchise reboot *Cobra Kai*, along with other genre-driven properties produced by Hollywood and YouTube creators. In early 2018, YouTube announced that it would no longer increase the budgets for original programming (Shaw, Bergen, and Sakoui 2018). By mid-2018, YouTube Red was renamed YouTube Premium and relaunched as a subscription-based video and music streaming platform, while YouTube Music became an ad-driven platform. YouTube also shut down its separate game app, which had been launched as a Twitch competitor in the game space, until Twitch began introducing other non-game verticals of livestreaming content (Peterson 2018a).

By the end of 2018, YouTube had issued a release to the industry trade press—conspicuously not posted on its official blog—announcing further dramatic changes to its original programming strategy. While some scripted programming would continue to be produced, no more scripted content was to be commissioned and all original programming would be available for free on its original ad-driven platform. The announcement was filled with confounding statements, like chief business officer Robert Kyncl's response to concerns that YouTube was abandoning original programming with "it is far too early to tell something that decisive" (Jarvey 2018). Hollywood and tech blogs exploded with commentary, asking whether YouTube Premium is a "flop" (Niu 2018), or blamed the shift in strategy on poor programming choices (Flynn 2018). Others suggested this was YouTube avoiding the "escalating arms race" between Netflix and Amazon (Jarvey 2018), further overshadowed by the impending "streaming wars" with the launch of SVOD platforms from Disney and Warner scheduled for 2019 (Byers 2018).

YouTube is hardly the outlier when it comes to repeated shifts in platform, content, and programming strategies. Facebook has experienced its own fails, most notably Facebook Live, where users witnessed murders, suicides, torture, sex, rape, and other crimes broadcast unfiltered across the platform (Baldas 2018). Desperate to maximize advertising income, for two years Facebook grossly exaggerated its video viewing metrics by as much as 80 percent (Vranica and Marshall 2016). Undeterred, in mid-2017, Facebook Watch, a separate, ad-driven platform to feature licensed and produced video IP, was launched. This IP would be referred to as "Facebook Shows" to offer differentiation from other video content on the platform by Facebook users and creators. With a healthy one-billion-dollar programming budget, the "shows" were to be produced by traditional media production companies, like National Geographic and Refinery 29, offered license fees comparable to Hollywood standards, and featured genre-driven episodic fare comparable to traditional TV (Patel 2017).

Less than a year later, Facebook relaunched the Watch platform, integrated into its Discovery feed on its main platform. The new Watch would include all videos, not just those produced and licensed by Facebook from legacy media producers, but including content generated by Facebook creators now securing partnership agreements similar to YouTube partnerships (Peterson 2018b). Pundits questioned Facebook's intended mark: "It's easy to think of this as Facebook's attempt to 'kill TV.' But while it's tempting to see this as the social network's answer to Netflix or even Disney's as-yet-unnamed streaming service, Watch's prime competitor out there actually seems to be YouTube" (Tsukayama 2017). Coupled with numerous scandals and declines in Facebook's user base and inclines in average age, Facebook Watch has not met expectations. Monthly views pale in comparison to YouTube. Programming executives have fled the company, and Facebook has "pared down the number of shows it's purchasing" (Castillo 2018). Whether or not Facebook Watch survives, the company's efforts may represent just standard tech experimentation: "Facebook's other game plan has been to throw things at the wall to see what sticks. In more flattering Silicon Valley parlance: Fail fast" (Solsman 2018).

Instagram TV (IGTV), which represents the most recent attempt by social media platforms to enter the video streaming game, launched in June 2018 as a long-form video app integrated within Facebook-owned Instagram (Systrom 2018). Unlike either Facebook Watch or YouTube Red, the player didn't cater to the IP models of main media and was not accompanied by programming generated by either Hollywood producers or native Instagram creators. Instagram launched in 2010 as a photo-sharing platform, but shortly after acquisition by Facebook in 2012, the platform introduced short-form video sharing designed to compete with the rapidly scaling Vine short video app. (Vine proved a short-lived experiment, acquired early on by Twitter in 2012, but shuttered less than four years later, in part due to Instagram's aggressive competition [Newton 2016].) In 2016, Instagram also added a recorded and live short form video player called "stories" designed to compete with Snapchat's similar "stories" feature. Whereas these video features were well received, IGTV has failed to appeal, and "executives at the company insist on referring to IGTV as a 'work in progress'" (LaPorte and Ifeanyi 2018).

Over the past decade, Western social media platforms have struggled to effectively compete in the PGC portal wars, despite numerous attempts. Such strategies will get only more difficult, as new entrants into PGC streaming (Apple TV, Disney, WarnerMedia, and Comcast) crowd in. In contrast, China's tech ecosystem features a diverse landscape of integrated online media portal-platforms. These sites have fostered a more viable and accelerated Chinese SME industry while also developing highly competitive, professionally generated, licensed, and originally produced entertainment IP.

China's Policy-Driven Platform Economy

The platformization of online video distribution in China has followed a different course, demanding some "understanding of the historicity of the Chinese Internet, that is, its distinct features in a historical process marked by both constraints and contingency" (Yang 2014, 136). Since the late 1970s, China's economy has evidenced an epochal move up the value chain from low-cost manufacturer to high-value-added tech innovator—from "made in China" to "created in China" (Keane 2007). The economy, while still massively servicing Western markets and brands, has shifted focus to higher domestic market demand, a transition from low-cost manufacturing to a service-based economy, while responding to a rising middle class and growing forms of nationalistic appeal for Chinese-owned and -operated platforms, brands, and services. The rapidity of this shift is due in part to the fact there has been comparatively little path dependency in technology, finance, and retail. "Unlike in the United States, where banks and retailers already have strongholds on customers, China's state-run lenders are inefficient, and retailers never expanded broadly enough to serve a fast-growing middle class" (Mozur 2016).

China's tech sector is a leading contributor, dominated by major conglomerates, Baidu, Alibaba, and Tencent, or BAT, which have launched a huge array of tech platforms, services, and features. The West has AFA (Alphabet, Facebook, Amazon). Each conglomerate owns an array of platforms and services: Alphabet operates search (Google), video streaming (YouTube), mobile payments (Google Pay), and more. Facebook's purchase of Instagram consolidated its primacy in social media; it was one of their many acquisitions that have included messenger apps and 3D firms. Amazon dominates e-commerce (Amazon) and livestreaming (Twitch), while also competing against Netflix with Amazon Prime. Similarly, Alibaba Group Holding contains Alibaba's e-commerce platform (like Amazon) but also their Taobao store (eBay is a pale comparator). Alphabet-owned Google acquired YouTube; Alibaba purchased leading video-streaming platform Youku Tudou. Along with dominating the game publishing industry, Tencent owns Tencent Video, a portal comparable to Netflix, and another dozen social media, messenger, and livestreaming platforms. These livestreaming game play platforms promote Tencent games. Baidu operates a search engine like Google's but also owns iQIYI, which is the closest comparator to Netflix. Other tech firms are operating successfully outside the BAT system, including Bytedance, which owns one of the fastest growing platforms in the world, and Bilibili, Inc. whose online video service is touted as the "largest online entertainment platform for generation Z in China" (Cherney 2018).

The early Chinese platform era in the mid-2000s was roughly concurrent with the launch of their Western counterparts. Video-sharing platform Tudou predates YouTube, although YouTube was not the first platform to offer short video services in the West. Some platforms emulated non-U.S. platforms, like Tencent's QQ messenger service, modeled after Israeli-owned ICQ. But many appeared to emulate, if not directly copy, Western platforms, such as Weibo, a microblogging site modeled on Twitter. This strategy affirmed an intrinsic part of Chinese strategic "soft power" rhetoric, to speak of following and learning from advanced Western tech practice and achievement (Keane 2015).

Over the past decade, however, China's platforms have become central to the nation's digital economy and global competitiveness, progressing "from imitation to innovation" (Larson 2018). Innovations in global online commerce (e.g., QR codes, digital wallets), messaging, and livestreaming have been incubated, popularized, and sometimes originated in China. Over a third of the top platforms in the world have been launched by China (Chen and Djankov 2018) and have traveled well "over the wall." In 2018, Shanghai-based Bytedance became "the world's most valuable startup" (Byford 2018) with the fastest growing app in China (Douyin) and its non-Chinese counterpart, TikTok. According to the Asian Video Industry Association (AVIA) (2018), China's online video sector features over two hundred platforms that have grown by a factor of five ($1.5 to $10 billion) from 2014 to 2017. It should be noted that these industry accounts typically conflate online video portals with social media platforms that may or may not feature video services and/ or PGC or UGC content.

A major reason for the strength of China's tech sector is that it is strongly aligned with state political and economic strategy. As Wang and Lobato (2019) argue, in contrast to the "essentially liberal values" of free speech and free markets, which are the constitutive conditions underlying much of Silicon Valley business practice, scholars of the Chinese internet do not see communication technologies as being *outside* the state's political domain; instead, media and communication technologies have always been conceptualized as part of the state's political apparatus. China's platform evolution reflects this, requiring as it does constant realignment in the wake of ongoing policy shifts. For example, these developments have exposed ongoing policy tensions between protection of China's traditional media industries and the pressure to keep their platform economy growing at rapid pace. Depending on how smart TV apps and service providers are defined, these tech firms are prohibited from eroding the broadcasting base by policy decree. An outstanding feature of the Chinese online video market "concerns the partnerships between video streaming services' smart TV apps and broadcast television networks. Since 2010, China's content regulations have stated that all Internet TV (*wangluo dianshi*) service providers must collaborate with one of the seven Internet TV license holders, all of which are state-owned. . . . The major effect of the licensing rule is that each video platform must be structurally linked to a state controlled television network that provides much of its content" (Wang and Lobato 2019, 363).

China's Portal-Platform Ecosystem

Chinese platformization strategies are bringing IP-based media industries in closer alignment with community-based SME, popularly referred to as the wanghong industry. "Wanghong" translates literally as "red internet," figuratively as "internet famous" as well as "online celebrity." But the term has also come to describe the emerging industry itself—China's version of SME.

Like their Western counterparts, China's wanghong platforms incorporate diverse features and modalities, including microblogging (Weibo), video (Youku), images (Little Red Box), game play livestreaming (Bilibili, Douyu), messaging (WeChat), e-commerce livestreaming (Taobao), and short form video (Kuaishuo, Douyin aka TikTok, Vigo). Operating across these platforms, wanghong creators appeal to the interests of fan communities across verticals such as comedy (Papi Jiang is a leading exponent), game play, and lifestyle. At the top tier, beauty vloggers like Zhang Dayi, likened to Kylie Jenner, secured over $46 million in 2015, earning twice as much as China's leading movie star (Tsoi 2016). Livestreaming game players competing as part of China's rapidly expanding game and e-sports industry can earn RMB1 million ($141,000) on a single stream in one sitting (Shea 2019).

The industry has adopted the Western term MCN (multichannel networks) to describe thousands of firms providing a suite of services as intermediaries between creators, brands, and platforms. For example, Xinpianchang manages the channels and provides branded content deals for wanghong, hosts an online network for creative talent, and runs a production studio for web series. As new platforms emerge and policy changes, the more successful MCNs have managed rapid change. Star Station TV, a Beijing-based MCN, pivoted from producing PGC-like recorded video content on their own channels to a "traffic company" providing a diverse suite of services to platforms, creators, and brands across the liveliest emerging short-form/livestreaming platforms (Heng 2019).

China's online video platforms offer SVOD, AVOD, and TVOD options while integrating on-demand and livestreaming video players. Chinese media platforms feature licensed and original professional content (PGC) alongside user-generated (UGC) fare, including channels and content generated by their Chinese creators (Cunningham, Craig, and Lv 2019). Whereas Netflix, Hulu, YouTube Premium, and Facebook Watch demand ownership or licensing of all content on their platform, platforms like iQIYI and Bilibili offer closed and open access, original and licensed PGC fare, and wanghong content like vlogs and game play.

In addition to a mix of UGC and PGC content, some of these platforms afford more dynamic synchronous forms of social media interactivity such as liking, sharing, and commenting, which have placed these platform "at the center of China's social video boom" (Magpie Kingdom 2018). Netflix, Hulu, and Amazon lack these features. For example, Bilibili's bullet messaging allows viewers to post on-screen comments on recorded as well as livestreaming video, a feature borrowed from Japan's Niconico platform. In comparison, Western platforms have avoided this feature. Chinese media platforms offer better integration between content distribution and user interactivity with multiple, or rather "stacked," services, like e-commerce stores (Taobao and Tmall) and online payment services (WeChat Pay and Alipay). As Wang and Lobato (2019, 356–60) note,

> Chinese video streaming services do not fit neatly into the categories of platform and portal as they have been established in the screen studies literature. For example, iQiyi is both *portal-like* (because it foregrounds professional content and established celebrities, offering a strongly curated and programmed TV-like experience) and *platform-like* (because it provides interactive functions such as online shopping, online payment, e-wallet, e-lending, and upload/sharing of user-generated video). Consequently, it is difficult to map the Chinese services onto a Silicon Valley taxonomy of video services. Additionally, it is not easy to connect these services to the same critical debates that characterize the literature on US-based platforms.

These significant differences from the Western models have not lessened the degree to which they engaged in intense and ongoing competition. China's "platform wars" around online video emerged relatively early with competition between iQIYI, Youku, and Tencent Video. Youku, launched in 2006 shortly after YouTube, has often been described as a YouTube wannabe with open access featuring UGC fare that would eventually "reward content creators with revenue" (Coonan 2013). However, in the wake of repeated policy shifts around infringing private platforms, piracy concerns, and IP licensing, Youku merged with Tudou, a portal-like enterprise that featured acquired domestic and international content (Zhao 2016). Crudely put, China's YouTube merged with its Netflix.

Comparable to Silicon Valley's agglomerative practices of both platforms and capital, Youku Tudou was acquired by Alibaba. This acquisition may resemble Google's acquisition of YouTube, but more readily compares with Amazon's purchase of Twitch, a "stacked" platform company integrating e-commerce and video services. A more significant comparison is that Alibaba took Youku private, allowing the platform to engage in even more rapidly beta innovation nurtured by ongoing investment from Alibaba's deep pockets. Like their Silicon Valley counterparts, China's BAT ecosystem stimulates risk taking, even at a massive scale. Emulating Netflix's rapid expansion strategies, Youku has been building its library of acquired and original programming, but unlike the U.S. service, Youku has also acquired expensive live programming, including the World Cup. As of late 2020, none of these platforms has proven profitable yet. For example, iQIYI (Sun 2020) claimed to have lost subscribers due to the competitive platform and portal landscape coupled with the lack of original content due to the COVID-19 crisis. Nonetheless, their deep-pocketed owners can allow these platforms to play the long game to pursue profit and sustainability.

Like Google-owned YouTube, Youku secures subscription and advertising revenue. Unlike YouTube, Alibaba has more successfully integrated its e-commerce platforms along with their online mobile payment system (Alipay) into Youku and other platforms, whether Alibaba-owned like Weibo or not. In turn, commercially empowered wanghong are sending their fan communities to Alibaba's e-commerce Tmall and Taobao platforms, where they can purchase product with nearly one-touch affordance. As Wang (2018) notes, "Chinese e-commerce giant Alibaba has been defying the country's economic slowdown by continuing to deliver strong revenue growth. Its secret? Internet celebrities, known as Wang Hong, who make real cash by turning their social media followers into loyal Alibaba customers."

Google/YouTube have failed to successfully introduce e-commerce features on their platform while struggling to launch their online payments system. They recently relaunched Google Wallet and Android Pay as Google Pay in 2018 (Gartenberg 2018). Amazon is attempting to emulate Alibaba through integration of video players on Amazon channels and e-commerce features on Twitch. Amazon added video reviews aimed "to keep shoppers on its own site, preventing them from migrating to YouTube or social media platforms" (Edwards and Edwards 2017). Twitch streamers were made eligible on an Amazon Associates affiliate program, "providing a seamless way for audiences to buy select products" (Krefetz 2017). Yet while Twitch dominates the Western livestreaming market, pundits predict "Twitch won't become a major growth engine for Amazon alongside its e-commerce and cloud businesses anytime soon" (Sun 2019).

Tencent has differentiated in its platformization strategies compared to its BAT rivals. Whereas Alibaba has focused on e-commerce integration, Tencent initially pursued a multiplatform strategy that serviced their world-leading game publishing business. In addition to their QQ messenger platform, they invested in livestreaming platforms comparable to Twitch, Huya, and Douyu, which are dominated by game players. Tencent Video is an on-demand video streaming service featuring licensed and original content to rival Youku and iQIYI. WeChat, Tencent's messaging service, offers more sophisticated and integrated features than Western comparators Facebook Messenger and WhatsApp. The quality of the service propelled WeChat to over one billion users, within and outside of China (Gray 2018). WeChat not only offers video chat features but also integrates the Tencent Video player that allows users to watch *Game of Thrones*, which Tencent licensed from HBO (Tao, Perez, and Lee 2018). Like Alibaba's Alipay online payments application, Tencent's rival WeChat Pay optimizes transactions across Tencent's multiplatform portfolio of social media, messenger, video, and game platforms.

Like Youku, Tencent's platforms have also embraced wanghong creators. WeChat creators launch public or official accounts, which grew from 1.44 million to 14 million between 2014 and 2018 and attracted millions of wanghong community members who share mutual interests including lifestyle, movies, celebrity gossip, and singing (Tao 2018). Across these channels and platforms, like their Western counterparts, Chinese wanghong engage in a diverse portfolio of revenue-generating strategies including influencer marketing, sponsored content, and e-commerce. In an effort to keep their wanghong in-house, in 2017 Tencent launched a competing e-commerce platform to rival Alibaba's (Chen and Tao 2017).

Baidu's iQIYI platform comes closest to emulating Netflix's PGC model of licensed and original content. This would explain why Netflix has entered into exclusive streaming partnerships with the platform in an attempt to bridge the Western and Chinese SVOD divide (Shen 2018). But, as previously noted, iQIYI also features UGC and platform affordances that fuel the wanghong industry. The next chapter in platform and media distribution strategies, including bridging the legacy and SME industries, is being written in China.

Conclusion

The differences between U.S. platforms and portals and Chinese platform-portals are, at present, stark. As Lobato points out, "Unlike Western portals, Chinese video services are multipurpose platforms that integrate free ad-supported video alongside many other services, including dating, shopping, real estate, and transport" (2019, 132). Behind these extraordinarily complex, "one-stop-shop" platform-portals lies China's world leadership in platform e-commerce integration, which is a classic case of tech "leapfrogging." At the time of writing in 2019, such frictionless ecommerce integrations remain at the planning and trial phases on many Western platforms. Quite apart from Chinese state action, which has bordered on the autarkic in strategy, there is the online and consumer culture fostered by these remarkable Chinese platform-portals, which has led Lobato to surmise, "Netflix's pure-play SVOD model would have been quite unfamiliar to most Chinese (and possibly somewhat boring)" (Lobato 2019, 132).

As Wang and Lobato (2019) argue, it is time to reevaluate the degree to which implicit Western-centrism in media and social media studies theory and frameworks may have inhibited a fuller understanding of Chinese strategy and achievement in the platform-portalization of screen distribution. This is brought more clearly into view when it is considered alongside the separation of platform and portal in Western media systems as well as the largely failed attempts by U.S. platforms to blur the platform-portal divide. The U.S. system has produced two online screen distribution industries that are highly successful and world leading—SME and IDTV. Despite many efforts to synergize the systems, they work in contrast to and contradistinction from each other. But the Chinese system has blurred these distinctions and arguably synergized them. "These parallel lines of development between SVOD, social media and livestreaming may eventually converge, but I suspect they are just as likely to keep diverging—with the effect that the internet video ecology becomes more complex and differentiated as it ages" (Lobato 2019, 187). The future of screen distribution online will of necessity grow out of the interaction between these two models.

BIBLIOGRAPHY

Asia Video Industry Association. 2018. "Online Video Industry China 2018." https://asiavia.org.

Baldas, Tresa. 2018. "Gang Rape. Suicides. Shooting Deaths. The Dark Side of Social Media." *Detroit Free Press*, April 13. https://eu.freep.com.

Bucher, Tania, and Anne Helmond. 2018. "The Affordances of Social Media Platforms." In *The Sage Handbook of Social Media*, edited by Jean Burgess, Alice Marwick, and Thomas Peoll, 233–53. London: Sage.

Byers, Dylan. 2018. "The Streaming Wars: How the New Kingdoms of Hollywood Are Battling It Out for the Future of Entertainment." *NBC News*, November 1. www.nbcnews.com.

Byford, Sam. 2018. "How China's Bytedance Became the World's Most Valuable Startup." *The Verge*, November 30. www.theverge.com.

Castillo, Michelle. 2018. "Facebook's YouTube Competitor Is Pivoting to Older Audiences as Teens Tune Out and Publishers Balk." *CNBC*, November 26. www.cnbc.com.

Chandra, Akshay. 2017. "YouTube Original Channel Initiative Report after 7 Years." *Vidooly*, January 16. https://vidooly.com.

Chen, Celia, and Li Tao. 2017. "Tencent Moves into Alibaba Turf with US$863 Million Retail Investment." *South China Morning Post*, July 20. www.scmp.com.

Chen, Rong, and Simeon Djankov. 2018. "Digital Platforms in China." *Let's Talk Development*, December 6. https://blogs.worldbank.org.

Cherney, Max A. 2018. "This Chinese App Maker Was Just Valued at More Than $3 Billion." *MarketWatch*, March 28. www.marketwatch.com.

Coonan, Clifford. 2013. "China's Internet Video Giant Youku Tudou Rewards Content Creators with Revenue." *Hollywood Reporter*, October 31. www.hollywoodreporter.com.

Cunningham, Stuart, and David Craig. 2019. *Social Media Entertainment*. New York: New York University Press.

Cunningham, Stuart, David Craig, and Junyi Lv. 2019. "China's Livestreaming Industry: Platforms, Politics and Precarity." *International Journal of Cultural Studies* 22 (6): 719–36.

Cunningham, Stuart, and Jon Silver. 2013. *Screen Distribution and the New King Kongs of the Online World*. London: Palgrave Macmillan.

de Moraes, Lisa. 2019. "Curiosity Stream's John Hendricks Predicts Survivors and Victims of SVOD War—TCA." *Deadline Hollywood*, February 9. https://deadline.com.

DTVE Reporter. 2016. "The Rise of SVOD: Africa's Homegrown Netflixes." *Digital TV Europe*, December 4. www.digitaltveurope.com.

Edwards, Helen, and Dave Edwards. 2017. "Amazon May Have Patented the Next Big Thing in Online Shopping." *Quartz*, December 1. https://qz.com.

Flynn, Kerry. 2018. "Why YouTube Premium Will Move Its Original TV Shows in Front of the Paywall." *Digiday UK*, December 24. https://digiday.com.

Gartenberg, Chaim. 2018. "Google Begins Replacing Android Pay and Google Wallet with New App." *The Verge*, February 20. www.theverge.com.

Gillespie, Tarleton. 2010. "The Politics of 'Platforms.'" *New Media & Society* 12 (3): 347–64.

Gray, Alex. 2018. "Here's the Secret to How WeChat Attracts 1 Billion Monthly Users." *World Economic Forum*, March 21. www.weforum.org.

Heng, Cai. 2019. CEO StarStation TV. Interview with David Craig, Beijing, May 17.

Jarvey, Natalie. 2018. "YouTube to Pull Back on Scripted in 2020 Amid Ad-Supported Push (Exclusive)." *Hollywood Reporter*, November 27. www.hollywoodreporter.com.

Jin, Dal Yong. 2013. "The Construction of Platform Imperialism in the Globalization Era." *tripleC—Communication, Capitalism & Critique* 11 (1): 145–72.

Keane, Michael. 2007. *Created in China*. London: Routledge.

———. 2015. *The Chinese Television Industry*. London: British Film Institute.

Krefetz, Nadine. 2017. "Twitch Embraces Ecommerce with Amazon Associates." *Streaming Media*, August 31. www.streamingmedia.com.

LaPorte, Nicole, and K. C. Ifeanyi. 2018. "Instagram's IGTV Was Supposed to Be the 'Next Generation's TV-Viewing Experience.' What Happened?" *Fast Company*, December 5. www.fastcompany.com.

Larson, Christina. 2018. "From Imitation to Innovation: How China Became a Tech Superpower." *Wired*, February 13. www.wired.co.uk.

Lobato, Ramon. 2016. "The Cultural Logic of Digital Intermediaries: YouTube Multi-channel Networks." *Convergence* 22 (4): 348–60.

———. 2019. *Netflix Nations: The Geography of Digital Distribution*. New York: New York University Press.

Lotz, Amanda. 2017. *Portals: A Treatise on Internet-Distributed Television*. Ann Arbor, MI: Maize Books.

———. 2018. *We Now Disrupt This Broadcast: How Cable Transformed Television and the Internet Revolutionized It All*. Cambridge MA: MIT Press.

Magpie Kingdom. 2018. "Bilibili Started Out as a Platform for Japanese Anime. It's Now the Center of China's Social Video Boom." *Splice*, January 11. www.splicemedia.com.

Mitroff, Sarah, and Taylor Martin. 2017. "Everything You Need to Know about YouTube Red." *CNet*, October 27. www.cnet.com.

Mozur, Paul. 2016. "China, Not Silicon Valley, Is Cutting Edge in Mobile Tech." *New York Times*, August 2. www.nytimes.com.

Newton, Casey. 2016. "Why Vine Died." *The Verge*, October 28. www.theverge.com.

Nieborg, David, and Thomas Poell. 2018. "The Platformization of Cultural Production: Theorizing the Contingent Cultural Commodity." *New Media & Society* 20 (11): 4275–92.

Niu, Evan. 2018. "Is YouTube Premium a Flop?" *Motley Fool*, November 28. www.fool.com.

Patel, Sahil. 2017. "Facebook Starts Rolling Out Funded Shows for Watch." *Digiday UK*, August 30. https://digiday.com.

Peterson, Tim. 2018a. "YouTube Gaming's Shutdown Could Be an Attempt to One-Up Twitch." *Digiday UK*, September 25. https://digiday.com.

———. 2018b. "'That's YouTube': Facebook Opens Watch to All Videos from Publishers, Creators." *Digiday UK*, June 19. https://digiday.com.

Popper, Ben. 2015. "YouTube Music Is Here, and It's a Game Changer." *The Verge*, November 12. www.theverge.com.

Shaw, Lucas, Mark Bergen, and Anousha Sakoui. 2018. "YouTube Holds Spending for TV, Films while Rivals Bulk Up." *Bloomberg*, February 23. www.bloomberg.com.

Shea, Sharon. 2019. "Douyu vs Huya: The Battle to Lead China's Esports Industry." *Dragon Social*, January 23. www.dragonsocial.net.

Shen, Xinmei. 2018. "What Happens When There's No YouTube? Welcome to China." *Abacus News*, October 17. www.abacusnews.com.

Solsman, Joan E. 2018. "Facebook Watch May Have Been the Best Thing in the Company's Bad Year." *CNet*, December 21. www.cnet.com.

Sun, Leo. 2019. "Amazon's Twitch Is Still Crushing the Competition." *Motley Fool*, June 15. www.fool.com.

———. 2020. "Better Buy: Iqiyi vs Huya." *Motley Fool*, November 20. www.fool.com.

Systrom, Kevin. 2018. "Welcome to IGTV." Instagram, June 20. https://about.instagram.com.

Tao, Li. 2018. "Want Fame and Fortune? China's Internet Celebrity Business Offers Both." *South China Morning Post*, June 9. www.scmp.com.

Tao, Li, Bien Perez, and Amanda Lee. 2018. "Game of Thrones Binge-Watching Helps Tencent Beat Estimates with US$2.7b Third-Quarter Net Profit." *South China Morning Post*, November 16. www.scmp.com.

Taplin, Jonathan. 2017. *Move Fast and Break Things: How Facebook, Google, and Amazon Cornered Culture and Undermined Democracy*. Boston: Little, Brown.

Tsoi, Grace. 2016. "Wanghong: China's Online Stars Making Cash." *BBC News*, August 1. www.bbc.co.uk.

Tsukayama, Hayley. 2017. "How to Make Sense of Facebook's New Video Platform, Watch." *Washington Post*, August 10. www.washingtonpost.com.

Vranica, Suzanne, and Jack Marshall. 2016. "Facebook Overestimated Key Video Metric for Two Years." *Wall Street Journal*, September 22. www.wsj.com.

Wang, Wilfred Yang, and Ramon Lobato. 2019. "Chinese Video Streaming Services in the Context of Global Platform Studies Debates." *Chinese Journal of Communication* 12 (3): 356–71.

Wang, Yue. 2018. "Is Alibaba Losing to Tencent in the China's Trillion-Dollar Payment War." *Forbes*, March 28. www.forbes.com.

Yang, Guobin. 2014. "The Return of Ideology and the Future of Chinese Internet Policy." *Critical Studies in Media Communication* 31 (2): 135–44.

Zhao, Elaine. 2016. "Professionalization of Amateur Production in Online Screen Entertainment in China." *International Journal of Communication* 10:5444–62.

8

Language, Culture, and Streaming Video in India

The Pragmatics and Politics of Media Distribution

ASWIN PUNATHAMBEKAR AND SRIRAM MOHAN

A television advertisement begins with a young woman introducing her mother to her roommate. As the roommate and the mother mouth pleasantries in Tamil (a major south Indian language), the voice track plays out in accented Hindi (the most widely spoken language in north India). The words make sense. But the expressions and the inflections simply do not add up. The video first cuts to a television viewer frustrated by this mismatch and then to an avuncular gentleman, who looks straight into the camera and asks, speaking in Hindi with a strong Tamil accent, "Don't you feel like strangling the guy who translated this ad?"

The advertisement here is a satirical take on lazily dubbed and poorly localized television commercials originally made in Hindi and translated into various south Indian languages. Part of a longer YouTube video made by a Chennai-based advertising agency, Mind Your Language, it tackles the enduring problem of media distribution having to address different cultural and linguistic regions within the Indian subcontinent. Titled "Southify," the video itself is a plea to presumably north Indian brand managers and marketers to take seriously the linguistic diversity and cultural specificities of the south Indian region. The avuncular protagonist, played by actor Delhi Ganesan, who reprises a persona solidified by years of being cast in similar parts in Tamil cinema, pleads with media industry professionals to "southify" and to "trans-create," not just translate. "We should also feel your brand's magic, no?" asks Ganesan before urging advertisers and marketers to work with the Southify division of Mind Your Language, an agency that will "carefully trans-create ads, select authentic south voices, get the dubbing exactly right, and produce original language ads."

The existence of an entrepreneurial class of "culture brokers" who promise access to local particularity (Mazzarella 2003), especially in the advertising and marketing domains, is hardly new. But the fact that this satirical ad was circulated on YouTube is telling. At a broad level, "Southify" speaks to the ferment that digitalization has sparked across the media industries in countries like India. The remarkable transformation in internet infrastructures—especially mobile broadband connectivity—and the emergence of a range of transnational digital media platforms since the late 2000s has transformed the production, circulation, and consumption of media entertainment. Even as powerful digital platforms and portals like YouTube, Netflix, and Amazon Prime have made inroads into a dense and highly competitive media market, media conglomerates with deep roots in the film, television, and music industries in India have launched their own portals and platforms. Hotstar (Star Network), ErosNow (Eros International), Hoichoi (SVF Entertainment), Sun NXT (Sun Network), and others have leveraged extensive media libraries and are producing enough original programming to make their presence felt in the streaming video universe.

Moreover, regardless of their origin story, every online portal and digital platform has had to contend with the sociocultural, political, and economic significance of regional languages in their quest to carve out distribution territories and stake a claim for audience shares. Even a cursory scan of trade/business publications and mainstream news coverage of the digitalization of media entertainment in India reveals the anxieties about regionalization coursing through streaming video companies. As we detail later in this chapter, industry lore about language-based media territories being the key to "scaling up" in the Indian context plays out along multiple vectors. In addition to investments in machine language and artificial intelligence tools for "smart dubbing" and "automated translation," the emphasis on all things regional is also shaping decisions in other closely linked media sectors including advertising, venture capital funding, and digital payments (Ahuja 2018; Goel 2018).

Taking stock of this rapidly evolving digital media terrain, this chapter examines the pragmatics and politics of distribution by focusing on the link between language-based cultural geographies and the making of media regions. In particular, we focus on the fortunes of Put Chutney, a

Tamil-language YouTube channel, to examine the industrial and cultural logics at work in imagining south India as a media region. Drawing on trade press materials and in-depth interviews conducted with executives at Put Chutney, we first map YouTube's trajectory in India and outline how the digital platform came to recognize and value south India's linguistic and cultural diversity as crucial for its national and global expansion. Through close readings of two videos produced by Put Chutney, we then show how distinct and competing conceptions of the south Indian region were mobilized to secure an online audience. As we outline in the next section, these negotiations in the Indian digital sector have broader implications for our understanding of how media regions are produced and reimagined over time.

Digital Media Platforms: Thinking Globally, Nationally, *and* Regionally

With the second largest number of internet users in the world and exponential growth potential, India features prominently in the ongoing transformation of online entertainment cultures. Indeed, the meteoric growth of local-language internet users from 42 million in 2011 to 234 million by 2016 also signals the emergence of vernacular practices that challenge our Anglo-centric understandings of digital cultures (KPMG 2017). Steinberg and Li's (2017, 173) argument, that "digital platforms have given rise to a sense of media regionalism and a renewed regional media geography through both transnational and transmedial processes," is an important reminder to not reestablish the Anglophone North Atlantic region as the basis for universal claims about emergent screen cultures. After all, media globalization is by no means solely a "Western" phenomenon. Beginning in the 1980s, the media landscape across Asia, Africa, Latin America, and the Middle East was altered dramatically as transnational and regional television networks displaced and, in some cases, reinvigorated centralized, public, and often state-regulated media systems. This process has only intensified in recent years as digital distribution and streaming video networks (both legal and extralegal) have expanded their footprints, creating new circuits for the flow of media content that crisscross national, linguistic, and other political and cultural borders.

Furthermore, since the early 1990s, a number of cities and regional hubs across the non-Western world—Hong Kong, Shenzhen, Mumbai, Bangalore, Accra, Lagos, Bogota, and so on—have emerged as important nodes in a transnational network of media and information and communication technology design, production, and circulation. In rich accounts of media industries (Curtin 2003; Govil 2015) and digital cultures (Chan 2013), scholars have shown how media and tech capitals emerge through a complex interaction of local, regional, global, as well as national forces and factors including state policy, technological advances, the built environment, talent migration, and the desires and ambitions of media moguls and venture capitalists. Far from leading to a homogenized world system in which Anglo-American media, culture, and values overwhelm local cultures everywhere, the globalization of media has given rise to new and highly hybrid scales and forms of cultural production.

The technological, institutional, and cultural changes that marked two decades of media globalization across Asia form the backdrop against which we need to examine the growing influence of digital media platforms and what Cunningham and Craig have termed "social media entertainment" (2019). Further, while scholarly attempts to outline the role of digital platforms as global economic actors in capitalist modes of production are valuable, notions of "platform imperialism" (Jin 2013) seldom allow for granular, experiential engagement with industry and user practices coalescing on these platforms. To be sure, the thoroughgoing "datafication" and "commodification" of every social interaction we have online are undoubtedly concerns that scholars and activists worldwide are grappling with. But we show that the "coded structures" (van Dijck 2013) that undergird digital platforms are indelibly cultural and not just technical and commercial ones. In particular, we focus on how enduring issues of cultural difference, as they play out in relation to linguistic and cultural regions, are worked out by streaming video platforms.

In doing so, we propose a broader analytical shift in relation to the problem of media distribution in an era of accelerated globalization and digitalization (Curtin, Holt, and Sanson 2014; Lobato 2019; Lotz 2017; Athique, Parthasarathi, and Srinivas 2017). We argue that media distribution should be understood as a scalar enterprise, one that involves a set of practices that continually imagine and produce the very scales—

local, urban, regional, national, global, and planetary—at which media circulate. We share anthropologist Anna Tsing's concern that "*scale* has become a verb that requires precision; to scale well is to develop the quality called *scalability*, that is, the ability to expand—and expand, and expand" (2012, 505). Indeed, even a couple of hours spent scanning business news is enough to see how much *scalability*—across a region, or nation, or even the entire planet—haunts executives in digital media companies. Building on a rich strand of scholarship in cultural geography and anthropology that approaches claims about scales in a reflexive fashion allows us to ask exactly how a particular media region is imagined, produced, maintained, and contested over a period of time (Marston 2000; Massey 1994; Moore 2008; Carr and Lempert 2016; Tsing 2000, 2005, 2012). As Carr and Lempert put it quite simply, "Scale is process before it is product" (2016, 4).

Taking a process-oriented approach entails setting aside well-worn antinomies of global/local and national/regional that have for far too long shaped our understanding of the transnational dimensions of media production, distribution, and consumption. And when it comes to the media industries, this also involves paying closer attention to the discursive dimensions of scale-making projects. For what Put Chutney's videos reveal is the gradual scaling "down" from a capacious peninsular imaginary to a more culturally and politically specific imagination of a linguistic region (in this case, the Tamil region) that also makes financial sense from the perspective of legible branding. Storytelling practices thus serve as fertile ground for us to understand how affective attachments to cultural spaces are organized over time into intelligible territories for media distribution.

Streaming Video and Localization: YouTube in India

As we contend with platforms moving from one cultural and industrial context to another, our understanding of localization and hybridity in relation to film and television proves particularly helpful (Kraidy 2005). Scholarship on MTV's national and regional avatars across the world has shown that localization is a complex process involving cultural translations and exchanges that can at times be politically fraught (Fung 2006; Cullity 2002). These accounts also foreground how localization is a multiscalar process whereby shifts in industrial and managerial logics (for instance, producing content locally) go hand in hand with highly charged representational moves that build on and often challenge dominant norms, values, and aspirations in relation to class, caste, gender, and sexuality (Kumar and Curtin 2002; Mankekar 2004). When assessed in relation to this longer media and cultural history, it is evident that localization in the era of streaming video cannot be merely about local language implementation, subtitling, and technological tweaks that respond to concerns like data speeds and cost.

To be sure, these are all crucial factors, and we do see platforms including Facebook, YouTube, and Twitter make precisely these moves as they get woven into the rhythms of users' daily lives in countries across the world. The YouTube Go project is a telling example of the localization that digital companies have engaged in as nation-states and telecom companies have invested in high-speed network infrastructures and ensured phenomenal growth in the number of users with smartphones and data connections. Framed as "lessons for building international products," a report from Google's Design team recounts how their YouTube Research team helped the company to "reimagine the app's experience" for users in India, Nigeria, Brazil, and other "emerging markets" (Next Billion Users 2018). With the understanding that "retrofitting would not work," the design team recommended a series of tweaks—video previewing, offline viewing, and proximate sharing—that addressed users' frustrations. The research team also recognized the importance of featuring "locally relevant content" and local language support but did not address the crucial question of what exactly locally relevant content meant (besides the metric of which videos were popular in a given region).

In other words, platforms like YouTube are able to address the concern about local relevance at an infrastructural level through moves such as offline availability of videos, sharing videos through mobile internet hotspots, and so on. Even language, the immanent domain of the cultural and the political, turns into an infrastructural concern that ought to be managed, not negotiated. The question of local languages has become fundamental to the future of the digital media industries in countries like India, given the meteoric growth of Indian-language internet users. The impact of the emergence of local language users as a powerful bloc is felt well beyond a platform's software and design domains to include the wider media ecosystem including the development of digital advertisements in local languages, digital payment interfaces, and, crucially, multilanguage data analytics (KPMG 2017). These industry-wide changes notwithstanding, the issue of developing and offering locally relevant content has been far more complex for platforms like YouTube.

For social networking platforms like Facebook or Twitter, locally relevant content is generated almost entirely by users, and the platform's primary function becomes one of enabling discovery and algorithmically prioritizing hashtags and user feeds (Marwick and boyd 2011). But for an online video platform like YouTube, localization has meant bridging the gulf between user-generated content and material sourced from established screen industries. As Cunningham and Craig (2019) show in their global mapping of "social media entertainment," it is with the emergence of a distinct "creator culture" centered on comedy, food, beauty, technology, children's culture, and web series that YouTube could claim a measure of success in producing content that resonates with users rooted in language-based cultural regions. It has become clear that streaming video platforms and portals (Lotz 2017) including Netflix, Amazon Prime, and YouTube are forging links with established film and television companies. Consider, if only briefly, YouTube's trajectory in the Indian mediascape. When YouTube India, the twentieth country-localized version of the online video platform, was launched in May 2008, press coverage of the announcement focused on institutional partnerships with top Bollywood content providers (Indiatimes News Network 2008). Google-owned YouTube also ensured that it lined up a series of partnerships with television news channels like NDTV, state institutions like the Ministry of Tourism and the Indian Institute of Technology, and sports content providers like KrishCricket.

In bringing together a range of partners to provide content across specific genres, YouTube was once again mobilizing industry lore about Indian audiences' proclivities, that is, their preference for cricket and Bollywood, and their investment in news and education. Sangeet Kumar is right to argue that the emergent scene of online video production in India has a "codependent relationship with hegemonic cultural institutions by being both in competition with it but also gaining from the technical, cultural labor, as well its archive of readily available content to be used and reused" (2016, 5609). At the same time, even a cursory examination of archived copies of the YouTube India site a month after its launch reveals that there were efforts undertaken to surface content created by individuals (in the "Featured Videos" tab on the home page, for instance). The online video platform also built on the momentum around comedy, curating content from collectives like All India Bakchod and the Viral Fever alongside clips from films in various regional languages (Pahwa 2012). If partnerships with the Indian Premier League to livestream cricket matches was one plank on which the platform sought to build its user base in the region and attract advertisers, satire, parody, and original comedy content represented another plank in the boardwalk of localization efforts. By the time the national general election results were livestreamed on YouTube in May 2014 (yet another marker of its growing importance as a site for political speech and resistance), the platform could boast of significant depth in terms of content availability in genres ranging from cooking and makeup tutorials to gadget reviews and devotional music.

This was rendered possible by the broader move toward "platformization" (Plantin et al. 2018) of splintered infrastructures (of language, network connectivity, etc.) that YouTube exemplifies. While YouTube India introduced a Hindi interface about a year after its launch (Preethi 2009), it took a few more years to broaden support for various Indic languages and expand the catalogue of content in regional languages apart from Hindi (Saxena 2012). But the biggest shift arguably was the introduction of the option to download videos for offline playback on Android phones in 2014, a feature that was initially introduced in only three markets (India, Indonesia, and Philippines) known for their mobile-phone-centric user base and expensive high-quality data plans. These were also three nations with the slowest average internet connection speed in the Asia-Pacific region (Bellman 2014).

While scholars like Larkin (2008) point to how media infrastructures and networks of circulation in precisely these kinds of places can connect people into collectivities, YouTube's infrastructuring impulse appears to be driven by the need to recast people as users. This is evident in proclamations by senior YouTube employees that the "next billion users . . . are going to come from a market like India" (indiantelevision.com Team 2015). This industry discourse about emerging markets is not off the mark given that India is one of the biggest online video markets in the world, with YouTube viewership on mobile phones alone hitting 180 million in early 2017 (Menon 2017). When we contend with streaming video platforms moving from one cultural and industrial context to another, we thus see how multiple layers and dimensions of existing infrastructures play a key role. As the work of infrastructure studies scholars has shown (Larkin 2008; Parks and Starosielski 2015), infrastructures are composed of both technical, material things (mobile phones, SD cards, set-top boxes, satellites, etc.) and the "soft" cultural practices that shape the formation of social collectivities and the circulation of media objects, ideas, and so on. Where a platform like YouTube is concerned, the importance of tracing telecommunication industry practices becomes as crucial as tracking content licensing and coproduction arrangements with established media industries including film, television, and music. But localization also rests on an elusive notion of "cultural fit," and the history of global media is littered with efforts by media companies to produce content that resonates with audiences rooted in particular social and cultural milieus.

Regions in Global Media History

From the perspective of the media industries, regions are at times regarded as sites of cultural and political coherence but at other times as spaces that have to be actively policed to ensure that audiences/users do not access content through various informal distribution circuits. Studies of global media industries make it clear that any straightforward mapping of geographic territories onto media regions is a fraught endeavor (Lobato and Meese 2016; Elkins 2016). However, in the Indian context, the region–language link does emerge as a powerful organizing principle given that the purportedly "national" Hindi-English language content producers have explicitly categorized the "south" of India not just as a market but as a distinctive cultural and political territory. This is not a new categorization; it has been held in place by film and television distribution practice for well over five decades.

The reorganization of independent India's states and territories along linguistic lines in 1956 helped to produce within the country a set of "regions," which continue to guide media production and distribution practices to this day. Specifically, the troubled imagination of Hindi as the *national* language and Hindi-language cinema as the *national* cinema has meant that other language-based cultural productions have historically been marginalized under the umbrella of the *regional*. This territorial imagination has been contested by intellectuals and activists from various sites for well over a century now, with the Indian diaspora's spread and influence also contributing to its instability. Moreover, forces of economic globalization and cultural globalization that led to the emergence of numerous translocal television networks like Sun TV or the development of new and diffuse regional formations around Bhojpuri-language cinema have also challenged this narrow mapping of region onto language (A. Kumar 2013).

Scholars have also pointed out that media and cultural regions, far from being fixed and pregiven, have to be continually produced and performed. It is not possible in the space of this chapter to detail the many inter- and intraregional struggles that define the history of language-based communities in South Asia and other world regions, but it is worth situating contemporary cultural and political dynamics within a history that extends back, as Mir (2010) and Orsini (2013) argue, well into the fifteenth and sixteenth centuries. It is crucial, then, to approach language-based formations by keeping in mind their inadequate yet necessary character. This broader history of languages and cultural regions proves helpful in decoding YouTube India's logics of scale and specifically, their purported "discovery" of south India as a distinct cultural region.

In an interview rounding up developments on YouTube in India in 2017, Satya Raghavan, the company's head of entertainment for the country, revealed that Hindi, Tamil, Telugu, and English remained the top four languages for the platform (Mathur 2017). Less than a year later, he acknowledged a rise in demand for content in south Indian languages, in another trade press article about the seven-hundred-million-dollar online video market in India (Singh 2018). Such narratives about languages and the scales of their appeal are reiterated in the platform's own annual global retrospective, YouTube Rewind. The 2017 version, for instance, marks the dominance of Hindi (and "Hinglish") by featuring the stars of popular north Indian YouTube channels like BB ki Vines, Technical Guruji, All India Bakchod, and fashion vlogger Shruti Arjun Anand.

But despite Raghavan's own claims about the importance of south Indian languages like Tamil and Telugu to YouTube at large, not a single south Indian channel finds mention in the Rewind video. The "Indian" market continuing to be spoken for by Hindi-language content creators in such global initiatives illuminates one of the foundational tensions of imagining and mobilizing media regions in a national context where the boundaries of the states have largely been drawn across linguistic lines.

Region, Storytelling, and Experiments in Scale Making

On YouTube, an early example of speaking back to such othering is *South of India*, the "viral" hit video produced by the Chennai-based theater company Stray Factory in association with Culture Machine and uploaded onto a channel called Rascalas in November 2014. Some members of the founding team of Rascalas went on to set up Put Chutney within a year. Set to the tune of Billy Joel's "We Didn't Start the Fire," *South of India* starts with the screen being split into a two-by-two grid and four actors in traditional attire occupying those spots, facing the audience. They then burst into song, listing the names of various states and union territories in the peninsula and briefly slipping into the four dominant south Indian languages before returning to register their complaints about the "Northies" in English.

The peninsular mapping and its limits are echoed in the chorus ("We are South of India")—that it is not a single state made up of *madrasi-s*; rather, they are all *padosi-s* ("neighbors" in Hindi). The rest of the song then proceeds with two verses highlighting widely regarded cultural, sociopolitical, and religious icons and places of note in each of the four large southern states, interspersed with the chorus that indexes both the legibility of the south Indian peninsula as a distinct entity and its role as a signifier of a more granular regional formation. As the performers mime their way through this survey of the south, their anger and frustration about being imagined as a monolith by Hindi-speaking northerners turns into pride and satisfaction of having set the record straight. The BBC's online magazine called the video "a musical guide to southern India" and declared it a "YouTube hit" (Brosnan 2014), with the song eventually clocking close to 2.6 million views on the online video platform and garnering press coverage in national and international news outlets. At

Figure 8.1. *South of India*: An Early Example of YouTube Channels Imagining a Peninsular Region

its heart, *South of India* represents what Michel de Certeau (1984) calls "spatial stories," where the text and its narrative enactments specify the practices organizing the peninsular space. Be it the song's reference to closing times of pubs in Bangalore or watching cricket at the Chepauk stadium in Chennai, the peninsular space mobilized here, while distinctly middle class and largely urban, is actuated in the aggregation of places and the everyday practices associated with them. It is articulated as a set of possibilities, with the urban elements in question offered as examples of both specificity and simultaneity. For Certeau, "space" does not possess the stability that "place" does. Instead, space, he argues, "occurs as the effect produced by the operations that orient it, situate it, temporalize it, and make it function in a polyvalent unity of conflictual programs or contractual proximities" (117). The narrators in *South of India* and the stories they tell, then, perform the labor of translating the peninsular space into a "practiced place," building on the territorializing impulse of the hegemonic Hindi-speaking north and establishing the itinerary charted as map. Central to these moves is the question of language, as the speech acts enabled by the narrators in service of region making faithfully abide by the linguistic reorganization of states in postindependence India. In so doing, they encounter an essential contradiction—the region-language mapping exceeds these territorial boundaries, as it invariably has.

The issue of language is central to discussions about regionalism and region making, as scholars like Ramaswamy (1997) and Mitchell (2009) have shown in relation to the construction of Tamil and Telugu identities around the languages themselves. These accounts chart how Tamil and Telugu identities and their regional moorings are stabilized through a history of emotional commitments to the language in question, made apparent through mass protests and even suicides. The creation of linguistically reorganized states in independent India must then be viewed as an accrual of these commitments over the nineteenth and twentieth centuries, with the south Indian states explicitly positioning themselves against the imposition of Hindi as a "national" language. Once again, the sociospatial dimensions of such efforts are significant, as attempts to establish Hindi as the primary language of administration or as a part of signage on roads and at train stations are seen as foundational challenges to the sovereignty of linguistic regions like *tamilakam*, or the Tamil region (Abraham 2003).

Thus, when the National Highways Authority of India started replacing English with Hindi on milestones on highways passing through Tamilnadu in 2017, the move unsurprisingly provoked significant backlash from social media users and regional political parties. This controversy then provided the background for Put Chutney to create *Hindi Thinnipu Pei* (*The Ghost That Imposes Hindi*; henceforth *HTP*), a satirical video that capitalized on the popularity of the horror-comedy genre in Tamil cinema to personify Hindi as a ghoul haunting the house of Tamils.

HTP opens with a shot of a father helping his school-age son with Tamil homework and being interrupted by a phone call. The father steps out of the house to talk on his cellphone, only to hear the phrase "Hindi is our national language" as static interference. He rushes back into the house upon hearing his wife call out to him. As he makes his way to the kitchen, his wife shows him how the *dosa* (a south Indian rice crepe) that she is preparing is turning into a *chapati* (a north Indian flatbread). As the lights go out and thunder and lightning strike, one horror film trope after another is deployed to lead up to the final and most troubling replacement—the transformation of the Tamil letter *om* into Hindi. A shaman-like character is then roped in to diagnose the cause of these mysterious happenings, who references the controversy around highway

Your house is haunted by "Hindi Imposition Ghost"

Figure 8.2. Echoing the *South of India* Video, Another Reference to the Widely Held Stereotype of All South Indians Being "Madraasee" in *HTP*

milestones and concludes that the house is haunted by a ghoul seeking to establish Hindi as the lingua franca. The shaman mediates between the ghoul and the family, as they argue about the merits and demerits of what is viewed by the latter as the imposition of Hindi upon hapless Tamils. The video ends with the father walking the weakened ghoul out of the house, stating that while he has been an Indian for just seventy years, he has been a Tamilian for thousands of years. *HTP* thus rehashes an argument that has been floated each time the specter of Hindi as a "national" language has been raised in the past century—Tamil is the "only case" (Shulman 2016, 2) among very ancient South Asian languages that still survives as a first language for tens of millions of speakers. However, in setting up this imposition of Hindi as a haunting, there is a clear effort to establish what Selby and Peterson (2008) refer to as a Tamil habitus. The "attack" on the house of the Tamils and on their lifeworlds (their food, their intimate space) in this video is then yet another effort to stabilize an imagination of the Tamil region, drawing on the long-standing history of emotional commitments to the language as the fount of culture. The narrative acts stabilize the antinomy of the creeping Hindi invaders against the denizens of the Tamil region, whose memories have fueled politics in the state (and in neighboring countries like Sri Lanka) for decades, and whose persistence is renewed by contemporary moves to establish Hindi as the language of the Indian nation, or Sinhala in the Sri Lankan case.

Here, the "localization" move toward a *tamilakam*, or a Tamil region, as opposed to the imagination of a unified southern peninsula or *thennakam*, must necessarily be read across multiple registers. In terms of industrial logics and algorithmic identification of audiences, it marks Put Chutney's recognition of their influence largely in relation to a Tamil audience and not a "south Indian" one. In an emergent field where such bona fides translate into users algorithmically discovering videos, issues, and themes in relation to one another through recommendation engines, texts such as *HTP* are also markers of struggles by creators to articulate their place as a "local" channel against other YouTube competitors (like Madras Central and Smile Settai). At the same time, in framing such efforts explicitly in relation to a longer history of language politics in the south and firmly against hegemonic north Indian formations, Put Chutney attempts to balance both specificity (a Tamil region, not a peninsular region) *and* collapse (a diverse cultural region united solely by the love of Tamil and a recognition of its centrality to notions of self-respect).

In this case, the Tamil region becomes the metaphorical "hub" around which the other linguistic "spokes" get constituted. For instance, one of the diagnostics run by the shaman-like figure in the *HTP* video, to determine whether the Tamil house is indeed haunted by a Hindi-loving ghoul, is to check using a political map of south India with all the different linguistic states marked out. As he chants and summons the ghost, the map transforms into an undifferentiated blob with the title *madraasee*, a catch-all term used almost exclusively by north Indians while referring to south Indians. Through visual gags such as these, it is clear that Put Chutney's vision of the "south" is one that responds to the hegemonic north with claims of multiplicity and calls for nuance. Such calls, however, also end up reinscribing Madras (or present-day Chennai) as the site of choice from where this hegemony of the north can be addressed and "fixes" Tamil as the lingua franca of this regionalism.

Conclusion

In a special issue on the topic of "regional platforms" in Asia, Steinberg and Li (2017, 174) contend that digital platforms are, in the first instance, "regional entities" and encourage us to "pay attention to how platforms construct regions and, indeed, often presume regions." In this essay, we have taken this perspective and drawn on scholarship on scales and scale making to examine the links between streaming video companies, storytelling practices, and language-based cultural geographies. In doing so, we have developed a broader claim about media distribution as a fundamentally scalar practice.

Of course, the ongoing transformation in media distribution is a multifaceted process, and we have focused on one dimension here to show that the history of language politics is woven into the warp and woof of the digital present. The emergent digital terrain that we have examined here also points to the enduring power of established scales inherited from film and television industries. It becomes clear that existing scalar fixes—for instance, media industry professionals' insistence on mapping language onto geographic territory—inform and in some instances constrain the future. Therefore, situating this moment within a longer cultural history of cable TV and regional media dynamics is critical if we are to develop more nuanced accounts of the ongoing digitalization of media and cultural industries.

Finally, we hope that this initial foray into investigating the pragmatics and politics of media distribution in relation to streaming video opens the door to research on the algorithmic processes at work here. Storytelling practices that we have drawn attention to here are underpinned and refracted by the growing reliance on algorithmic systems. Industry professionals now routinely invoke "data" to make claims about scales—urban, regional, national, etc.—as well as audience and user desires. Mapping both the material and discursive dimensions of varied industrial practices is crucial for understanding the changing relations between digital media industries, culture, and space.

BIBLIOGRAPHY

Abraham, Shinu Anna. 2003. "Chera, Chola, Pandya: Using Archaeological Evidence to Identify the Tamil Kingdoms of Early Historic South India." *Asian Perspectives* 42 (2): 207–23.

Ahuja, Aakanksha. 2018. "Regional Language Content Startups See Spurt in Ad Revenues." *LiveMint*, December 14. www.livemint.com.

Athique, A., V. Parthasarathi, and S. V. Srinivas, eds. 2017. *The Indian Media Economy: Industrial Dynamics and Cultural Adaptation*. Vol. 1. New Delhi: Oxford University Press.

Bellman, Eric. 2014. "Chart: India's Internet Speed Is the Slowest in Asia." *Wall Street Journal*, June 30. https://blogs.wsj.com.

Brosnan, Greg. 2014. "A Musical Guide to Southern India Is a YouTube Hit." *BBC News*, November 8. www.bbc.co.uk.

Carr, E. Summerson, and Michael Lempert, eds. 2016. *Scale: Discourse and Dimensions of Social Life*. Oakland: University of California Press.

Certeau, Michel de. 1984. "Spatial Stories." In *The Practice of Everyday Life*, translated by Steven Rendall, 115–30. Berkeley: University of California Press.

Chan, Anita Say. 2013. *Networking Peripheries: Technological Futures and the Myth of Digital Universalism*. Cambridge, MA: MIT Press.

Cullity, Jocelyn. 2002. "The Global Desi: Cultural Nationalism on MTV India." *Journal of Communication Inquiry* 26 (4): 408–25. https://doi.org/10.1177/019685902236899.

Cunningham, Stuart, and David Craig, eds. 2019. *Social Media Entertainment: The New Intersection of Hollywood and Silicon Valley*. New York: New York University Press.

Curtin, Michael. 2003. "Media Capital: Towards the Study of Spatial Flows." *International Journal of Cultural Studies* 6 (2): 202–28. https://doi.org/10.1177/13678779030062004.

Curtin, Michael, Jennifer Holt, and Kevin Sanson, eds. 2014. *Distribution Revolution: Conversations about the Digital Future of Film and Television*. Oakland: University of California Press.

Elkins, Evan. 2016. "The DVD Region Code System: Standardizing Home Video's Disjunctive Global Flows." *International Journal of Cultural Studies* 19 (2): 225–40. https://doi.org/10.1177/1367877914547300.

Fung, Anthony. 2006. "'Think Globally, Act Locally': China's Rendezvous with MTV." *Global Media and Communication* 2 (1): 71–88. https://doi.org/10.1177/1742766506061818.

Gillespie, Tarleton. 2010. "The Politics of 'Platforms.'" *New Media & Society* 12 (3): 347–64. https://doi.org/10.1177/1461444809342738.

Goel, Vindu. 2018. "Amazon's Plan to Reach 500 Million Indians: Speak Their Language." *New York Times*, November 1. www.nytimes.com.

Govil, Nitin. 2015. *Orienting Hollywood: A Century of Film Culture between Los Angeles and Bombay*. New York: New York University Press.

indiantelevision.com Team. 2015. "'The Next Billion YouTube Users Are Going to Come from India.' Ajay Vidyasagar." *Indian Television*, December 4. www.indiantelevision.com.

Indiatimes News Network. 2008. "YouTube Launched in India." *Economic Times*, May 7. https://economictimes.indiatimes.com.

Jin, Dal Yong. 2013. "The Construction of Platform Imperialism in the Globalization Era." *tripleC—Communication, Capitalism & Critique* 11 (1): 145–72.

KPMG. 2017. "Indian Languages—Defining India's Internet." https://assets.kpmg/content/dam/kpmg/in/pdf/2017/04/Indian-languages-Defining-Indias-Internet.pdf.

Kraidy, Marwan M. 2005. *Hybridity, or the Cultural Logic of Globalization*. Philadelphia: Temple University Press.

Kumar, Akshaya. 2013. "Provincialising Bollywood? Cultural Economy of North-Indian Small-Town Nostalgia in the Indian Multiplex." *South Asian Popular Culture* 11 (1): 61–74. https://doi.org/10.1080/14746689.2013.764642.

Kumar, Sangeet. 2016. "YouTube Nation: Precarity and Agency in India's Online Video Scene." *International Journal of Communication* 10. http://ijoc.org.

Kumar, Shanti, and Michael Curtin. 2002. "'Made in India': In between Music Television and Patriarchy." *Television & New Media* 3 (4): 345–66. https://doi.org/10.1177/152747602237279.

Larkin, Brian. 2008. *Signal and Noise: Media, Infrastructure, and Urban Culture in Nigeria*. Durham, NC: Duke University Press.

Lobato, Ramon. 2019. *Netflix Nations: The Geography of Digital Distribution*. New York: New York University Press.

Lobato, Ramon, and James Meese, eds. 2016. *Geoblocking and Global Video Culture*. Amsterdam: Institute of Network Cultures.

Lotz, Amanda. 2017. *Portals: A Treatise on Internet-Distributed Television*. Ann Arbor, MI: Maize Books.

Mankekar, Purnima. 2004. "Dangerous Desires: Television and Erotics in Late Twentieth-Century India." *Journal of Asian Studies* 63 (2): 403–31.

Marston, Sallie A. 2000. "The Social Construction of Scale." *Progress in Human Geography* 24 (2): 219–42. https://doi.org/10.1191/030913200674086272.

Marwick, A., and d. boyd. 2011. "To See and Be Seen: Celebrity Practice on Twitter." *Convergence* 17 (2): 139–58. https://doi.org/10.1177/1354856510394539.

Massey, Doreen. 1994. *Space, Place, and Gender*. Minneapolis: University of Minnesota Press.

Mathur, Nandita. 2017. "We Have a Content Ecosystem That Is Wide, Deep, Well Balanced: YouTube." *LiveMint*, December 11. www.livemint.com.

Mazzarella, William. 2003. *Shoveling Smoke: Advertising and Globalization in Contemporary India*. Durham, NC: Duke University Press.

Menon, Bindu. 2017. "YouTube Mobile Viewership Hits 180 m in India." *Hindu BusinessLine*, March 23. www.thehindubusinessline.com.

Mir, Farina. 2010. *The Social Space of Language: Vernacular Culture in British Colonial Punjab*. Berkeley: University of California Press.

Mitchell, Lisa. 2009. *Language, Emotion, and Politics in South India: The Making of a Mother Tongue*. Bloomington: Indiana University Press.

Moore, Adam. 2008. "Rethinking Scale as a Geographical Category: From Analysis to Practice." *Progress in Human Geography* 32 (2): 203–25. https://doi.org/10.1177/0309132507087647.

Next Billion Users. 2018. "The Making of YouTube Go." *Google Design*, February 1. https://design.google.

Orsini, Francesca. 2013. *The History of the Book in South Asia*. London: Routledge.

Pahwa, Nikhil. 2012. "YouTube India Is Bigger Than MTV India in Revenues—Rajan Anandan." *MediaNama*, January 18. www.medianama.com.

Parks, Lisa, and Shanti Kumar, eds. 2003. *Planet TV: A Global Television Reader*. New York: New York University Press.

Parks, Lisa, and Nicole Starosielski, eds. 2015. *Signal Traffic: Critical Studies of Media Infrastructures*. Champaign: University of Illinois Press.

Parthasarathi, Vibodh. 2018. "Market Dynamics of the Media Economy." In *The Indian Media Economy: Market Dynamics and Social Transactions*, edited by Adrian Athique, Vibodh Parthasarathi, and S. V. Srinivas, vol. 2, 1–22. New Delhi: Oxford University Press.

Plantin, Jean-Christophe, Carl Lagoze, Paul N. Edwards, and Christian Sandvig. 2018. "Infrastructure Studies Meet Platform Studies in the Age of Google and Facebook." *New Media & Society* 20 (1): 293–310. https://doi.org/10.1177/1461444816661553.

Preethi, J. 2009. "YouTube India Embraces Hindi; No Transliteration; Subtitles?" *MediaNama*, August 17. www.medianama.com.

Ramaswamy, Sumathi. 1997. *Passions of the Tongue: Language Devotion in Tamil India, 1891–1970*. Berkeley: University of California Press.

Saxena, Anupam. 2012. "YouTube Adds Support for More Indic Languages." *MediaNama*, February 27. www.medianama.com.

Selby, Martha Ann, and Indira Viswanathan Peterson. 2008. *Tamil Geographies: Cultural Constructions of Space and Place in South India*. Albany: State University of New York Press.

Shulman, David D. 2016. *Tamil*. Cambridge, MA: Harvard University Press.

Singh, Manish. 2018. "Netflix and Amazon Are Struggling to Win over the World's Second-Largest Internet Market." *CNBC*, July 5. www.cnbc.com.

Steinberg, Marc, and Jinying Li. 2017. "Introduction: Regional Platforms." *Asiascape: Digital Asia* 4 (3): 173–83. https://doi.org/10.1163/22142312-12340076.

Tomlinson, John. 1991. *Cultural Imperialism: A Critical Introduction*. Baltimore: Johns Hopkins University Press.

Tsing, Anna. 2000. "The Global Situation." *Cultural Anthropology* 15 (3): 327–60.

———. 2005. *Friction: An Ethnography of Global Connection*. Princeton, NJ: Princeton University Press.

———. 2012. "On Nonscalability: The Living World Is Not Amenable to Precision-Nested Scales." *Common Knowledge* 18 (3): 505–24. https://doi.org/10.1215/0961754X-1630424.

van Dijck, José. 2013. *The Culture of Connectivity: A Critical History of Social Media*. Oxford: Oxford University Press.

9

"Sorry about That"

Hopes and Promises of Geoblocking's End

EVAN ELKINS

Most of the digital technologies we use to watch, listen to, and play media—video game consoles, DVDs, streaming platforms, and so forth—have been installed with some form of "regional lockout." This refers to intentionally installed technological mechanisms that block particular platforms within certain geographic locations. While regional lockout has existed in digital technologies since at least the 1980s, its most recent incarnation is geoblocking, or the practice of blocking all or part of an online platform in a specific location. Though the practice has long been frustrating for users, the 2010s has seen a pushback against geoblocking by executives of major entertainment companies, regulators, and digital rights activists. This chapter explores this emergent, public-facing discourse, primarily in European and North American contexts, that heralds the end of geoblocking in digitally networked entertainment. The "end of geoblocking discourse," as I call it, reveals much about how media industries draw on the long-standing public hope for universally available "celestial jukeboxes" of digital entertainment (Goldstein 1994). It also shows how such stakeholders publicly discuss, and at times ignore, the boundaries and friction that still mark global media flows. In this chapter, I illustrate commonalities and differences in anti-geoblocking rhetoric and explore what they illustrate about industrial and regulatory understandings of digital entertainment's global geography. To do so, I trace the end of geoblocking discourse across three public instances of mainstream, Western industrial practice and media governance: first, the "not available in your country" messages that appear on geoblocked platforms like Hulu, YouTube, and Spotify and that often promise that the platform will be available in one's country soon; second, Netflix's 2016 announcement that it would be dropping nearly all of its national geoblocks; and finally, the European Union's 2010s promotion and implementation of a Digital Single Market that was meant, in part, to eliminate geoblocking within EU borders. I choose these parameters not to present a survey of how geoblocking's end has been imagined all over the world, but rather to show how it has been promoted primarily to a Euro-American public through Westernized logics of liberal markets and consumer-driven governance.

Whether prematurely pronouncing geoblocking's death or calling for its swift elimination, the end of geoblocking discourse posits that the time has come to abolish the practice. Major streaming entertainment platforms have promoted their services within the disruption-laden rhetoric of "everywhere," a hoped-for condition of making the platform available in (virtually) every market around the world. However, such calls tend to treat geoblocking as a historical blip—an extended accident of media industries trying to integrate digital technologies into existing distribution practices and intellectual property rules rather than simply the newest manifestation of long-standing business models based on market segmentation and windowing. Such rhetoric sees the industrial abandonment of geoblocking as part of a natural evolution into an idealized, globally open mediascape rather than the more banal reality of media industries attempting to enter new markets within a media environment increasingly marked by global simultaneity rather than staggered windowing. By hoping for and heralding an end to geoblocking, various stakeholders promote a vision of digital media technologies as following a straight path toward increased global openness and accessibility. As a result, the end of geoblocking discourse smooths over the fact that regional hiccups are in fact produced through a variety of means: poor infrastructure, national content regulations, variable pricing in different territories, and digital entertainment companies' hesitance to expand into new markets too quickly. They view the digital entertainment landscape, and the internet as a whole, as either open or closed, rather than a complex series of networks operating at various levels of openness and closedness. Geoblocking's heterogeneity means that its elimination is more a utopian ideal than a realistically attainable goal.

I argue that the end of geoblocking discourse blurs the lines among utopian hopes for an open, public digital commons, a celestial jukebox where consumers can access anything at any time, and the internet as a potential landscape for borderless commercial exchange and free-market capitalism. Such rhetorics can be seen across a wide range of examples, from commercial and public service platforms to the expressed desires of corporate platform owners, regulators, and digital rights activists. Indeed, figures as dissimilar as Netflix CEO Reed Hastings and members of the anti-corporate Pirate Party have all called for the end of geoblocking. While the latter, for instance, has levied its critiques from a political platform fighting for an open commons, information privacy, and intellectual property reform, entertainment CEOs see geoblocking as an outmoded barrier to digital entertainment services' ambitions of global dominance. Such institutions are interested in geoblocking's end for different reasons, but in the end of geoblocking discourse their reasonings swirl together into a familiar blend of technological freedom and libertarian capitalism that heralds the arrival of digital services "everywhere."

Geoblocking in Digital Entertainment

Geoblocking specifically refers to when online platforms use IP address detection systems to ascertain a user's location and use the address's geolocative information in order to ban that user from the service (Lobato 2016, 10). While someone in a geoblocked country might be able to visit a service's website or open the app, if they try to watch a video or play a song they will generally see a message on-screen that says something like, "This content is not available in your country" (more on these notices shortly). For the purposes of this chapter, I distinguish geoblocking from state-mandated forms of internet restriction such as China's Great Firewall. While not wholly unrelated, these kinds of restrictions operate more as a top-down, content-based censorship of platforms and ideas rather than a mechanism to direct the routes of entertainment circulation. In contrast, the kinds of geoblocking discussed here are primarily tools of media distribution. They are implemented by digital platforms as a way of maintaining nation- and region-based distribution licenses and market segmentation practices in order to shape the global distribution of commercial intellectual property. Geoblocking's most direct antecedent is the region code, a technology implemented

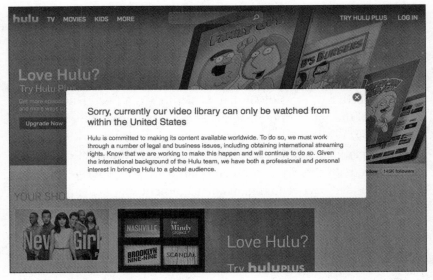

Figure 9.1. The Geoblocked Hulu Platform

in disc-based technologies like the DVD wherein discs and players distributed to a particular region of the world are encoded with the same numbered region—region 1 being the United States and Canada, region 2 being much of Europe and Japan, and so on—with the regions needing to match before the user is able to play the disc. While these technologies resulted in similar public and industry debates about the appropriateness of region-based regulation in a digital age, they were more about directing the distribution of physical goods—discs, players, consoles—than geoblocking, which is more about directing internet traffic and platforms. Even earlier, home entertainment technologies like VCRs also had regional incompatibilities, but these were usually the result of globally divergent technological standards than territorial distribution agreements. So regional lockout has a longer history of ensuring that media circulates globally along restrictive routes that are sanctioned by powerful industrial players.

At the same time, geoblocking is about more than industrial bottom lines. Regional lockout both reflects and shapes global geocultural divisions and hierarchies. As I have argued elsewhere, it does so by affecting digital technologies' affordances, media distribution paths, and cultural practices of media circulation and reception (Elkins 2019). Because geoblocking carries social importance beyond the media industries, it has long been a target for audience frustration. When someone from Nigeria tries to use the Spotify app to listen to a particular song, they find a message telling them they are unable to do so. When a viewer in Latin America wants to watch Hulu, they encounter a similar message. The experience is akin to the frustration in discovering your internet is temporarily down, but it is an intentionally installed form of frustration. Geoblocking has also stymied certain platforms and other media-industrial stakeholders who are interested in a more international reach free from the constraints of territory-based distribution agreements. While tussles over regional lockout in a pre-streaming era were marked by a perceived battle between consumers and a monolithic entertainment industry, the rise of platforms as intermediaries has complicated these debates. Services like Netflix, Spotify, and Hulu, as well as governance bodies like the European Union, have at times aligned with members of the public against geoblocking—but with their own goals in mind.

Coming to Your Area Soon: The Promises of the "Not Available" Message

One perhaps unexpected place we see the end of geoblocking discourse is within geoblocked digital entertainment platforms themselves. In various consumer-facing and public relations contexts, company executives will often promise that their platform will soon be available in more countries. Such promises also tend to appear within on-screen messages to users found in FAQ pages as well as notifications that pop up when one tries to access a platform from a blocked country. Usually, the latter incorporate some variant on the "not available in your country" message followed by a vague explanation and promise that the platform is working to bring its product to as many global users as possible. In one representative example, U.S.-based streaming video platform Hulu has informed would-be viewers via an on-screen graphic that "Hulu is committed to making its content available worldwide." The message continues, "To do so, we must work through a number of legal and business issues, including obtaining international streaming rights. Know that we are working to make this happen and will continue to do so. Given the international background of the Hulu team, we have both a professional and personal obligation in bringing Hulu to a global audience." The statement doubles as an apology for keeping the platform closed off from many around the world and a broad promise that the platform will attempt to become more globalized in the future, all while drawing on a vision of globalization steeped in consumer choice. At the same time, Hulu positions itself as a cosmopolitan, globally diverse service even as it remains nation-bound.

Referencing "obtaining international streaming rights," Hulu in particular directs the blame for geoblocking to the content owners who refuse to license content globally—a refusal that acts in opposition to the platform's putative goal of opening up global access. But in Hulu's case, we are asked to accept this simple proposition rather than acknowledge the complexity of the platform's ownership structure (it is not an independently owned platform but is in fact owned by Disney and Comcast, two conglomerates that run three of the four major broadcast networks) as well as the fact that Hulu sees some benefit in keeping the platform nation-bound. As Kevin Sanson and Gregory Steirer (2019, 1217) point out, the platform's U.S.-based reach helps it negotiate more traditional deals that allow content producers to retain an ownership stake in their productions and negotiate their own international distribution rights. This gives Hulu an edge with media producers who may not want to sign a production and global distribution deal with Netflix wherein they get more money up front but lose out on back-end revenue. As opposed to Hulu's implied narrative—i.e., that producers are holding their films and programming hostage from platforms—the licensing agreements that keep geoblocking in place are clearly more complicated than a two-sentence blurb might suggest. They involve contractual issues about when and where certain content can be distributed for any number of reasons—content regulations, international marketing practices, sufficiency of internet infrastructure, and so forth. Since all of these issues are likely uninteresting or confusing to the lay user, it is expedient and convenient for the platform to shift blame.

Masking the business of global media distribution even while vaguely pointing to it is part of a general trend among other digital entertainment platforms. They similarly use their on-screen "not available in your country" messages to emphasize that distribution structures media accessibility while pointing to supposedly natural and uncontrollable industry forces as the reason viewers are unable to access the media experience that they desire. BBC's iPlayer platform simply says, "BBC iPlayer only works in the UK. Sorry, it's due to rights issues," and leaves it at that. Rather, there are important regulatory and commercial reasons that the iPlayer has remained geoblocked, many of which relate to the platform's attempts to adapt to a global, digital environment wherein the national public service broadcaster volleys various threats (Elkins 2019). Turning to another example, YouTube has recently become more commercialized and less steeped in amateur media through its intensified advertising and monetization program as well as its partnerships with major entertainment institutions. As a result, it has more thoroughly incorporated geoblocking into the platform. In its own "not available" messages, YouTube tells viewers, "The uploader has not made this video available in your country. Sorry about that." As in the Hulu and iPlayer messages, this is technically accurate. YouTube does not directly geoblock content but allows users who enroll in the YouTube Partner Program—i.e., those who want to monetize their copyrighted content—to geoblock their uploaded material if they choose. But also like the other messages, it defers blame to other parties besides YouTube, thereby positioning the platform as a more passive entity within the institutional tussles that accompany geoblocking.

One example from Germany shows how YouTube positions itself as the passive receiver of geoblocking and would-be viewers as the victims. It also shows how "not available" messages communicate to users that geoblocking is an artificial imposition on an ideally open platform. During the 2010s, the German royalty collection and rights agency Gesellschaft für musikalische Aufführungs-und mechanische Vervielfältigungsrechte (GEMA) engaged in a dispute with YouTube over the platform's exhibition of videos containing royalty-protected music. In 2010, GEMA took YouTube to court, which resulted in the platform blocking such videos within Germany's borders. The accompanying notice on a blocked video initially read (in German), "Unfortunately, this video is not available in Germany, because it may contain music for which GEMA has not granted the respective music rights. Sorry about that." As Philip Stade (2014) points out, the phrasing blames GEMA for the dispute, which resulted in public critics calling GEMA "bureaucratic posers" and a "dinosaur" that "is denying cultural diversity."

Such examples illustrate that "not available" messages are crafted texts that muddy the reality of geoblocking and imply a possible state of affairs where it would not exist; if only the party supposedly *causing* the geoblocking would open up access to the world. The colloquial, almost intimate nature of the messages (both examples above use the familiar "Sorry about that" phrasing) likewise position the platform as a friend to consumers—the institution that is on *our* side in trying to convince the stubborn content providers that they should give us what we want. The delayed promises of global expansion as well as the occasionally passive-aggressive redirection of blame suggest that geoblocking is only a temporary condition rather than a long-standing reality of territorial licensing agreements and geographically limited media infrastructures.

On some level, these messages' oversimplifications make sense. The vast majority of viewers likely do not care about the ins and outs of licensing agreements, global market segmentation, and media distribution. At the same time, the messages obfuscate the reality that geoblocking works to maintain the interests of various industry stakeholders—including, often, the platforms themselves. There are additional reasons that platforms do not expand globally beyond simply a lack of globally licensed content. These have more to do with the various costs and logistical headaches that accompany global availability, like dealing with local content and technology regulations, paying for increased market research, adapting algorithmic recommendation systems, building language and subtitling tracks, and allowing for sufficient infrastructure on the platform and user ends to run the service. In Hulu's case, such processes might fall under the vague rubric of "legal and business issues," further confusing the messy issues of infrastructural and institutional expansion—costs of entering new markets, quality of internet service, content regulations, needs for broadcasting licenses—that keep digital platforms nation- and region-bound.

Like Hulu, other platforms use their public messages about geoblocking to signal that they are *in fact* global services. One such platform is the streaming music service Spotify. Founded in Sweden but now "operat[ing] increasingly like a traditional American media company" due to its financial backing by major American corporations as well as its increasingly multimedia approach, the platform regularly promotes its globalness—not just in terms of its growing availability and audience but also in how it brands the platform (Vonderau 2019, 9). Ironically, one space where we can see this global brand is on a web page where would-be users can enter their email address and be notified when the platform launches in their country. The site contains a large banner with the message, "Spotify is currently not available in your country. Be the first to know when we launch." "When we launch" suggests that it is only a matter of time before Spotify is available everywhere. True or not, this reflects the characteristic idea that geoblocking is a temporary hurdle on a forward path toward a more open internet. It therefore presents an end-of-geoblocking discourse that presumes that an unblocked online world is inevitable. Further underlining the irony, just below the large "currently not available message" is a promise that with Spotify, you can "listen everywhere." While "everywhere" in this context refers to the mobile nature of the platform (it is followed by a notice that "Spotify works on your computer, mobile, tablet and TV"), it invokes conditions of "ubiquitous listening" or the "celestial jukebox" that have been associated with music in the digital era (Kassabian 2013; Goldstein 1994). If "listen everywhere" in this context is aspirational rather than an empirically correct description of how Spotify works on a global scale, it nevertheless expresses the possibility that the platform could and should be a truly ubiquitous music service.

"A Better Experience": Reed Hastings and Netflix's Global Brand

For a clear look at how the end of geoblocking discourse at once crystalizes a host of dominant ideologies regarding commercial digital entertainment and unveils even more complexities about how globalized digital platforms operate, we can turn to a moment when streaming video service Netflix celebrated the supposed end of its own geoblocking practices. In January 2016, Netflix CEO Reed Hastings gave a keynote address at the Consumer Electronics Show (CES) in Las Vegas. As Ramon Lobato (2019, 2) has argued, this keynote marked the point when Netflix credibly positioned itself as a truly *global* media company, as it was in this address that Hastings announced that the platform would be dropping almost all of its geoblocks. It would be difficult to find a more perfectly distilled blend of the Silicon Valley–espoused ideology that "technological progress driven by capitalism not only provides personal convenience and raises the standard of living but also spurs social change" and the neoliberal entertainment industry dogma that consumer choice is equivalent to the empowerment of individuals and communities (Levina and Hasinoff 2017, 490). At the beginning of the address, Hastings presented Netflix as the result of a century-old process of consumer-media development: "From radio to broadcast TV. From broadcast TV to cable TV. And now to internet TV . . . with each of these bringing a better experience." By presenting media convergence as a tidy, linear evolution rather than a messy and conflictual process, Hastings sets up the premise that Netflix's advanced technological architecture, ease of use, and diversity of content make the platform uniquely poised to offer consumers the viewing experiences they have long desired. Proposing media history as a straight line, Hastings argues, "We live in an on-demand world, and there's no going back."

This forward-progress rhetoric sets up a major announcement that comes later in Netflix's CES presentation. After a half hour or so of promos and interviews with Netflix talent, Hastings returns to the stage. Toward the beginning of this segment, he channels Marshall McLuhan by folding Netflix into an even longer history of technical ingenuity and connection: "Just as the power we once harnessed from the horse gave way to the combustion engine and the transistor brought us into the information age, the internet is transformative." Drawing on the longstanding links between electronic connection and transportation, the quotation proposes a lineage of which we are meant to consider Netflix a part. Hastings segues into a discussion about how Netflix's job is, in part, to help consumers discover new things. Echoing the earlier discussed example of Spotify pushing blame for geoblocking to the content providers, he points out that "it's a big and challenging task to [deliver content] globally" because "content rights are sliced and diced" among various global outlets. Noting that internet access is steadily improving around the world, he suggests that conditions are right for Netflix to be the force that finally uses the infrastructural accomplishment of global high-speed internet to its fullest potential. Pointing to an oft-repeated question about when Netflix will be available across the world, Hastings excitedly lets the audience know that while he has been on stage, the Netflix service was introduced in 130 new countries.[1] As he tells the audience that the service has "gone live in nearly every country of the world but China," the hashtag #NetflixEverywhere pops up on-screen in front of an animated map of the world constructed of TV-screen-shaped rectangles. Hastings puts a cap on the announcement, telling the audience that they are "witnessing the birth of a global TV network."

The address is rich with what David Morley and Kevin Robins (1995, 11) call the "mythology of global media," which suggests that media help eliminate national borders and foster cross-cultural understanding and that global corporate media institutions have the resources and will to best achieve such a state of affairs. Indeed, the talk offers a now-familiar blend of neoliberal Silicon Valley disruption rhetoric and the entertainment-industrial dogma that consumer choice equals individual agency and freedom. At one point, Hastings notes that Netflix offers a "simple shift from corporate to consumer control." Of course, such rhetoric ignores the fact that Netflix's interactive interfaces and data-collection practices seek to construct an image of the viewer's identity and preferences as much as—or more than—they purport to offer her a true choice in the content that she wants (Arnold 2016, 59). Beyond this, the celebration of consumer choice, conflated with utopian visions of a borderless world, position Netflix as a benevolent force that can connect the world, once and for all—a global watercooler of sorts. This, of course, asks us to accept the premise that a Netflix platform available in 190 countries exemplifies a more connected, cosmopolitan world rather than simply an achievement of infrastructure, content licensing, and marketing.

There is an even simpler and more straightforward criticism that one could raise of Hastings's announcement of a universally available Netflix: it is not even accurate. Here, we can return to his caveat that the platform is available "nearly everywhere except China." Though not a joke, the line gets a laugh from the audience of CES industry types, undoubtedly reflecting on their own experiences attempting to break into the tightly regulated Chinese market. The remark cannot help but produce cognitive dissonance, as it glosses over the fact that the platform is still not available all over the world even with #NetflixEverywhere placed on-screen. When he makes his announcement about Netflix dropping its geoblock, Hastings takes the more expedient but less precise route of claiming that the platform is now ubiquitous. His comment about hoping to enter China soon reads as an aside, but it serves as a reminder that roughly 1.4 billion people do not factor into "everywhere." Likewise, going unmentioned in Hastings's address is the fact that the platform remains unavailable in Crimea, North Korea, and Syria due to sanctions. Furthermore, he notes that there are 3.2 billion internet users around the world, invoking the possibility for the internet to foster global connection while implying that these 3.2 billion represent a massive potential market for the platform. Even accounting for the fact that not all of those left out of this number would be counted as internet users even if they did have access, it calls attention to the impressive positive number rather than acknowledge the gaps in access that remain. This is more than simply a pedantic fact check of Hastings's rhetoric. Rather, it illustrates how the service's celebration of its new accessibility ignores the de facto geoblocking that occurs through means beyond simply the vagaries of content licensing agreements. Political and infrastructural realities keep various forms of geoblocking intact.

Following the address, Netflix amplified the global dimensions of its brand. Hastings and other representatives of the company showed up regularly in the trades and popular press, which were eager to publish stories celebrating the company's newly global image (Roettgers 2017; Adalian 2018). Case in point: the headline of a 2019 *New York Times* editorial called the platform an "intoxicating portal to Planet Earth." Highlighting the surfeit of international films and programming on Netflix, as well as its global availability, the piece argued that the platform embodied a kind of "open-border digital cosmopolitanism" (Manjoo 2019). While there is undoubtedly truth to the idea that the platform helps people engage with international culture, the piece nevertheless offers an uncritical repetition of the platform's public relations rhetoric that has promoted its global expansion during the last half of the 2010s. Indeed, the piece's argument that the platform "[aims] to sell international ideas to a global audience" echoes directly a statement by Reed Hastings in an interview that Netflix is trying to "curate some of the world's best stories and provide them to the whole world" (Anashkina and Fink 2016). Furthermore, the evocation of open borders further erases the real infrastructural, economic, cultural, and linguistic barriers to access that do exist, all while promoting massive corporate platforms as the forces that have supposedly erased such barriers.

A Digital Single Market: Europe's Consumer-Oriented Anti-Geoblocking Measure

Netflix's promise to end geoblocking was characterized by the wills of corporate global expansion wrapped up in the evolutionary rhetoric of open communications systems. A concurrent attempt to end geoblocking in the European Union likewise pitched its proposal to a public long frustrated with geoblocking, but with a solution drawn from international governance rather than from a single platform's corporate priorities. In 2015, the EU's legislative body, the European Commission, introduced the Digital Single Market (DSM), a set of regulations meant to eliminate various impediments to doing business in digital arenas across its regional market and facilitate increased, yet still limited and controlled, digital access and mobility across national borders. These involved opening up access to e-commerce services, changing copyright laws, eliminating roaming charges for Europeans traveling within the EU, and a host of other regulatory reforms on Europe's digital landscape. One of these promised regulations was an end to "unjustified geoblocking" (European Commission 2019). Though this was widely reported as the EU's attempt to eliminate geoblocking, the use of the qualifier "unjustified" highlights a caveat that would make the end of geoblocking more complicated than it might have initially seemed.

By the DSM's logic, geoblocking clashes with a culturally and economically borderless Europe envisioned as more modern than one split up by national boundaries. This is apparent in a press conference from European Commission vice president Andrus Ansip, wherein he says that he "hate[s] geoblocking" because it is "old-fashioned," and "we don't have to use . . . [these] instruments in the twenty-first century" (Reda 2015). Similar to Hastings, though from a different perspective, Ansip posits geoblocking as an outdated technology. In the same address, he makes clear that the EU's anti-geoblocking proposals are best understood through the (de)regulatory mechanisms of liberal, transnational capitalism: "There are two logics: the logic of geoblocking and the logic of the internal [i.e., single] market. . . . Those two, they cannot coexist. We have to abolish geoblocking" (Reda 2015). Taken together, these statements draw together an empathetic personal frustration with encountering the "not available in your country message" and a larger-scale question about how a regional market should operate, particularly in an era when cultural policy within film and television industries promotes international distribution via mechanisms like coproductions and simultaneous releasing. The experiences of consumers, individuals, communities, and national and regional economies are all blurred together and folded into one common frustration that can be solved through EU governance.

The European Commission, thus, asks its constituents to envision a deregulatory economic policy as a path toward less frustrating online experiences. The EU website promoting and explaining the DSM amplifies its fiscal-regulation aspects: "Making the EU's single market fit for the digital age requires tearing down unnecessary regulatory barriers and moving from individual national markets to one single EU-wide rulebook. These steps could contribute €415 billion per year to economic growth, boosting jobs, competition, investment and innovation in the EU" (European Commission 2018). When the issue is discussed at the level of the consumer, geoblocking is presented less as an impediment to the internet as a global medium and more as a force that can enable people to save money and generally have an easier time online. One European Parliament–produced video contains narration that discusses geoblocking in the context of e-commerce, all while we see would-be shoppers running into higher prices and geoblocked content (European Parliament 2017). All told, consumption and economic growth are the primary mechanisms through which constituents are asked to envision the end of geoblocking, rather than a broader investment in the internet as an open communications system. As a result, the commission regularly blurs the line between the DSM's market-based benefits and the purported freedom that it will offer digital consumers (with "consumers" being the operative word here). To be fair to the EU, the European Commission does not officially present the DSM as more than a way to ease cross-border economic exchange. It is called the Digital Single *Market*, after all, and it is geared primarily at eliminating economic hurdles for consumers and media companies alike. Furthermore, there is no doubt that some of the DSM policies will ease the frustrations of EU denizens who regularly run into geoblocked services. At the same time, promotional material and commissioners' rhetoric draw on sweepingly humanistic visions of a free internet in order to promote what is fundamentally an economic regulation.

Given its blend of ideas regarding internet freedom, personal choice, and economic liberalism, the DSM has been promoted with various levels of enthusiasm by members of the European Parliament existing on a spectrum ranging from centrist free-market advocates to more internet-freedom-oriented cyber-activists. While many public representatives of the DSM present it as a fiscal policy wrapped in the trimmings of cross-border communication and digital liberty, members of the more stridently anticapitalist Pirate Party, for instance, reject the DSM's framing as overly reliant on a consumer logic that still benefits big business. The most vocal representative of this view is Julia Reda, a former member of the European Parliament who represented the Pirate Party Germany and was part of the Parliament's left-wing Greens / European Free Alliance. She usually articulates her support and subsequent criticism of the DSM not primarily in terms of cross-border economics but rather through the Pirate Party platform that Patrick Burkart (2014, 2) characterizes as "moral and economic notions of a commons, or a public domain." Reda has consistently represented a view that envisioned the DSM as oriented toward the public and lamented its ultimately watered-down approach to copyright and geoblocking. One of her blog posts, published just after the European Parliament agreed on the DSM's anti-geoblocking measures, carries the blunt title, "No, the EU Did Not Abolish Geoblocking Today" (Reda 2018). In the post, she points out that the EU measures are "timid baby steps" that eliminate geoblocking only within certain e-commerce and web-hosting contexts but do not offer European citizens access to a number of blocked platforms. Furthermore, while not wholly avoiding the consumer logic that dominates discussion of the DSM, she presents the issue as one that can offer a more substantial *cultural* benefit to European media makers and audiences, pointing out that geoblocking has long served to "deny European works access to a pan-European audience." Here, Reda gestures toward possible consequences of geoblocking, and benefits to its abolishment, that dig deeper than the dominant consumer-oriented argument.

However, the end result was a version of the DSM that retained many of geoblocking's most common and frustrating instances. While it eliminated geoblocking among online shopping site services, platforms exhibiting copyrighted content—streaming platforms, digital games, e-books—were made exempt from the regulations. This can be attributed to a combination of Hollywood's and other entertainment industry giants' powerful influence as well as the difficulty in balancing regional governance with divergent laws among member nations (Lomas 2018; Trimble 2016, 61–62). As in some of the earlier discussed examples, this outcome illustrates how the end of geoblocking discourse can be mobilized toward governance and (de)regulation that carry overtones of internet freedom but are softened by, or even geared toward, the wills of powerful entities.

Conclusion: What Does the End of Geoblocking Discourse Actually Tell Us?

The preceding examples indicate that, in spite of their differing goals, a wide range of industrial and regulatory actors speak about geoblocking's end in many of the same ways. A number of themes emerge, all of which tell us a great deal not just about how powerful institutions envision geoblocking but also about dominant discourses regarding digital entertainment in general. One is the ignorance or evasion of internet-access problems and gaps that persist beyond geoblocking. Another presents geoblocking and its end as an issue primarily of interest to people envisioned as *consumers* and the attendant idea that the internet is a space of economic activity and consumption rather than a communication medium or a commons built for information sharing and gathering. There is also the related issue that geoblocking is an impediment to media industries' abilities to sell and distribute their products around the world, and it is therefore an external force prohibiting these industries from giving the people what they want. We also see a shifting of blame for geoblocking onto other stakeholders like content providers, with this blame passing often acting as part of a broader series of negotiations among these stakeholders. More broadly, we notice a proposition that the development of media should be viewed as a linear history moving toward greater advancement and freedom, and one wherein geoblocking would inevitably be a thing of the past. Similarly, such discourses also repeat the idea that a globally accessible, single internet is a good thing and that it is the medium's ultimate, ideal state. Finally, this is accompanied by an argument that geoblocking is an impediment to this ideal state rather than one example of the internet's relationship to material geography.

Taken together, these premises show that industrial and governance-based visions of geoblocking's end in fact reflect some rather traditional ideologies about digital entertainment. Although they ostensibly promote a more universally available internet, the end of geoblocking discourses discussed here view the internet as a commercial space marked by what Cameran Ashraf and Luis Felipe Alvarez León (2016, 52) call a "binary open/closed model" that fails to recognize the internet for what it is: a heterogeneous set of networks and experiences functioning along a variety of different territorial logics. The end of geoblocking discourse views the internet as a store with "yes, we're open" and "sorry, we're closed" signs, with all the attendant implications of commerce and consumption.

Such ideas blend utopian rhetorics from two spheres often erroneously seen as distinct and counterpoised: the entertainment industry and the information technology industry. Indeed, Hastings begins his CES keynote by suggesting, "Entertainment and technology are continuing to transform each other as they have for the last 100 years," positioning the two as forces that are interacting but distinct rather than mutually constitutive. The end of geoblocking discourse blends neoimperialist desires of global market expansion with digital-libertarian dreams of universal accessibility, offering a consumerist twist on Stewart Brand's oft-quoted aphorism, "Information wants to be free." As Fred Turner (2006, 254) reminds us, however, Brand prefaced this statement with, "Information wants to be expensive because it is so valuable." The end of geoblocking discourses reflect a similar duality; these narratives rest on a vision of internet freedom while acknowledging the commercial logics of content value that have long structured digital entertainment accessibility. Given geoblocking's presence within the intertwined worlds of global entertainment and the digital economy, neither the commercial/creative and rights-based logics of global media distribution nor the information and infrastructure-dominated discourses of the global tech industry are sufficient on their own to make sense of it. Taken together, they illustrate how geoblocking and the collective hopes for its abolishment bind together the notions that the internet is a space for the commercialized promotion and circulation of creative material and a more personalized, ideally (to many) noncommercial space of information access. They also indicate how entertainment media distribution still does much to shape the internet's economic and cultural geography.

NOTE

1 Before this point, Netflix was already available in a number of regions around the world, having been introduced to Canada in 2010, to Latin America in 2011, and throughout parts of Europe, Asia, and Oceania in subsequent years. Hastings's announcement thus effectively promoted a once multiregional platform as a now-global one.

BIBLIOGRAPHY

Adalian, Josef. 2018. "Inside the Binge Factory." *Vulture*, June 10. www.vulture.com.

Anashkina, Anastasia, and Erica Fink. 2016. "Inside Netflix's Plan to Get the Entire World Watching." *CNN Money*, January 6. https://money.cnn.com.

Arnold, Sarah. 2016. "Netflix and the Myth of Choice/Participation/Autonomy." In *The Netflix Effect: Technology and Entertainment in the 21st Century*, edited by Kevin McDonald and Daniel Smith-Rowsey, 49–62. New York: Bloomsbury.

Ashraf, Cameran, and Luis Felipe Alvarez León. 2016. "The Logics and Territorialities of Geoblocking." In *Geoblocking and Global Video Culture*, edited by Ramon Lobato and James Meese, 42–53. Amsterdam: Institute of Network Cultures.

Burkart, Patrick. 2014. *Pirate Politics: The New Information Policy Contests*. Cambridge, MA: MIT Press.

Elkins, Evan. 2019. *Locked Out: Regional Restrictions in Digital Entertainment Culture*. New York: New York University Press.

European Commission. 2018. "Digital Single Market." https://ec.europa.eu.

———. 2019. "Geo-blocking." January 7. https://ec.europa.eu.

European Parliament. 2017. "Common Goals: Digital Single Market." YouTube, February 7. https://www.youtube.com/watch?v=_MO6nEd_Vqo.

Goldstein, Paul. 1994. *Copyright's Highway: From Gutenberg to the Celestial Jukebox*. New York: Hill & Wang.

Kassabian, Anahid. 2013. *Ubiquitous Listening: Affect, Attention, and Distributed Subjectivity*. Berkeley: University of California Press.

Levina, Marina, and Amy Adele Hasinoff. 2017. "The Silicon Valley Ethos: Tech Industry Products, Discourses, and Practices." *Television & New Media* 18 (6): 489–95. https://doi.org/10.1177/1527476416680454.

Lobato, Ramon. 2016. "Introduction: The New Video Geography." In *Geoblocking and Global Video Culture*, edited by Ramon Lobato and James Meese, 10–22. Amsterdam: Institute of Network Cultures.

———. 2019. *Netflix Nations: The Geography of Digital Distribution*. New York: New York University Press.

Lomas, Natasha. 2018. "At Last an End to Geoblocking in Europe? Nope, Not by a Long Chalk. . . ." *TechCrunch*, February 6. https://techcrunch.com.

Manjoo, Farhad. 2019. "Netflix Is the Most Intoxicating Portal to Planet Earth." *New York Times*, February 22. www.nytimes.com.

Morley, David, and Kevin Robins. 1995. *Spaces of Identity: Global Media, Electronic Landscapes, and Cultural Boundaries*. London: Routledge.

Reda, Julia. 2015. "'I Hate Geoblocking!' Says EU Commission VP Ansip." YouTube, March 26. https://www.youtube.com/watch?v=JCRG6BV0AYI.

———. 2018. "No, the EU Did Not Abolish Geoblocking Today." *Julia Reda*, February 6. https://juliareda.eu.

Roettgers, Janko. 2017. "How Netflix Wants to Rule the World: A Behind-the-Scenes Look at a Global TV Network." *Variety*, March 18. https://variety.com.

Sanson, Kevin, and Gregory Steirer. 2019. "Hulu, Streaming, and the Contemporary Television Ecosystem." *Media, Culture & Society* 41 (8): 1210–27. https://doi.org/10.1177/0163443718823144.

Stade, Philip. 2014. "'This Video Is Not Available in Germany': Online Discourses on the German Collecting Society GEMA and YouTube." *First Monday* 19 (10). https://doi.org/10.5210/fm.v19i10.5548.

Trimble, Marketa. 2016. "Geoblocking, Technical Standards and the Law." In *Geoblocking and Global Video Culture*, edited by Ramon Lobato and James Meese, 54–63. Amsterdam: Institute of Network Cultures.

Turner, Fred. 2006. *From Counterculture to Cyberculture: Stewart Brand, the Whole Earth Network, and the Rise of Digital Utopianism*. Chicago: University of Chicago Press.

Vonderau, Patrick. 2019. "The Spotify Effect: Digital Distribution and Financial Growth." *Television & New Media* 20 (1): 3–19. https://doi.org/10.1177/1527476417741200.

10

Global TV Markets and Digital Distribution

JOONSEOK CHOI

The recent emergence of streaming platforms has shaken the television business around the world. Their global scale, high-quality content, and sheer volume of audience data, enabled by digital distribution, have led to much contemplation and debate over the future of television. Speculation is rife that digital distribution is revolutionizing and disrupting not only the way we watch television, but the way television businesses operate (Alsin 2018).

Indeed, large streaming platforms (e.g., Netflix, Amazon, Facebook, and YouTube) are disrupting not only national television markets but also the structure of the global television trade, which has been sustained by the value chain from content producers and distributors to broadcasters and pay TV providers (Chalaby 2016). The relationships among businesspeople in these three segments have been produced, maintained, and reproduced via annual trade fairs, often called global television markets or global content markets. The markets are must-attend events for television businesspeople around the world, who gather to make sales, build social networks, gather information on new trends, and establish their identities (Havens 2006). They are crucial in forming a cohesive identity as a global television community and sharing knowledge of what can travel well around the world.

The streaming platforms are now threatening to disrupt this existing order in global television business. Their direct-to-consumer services via digital distribution demonstrate an alternative value chain that bypasses the traditional distribution route. By untethering themselves from the traditional structure of trade, such platforms cause the global television business community to be concerned that they may alter the need for the global television markets such as MIPTV and MIPCOM, which are "institutions of economic and cultural exchange in the creative industries" (Moeran and Pedersen 2011, 1). Can they survive in an era of digital distribution? How disruptive to the markets will digital distribution be?

Despite the power of Netflix and Amazon in the global television business, little is known about the impact of the new technology of digital distribution on global television markets and the community of television businesspeople. In this chapter, to answer the questions I have posed, I examine the global television business culture that shapes the value of digital distribution. Technology is malleable in that its form and function are shaped by not only materials but also discourses around how its value is imagined and reimagined in culture (Edwards 1996; Streeter 1996). In a Foucauldian sense, discourses produce realms of truth that reveal and conceal the possibilities and limitations of digital technology in the global trade of television. They make sense of the advent of new technologies relevant to the business. As such, I analyze discourses around the value of digital distribution in the global television business community.

In broad terms, two discourses exist at present. On the one hand, digital distribution is being imagined as a new architecture for a television system that can connect directly to a global audience as opposed to an assemblage of national audiences. The new architecture promises to help producers and creators by providing them with more creative freedom and a better understanding of their audience. At the same time, however, access to digital distribution is limited to a select few large streaming platforms, which are the main producers of this discourse.

On the other hand, digital distribution is imagined as an extension of traditional broadcast networks, as just another add-on to the existing structure of global television. Therefore, the existing structure of the trade, which is based on territories, remains. Moreover, this discourse reclaims the cohesion of a global television business community whose players cooperate with each other. This in turn reaffirms the role of distributors as not only sellers and buyers of television commodities but also creators of global television. The major actors in the production of this discourse are large distributors.

In this chapter, based on my visits to Marché International des Programmes de Télévision (MIPTV) and Marché International des Films et des Programmes pour la Télévision, la Vidéo, le Câble et le Satellite

(MIPCOM) and my readings of market publications and trade journal articles, I argue that digital distribution cannot simply replace global television markets. A resistance against streaming platforms is evident from the existing structure of trade—particularly that of distributors. More importantly, the two discourses are battling one another in the global television markets to shape the value of digital distribution. In this chapter, I first explain what global television markets are and do. I then discuss some aspects of digital disruption. Next, I analyze the two discourses that are produced and supported by large streaming platforms and large distributors. In the conclusion, I draw some implications regarding this discursive struggle.

Global Television Markets

Global television markets are among the major institutions to have supported the distribution of television commodities—both finished television programs and television formats—around the world. There are three major global television markets: MIPTV, MIPCOM, and the National Association of Television Programming Executives (NATPE) (Bielby and Harrington 2008; Havens 2006). Although MIPTV, MIP-COM, and NATPE are often called markets, they differ from regular markets in which sellers and buyers exchange goods and services based on prices. They more closely resemble trade fairs, which appear in the form of temporary townships or cities that "in social and symbolic ways contribute to the global needs of a particular industry and those who work therein" (Moeran and Pedersen 2011, 8).

Global television markets are annual events, running for three or four days each, in tourist destinations such as the French Riviera or Miami Beach. NAPTE is a January event that takes place in Miami. MIPTV is an April event and MIPCOM an October event, both held in Cannes, France. They are events for members of the global television business community, including creators, producers, distributors, broadcasters, advertisers, technology manufacturers, journalists, and so on, but are not open to the general public.

These events serve multiple functions. One primary function is to provide participants with space and time for networking. Creators, producers, distributors, broadcasters, advertisers, technology manufacturers, and journalists from various countries attend the markets to forge business relationships, which are an important part of the decision-making process during and after the events. One experienced buyer told me that the markets are all about building and renewing relationships with fellow participants. Another function is to provide conference sessions at which industry leaders discuss new, cutting-edge trends and technologies. Each session has its own specific topic (e.g., over-the-top services, new content, coproduction, acquisition). For example, at MIPCOM 2017, I attended a conference session titled "Beyond Coproduction: Making Global Creative Connections." In an auditorium, four industry experts and one moderator held a panel discussion on the strategy of coproduction, offering their experiences and thoughts on the topic. In addition, the markets provide exhibitors with floor space to set up booths where sellers and buyers meet and make sales and coproduction deals. Through the booths, exhibitors establish their brands and articulate their differences from competitors (Havens 2006).

The global television markets allow participants to think of themselves as parts of a cohesive global business community of television through networking, conference sessions, and meetings on exhibition floors. The community shares discourses of knowing which commodity is more valuable than another and how to add more cultural values to television products and creative projects to produce more economic values. The discourses produce conventional knowledge and practices that guide the participants to understand the highly uncertain and complex process of exchanging the cultural values of television for economic values.

Discourses in global television markets are supported and used strategically by institutions. Large distributors, such as the distribution arms of the major Hollywood studios (e.g., NBCUniversal International Television) and international TV production groups (e.g., Endemol Shine Group), have long been the most responsible for producing and reproducing conventional knowledge and practices in the markets. They have been the leaders of the global television business because they have not only the financial power but also the knowledge to connect producers and broadcasters around the world. Distributors' discourses, shared by the global television community, have been the guidance allowing market participants to discover global taste and, therefore, economic value.

However, this conventional knowledge is being disrupted by the emergence of streaming platforms. Major players in this area, such as Netflix and Amazon, use a different kind of discourse about how television commodities and creative projects can be digitally distributed to bypass traditional distributors and global television markets. The concern emerges as to whether digital distribution can possibly render the distributors and markets obsolete.

Digital Disruption

The emergence of the streaming platforms disrupts conventional knowledge and practices that have been orchestrated by distributors. Instead of relying on traditional distributors, platforms have introduced a new logic of doing television business via their direct-to-consumer services (Burroughs 2019).

It is well known that streaming platforms use their algorithms to better understand and target audiences. Via digital distribution powered by algorithms and big data analysis, they accumulate data on audiences' engagement with programs. As Ted Sarandos, chief content officer of Netflix, claimed, the platform has "insight into every second of the viewing experience" (Curtin, Holt, and Sanson 2014, 136).

The power of algorithms—which are essentially rearticulated audience data—is influencing traditional media conglomerates and television players. Dominique Delport, then president of Vivendi Content, claimed in MIPCOM 2017's keynote speech that the global television business is experiencing a shift in the way of reaching audiences from managing media content to assembling different data about individual audience members' identities, values, and behaviors. Delport urged media corporations to understand and master algorithms and data analysis to adapt to the shifting television ecologies. The traditional day-to-day activity of television business, which consists primarily of meeting people and creating stories, is being pressured to transform into the collection and analysis of data.

In addition, by expanding their services to multiple countries, streaming platforms are disrupting the traditional strategy of windowing, "the process of managing the release sequence for content so as to maximize the returns from intellectual property rights" (Doyle 2016,

629). The traditional strategy of windowing has been characterized by "neatly delineated territorial and time segments" (641). However, these platforms can distribute television programs to a large number of audiences in various countries with no temporally delayed windows. For example, Netflix reaches 125 million subscribers in all countries except China, Crimea, North Korea, and Syria (Usborne 2018). Amazon has 100 million subscribers for its Amazon Prime service (Spangler 2019a). Digital distribution forces the television business community to rethink its windowing strategies.

Streaming platforms are also galvanizing producers and creators because they are spending billions of dollars to acquire content for their catalogues; their budgets, too, are increasing. Netflix spent $12.04 billion on content in 2018 and planned to spend $15 billion in 2019 (Spangler 2019b). Amazon was also expected to spend $5 billion in 2018 and $7 billion in 2019 (Roettgers 2019; Weprin 2018). Apple was also willing to spend $6 billion in 2019, a massive increase from $1 billion in 2017 (Nicolaou and Bradshaw 2019). In addition, YouTube and Facebook were willing to spend millions of dollars on dramas and short-form content in 2017 (Sandberg and Rose 2017). Given that Disney, the biggest spender, expected to spend $16.4 billion in 2019 on content, excluding sports-related properties (Littleton 2019), streaming platforms—Netflix in particular—are attracting the attention of producers and creators from around the world.

Although digital distribution through streaming platforms is disrupting the television industries, little is known about how such platforms are upsetting global television markets. All we have are concerns and speculations that digital distribution may make global television markets obsolete because it can replace distributors who have played a central role in disseminating television programs and creative projects through the markets.

However, in the following analyses, I find that the markets will retain their position for the foreseeable future because distributors are striving to demonstrate that they are not obsolete and that they are, and will be, an important segment of the global television business that links producers and creators with broadcasters and pay TV providers. To do so, they are attempting to reshape the value of digital distribution against streaming platforms that also participate in the markets to construct new perceptions on the global television business. Global television marketplaces have become a battleground where discourses around digital distribution are struggling to shape its value.

Constructing Digital Distribution: Streaming Platforms

The entrance of streaming platforms into global television markets began in 2014, when Ted Sarandos of Netflix participated in MIPCOM. However, these platforms do not engage in buying television programs in the markets; instead, they participate in the markets to reshape the distribution of global television. They are demonstrating that they are not simply tech companies but also global television corporations similar to but better than traditional distributors, broadcasters, and networks. They are building legitimacy as television players. At the same time, they are articulating their difference from the traditional movers by constructing digital distribution as an enabler of a new architecture of television. They are making this distribution desirable by creating scarcity of access to the new architecture through restricting producers and creators in the markets.

Executives—often heads of global television divisions—participate in market events as keynote speakers. In the "Media Mastermind Keynotes" series at MIPTV and MIPCOM, one executive and one interviewer conducted a thirty-minute interview in the largest auditorium of the main building, the Palais des Festivals. They shared stories of their success and visions for global television. They also announced the latest developments in their creative projects and business plans. Interviewers asked the executives what they sought in the marketplaces on behalf of producers and distributors.

Since 2014, streaming platforms have sent their executives to appear as keynote speakers. For example, Netflix, Hulu, YouTube, Amazon, Facebook, and Snapchat sent their heads of content to MIPTV, MIPCOM, and NATPE. This signaled a departure from past practices, as the keynote series had long been occupied by representatives from traditional players, such as NBCUniversal, Endemol Shine Group, and the BBC. By standing onstage in front of the global television business community, executives from the streaming platforms have established both their identity as part of the community and their leadership in the business. These large streaming platforms, however, imagine digital distribution not as a technological tool for distribution but as a new architecture of television with different governing rules, with audience data collected via digital distribution becoming central to the value of television commodities. For instance, when asked whether the value of television lies in the copyright or in the consumer experience, Sarandos acknowledged that "there's an underlying asset value in the copyright," but emphasized that Netflix tries to "focus on what the consumer value is" (Sarandos 2014). Roy Price (2017), then vice president of Amazon Studios, echoed Sarandos by saying he paid attention to the audience's engagement with shows and its influence on subscriptions.

These streaming platforms express their willingness to share massive audience data with producers and creators to tell better stories and therefore add more value to their commodities. At MIPCOM 2017, when Snapchat announced the launch of a digital studio with NBCUniversal, NBC Entertainment's senior vice president of prime-time programming, Lauren Anderson, expressed her excitement over using data, finding patterns, and shaping ideas and stories (Mills 2017). The platforms' algorithms and audience data equate to ways of reducing risk and uncertainty in the business. According to Tom Wright, CEO of Vertical Networks, which has produced content for Facebook and Snapchat, digital distribution is a new architecture where creators "can have the discipline of refine and optimize [creative works] based on [the platforms'] metrics" (mipmarkets 2018b). Optimization in telling stories is the central idea in the discourse of digital distribution.

Second, the executives emphasized that their platforms are the best way to connect with *global* audiences. Ricky van Veen, head of global creative strategy at Facebook, proudly said that Facebook Watch, Facebook's video platform, has the potential to create a global show to reach an audience of two billion (van Veen and Danker 2017). Susanne Daniels of YouTube also emphasized the platform's "global community" to which producers and creators can connect (mipmarkets 2016). Needless to say, Netflix and Amazon have also articulated their global connection with the audience.

Discourses of "global show," "global community," and "global connection" serve two functions. On the one hand, they are useful to craft the streaming platforms' corporate identities as global brands, demonstrating their capacity to "brand program content at the broadest possible level" (Havens 2018, 321). This branding strategy, as Havens argues, can be understood as an extension of the branding strategy that has been used by television networks. It allows the streaming platforms to function as networks and to build legitimacy as television players in the global television business community.

On the other hand, these executives used the term "global" without referencing specific national television markets, distinguishing themselves from traditional distributors whose use of the term "global" has always had the sense of "multinational." The streaming platforms imagine digital distribution as a global architecture free from the constraints imposed by national television markets. For example, the streaming platforms do not have set rules for the length, time slot, geographical characteristics, and language of a show. Producers and creators need only to concentrate on their best stories that induce engagement and attract more subscribers. As one producer said at a conference, working with streaming platforms requires a different mind-set (mipmarkets 2018b).

Executives from the large streaming platforms at the global television markets imagine digital distribution as a new architecture with which producers and creators can tell a better story for a larger audience. Their participation in the markets is aimed at building legitimacy and articulating the capability of digital distribution for the global television business. What is threatening to traditional distributors is more than the encroachment of the platforms on their positions in the markets. The real problem of digital distribution is that the streaming platforms use the technology as leverage to create another kind of distribution that does not depend on traditional distributors and marketplaces.

While streaming platforms have been working to articulate digital distribution as a new architecture via the presence of executives and their speeches at the conferences of global television markets, a companion discourse has also developed on the sales floors of these markets. These large platforms are molding the new architecture enabled by digital distribution as a prestigious institution to which access is restricted. Buyers from the large platforms are abandoning the sales floor for private meetings while still maintaining their presence in the markets. Havens (2011, 152) described this particular strategy, which major Hollywood studios used in the early 2000s, as "absent presence." Streaming platforms are the inheritors of this strategy but use it in a slightly different way.

Most of the large platforms sent teams of buyers to the marketplaces. Table 10.1 shows the number of buyers who were present at MIPCOM 2017. The numbers of buyers, especially those from Amazon and Netflix, were comparable to those from other major players such as the BBC, NBCUniversal, and Endemol Shine Group, which respectively sent forty, twenty, and thirteen buyers to MIPCOM 2017. Facebook, Hulu, and YouTube, although sending fewer delegates than Amazon and Netflix, nevertheless were represented by sizable teams of buyers at the marketplace. By sending such teams, digital players marked their presence as well as their willingness to spend money in the markets.

TABLE 10.1. Number of Buyers from Large Streaming Platforms at MIPCOM 2017

Large Streaming Platforms	Number of Buyers at MIPCOM 2017
Amazon	64
Netflix	23
Facebook	9
Hulu	7
YouTube	5
Apple	1

Source: MIPCOM (2017).

However, despite the numbers present on the sales floors, these buyers were not available to all market participants. They were "absent" from the sales floors except at arranged meetings. Amazon, Facebook, Hulu, YouTube, and Apple, for example, did not place their booths on the sales floors at MIPCOM 2017. In fact, as buyers, they did not need booths. Netflix, on the contrary, had its office on the fourth floor of the Palais and a small booth called the Waiting Lounge on the main floor at MIPCOM 2017. The presence of the booth was subdued, being located at the far end of the main floor next to the large and extravagant stands of other companies such as Turner, Dick Clark Productions, and Pokémon. In contrast to the extravagant decorations of other corporations, Netflix's booth simply had the red letter "N" as an identifier of the company. Its office on the fourth floor, meanwhile, was accessed by a small eleva-

Figure 10.1. Netflix's Office on Floor 4 of the Palais. Source: Photo by the author.

tor. It was almost isolated from the rest of the marketplace. The space was quite small compared to those of other large distributors, broadcasters, and networks. In addition, Netflix did not decorate the office; no posters, promos, giveaways, or shiny logos were present. The company used a room and a terrace only to have conversations with its partners. However, as with other large players in the markets, access to the Netflix office was controlled by a receptionist who managed meetings. By having a gatekeeper to the office, Netflix signaled to market participants that only a select few were allowed access to its digital distribution. Restricting access in the marketplaces is a strategy that adds value to the commodity by creating scarcity (Havens 2006). It is a strategy of creating temporal scarcity (i.e., by means of formulations such as "our schedules are already packed with meetings") to demonstrate that many producers and creators desire meetings with the streaming platforms for access to digital distribution even before the marketplaces open.

Netflix's restrictive access is hardly different from the methods that traditional distributors have used. However, what marks out Netflix's strategy is its *inaccessibility* during the marketplaces. While MIPCOM 2017 was running, I learned that Netflix had meetings only with producers and creators with whom they already had business relationships. The purpose of participating in the marketplace was not to buy third-party products or to make new partnerships but to maintain existing relationships and develop projects. Acquisitions of third-party programs, instead, are handled by the company's Los Angeles office (Ravindran 2018). While talking to the receptionist, I witnessed an Italian producer who was eager to make an appointment with a delegate of Netflix but came away from the reception desk disappointed. One Spanish independent producer whom I met also described the difficulty of making an appointment with Netflix at MIPCOM 2017.

This inaccessibility shows that Netflix is not interested in buying projects that have been "shopped around" (mipmarkets 2018b); instead, the company hopes that the best original projects will come to its office in Los Angeles first. As such, scarcity of access can encourage more competition among producers and creators, which in turn can lead to the enhancement of the quality of creative ideas and programs in the input pools of streaming platforms. In a market of overabundance, particularly as a result of the creative freedom promised by the streaming platforms, the quality of projects cannot be guaranteed. Scarcity of access, then, is a strategy of quality management.

The "absent presence" of large streaming platforms in global television markets is a way of discursively shaping digital distribution as a valuable infrastructure. However, their inaccessibility to creative ideas and third-party programs in the marketplaces shows a desire to become "quality television" independently of the existing distribution through markets. The platforms are trying to reshape the global television business culture by taking the best ideas and television programs out of the markets and into this new exclusive architecture and leaving the leftovers for traditional distributors, broadcasters, and networks.

Reshaping Digital Distribution: Distributors

The separation of digital distribution from the existing world of television is a threat to the distributors who have reigned over global markets. In fact, at MIPCOM 2017, at an acquisition panel discussion, broadcasters and networks expressed their frustration over shows they had expected to see in the market disappearing into the hands of large streaming platforms, which often require worldwide rights from producers and creators to control exclusive rights to distribute content (Clarke

2018a). Maybe unsurprisingly therefore, inside and outside global television markets an important topic of conversation is the obsolescence of traditional distribution. To demonstrate that traditional distribution is not obsolete, large distributors are developing discursive strategies to rearticulate the value of digital distribution. First, they demystify the word "digital" by arguing digital distribution is merely a delivery system. Second, they reimagine digital distribution as an extension of the existing structure of broadcasting systems in nation-states. Distributors are attempting to reproduce a coherent mentality for the global television business community and to reaffirm the roles of distributors and markets in the global television trade.

The demystification of digital began in the conference sessions of the markets. In sessions covering the state of distribution in a digital era, distributors rejected the notion that digital distribution would replace the markets. In a conference session at MIPTV 2018 titled "Just How Disrupted Is the Distribution Game?" the conversation began with a thesis—independent distribution is dead—a view meant to be rejected by the distributors on the panel. In another conference session at MIP-COM 2018 titled "Disrupting Distribution: Welcome to the Shakeout," the moderator explicitly said, "We're going to try to kill the word '[digital] disruption'" (mipmarkets 2018a). Distributors insisted on the absurdity of the idea of digital disruption by arguing that it is merely a form of delivery rather than a value that can be produced and exchanged. They emphasized that value in the global television business is based on intellectual property (IP) rights and that the management of such rights is the backbone of the television trade. Because they are the experts in managing rights, they showed confidence in their roles and the existing structure of the global television trade.

Some of the most active and vocal players in reshaping digital distribution and reproducing the global television business community are international TV production groups (Esser 2016). Such groups are sometimes called international TV production supergroups (Chalaby 2012) or mini-major companies (Moran 2013). Such a production group is composed of a headquarters, local production houses in multiple territories, and a distribution arm. For example, the Endemol Shine Group (2019) operates 120 production companies in twenty-three countries. Such groups are often categorized as producer-distributors.

These groups are heavily involved in producing, coproducing, and licensing local versions of their formats in multiple national television markets. Their business model is dependent on the performance of these versions in multiple territories. The value of IPs can grow if a local version performs well in one territory, resulting in the licensing of another version in another territory. The repeatability of a format property in multiple territories provides buyers with more certainty of success in their own national television markets. Therefore, for the production groups, the central focus of this business model is to maintain repeatability via territory-by-territory distribution of formats without overselling them (Bylykbashi 2018).

From the perspective of international TV production groups, the model of acquiring global rights used by the large streaming platforms is simply incompatible with the television format business. Compared to the territory-by-territory model, selling global rights for formats to streaming platforms would reduce the economic value of these properties, while also losing control over IP. Stephen Lambert, CEO of Studio Lambert, owned by international TV production group All3Media, argued that selling global rights to the large streaming platforms would mean a "work-for-hire" model (Waller 2017). Therefore, executives of the production groups, such as Cathy Payne, CEO of Endemol Shine International, strongly argued that digital disruption is a mirage that cannot fundamentally change the fact that broadcasters and networks in national and regional television markets are here to stay (Fry 2019).

In the format conference sessions titled "Will Digital Save Formats?" (MIPFormats 2016, 2017, 2018), discussions were ongoing between the two parties to develop a new hybrid model for the format trade, yet reconciliation seemed elusive. Even in a recent deal between Netflix and Voltage TV to localize *The Big Family Cooking Showdown* (2017–) for various national television markets, Creative Artists Agency (CAA), an American talent agency rather than an international TV production group was involved in the distribution.

In addition to the demystification of digital, international TV production groups and other distributors are striving to dissociate digital distribution from the discourse of global connection. They point out that the majority of digital players are actually digital extensions of national broadcasters. In fact, digital buyers attending the markets are not just from Netflix, Amazon, Apple, Facebook, YouTube, or Snapchat, but from various countries, with their numbers increasing (table 10.2). Broadly speaking, there are two kinds of national and regional digital platforms. One is a homegrown digital player. For example, China's Tencent and Mexico's Claro Video are subscription video-on-demand (SVOD) services that compete against Netflix and Amazon and have participated as buyers in the global television markets since 2017 (Clarke 2018a). Other types of digital player entering the markets, however, are online extensions of the services provided by national or regional broadcasters and networks. CBS All Access, Channel 4's All4 service in the United Kingdom, and Globo's Globoplay in Brazil, for example, seek content for their national markets in addition to supplying for their catch-up services (Clarke 2018a). Regional players such as Hooq for Southeast Asia and India and Viaplay for the Nordic region also seek content that works specifically for their regional markets (Clarke 2018a). BritBox, a joint venture between the BBC and ITV for the North American region, participated in the markets to buy more English-language programs. Starz attended MIPCOM 2018 to buy programs for its regional streaming services, which still need more content other than popular programs such as *Outlander* (2014–) and *Power* (2014–) (Littleton 2018).

TABLE 10.2. Number of Digital Buyers at MIPCOM 2015–18

	Number of Digital Buyers / All Buyers	Percentage
2015	1,375 / 4,700	29.26
2016	1,500 / 4,900	30.06
2017	1,760 / 4,700	37.45
2018	1,800 / 4,800	37.50

Sources: Clarke (2018a), Hopewell (2015), Hopewell and Keslassy (2016), MIPCOM (2018).

Fremantle, an international TV production group, has demonstrated how to use large streaming platforms as a secondary domestic window. For example, instead of selling global rights to the platforms, Fremantle licensed Netflix and Amazon to stream *America's Got Talent* and *American Idol*, respectively, in the United Kingdom (Clarke 2018a, 2018b). In these deals, Netflix and Amazon could stream the television programs only two days after the shows aired on NBC and ABC in the United States. By apportioning rights in this way, Fremantle divided the streaming platforms in order to fit its territory-based business model. Distributors therefore point out that national and regional deals, involving the broadcasters and networks with which they have preexisting relationships, still account for the majority of the television trade. Although distributors feel the need to be more agile in searching for creative projects and more flexible in acquiring funding sources to support them, they argue that the fundamentals of the television business have remained the same, for their day-to-day business activity has not radically changed. They point out that the best practices remain acquainting themselves with national television markets by going to the relevant countries, attending global television markets, building strong relationships via face-to-face interactions, negotiating the values of television commodities, and managing their IPs (mipmarkets 2018c).

To deal with disruption, distributors have contained digital distribution both economically and discursively within specific geographical territories. Economically, they refuse to sell global rights to streaming platforms because territory-by-territory sales are the way to add value to their properties. As Fremantle showed, selling territory rights to the platforms is viable. Discursively, they simplify the cognitive map of market participants by defining digital players as mere extensions of existing broadcasters and networks. By doing so, they can reduce the complexity of the dynamics in the market and maintain the global television business community and its business culture.

Conclusion

This chapter has demonstrated the impact of digital distribution on the global television markets. Rather than assuming that streaming platforms are an agent of revolution in the global television business, I examined how various discourses on digital distribution within the global television business community are struggling to shape and reshape digital distribution in the marketplaces. The main players in this struggle are large streaming platforms and international TV production groups.

Streaming platforms emphasize that the value of digital distribution resides in the ability to reach a global audience as well as increasing the efficiency of telling stories by using massive audience data and providing more creative freedom for producers and creators. At the same time, however, to ensure the quality of creative projects in their input pools, platforms signal to producers and creators that access to their systems is a scarce commodity. They are attempting to establish a prestigious reputation for the new architecture of the global television system that they promote. Distributors, on the other hand, emphasize that digital distribution is nothing but a delivery system, which does not produce any independent value for the global television business. Instead, distributors, particularly international TV production groups, argue IP rights remain the key source of value, particularly the repetition of IP through production of local versions of formats for national television markets. By encouraging the view that digital players are national and regional players, distributors redefine digital distribution as merely an extension of the existing structure of the television trade, thereby reducing the complexity of dynamics in the digital market by claiming nothing has really changed.

By examining the discourses on digital distribution at work in the global television markets, in this chapter I have shown that global television distribution is not determined by technological change alone. Distribution is more than the technological delivery of media; it is also a cultural process supported by institutional discourses. The struggle between the discourses promoted respectively by the platforms and the distributors shows that it is important to understand how businesspeople imagine the possibilities and limitations of digital distribution. How they imagine and communicate their visions of technology will determine their business relationships, their creative ideas, and the form and content of the television programs they circulate around the world.

I would also like to emphasize that global television markets are an excellent object for studying distribution of television especially in the years to come as we witness the expansion of numerous streaming platforms (e.g., Disney+ and HBO Max) and the growing complexity of distribution of television. Influenced by Moeran's (2011) attention to trade fairs, studies of the television markets can make the changing distribution landscape of digital television more visible, providing a point of focus through which to see how the desire for order is being envisaged and articulated within the global television business community.

BIBLIOGRAPHY

Alsin, Arne. 2018. "The Future of Media: Disruptions, Revolutions and the Quest for Distribution." *Forbes*, July 19. www.forbes.com.

Bielby, Denise D., and C. Lee Harrington. 2008. *Global TV: Exporting Television and Culture in the World Market*. New York: New York University Press.

Burroughs, Benjamin. 2019. "House of Netflix: Streaming Media and Digital Lore." *Popular Communication* 17 (1): 1–17. https://doi.org/10.1080/15405702.2017.1343948.

Bylykbashi, Kaltrina. 2018. "TBI Distributors Survey 2018: Part Two." *Television Business International*, October 15. https://tbivision.com.

Chalaby, Jean K. 2012. "Producing TV Content in a Globalized Intellectual Property Market: The Emergence of the International Production Model." *Journal of Media Business Studies* 9 (3): 19–39. https://doi.org/10.1080/16522354.2012.11073550.

———. 2016. "Television and Globalization: The TV Content Global Value Chain." *Journal of Communication* 66 (1): 35–59. https://doi.org/10.1111/jcom.12203.

Clarke, Stewart. 2018a. "Why So Many at Mipcom Are Shifting Focus to Streaming." *Variety*, October 10. https://variety.com.

———. 2018b. "Netflix Lands 'America's Got Talent' for the U.K." *Variety*, June 1. https://variety.com.

Curtin, Michael, Jennifer Holt, and Kevin Sanson. 2014. *Distribution Revolution: Conversations about the Digital Future of Film and Television*. Oakland: University of California Press.

Doyle, Gillian. 2016. "Digitization and Changing Windowing Strategies in the Television Industry: Negotiating New Windows on the World." *Television & New Media* 17 (7): 629–45. https://doi.org/10.1177/1527476416641194.

Edwards, Paul N. 1996. *The Closed World: Computers and the Politics of Discourse in Cold War America*. Cambridge, MA: MIT Press.

Endemol Shine Group. 2019. "Who We Are." www.endemolshinegroup.com.

Esser, Andrea. 2016. "Challenging U.S. Leadership in Entertainment Television? The Rise and Sale of Europe's International TV Production Groups." *International Journal of Communication* 10:3585–614.

Fry, Andy. 2019. "Who Needs Distributors? Roadmaps for the Streaming Offensive—Endemol Shine's Cathy Payne." *MIPTrends*, September 6. https://mipblog.com.

Havens, Timothy. 2006. *Global Television Marketplace*. London: British Film Institute.

———. 2011. "Inventing Universal Television: Restricted Access, Promotional Extravagance, and the Distribution of Value at Global Television Markets." In *Negotiating Values in the Creative Industries: Fairs, Festivals and Competitive Events*, edited by Brian Moeran and Jesper Strandgaard Pedersen, 145–68. Cambridge: Cambridge University Press.

———. 2018. "Netflix: Streaming Channel Brands as Global Meaning System." In *From Networks to Netflix*, edited by Derek Johnson, 321–31. New York: Routledge.

Hopewell, John. 2015. "Mipcom: Hot Titles, Booming Biz Add Sizzle to Market Despite Weather Woes." *Variety*, October 4. https://variety.com.

Hopewell, John, and Elsa Keslassy. 2016. "Drama, Local Business, Digital, Women's Empowerment, Energize Mipcom 2016." *Variety*, October 20. https://variety.com.

Littleton, Cynthia. 2018. "International Broadcasters Plan Netflix Counterattack." *Variety*, October 25. https://variety.com.

———. 2019. "A Stream of Questions." *Variety*, January 29. https://variety.com.

Mills, Sean. 2017. "Media Mastermind Keynote." In *MIPCOM*, edited by Kate Bulkley. Take 1 Transcription. www.miptrends.com.

MIPCOM. 2017. "Full List of Buyers MIPCOM 2017." www.my-mip.com.

———. 2018. "Overview of MIPCOM." www.mipcom.com.

MIPFormats. 2016. "Conferences & Events Programme." Boulogne-Billancourt: Reed MIDEM.

———. 2017. "Conference Programme." Boulogne-Billancourt: Reed MIDEM.

———. 2018. "Conference Programme." Boulogne-Billancourt: Reed MIDEM.

mipmarkets. 2016. "Keynote: Susanne Daniels, YouTube, with Rooster Teeth & Lionsgate—MIPCOM 2016." YouTube, October 17. https://www.youtube.com/watch?v=s3CjaQvmlIw.

———. 2018a. "Disrupting Distribution: Welcome to the Shakeout—MIPCOM 2018." YouTube, November 16. https://www.youtube.com/watch?v=y8akbCkzYA8.

———. 2018b. "FAANGS: How to Work with the New Players—MIPFormats 2018." YouTube, September 5. https://www.youtube.com/watch?v=UUx3MJZWpI8&feature=emb_logo.

———. 2018c. "Just How Disrupted Is the Distribution Game? MIPFormats 2018." YouTube, April 10. https://www.youtube.com/watch?time_continue=4&v=7Lsboko_4Go&feature=emb_logo.

Moeran, Brian. 2011. "Trade Fairs, Markets and Fields: Framing Imagined as Real Communities." *Historical Social Research* 36 (3): 79–98.

Moeran, Brian, and Jesper Strandgaard Pedersen. 2011. "Introduction." In *Negotiating Values in the Creative Industries: Faris, Festivals and Competitive Events*, edited by Brian Moeran and Jesper Strandgaard Pedersen, 1–35. Cambridge: Cambridge University Press.

Moran, Albert. 2013. "Global Television Formats: Genesis and Growth." *Critical Studies in Television* 8 (2): 1–19. https://doi.org/10.7227/CST.8.2.2.

Nicolaou, Anna, and Tim Bradshaw. 2019. "Apple Splashes $6bn on New Shows in Streaming Wars." *Financial Times*, August 19. www.ft.com.

Price, Roy. 2017. "Media Mastermind Keynotes." In *MIPTV*, edited by Scott Roxborough. Take 1 Transcription. www.miptrends.com.

Ravindran, Manori. 2018. "MIPCOM 2018: The Inside Scoop." *Television Business International*, October 19. https://tbivision.com.

Roettgers, Janko. 2019. "Amazon Spent $1.7 Billion on Content in Q1, but Original Video Investments Still Unknown." *Variety*, April 26. https://variety.com.

Roxborough, Scott. 2018. "Amazon Prime Takes 'American Idol' in U.K. in Landmark Deal." *Hollywood Reporter*, March 15. www.hollywoodreporter.com.

Sandberg, Bryn Elise, and Lacey Rose. 2017. "A Seller's Guide to the Streaming Universe." *Hollywood Reporter*, October 4. www.hollywoodreporter.com.

Sarandos, Ted. 2014. "Media Mastermind Keynote." In *MIPCOM*, edited by Eric Scherer. Take 1 Transcription. www.my-mip.com.

Spangler, Todd. 2019a. "Amazon Has More Than 100 Million Prime Subscribers, Jeff Bezos Discloses." *Variety*, April 18. https://variety.com.

———. 2019b. "Netflix Spent $12 Billion on Content in 2018. Analysts Expect That to Grow to $15 Billion This Year." *Variety*, January 18. https://variety.com.

Streeter, Thomas. 1996. *Selling the Air: A Critique of the Policy of Commercial Broadcasting in the United States*. Chicago: University of Chicago Press.

Usborne, Simon. 2018. "Netflix's 'New World Order': A Streaming Giant on the Brink of Global Domination." *Guardian*, April 17. www.theguardian.com.

van Veen, Ricky, and Daniel Danker. 2017. "Media Mastermind Keynotes." In *MIPCOM*, edited by Marjorie Paillon. Take 1 Transcription. www.miptrends.com.

Waller, Ed. 2017. "SVOD Takes Spotlight." *C21*, April 3. www.c21media.net.

Weprin, Alex. 2018. "Amazon Expected to Spend $5 Billion on Video Content This Year." *Mediapost*, February 23. www.mediapost.com.

White, Peter. 2017. "Netflix Inks UK Format Deal." *Broadcast*, September 28. www.broadcastnow.co.uk.

11

Children's Television in an Era of Digital Distribution

Arab and European Responses

NAOMI SAKR AND JEANETTE STEEMERS

The ubiquity of digital distribution makes the very idea of children's "television" seem almost antiquated, particularly when we are repeatedly told that children are deserting television for on-demand entertainment, distributed globally online. Yet the truth is more nuanced, not least because of inequalities in distribution and the policy and industry contexts that shape these inequalities. As Evans and colleagues (2016, 410–11) indicate, digital distribution is shaped not only by "differences in network coverage, broadband access and speed, levels of device ownership, corporate strategies and IT internet policy or media regulation," but also by disparities in wealth between the Global North and Global South, different social, cultural, and political contexts, and the degree to which governments either promote or hinder new developments. These inequalities are evident in what gets distributed, and by whom, and are also reflected in children's different experiences of content in different geographical settings (Steemers, Sakr, and Singer 2018). Industry stakeholders frequently focus on the liberating potential for children of new forms of digital distribution, which afford children opportunities to participate on their own terms, including as producers. In the words of the last Children's Global Media Summit held in Manchester in 2017, digital distribution opens up "a digital world without limits or end, an unlimited resource with unlimited possibilities for the unlimited generation" (Children's Global Media Summit 2017, 2). Yet this stance ignores evidence, which suggests that many children do not enjoy unfettered access to global distribution networks created by YouTube, subscription video-on-demand (SVOD), and social media, for various reasons including inability to pay or lack of access where they live.

In light of these disparities, does the new distribution landscape change everything in the children's television market, or are there fundamental continuities? This chapter addresses this question, drawing evidence from multilingual Europe, with its tradition of public service broadcasting (PSB), and the Arab region, where a shared language opens up a regionwide market, but where PSB provision is nonexistent. Comparing distribution in Europe and the Arab world provides insight into rarely researched children's content distribution as well as alternatives to North American distribution practices in those parts of the world where children have limited access to smartphones, tablets, and social media (Lemish 2019, 119–20).

The chapter compares levels of change and continuity along three axes: the particularities of regional markets including audience size, connectivity levels, and changes in how children's screen content is consumed; the challenge posed by platform convergence and the rise of YouTube, and how broadcasters and pay TV operators are responding to shifts in children's media use; and the impact of these responses on rights procurement, which are fundamental for distribution but also have implications for production. It concentrates on distribution directed by industry and tied to professionally produced content *for* children rather than production *by* children, which may be circulated more informally. It focuses predominantly on distribution as an industry activity involving new and old infrastructures, services, and formats, as it delivers television content through TV channels, subscription TV services provided by cable, satellite, and telecoms operators, as well as online on-demand services such as Netflix (see Johnson 2019, 28; Lotz 2014, 113). Linked to this is a second definition that refers to the "sale" or "licensing" of content rights by rights owners to channel and service providers (Steemers 2014). Analyzing change and continuity along these three axes provides insights into how digital distribution complicates the creation and circulation of children's TV outside the United States because of shifts in the way that rights are sold and exploited, based on platform and territory (Steemers 2016; Lobato 2019).

Regional Contexts in the Market for Children's Screen Content

Distribution of children's content in European and Arab markets is undoubtedly affected by regional particularities. One thing both have in common is the overwhelming prevalence of imported animation, chiefly from the United States but also from Europe and Asia (D'Arma and Steemers 2012; Awan and Steemers 2017). Yet the number of children's channels varies hugely. In a 2017 Council of Europe audit, 329 children's channels were counted across 40 European countries belonging to 127 networks (Ene 2017, 8 and 20). Of these, 69 percent were multiple language channel versions of U.S. transnational operators—including Disney, Viacom, WarnerMedia, and AMC Networks (24), accounting for 60 percent of European children's channel ratings in 2017 (9). National PSB children's channels in Europe accounted for only 6 percent of the total (24) but are often among the top performing channels in their markets. In a few cases U.S. companies have established new channel brands in collaboration with European partners—including Boing (available since 2004 in Italy and later Spain as a joint venture between WarnerMedia and Italian conglomerate Mediaset) and the preschool channel Cartoonito (WarnerMedia and Mediaset in Italy). Minimax, established in 1999 as a European-owned network for Central and Eastern Europe, and broadcasting up to 80 percent European content (Lustyik and Zanker 2013, 193), has become more focused on U.S. and nondomestic European imports since its takeover by U.S.-owned Chellomedia (part of Liberty Global) in 2007, and incorporation by AMC in 2014 (Lustyik and Zanker 2013, 193–94; Lustyik 2015).

In the Arab region there are fewer children's channels, approximately a tenth of what is on offer in Europe, because U.S. and Arab providers mostly broadcast one feed for the whole region, stretching from the Arabian Sea to North Africa (Cartoon Network 2014; Sayfo 2012). At the start of 2019, there were approximately thirty-five mostly pan-Arab children's TV channels, distributed as free-to-air satellite channels or as part of Arab-owned, satellite-delivered pay TV packages (OSN, beIN), with over two-thirds based in the United Arab Emirates (UAE), Qatar, and Saudi Arabia.

Discrepancies between channel numbers in European and Arab regional markets highlight the degree to which children are able to access screen content distributed in their own language or dialect. In multi-language Europe there is a tradition of PSBs scheduling blocks of children's programming as part of generalist channels and now dedicated children's channels. Most European PSBs also commission content from local producers, an activity that has grown in importance, as European-owned commercially funded channels, such as the United Kingdom's ITV, commission less children's content because of competition from U.S. transnationals and online, combined with advertising restrictions around children's content (D'Arma and Steemers 2013, 131; Ofcom 2018). Although PSB provision for children is less adequately resourced in Central and Eastern Europe, children here can nevertheless still view transnational channels in their own languages because there are separate language feeds.

In Arab countries provision for children has always been sparse, with little domestic content provided by local broadcasters (Sayfo 2012). Since the 1990s both U.S. providers such as Nickelodeon as well as Arab regional providers such as Dubai-based, Saudi-owned MBC have taken advantage of Arabic being a common language, targeting at least eighteen Arabic-speaking countries in order to reduce the distribution and content management costs associated with multiple language feeds. As most children's channels use a standardized literary version of Arabic, children rarely get to hear their local or regional dialects. This consolidation of Arabic-speaking audiences is being replicated online by SVOD players Netflix and Amazon Prime and also by regional SVODs such as Icflix, Shahid Plus (owned by MBC), and Starz Play Arabia. So, although European and Arab children are watching the same cartoons from North America, Europe, and Asia, for Arab children this content is rarely in their dialect because there is insufficient advertising or subscription revenue to support distribution in local languages (Sakr and Steemers 2019, 28–29).

The lack of advertising and subscription revenue to support the distribution of children's content in individual Arab dialects is related to income levels rather than market size. Over 512 million people live in the European Union including the United Kingdom, with 16 percent under fifteen (Eurostat 2017), yet there is separate provision for children in every EU market, both large and small. Over 350 million people live in eighteen Arabic-speaking countries of the Middle East and North Africa (MENA) region (UN 2017, 14–15), and the proportion under fifteen is significantly higher, accounting for approximately one-third of Egypt's population and rising to 40 percent in Iraq, Palestine, and Yemen (14–15). However, the most populous country, Egypt (97.5 million), accounted for only 7 percent of regional advertising spending in 2016, less than the UAE with 11 percent and a population less than a tenth of Egypt's (Northwestern University 2016a). Only Saudi Arabia has a sufficiently large and affluent population to sustain children's channels supported from advertising and subscription, bearing out long-established rules of media economics relating to market size and income (Hoskins, McFadyen, and Finn 1997, 38–39 and 47–48). At the same time disparities of wealth among Arabic-speaking countries are reflected in disparate levels of advertising spending within the region (Northwestern University 2016a) and between regions, with Arab TV advertising averaging seventeen dollars per capita in 2016, compared to eighty dollars in Western Europe (Northwestern University 2016b).

Another difference relates to levels of connectivity and access. While 86 percent of households in the twenty-eight EU countries had access to broadband internet in 2018 (Eurostat 2019), connection rates in Arab countries diverge more widely and in some instances are significantly lower than in Europe. Bulgaria has the lowest EU penetration rate at 72 percent. Estimates for the whole of the Middle East claim an average internet penetration rate of 67.2 percent in April 2019 (Puri-Mirza 2019), but this aggregate figure masks a patchy picture for the kind of high-speed broadband connectivity needed for comfortable viewing of video content. Other reports suggest that less than 10 percent of 48 million TV households in twelve Arab markets, including Egypt, subscribe to pay TV and that only 20 percent view online video on a regular basis (Maurell, Reda, and Singh 2018, 10). The UAE and Qatar recorded almost universal internet penetration in 2018, closely followed by Saudi Arabia, Lebanon, and Jordan exceeding 86 percent, but penetration in Egypt was only 50 percent (Northwestern University 2018). In countries affected by war, such as Syria, Yemen, and Libya, online access is rarer still.

A further marker of disparity involves the structures that are evolving to serve the children's market. In Europe the market for linear children's channels is clearly being disrupted by widespread nonlinear viewing on multiple devices. Research in 2018 by U.K. regulator Ofcom shows that while U.K. children aged five to fifteen still watch over thirteen hours a week of TV on a television set, this has declined by almost three hours since 2011, with less time spent viewing live TV and more time spent online, at over fifteen hours a week, rising to over twenty hours for those aged twelve to fifteen (Ofcom 2019b, 3 and 8). However, more children are watching TV online on other devices; 58 percent of U.K. children aged five to fifteen now watch video-on-demand services online, and 80 percent use YouTube (Ofcom 2019b, 31 and 34). Research in 2018 by Ampere Analysis in nine European countries and the United States revealed that up to 60 percent of viewing on TV sets in homes with children under ten years of age now takes place on a nonlinear basis as catch-up TV (25 percent), SVOD (16 percent), or digital video recorder (DVR) (9 percent) or on free online platforms like YouTube (7 percent) (Bisson and Deane 2018, 5).

Reliable research about children's media consumption in Arab households is rarer but echoes European experiences, particularly in affluent Gulf markets (Bahrain, Kuwait, Qatar, UAE) and Saudi Arabia, where 60 percent of households subscribe to pay TV, in contrast to low take-up of 3 percent in Egypt (IHS Markit, cited in Hamid 2017). A report by IHS Markit in 2018 revealed that SVOD is growing in MENA, accounting for 1.38 million subscriptions by the end of 2017, but at the expense of pay TV by cable and satellite, which fell 21 percent to just over 4.2 million subscriptions (McDonald 2018). The SVOD market leader in 2018 was Dubai-based Starz Play Arabia, with an estimated 24 percent share, closely followed by MBC-owned Shahid Plus (21.7 percent) and Netflix (18.4 percent) (Papavassilopoulos 2018). Starz Play Arabia was formed in 2014, with investment from the U.S. premium cable and satellite company Starz, among others.

With online viewing identified as a key family activity in both regions, SVOD services such as Netflix and Amazon Prime have been keen to add children's and family content (Flint 2016). However, this does not necessarily translate into significantly more new content. According to one report, although Amazon Prime and Netflix added 2,718 hours of children's content in 2017, only 98 hours were original commissions or first-run acquisitions (Bisson and Deane 2018, 9). What is commissioned is also more likely to be directed at global rather than national or local audiences, and according to one researcher, children's content functions more as "a retention platform" to prevent churn (Anon 2018a). In May 2019 it was announced that Amazon, having commissioned twenty original series for children since 2012, would be concentrating on content for families and young adults and dropping children's commissions (Franks

2019a). As in Europe, children's and family content has proved popular on SVOD platforms in the Gulf, with family films accounting for three of Netflix's top ten shows in the UAE during the Eid al-Adha holiday in 2017 (Hamdan 2017). These included *The Worst Witch* (2017–), a Netflix coproduced live action series with the BBC and Germany's ZDF, the Netflix series *A Series of Unfortunate Events* (2017–19), and *Anne with an E* (2017–), a Canadian children's drama, commissioned by the Canadian Broadcasting Corporation and Netflix.

Looking at the distribution of children's content on TV channels, cable and satellite services, and online SVOD, European and some Arab children are watching the same kind of internationally driven content, largely developed and funded for North American or global markets. Key differences relate to the wealth and connectivity of individual countries, with large parts of the Arab world lagging behind Saudi Arabia and the Gulf states. The experience of Arab children also differs because they rarely get to access children's content in their own vernacular language because of a pan-Arab approach by transnational and regional providers.

Distribution Strategies for Platform Convergence

The second axis for analyzing distribution of children's content is the shifts caused by platform convergence. Distribution of European children's TV shifted after the 1980s from limited provision in blocks of one or two hours on general mixed programming channels to dedicated children's channels, distributed via cable or satellite, and from predominantly local to more globalized, predominantly U.S.-sourced content (Steemers 2013, 109). These shifts were accelerated by the liberalization of regulatory regimes, facilitated by the EU's 1997 Television Without Frontiers Directive (1989, replaced in 2010 by the Audiovisual Media Services Directive), which enabled cross-border transmission and the rapid advance of channels owned by Disney, Viacom, and WarnerMedia, which headquartered in London and utilized their libraries and economies of scale in production and distribution to repurpose content for different European markets (Potter 2011). As capacity grew on round-the-clock channels, there was no need to invest in many new originations because library content could be repeatedly run for new child audiences as each successive generation grew up. As a consequence, imports of

U.S. and Japanese animation soared (Ene 2017). U.S. transnationals do commission small amounts of European content (D'Arma and Steemers 2012), but generally they continue to "exhibit a marked preference for using wholly owned content because of a combination of economies of scale and low cultural barriers" (152), reflecting their objective of projecting a global brand image. Having launched their principal brands in the United States, they began to roll out versions for individual European markets from the mid-1990s, localizing these mainly through dubbing, locally targeted advertising, channel idents, and programming selections. In some cases they outsourced or commissioned a limited number of globally appealing animation series in Europe, benefiting from tax relief and other subsidies in these countries, but usually retaining global rights ownership. Examples include *Doc McStuffins* (2012–, Brown Bag Films, Ireland, for Disney) and *Chip 'n' Dale* (2019–, Xilam Animation, France, for Disney); teen dramas such as *Evermoor Chronicles* (2014–17, Lime Pictures, UK, for Disney) and *House of Anubis* (2011–13, Lime Pictures, UK, for Nickelodeon); and entertainment, notably *Lazy Town* (2004–14, Lazy Town Entertainment, Iceland, for Nickelodeon).

As commercial children's channels multiplied in Europe from the 1990s, European PSBs launched their own children's channels. These included KiKa in Germany, a joint initiative by ARD and ZDF (1997); the BBC's CBeebies for preschoolers and CBBC for those aged over six (2002) in the United Kingdom; VRT's KetNet in Belgian Flanders (2012); NPO's Zappelin Extra (2009) in the Netherlands; Rai YoYo (2006) and Rai Gulp in Italy (2007); NRK Super (2006) in Norway; DR Ramasjang (2009) and DR Ultra (2013) in Denmark; and France 4 (2009) in France. In some countries, including Wales (S4C), Scotland (BBC Alba), and Ireland (TG4), there is additional support for content in minority languages. What marked PSBs out was their greater focus on commissioning homegrown drama and factual content, which children in these countries would recognize as rooted in their linguistic and cultural experiences. Even so, PSB provision for children across the European Union is patchy, especially in Southern, Central, and Eastern Europe, where PSB generally enjoys less political and financial support (D'Arma and Labio 2017; Lustyik and Zanker 2013), leading public channels and transnational operators like AMC to license content from suppliers in other European countries as well as from North America.

From the late 1990s, the rise of children's channels, both in Europe and internationally did boost the growth of independent European producers, ranging from medium-sized entities (HIT Entertainment, Chorion, Entertainment Rights in the United Kingdom; EM.TV and TV Loonland in Germany; Marathon in France) to smaller production companies. With broadcaster commissions declining in value, those with internationally appealing animation or preschool properties were incentivized to seek funding from commissions, international presales, coproduction arrangements (particularly in Canada), tax reliefs, and subsidies in the hope of recouping investments later from licensed merchandise if they had a hit (Steemers 2013, 105–6; Steemers and Awan 2016). Yet this ecosystem is changing as U.S.-headquartered toy companies Hasbro (*Transformers, My Little Pony*) and Mattel (*Barbie*) as well as Danish giant Lego move into content creation and distribution themselves, instead of simply licensing brands. The shift was accelerated after the financial crisis of 2008, when a number of European companies either were acquired or went out of business. The brand assets (*Octonauts*, 2010–; and others) of U.K.-based Chorion were sold in 2011 to companies in Europe, Asia, and North America. Mattel acquired U.K.-based Hit Entertainment (*Bob the Builder*, 1998– [various versions]; *Thomas and Friends*, 1984– [various versions]) in 2012. DreamWorks (part of NBC Universal since 2016) took on the assets of U.K.-based Entertainment Rights (*Postman Pat*, 1981– [various versions]) after it entered administration in 2009, as had Germany's TV Loonland. In 2016, French group Banijay absorbed the children's properties of Zodiak Media, which included Marathon (*Totally Spies!*, 2001–13). In August 2019 Hasbro acquired the Canadian company Entertainment One, owner of U.K.-originated global brand *Peppa Pig* (2004–), created by boutique animation company Astley Baker Davies, since 2015 itself a subsidiary of Entertainment One. What these consolidations accentuate are the high risks of developing and funding global children's properties, where returns from sales and merchandising are never guaranteed for producers without deep reserves and where the cultural origins of brands are increasingly blurred following incorporation within larger, mainly North American transnational enterprises with global licensing ambitions.

Arab countries also experienced growth in children's transmissions as channel numbers increased. In the absence, however, of PSB institutions with a remit to provide for local child audiences, and given the obstacles to building a sufficiently strong production community (Sakr and Steemers 2019, 61–62), privately owned Arab channels filled their schedules with U.S., Japanese, and European imports aimed at a pan-Arab audience. The first, Spacetoon Arabic, was established in Dubai in 2000. Dubai-based MBC3, the market leader, operated by the MBC Group, started in 2004 as a free-to-air channel and has an output deal with Nickelodeon. As in Europe, U.S. players such as Disney, Cartoon Network, and Nickelodeon have been able to rely heavily on their own libraries of U.S.-made and U.S.-European coproductions, which account for their popularity with Arab pay TV providers such as OSN and beIN (see below). In June 2017, they were joined by Gulli Bil Arabi, an Arabic version of French channel Gulli, owned by Lagardère Active and distributed to eighteen territories on the Dubai-based My-HD pay TV platform. There have been occasional forays into local production, such as three seasons (2015–19) of *Iftah ya Simsim*, an Arabic version of *Sesame Street* made primarily for Gulf children by Sesame Workshop, with companies based in the UAE, and Cartoon Network's support for UAE animation series *Mansour* (2013–17), produced in local dialect (Sakr and Steemers 2019, 78). There were also coproductions involving mainly U.K. companies working with Qatar's Al-Jazeera Children's Channel (now Jeem) and Baraem before 2011 (Sakr and Steemers 2016, 245–46).

A key competitor to professionally distributed, channel-led content for children in both Europe and the Arab region is YouTube, driven by widespread tablet and mobile phone ownership. In March 2019, roughly half of the top thirty most subscribed YouTube channels globally were targeted at children. In a 2018 study of eight European and two Arab markets, Saudi Arabia had the highest level of tablet ownership among children aged five to ten at 74 percent, followed by the UAE and United Kingdom at 69 percent each (Norton 2018, 11). The most popular content includes children or adults unpacking toys and confectionery in so-called unboxing videos, instructional how-to videos that show children or young adults playing video games, and channels featuring popular cartoons. The proliferation of nursery rhyme channels (e.g., Cocomelon, Little Baby Bum, ChuChu TV, Super Simple Songs), often from India and China, and toy review channels (Ryan ToysReview; Fun Toys Collector) may even be behind a reported 25 percent drop in time spent watching linear television in 2018 among two- to four-year-olds (Woodgate 2018, 6).

YouTube is extremely attractive to young Gulf audiences, who have grown up accustomed to strict censorship and little locally produced content. At time of writing, YouTube Kids, the curated children's app launched in 2015, was not available in the Middle East. Self-publishing on YouTube by young people took off during the Arab uprisings of 2011 (Atia 2017). Saudi Arabia became the world's biggest user of YouTube in terms of the average number of views each day per capita in 2013 (Smith 2013), as young creators and audiences searched for lifestyle vlogs and entertainment in a country where cinemas were illegal until recently and where music concerts are still restricted (Britton 2017). Published in January 2017, one music video, "Hush," by Khamsa Adwaa, a Saudi band of young girls, had over 149 million views by December 2018 and was the top Arab YouTube music video in 2017 (*Arab News* 2017). A study of social media use in MENA in 2017 suggested that fifteen- to twenty-four-year-olds spend about seventy-two minutes a day watching YouTube videos, with short-form content curated by "Arab youth" constituting the fastest-growing "video segment" (Radcliffe and Lam 2018, 12). YouTube is also emerging as a means of distributing educational materials for younger children in the region, as demonstrated by the examples of Pacca Alpaca, owned by a Saudi entrepreneur, and Jordanian-owned Adam wa Mishmish (Sakr and Steemers 2019, 34–35). According to WildBrain, a subsidiary of Canada's DHX Media that creates YouTube channels from international brands, the Arabic version of the 2014 remake of costumed character series *Teletubbies* (1997–2001) is the most popular version after those in English, Italian, and French (WildBrain 2017), racking up 478,000 subscribers and 2.5 million views in three years since launching in April 2016.

Broadcasters and pay TV providers have responded with their own catch-up and on-demand services. Assuming they have access to rights, some European PSBs (e.g., VRT in Flanders and DR in Denmark) are embracing YouTube as an additional distribution mechanism (Steemers, Sakr, and Singer 2018, 7), while others (e.g., NRK in Norway and the BBC) use it to draw attention to their own online offerings and apps. In the United Kingdom the BBC took a decision in 2017 to reallocate

25 percent of its children's budget by 2019–20 to streamed online content and apps (BBC 2017). In 2018 the French government announced that children's channel France 4 would close by 2020, to be replaced from 2019 by an advertising-free online streaming service for two- to thirteen-year-olds (Franks 2019b). This decision was put on hold in June 2019 following opposition from the French animators' association due to France 4's role as the country's largest animation commissioner. Denmark's DR Ultra for children aged seven to twelve will go online-only in 2020 and is unlikely to be the last to follow this route.

With fierce competition from SVODs and YouTube, regional broadcasters and service providers in the Arab pay TV market are also protecting market share by adding SVOD and streaming services for all audiences. In 2012 Dubai-based regional pay TV provider OSN created the streaming service OSN Play for existing subscribers, followed in 2017 by the contract-free and cheaper streaming platform Wavo, intended to serve less affluent countries like Egypt (Stuart 2018). OSN has exclusive access to first-run Disney movies and renewed its right to carry Disney Channel, Disney HD, and Disney Junior in Arabic in 2017. In February 2015 it added Nickelodeon HD, Nicktoons, and Nick Jr. in both Arabic and English. In March 2017 it launched a new children's channel, OSN Kids Zone, in Arabic and English in partnership with Magmedia International and Mega Mix Media. In 2018 it concluded a deal with Netflix to embed the Netflix app in a new set-top box.

OSN's Qatar-based pay TV rival, the beIN Media Group, established in 2014, has also sought to reinforce its roster of international children's channels to attract subscribers. In 2015 it concluded distribution deals with Turner for Cartoon Network and Boomerang, which moved from rival OSN. In April 2016, beIN incorporated Qatari channel Jeem and preschool channel Baraem behind its pay wall and partnered with Belgium-based Studio 100 to replicate German-language channel Junior in Arabic as beJunior, featuring European animation favorites *Maya the Bee* (2012–) and *Vic the Viking* (2013–). The same year, beIN added the United States' Discovery Kids and the BBC's English-language preschool channel CBeebies, while U.S.-owned AMC signed a deal to launch five channels on beIN including preschool service JimJam. A deal with Universal Pictures–owned DreamWorks in August 2016 gave beIN access to the DreamWorks Channel in Arabic.

As the region's main free-to-air satellite channel operator, MBC launched Shahid.net as a free VOD and catch-up service in 2011, followed in 2015 by an advertisement-free SVOD service, Shahid Plus. Regional SVOD rival Icflix launched the Icflix Kids app in 2014, at which point MBC started working on Goboz, a separate SVOD platform for curated children's content in app form to shore up reception of content on its children's channel, MBC3, and reassure parents they could find a safe source of what MBC group director of brand management and digital businesses Fadel Zahreddine called "engaging edutainment," "unlike the unboxing model which is a hard sell, and that obviously parents wouldn't appreciate" (quoted in Bisson 2018). Goboz was finally launched in March 2018 but was quietly dropped a year later, presumably because it was not meeting business expectations in terms of access to rights or subscriptions. In November 2018, MBC secured a partnership with Fox to add the Fox+ streaming service including Baby TV to Shahid Plus. What would be concerning for those responsible for the free-to-air children's channel MBC3 is that Nickelodeon, with which MBC has had a long-term content deal for shows like *Dora the Explorer* (2000–2015), *SpongeBob SquarePants* (1999–), and *PAW Patrol* (2013–), has subsequently concluded distribution deals for its channels with OSN. According to one researcher, "MBC3 has built an audience for another channel," with potential problems in future "as those deals come to an end" and "the content reverts to Nickelodeon" (Anon 2018a).

For both OSN and beIN, the strategy has been to retain audiences against competition from SVOD rivals by securing key U.S. and European channels within their packages, rather than seeking to invest in originals, thereby continuing the lack of investment in local children's content that has plagued Arab markets. In Europe, PSB channels, following their remit, continue to invest in original content, albeit in declining amounts, but are embarking on online distribution to meet children's changing consumption habits.

Rights Implications of Distribution

The appearance of YouTube and SVOD services in both regions is forcing decisions about distribution and a shift away from channels toward streaming and on-demand services on online platforms. This has implications for funding mechanisms in two areas. The first relates to the securing of rights and the second to the exploitation of ancillary revenues from licensed merchandise.

In Europe the positioning of PSB continues as a free publicly funded national offering for children, even as some broadcasters (DR Ultra, France 4) attempt to shift more or all of their activities online. Of crucial importance to PSB's future relevance and legitimacy is a commitment not to cut commissioning budgets as a result of the shift and to offer both a distinctive curated alternative to YouTube and a free alternative to Netflix and Amazon Prime. This means commissioning domestic content, supported by policy-related funding mechanisms such as tax incentives and independent ring-fenced funds (available in Denmark, France, Ireland, and the United Kingdom), which address market failure in domestic production and allow local producers to pool limited resources alongside international partnerships, if content has international appeal (Steemers 2017). Backed by public funding, a public service remit, some degree of political support, and reputations that can attract coproducers for internationally attractive content, European PSBs in the United Kingdom, Germany, France, the Nordics, and Benelux are the main commissioners of domestically originated screen content for children in their respective countries. Yet there are pressure points. Not all European PSBs, notably in Central, Eastern, and Southern Europe, enjoy the same degree of political and public support. Moreover, in future battles for rights, PSBs, which are not always the largest funders of high-profile animation and drama, may find it more difficult to secure a full range of rights for their commissions from rights owners for transmission online. Equally, commercial subsidiaries like BBC Worldwide do not always have distribution and ancillary rights to PSB commissions, which might feed additional revenues back into PSB coffers.

In the absence of PSB and motivated by commercial priorities, responses in Arab markets are more focused on securing regional distribution coverage and pan-Arab program rights, rather than on commissioning content (Bisson 2018). Pay TV platforms such as OSN and beIN and regional SVODs such as Dubai-based Icflix and Starz Play Arabia have secured deals with local telecom companies and internet providers to ensure distribution (Stuart 2018). These partnerships are also important because they provide delivery and billing solutions, allowing payments to be added to telephone bills in a region where credit card payments are not universal.

However, in aiming for pan-Arab coverage, Arab providers must also invest in multiple forms of rights for desirable properties across several platforms. This is especially important if they wish to generate revenues from licensed merchandise associated with well-known children's brands. By contrast, local productions without ancillary rights are less attractive than imports with a track record of success in the United States and other markets (Bisson 2018). For example, Qatar-based Jeem's decision in 2013 to replace Arabic-language commissions with packages from Disney and the BBC can be attributed to its wish not only to compete with pan-Arab rival MBC3 but also to pursue ancillary revenue streams (Sakr and Steemers 2016). According to an MBC executive, "When I make any acquisition of any content it is imperative to make sure that that content has digital rights with it, merchandising rights with it, and if there are theatrical shows then obviously that's a plus point. So, it's no longer acquiring content in isolation of other stuff" (Anon 2018b). For example, in July 2018 MBC3 acquired 52 seven-minute episodes of *Wissper* (2012–), an animated series about a girl who talks to animals, from European media companies Studio 100 and m4e (Dickson 2018). In addition to cable and satellite rights, the deal also included SVOD and advertising video-on-demand rights and exclusivity for MBC Group as the licensing agent for IP rights in the MENA region.

However, this approach to rights acquisition is problematic. First, the practice of treating all Arabic-speaking territories as a single market comes up against existing rights agreements, which may have been made with national television operators in individual countries. One U.K. researcher explained, "So say you've got linear rights to *Shaun the Sheep*, which you've acquired from Aardman. What happens if you go to Aardman and ask politely for the SVOD rights? . . . And they go 'well, a bit of a problem there, LBC in Lebanon has rights for there, and in Egypt national state-run TV has the rights, and actually we've just checked and it's on CBeebies in that part of the world as well because that's through beIN'" (Anon 2018a).

Such an approach is also at odds with the ambitions of transnational corporations. As Disney launched its own global streaming service, Disney+, across Europe and the Middle East in 2020, there was a risk of both Arab and European operators losing Disney-licensed shows and channels, although according to the revised EU Audiovisual Media Services Directive, SVODs will have to give over 30 percent of their catalogue to European content, providing some protection in EU markets (European Commission 2019).

Another issue for Arab players is that perennial reliance on well-known brands is inimical to the development of homegrown originals from the start because local content can never compete with properties that have proved their value in North America and Europe. This need for proven success overseas was underlined by Zahreddine's observation that there are "certain strong IPs that have strong international appeal" and "what is produced in the US seems to have a more universal appeal than the rest." He even suggested that local characteristics could be an impediment in the Arab marketplace because some locally produced content may "not at times work locally" because of the region's diverse "dialects, customs and protocols" (Bisson 2018, 23), thus crucially providing "no sound ROI" (Bisson 2018, 22).

Conclusion

From this overview it emerges that changes in children's consumption of screen content are having an impact on the underlying economics, resource allocation, and sustainability of professionally distributed content for children in both regions. Three key conclusions can be drawn that relate to the distribution component of the screen media business. First, although the volume of original production needed to sustain diverse or pluralistic distribution in both regions is limited, in Europe there is greater commitment to investment by European PSBs in culturally relevant content. In the Arab region institutional and regulatory frameworks to encourage production and distribution of local content are widely lacking, and operators have little incentive to engage in it, even for the whole pan-Arab market, because of low returns on investment and an overabundance of readily available, low-cost, easily dubbed animation series produced for North American, European, and Asian markets. Second, new complications in rights acquisition, occasioned by the rise of SVOD providers and the competition between them in different territories, work particularly to the disadvantage of Arab distributors who seek to serve a single pan-Arab region of eighteen countries where Arabic is the primary language. It remains to be seen whether this situation will ultimately trigger greater interest in local content production; to date the response has been for Arab operators to compete among themselves for rights to imported animation associated with toy brands and other merchandise that have already proved their worth in foreign markets. Finally, traditional rules of media economics pertaining to market size and affluence and these indicators' implications for a country's spending on advertising and subscriptions continue to influence distribution. They account for differences among European and Arab countries and between the two regions, explaining why there is such a strong preference in the latter to buy ready-made content rather than risk investing in originals. Since sales of licensed merchandise depend on content distribution, the deterrents to investment in local screen media IP in most of the Arab world have a knock-on effect in also deterring development of locally originated merchandise. This perpetuates a vicious cycle.

BIBLIOGRAPHY

Anon. 2018a. Interview with U.K.-based market researcher, July 12.

———. 2018b. Interview with MBC executive, September 20.

Arab News. 2017. "Mmoshaya 2017's Most Trending YouTube Video in MENA." December 8. www.arabnews.com.

Atia, Tarek. 2017. "A Channel for Every Child." In *Children's TV and Digital Media in the Arab World*, edited by Naomi Sakr and Jeanette Steemers, 122–37. London: I. B. Tauris.

Awan, Feryal, and Jeanette Steemers. 2017. "Arab and Western Perspectives on Childhood and Children's Media." In *Children's TV and Digital Media in the Arab World*, edited by Naomi Sakr and Jeanette Steemers, 20–44. London: I. B. Tauris.

BBC. 2017. "BBC Announces Biggest Investment in Children's Content and Services for a Generation." July 4. www.bbc.co.uk.

Bisson, Guy. 2018. "Interview with Fadel Zahreddine." *Mipblog.com*, August 27. https://mipblog.com.

Bisson, Guy, and Olivia Deane. 2018. "Where Next for Kids' TV." *Mip Trends*, April 24. https://www.miptrends.com/tv-business/where-next-for-kids-tv-predicting-the-future-of-childrens-content-exclusive-white-paper/.

Britton, Bianca. 2017. "Why Women Are Talking to YouTube in Saudi Arabia." CNN, April 5. https://edition.cnn.com.

Cartoon Network. 2014. "Ipsos Kids Telemetry Study: KSA 7–14 Commercial Report." Dubai: Cartoon Network.

Children's Global Media Summit. 2017. "Generation U. The Future of Media for an Unlimited Generation." http://cgms17.com.

D'Arma, Alessandro, and Aurora Labio. 2017. "Making a Difference? Public Service Broadcasting, Distinctiveness and Children's Provision in Italy and Spain." *International Journal of Digital Television* 8 (2): 183–99.

D'Arma, Alessandro, and Jeanette Steemers. 2012. "Localisation Strategies of US-Owned Children's Television Networks in Five European Markets." *Journal of Children and the Media* 6 (2): 147–64.

———. 2013. "Children's Television: Markets and Regulation." In *Private Television in Western Europe*, edited by Karen Donders, Caroline Pauwels, and Jan Loisen, 123–35. Basingstoke: Palgrave Macmillan.

Dickson, Jeremy. 2018. "Studio 100/m4e's Wissper to Make noise in MENA." *Kidscreen*, July 5. http://kidscreen.com.

Ene, Laura. 2017. "Media Ownership: Children's TV Channels in Europe—Who Are the Key Players?" Strasbourg: European Audiovisual Observatory. https://rm.coe.int.

European Commission. 2019. "Revision of the Audiovisual Media Services Directive." https://ec.europa.eu.

Eurostat. 2017. "Being Young in Europe Today—Demographic Trends." December. https://ec.europa.eu.

———. 2019. "Digital Economy and Society Statistics—Households and Individuals." June. https://ec.europa.eu.

Evans, Elizabeth, Paul McDonald, Juyeon Bae, Sripama Ray, and Emanualle Santos. 2016. "Universal Ideals in Local Realities: Online Viewing in South Korea, Brazil and India." *Convergence* 22 (4): 408–25.

Flint, Joe. 2016. "Netflix to Ramp up Originals Targeting Kids." *Wall Street Journal*, January 17. www.wsj.com

Franks, Nico. 2019a. "Amazon Shifts Away from Preschool, Kids." *C21*, May 25. www.c21media.net.

———. 2019b. "Plus ça change." *C21*, March 8. www.c21media.net.

Hamdan, Lubna. 2017. "Netflix Saw Highest Streaming Traffic during Eid al-Adha." *Arabian Business*, December 17. www.arabianbusiness.com.

Hamid, Triska. 2017. "MENA Viewers Tune into Pay-TV." *The National*, May 8. www.thenational.ae.

Hoskins, Colin, Stuart McFadyen, and Adam Finn. 1997. *Global Television and Film*. Oxford: Oxford University Press.

Johnson, Catherine. 2019. *Online TV*. London: Routledge.

Lemish, Dafna. 2019. "'A Room of Our Own': Farewell Comments on Editing the Journal of Children and Media." *Journal of Children and Media* 13 (1): 116–26.

Lobato, Ramon. 2019. *Netflix Nations: The Geography of Digital Distribution*. New York: New York University Press.

Lotz, Amanda. 2014. *The Television Will Be Revolutionized*. 2nd ed. New York: New York University Press.

Lustyik, Katalin. 2015. "From a Socialist Endeavor to a Commercial Enterprise: Children's Television in East-Central Europe." In *Popular Television in Eastern Europe During and Since Socialism*, edited by Timothy Havens, Aniko Imre, and Katalin Lustyik, 105–22. New York: Routledge.

Lustyik, Katalin, and Ruth Zanker. 2013. "Is There Local Content on Television for Children Today?" In *The International Encyclopedia of Media Studies*, edited by Angharad N. Valdivia, 179–202. Oxford: Blackwell.

Maurell, Frederique, Ahmed Reda, and Nripendra Singh. 2018. "Videonomics: Video Content Consumption, Production and Distribution in the MENA Region." EY Advisory Services. www.ey.com.

McDonald, Andrew. 2018. "IHS Markit: MENA Pay TV in Decline as SVOD Subs Grow 48%." *Digital TV Europe*, April 24. www.digitaltveurope.com.

Northwestern University in Qatar. 2016a. "Advertising." In *Media Industries in the Middle East 2016*. Doha: Northwestern University in Qatar and Doha Film Institute. www.mideastmedia.org.

———. 2016b. "Television." In *Media Industries in the Middle East 2016*. Doha: Northwestern University in Qatar and Doha Film Institute. www.mideastmedia.org.

———. 2018. "Online and Social Media." In *Media Use in the Middle East, 2018*. Northwestern University in Qatar. www.mideastmedia.org.

Norton. 2018. "Norton's My First Device Report." Edelman Intelligence. http://now.symassets.com.

Ofcom. 2018. "Children's Content Review: Update." July 24. London: Ofcom.

———. 2019a. "Children and Parents: Media Use and Attitudes Report 2018." London: Ofcom.

———. 2019b. "Children and Parents Media Use and Attitudes Report 2018—Research Annex." London: Ofcom.

Papavassilopoulos, Constantinos. 2018. "The Online Subscription Video Market in MENA in 2018—Presentation at TV Connect MENA 2018 in Dubai." *Omdia*, November 8. https://technology.ihs.com.

Potter, Anna. 2011. "It's a Small World After All: New Media Constellations and Disney's Rising Star—the Global Success of High School Musical." *International Journal of Cultural Studies* 15 (2): 117–30.

Puri-Mirza, Amna. 2019. "Internet Penetration Rate in the Middle East Compared to the Global Internet Penetration Rate from 2009 to 2019." *Statista*, May 28. www.statista.com.

Radcliffe, Damian, and Amanda Lam. 2018. "Social Media in the Middle East. The Story of 2017." Eugene: University of Oregon.

Sakr, Naomi, and Jeanette Steemers. 2016. "Co-producing Content for Pan-Arab Children's TV." In *Production Studies: The Sequel*, edited by Miranda Banks, Bridget Conor, and Vicky Mayer, 238–50. London Routledge.

———. 2019. *Screen Media for Arab and European Children: Policy and Production Encounters in the Multiplatform Era*. Basingstoke: Palgrave Macmillan.

Sayfo, Omar. 2012. "The Emergence of Children's Media and Animation Industry in the Gulf States." Paper presented at the 3rd Gulf Research Meeting, University of Cambridge, July 11–14. www.academia.edu.

Smith, Matt. 2013. "Young Saudis Getting Creative on YouTube." Reuters, November 18. www.reuters.com.

Steemers, Jeanette. 2013. "Children's Television Culture." In *The Routledge International Handbook of Children, Adolescents and Media*, edited by Dafna Lemish, 103–10. London: Routledge.

———. 2014. "Selling Television: Addressing Transformations in the International Distribution of Television Content." *Media Industries Journal* 1 (1): 44–49.

———. 2016. "International Sales of UK Television Content: Change and Continuity in the 'Space in Between' Production and Consumption." *Television & New Media* 17 (8): 734–53.

———. 2017. "International Perspectives on the Funding of Public Service Media Content for Children." *Media International Australia* 163 (1): 42–54.

Steemers, Jeanette, and Feryal Awan. 2016. "Policy Solutions and International Perspectives on the Funding of Public Service Media Content for Children: A Report for Stakeholders." May. https://westminsterresearch.westminster.ac.uk.

Steemers, Jeanette, Naomi Sakr, and Christine Singer. 2018. "Facilitating Arab-European Dialogue: Consolidated Report on an AHRC Project for Impact and Engagement: Children's Screen Content in an Era of Forced Migration—8 October 2017 to 3 November 2018." London: King's College London. https://kclpure.kcl.ac.uk.

Stuart, Jay. 2018. "By Popular Demand." *TVMEA—MIP Edition*, April, 6–11. https://issuu.com.

United Nations. 2017. "World Population Prospects: Data Booklet—2017 Revision." https://population.un.org.

WildBrain. 2017. "Teletubbies Available in Twenty Languages on YouTube." December 19. www.wildbrain-spark.com.

Woodgate, Adam. 2018. "Is Kids' Preferred TV Content Changing?" *MIPTV Trends*, November 13. www.miptrends.com.

12

Distribution, Infrastructure, and Markets

SVOD Services in Latin America

JUAN PIÑÓN AND EZEQUIEL RIVERO

Across Latin America, the adoption and growth of the new digital and mobile platforms for television content delivery show how the dynamics of digital television distribution produces a different set of structured opportunities, as well as obstacles, for new and traditional players in the region's television industry.[1] At the core of these differentiated opportunities, or the lack of them, are the different legal, technological, material/immaterial, and institutional frameworks that have shaped the three industrial sectors—media, telecommunications, and computing—that are fighting to reign over the subscription video-on-demand (SVOD) market. The success of the U.S. computing industry in Latin America's SVOD markets reveals a strong and commanding presence, not only as providers of television content but also as full participants across the very infrastructure that supports this digital distribution network as a whole. U.S. corporations such as Netflix and Amazon face limited resistance from the large national television networks, which have long commanded their respective domestic national markets. In contrast, telecom corporations with a dominant *regional* presence have taken advantage of their position in the digital infrastructure to pursue their own audience niches in the SVOD market. In this context a problematic reality arises with the lack of Latin American computing corporations as either content providers or key participants in the support of the infrastructure for the VOD market across the region.

In this chapter we analyze the infrastructure of internet-distributed television as a force transforming the production, distribution, and consumption circuits of television content in Latin America. A media infrastructure approach allows us to situate new distribution scenarios in the digital media ecology by identifying the participant entities and their role in internet-distributed television. The market conditions of entry, which determine the presence and opportunities for success of particular players, including national or multinational media, telecommunication, and computing corporations, are located in the distribution infrastructure.

Our study is situated at the crossroads of distribution studies and approaches to media infrastructures. It presents research on internet-distributed television through the examination of the seven main SVOD services in the region—Netflix, Amazon Prime Video, Claro Video, Movistar Play, HBO Go, Blim, and Globoplay—and the impact of these services on the six main audiovisual Latin American markets: Argentina, Brazil, Chile, Colombia, Mexico, and Peru.

An Introduction to Latin American Television Industries

When it comes to television content, Latin American national broadcasting networks still enjoy substantial reach and captive audiences. These broadcast corporations cemented their positions in their respective domestic industries through monopolistic or duopolistic market structures, including various alliances with national governments. This industrial scenario largely resulted in the rise of one or two highly dominant television networks in each domestic market, with smaller networks providing minimal competition in each market. Transnational television flows from and within Latin America have been an industrial reality too, mostly triggered by the early success of telenovelas in prime-time television that created a regional space for the circulation of this audiovisual commodity (Straubhaar 2012).

The dominance of the main national broadcast corporations in their domestic markets was preserved by means of several, interrelated technological, legal, political, economic, and cultural barriers of entry. These include a partial or total ban on foreign entities or individuals holding broadcasting licenses or owning broadcasting media corporations; relatively low penetration of pay TV across the region; monopolistic or duopolistic television market structures, mostly encouraged under economic and political alliances with national governments; and audience preferences for culturally proximate content (Straubhaar 1991) in the form of national or regional television programs. These barriers did not stop the flow of television programing from the United States, which in total numbers has been the source of the largest amount of content flowing across the region (Miller et al. 2004). However, the dynamics of popular culture and the quotidian lives of Latin American audiences have found in the daily seriality of telenovelas (Martín-Barbero 2004) a space in which fiction and reality seem to overlap, making these audio-visual media the most important commodity in prime-time television nationally and regionally. The success of telenovelas in prime time has been critical in maintaining the dominant role that larger Latin American broadcast networks continue to play in domestic and regional markets (Burnay, Lopes, and Neves de Sousa 2018).

The supremacy of the leading national broadcasters in the largest markets resulted in a rather early transnational regional dominance of television flows by networks such as Rede Globo (Brazil), Televisa (Mexico), and Venevisión (Venezuela). Recent decades, however, have witnessed the emergence of new competitors such as Rede Record (Brazil), TV Azteca (Mexico), Caracol TV and RCN (Colombia), El Trece and Telefe (Argentina), TVN and Mega (Chile), and América TV (Peru). These twelve networks not only command their own markets but are the main producers and distributors for the region.[2]

Uneven penetration of pay TV and internet as well as broadband connectivity have not yet tipped the scale of viewership from broadcast television channels to other platforms for television content distribution. Despite the fact that these corporations enjoy a commanding lead, looking at the way television is impacted regionally by transformations in consumption behavior afforded by new digital and mobile technologies allows us to reflect on how the position of broadcast television is threatened by the gradual penetration of other powerful players such as Netflix, Amazon Prime, Claro Video, and Movistar Play. In this sense, cable, digital media, and VOD services, particularly internet-distributed television, are now shaping the industries, not because of their massive audience reach but rather because young and upscale audience segments have adopted these technologies and the new forms of television consumption they afford.

The increasing presence of internet-distributed television in Latin America and the rise of VOD services, particularly SVOD services led by Netflix, offer opportunities for academic inquiries into the tenets of cultural proximity (Straubhaar 1991) as a way to revisit the assumed advantages of national broadcast television networks in their domestic markets. Such research requires reframing the political economy perspective on how national and regional corporations have maintained their power (Birkinbine, Gómez, and Wasko 2016) while reconsidering the role of U.S. SVOD services (Netflix, Amazon) through their newfound leadership.

Distribution and the New Digital Media Landscape

The digital and mobile media landscape has been shaped by the growth of large telecom corporations (mobile telephone, cable, and internet providers), such as América Móvil (Mexico), Telefónica (Spain), and DirecTV and Liberty Media (United States), that have become the dominant players in most national markets across Latin America and the Caribbean. Their presence, along with corporations from the computing sector, are threatening the dominance of the national television broadcasting networks. At the core of this threat is the way television content is being accessed and consumed due to changes in distribution dynamics.

The rise of regional players from the telecom sector begs the question of whether internet service providers enjoy an initial industrial advantage in the emergent SVOD market. In this context, we are thinking about the site of distribution as the space in which a complex set of decisions and transactions are made, thus largely defining the kind of television content that is produced and circulated online as well as the very infrastructure that made possible that circulation in the first place. Drawing on infrastructure studies that emphasize the impact of the materiality of media in our social and cultural lives, we look to make visible the players and their shaping and unequal role as participants that constitute the very network that supports the internet infrastructure of distribution. Perren recognizes that the entry of hardware and software corporations as "distributors of media—and the extent to which those activities intersect with their roles as retailers-exhibitors—merit further examination" (2013, 171). As part of this effort, we conceptualize SVOD distribution in Latin America as a site of opportunities and obstacles for possible contenders, largely shaped by their participation in the infrastructure that supports internet-distributed television. The emerging large regional players are now mostly composed of corporations from the computing and telecom sectors that seem to have had an edge in the surging digital television market.

Our focus is on internet-distributed television, which Amanda Lotz, Ramon Lobato, and Julian Thomas (2018, 36) define as "a subset integrated by online portals distributing television content produced in accord with professionalized, industrial practices of the market." It is key to understanding the entities constituting the infrastructure of internet-distributed television and how they have access to success in this new digital market. Particularly in the case of distribution, who is the best equipped to have an important or even a dominant role in an increasingly competitive digital market?

Examining the corporate players in the infrastructure of internet-distributed television in Latin America shows differentiated industrial development across the three main industrial participant sectors: media, telecoms, and computing. When we analyze the corporations that constitute the main SVOD platforms across the region, we find the relevance of major Latin American television corporations and major telecom firms across the region, but almost no companies from the region's computing sector. This unbalanced scenario is not only a by-product of the uneven state of innovation in the informational and computational sector but also the result of the regulatory landscape governing these industries.

The VOD Market in Latin America

To understand the possible impact of internet-distributed television in the media ecology of Latin America, it is crucial to recognize how the state of internet broadband and mobile device penetration sets the conditions of access and possible success for the growth of SVOD services. For the purposes of our study, we concentrate on the media markets of Argentina, Chile, Colombia, Brazil, Mexico, and Peru. In the analyzed countries, the average penetration of fixed broadband services is about 14 percent in relation to their total population (ITU 2018a). According to the International Telecommunications Union (ITU), the rate of adoption in Latin America has shown sustained growth over recent years but is far from that of OECD member countries, where the average penetration is 30.4 percent (ITU 2018a; Baladron and Rivero 2019). At the same time, there are still internal asymmetries in each country due to deficiencies in, or lack of, infrastructure, hindering access to fixed broadband services in terms of quality and costs for the entire population.

Mobile phone penetration and use have grown (ITU 2018b) as these devices remain the most widespread technology for internet connectivity in the countries analyzed. Reduced prices for smartphones plus greater geographical access to 4G mobile broadband have turned mobile phone usage into a strategic way to access content. However, according to each country, between 50 and 70 percent of mobile phone clients are prepaid, being the most popular payment option among lower income segments of the population (Becerra and Mastrini 2017). This situation limits general access to streaming VOD due to the huge amount of mobile data consumed. Pay TV shows unequal penetration levels in different countries. In general, the pay TV penetration rate across is 44 percent of TV homes across the region, with recent signs of stagnation or at least a minor contraction in subscriber numbers (McDonald 2018).

For VOD services, Latin America represents a huge market with about 650 million people, a relatively stable political environment, economic growth, and an expanding middle class. VOD in Latin America is growing at a fast pace, alongside increasing investment in telecommunications infrastructure aimed at overcoming constraints imposed by low broadband connection and poor broadband speed. The surge of VOD is in part fueled by the increase of digital mobile platforms by 450 million connections (Punt and Schuman 2019). There will soon be 289 million people watching digital video or VOD, an estimated 45 percent of the region's population (Ceurvels 2019). Also, the different modalities of VOD, represented by various business models—advertising VOD (AVOD), subscription VOD (SVOD), transactional VOD (TVOD), TV everywhere (i.e., offering internet or mobile access to authenticated subscribers of pay TV providers), catch-up TV (i.e., online access to shows previously shown on free-to-air broadcast networks), and a variety of hybrid models—have also grown. In spite of the attention given to the rise of SVOD services, the most important player in the region by far is the AVOD service YouTube, the second largest regional viewing service, with 270 million viewers, constituting 15 percent of total users globally (Ceurvels 2019). It is important to note that YouTube hosts the digital channels of almost all the television broadcasting networks across the region, alongside multiple amateur or professional video channels from different entities and individuals. YouTube's prevalence in Latin America not only comes from how consumers obtain "free access" but also from how Google, the parent company of YouTube, has been able to dominate the AVOD business model in the region. The problem is that because "there are so few streaming video services, ad inventory remains small, and advertisers do not allocate budget to it" (Punt and Schuman 2019).

SVOD in the region is booming, with 27 million subscribers in 2018, forecasted to reach 51 million by 2024 (Digital TV Research 2019). The SVOD surge, particularly after Netflix debuted in the region in 2011, has triggered a series of changes in the television industry as a whole, as the national networks fight back against the presence and success of services such as Netflix, Amazon, and HBO Go (Ceurvels 2019). Triggered by the success of SVOD, TVOD is also growing. By offering better release windows for specific premium content, TVOD providers can differentiate their services from the more general offerings of SVOD providers. In countries such as Mexico, TVOD growth has been driven by corporate giants like América Móvil (the largest telecom corporation in the region), followed by iTunes and Google Play (Blanco and Couce 2016). The TVOD market shows signs of increasing opportunities for content distribution and diversification as the regional market grows. With the six largest territories still attracting significant pay TV revenues, SVOD services are complementing rather than replacing pay TV offerings (Ceurvels 2019). So far the six largest markets in the region represent around 85 percent of the region's SVOD market, with Brazil and Mexico taking two-thirds of the whole regional market (Digital TV Research 2019). Piracy also plays an important role in audiences' consumption of SVOD content and has grown as a parallel industry across the region (Franklin 2019).

Mapping the Infrastructure of Internet Distributed Television

The infrastructure built to support the efficient distribution, traffic, security, storage, and analysis of internet-distributed television has required the participation of multiple industrial sectors, with their different technological resources, to ensure a streaming experience that is pleasurable for audiences and productive in information for the market. The routes of media distribution, as infrastructure, can be characterized as a paradoxical condition; on the one hand, there is a complex landscape of many different players in which industrial necessity has triggered codependency, cooperation, and convergence in order to effectively operate in the internet regionally or globally (Sandvig 2015). On the other hand, however, at the end of the pipeline there is a scenario in which different corporations, along with their technologies and products, compete ferociously for digital markets. The infrastructure of internet-distributed television is a universe in which participants both need and compete with each other.

In order to identify the key players in this infrastructure, we must map the interrelated levels and functions formed by participants, including the pipes that offer content, the providers of internet service who facilitate access to digital portals, the digital networks that optimize the distribution of content regionally and globally, and the growing number of entities involved with curating, protecting, or commercializing content, plus those involved with gathering and mining data to allow VOD services to maximize their business models. Here we identify four levels in the infrastructure of internet-distributed television that have played key roles in the growth of Latin America's SVOD: (1) SVOD service providers, (2) Internet service providers, (3) content delivery networks, (4) digital intermediaries.

Dominant SVOD Service Providers

Latin America's key players in SVOD come from mass media (Blim, Globoplay, HBO Go), telecommunications (Claro Video, Movistar Play), and the computing sector (Netflix, Amazon Prime). Their possible presence is based on the specific assets that give them a relative competitive advantage in an emergent changing distribution landscape increasingly defined in terms of infrastructure resources.

In the region, there are around 274 video platforms: 114 are subsidiaries of mass media corporations, 69 are owned by corporations from the telecommunications sector, and 91 were launched by corporations from the computing sector specializing in digital platforms services (PRODU 2019, 35). While the expansion of services might suggest there is a promise of competition for audiences, the region shows a high level of concentration. By the end of 2018, there were 27.2 million SVOD subscribers, of whom 90 percent were subscribers to at least one of the seven dominant SVOD providers: Netflix, Claro Video, Amazon Prime Video, HBO Go, Globoplay, Blim, and Movistar Play. This landscape becomes even more concentrated once it is noted that Netflix, enjoying the competitive edge of first-mover advantage, dominates 65 percent of the market (Digital TV Research 2019). Arguably, Netflix's success can be attributed to the company's early expansion into Latin America, beginning in 2011. This was followed in 2015 by an aggressive plan to produce local content, making important investments in Mexico and Brazil. Amazon lagged behind, reaching Latin American territories in late 2016 as part of the international rollout of Prime Video and adopting a more conservative approach to the commissioning of original productions from the region.

Telecom and Larger Internet Service Providers

Mainly emerging from the telecommunication sector, internet service providers form a gateway to internet-distributed television. While telecommunication operators have strong control over the provision of internet services, some of the larger media corporations in national markets have also entered the business of telephony and internet services, in many cases afforded by their long-standing presence in the business of providing pay TV.

The region's main internet providers are Claro (América Móvil from Mexico), Movistar (Telefónica from Spain), Vrio (DirecTV/AT&T from the United States), Tigo (Millicom from Sweden), and Liberty Latin America (Liberty from the United States). América Móvil is present in seventeen countries, attracting 278 million subscribers, but there are still many local and national telecommunications corporations with significant shares at national levels and with considerable size relative to their domestic markets, such as Oi and TIM (Telecom Italia) in Brazil, Izzi (Televisa) and Total Play (TV Azteca) in Mexico, ETB and UNE in Colombia, and Telecom in Argentina.

Content Delivery Networks

Most VOD services operate as over-the-top (OTT) services, meaning they provide end users with video content over the open internet. To work efficiently, any OTT therefore requires the optimization of internet traffic. Content delivery networks (CDNs) are systems of interconnected servers that deliver content based on the proximity to the user requesting the video. By providing a service from a server physically close to the user, CDNs speed the delivery of content as well as prevent jamming in the context of high traffic, whether regionally or globally. According to Team Intricately (2018), the leading CDNs in Latin America are Akamai, Amazon CloudFront, CloudFlare, Imperva Incapsula, and Stack Pack. But focusing only on the CDNs providing services to Netflix, Amazon, HBO, Blim, Claro Video, Globo.com, and Movistar within the Intricately database (Intricately.com n.d.), we found that the dominant corporations are Amazon, Akamai, CloudFlare, and the Swedish Varnish Software Group.

Many of the main CDNs have spent resources on server infrastructure for the purpose of delivery and storage of data in big quantities, creating a distinctive subsector: the data cloud business. Amazon Web Services (AWS) is the leading provider of cloud services for the region, followed by Microsoft Azure, IBM Cloud, América Móvil, and Google Platform (Team Intricately 2018). But if we look at cloud services for the leading seven SVOD providers, the landscape is more dispersed. A search on the Intricately database for corporations providing cloud services for these SVOD providers resulted in a list of seventy-five companies, of which fifty-five were from the United States, representing 77 percent of the market. From this segment, Amazon is followed by Google, Microsoft Azure, and Yahoo (Verizon), along with Latin American players such as the Mexican Telmex and Argentine Impsat providing services to América Móvil, and Brazilian Locaweb to Globo.com, as well as companies from Canada, France, Sweden, Australia, and Israel (Intricately.com n.d.).

Digital Intermediaries

Digital intermediaries compose a variety of different corporations giving services through algorithms, curatorial resources, user tracking, advertisements, and any other services that allow different forms of data mining that mediate the operations and possible decisions of different SVOD providers (Braun 2014). This is the most opaque of the four levels, for the participation of corporations goes largely unnoticed and seems invisible through the whole process of distributing video content. Through the Intricately database, we found 225 corporations giving specialized software support to the seven main SVOD providers in Latin America. Among these, the main players were Google, Amazon, Facebook, and Microsoft. But there were twenty-one Latin American entities, all of them supporting the three SVOD corporations actually from Latin America: Claro, Blim, and Globo.com. It is important to underscore that many of these entities are actually subsidiaries of their Latin American SVOD's parent corporations and companies from their domestic markets: Claro (América Móvil) has ten Latin American corporations, Globo.com has ten Brazilian entities, and Televisa has one Mexican subsidiary (Intricately.com n.d.).

The Latin American Market for SVOD

According to OVUM (2018), in 2018 there were 28.5 million SVOD subscribers in Latin America, which represented an increase of 22 percent in relation to the 23.3 million in 2017. SVOD has mainly grown in urban centers due to the better infrastructural conditions for connectivity, with most subscribers found among the middle- and high-income demographics.

Despite the decline in broadcast television audiences in almost all countries across the region, content produced by national television networks has a large presence in SVOD catalogs. In the analyzed markets, traditional television retains a privileged position as the first window of exhibition through free-to-air television, even though in most of the cases this content then is moved and offered through several VOD services, either after the broadcasting of each episode or at the end of the whole season, giving the content a second and larger life through digital archives. This is applicable to the coproduction agreements among local broadcast corporations and global SVOD providers, in which the television networks reserve the first window of distribution.

In the largest media markets of Latin America, television broadcasters and pay TV entities have better capacity to be competitive with their own VOD services and offer the possibility of succeeding as full-fledged participants against regional and global players. For instance, in Brazil, Rede Globo is the dominant television network and has its own SVOD platform, Globoplay, offering programming that has already been broadcast on the network along with content produced exclusively for the platform. Also, Globoplay premieres some content that is later scheduled for broadcast television. In Mexico, Televisa launched Blim, later rebranded as BlimTV, an SVOD service with a presence in seventeen countries across the region. Blim's original approach was to offer successful Televisa content through the platform, but the network shifted toward producing original programming as well as offering live television channels and content from international television and film corporations such as Disney, Paramount, MGM, and the BBC. In Argentina, the main pay TV provider, Cablevisión, a subsidiary of the Clarín Group, launched its own SVOD service in 2017 under the brand Flow. With a content strategy similar to Globoplay, Flow combines programming from free-to-air television with other content exclusive to the platform. Flow now has a 20 percent share of the SVOD market in the country.

In contrast, in small media markets there is little opportunity for local corporations to become important contenders. Mega and América TV, the leading networks in Chile and Peru, respectively, use their official websites or YouTube channels to distribute for free programming that has already been broadcast. Neither, however, has consolidated its own VOD platform by producing original content to compete against the regional players, as is the case in Argentina, Mexico, and Brazil.

After a period of struggle and requests for a stronger regulatory framework to "level the playing field," telecom operators and pay TV corporations now seem to be convinced that players such as Netflix are complementary and are opting to forge alliances of a different nature and reach. Meanwhile, broadcast corporations are taking advantage of the opportunities to provide production services to the global SVOD players by making local content for them. However, the latter is a collaborative scenario mostly in the larger developed audiovisual markets. Caracol TV, Colombia's leading broadcast television network, has an agreement to provide production services to Netflix. In the context of this agreement, *Siempre Bruja* (2019–) was produced as exclusive content for the platform, as well as the series *Sobreviviendo a Escobar, Alias*

JJ (2017), *La Niña* (2016), and *La Ley Secreta* (2018). In Brazil, Globo Group created the company Globo Studios to design, develop, and deliver content. They established an agreement to produce content for Sony and have also created content for Globoplay. Amazon Prime Video launched its first Latin American studios in Rio de Janeiro. In Mexico, the main television networks offer production services to international corporations. Televisa produces for Amazon as part of the strategy to launch a new premium content division. Meanwhile, TV Azteca produces content with Sony Pictures Television, creating its own production company and seeking to make programming for the international television marketplace.

In relation to original content production in the region, Netflix has gone after the largest markets: Argentina, Brazil, Colombia, and Mexico. In 2018, Netflix produced seven series in Brazil—*3%* (2016–), *O Mecanismo* (2018–), *Samantha!* (2018–), *Borges* (2018), *Gamebros* (2018–), *Velhas Amigas* (2018–), and *Se Beber, Não Ceie* (2018); seven in Mexico—*El Chapo 3* (2018), *Club de Cuervos 3* (2017), *Ingobernable 2* (2018), *La Balada de Hugo Sánchez* (2018), *Yo, Potro* (2018), *La Casa de las Flores* (2018–), and *Diablero* (2018–); two in Colombia—*Distrito Salvaje* (2018–) and *La Ley Secreta*; and one in Argentina—*Edha* (2018). But in Chile, Peru, and other smaller markets across the region, there has been no original production.

Even though Netflix is by far the dominant player, with an average of 65 percent of subscribers in the domestic markets in all analyzed countries, according to Digital TV Research (2019) the emergence and growth of many different SVOD players in the region will reduce the company's commanding presence. Smaller players are emerging to serve specific audiences with niche content. In some cases, these services have been launched by private entrepreneurs supported by national capital. Others are supported by the state, which has entered the VOD market as a player with its own platforms offering local and national content produced using public funding. These trends are visible in the case of Argentina. MUBI (mubi.com), the international niche SVOD service launched by Turkish-born entrepreneur Efe Çakarel, addresses an audience of cinephiles by offering a small rolling program of films focused on *auteur cinema*, with contemporary and avant-garde work in different languages. Homegrown service QubitTV (qubit.tv) offers a catalogue of classic and independent film titles. Meanwhile, in 2015 the Argentinean state created Cine.ar Play (play.cine.ar) to offer free Argentinean content together with premiere titles as a TVOD service. In 2018, Cine.ar Play premiered 170 new films simultaneously with movie theaters. Similarly, in Chile the National Television Council (CNTV) has a content streaming platform, Plataforma Audiovisual (prontus.cntv.cl/videoteca), that makes available a library of productions financed by the state that the Chilean public can access for free.

As these initiatives intentionally serve niche audiences, they do not have the goal of directly competing with the global players such as Netflix or Amazon. Nonetheless, as mentioned earlier, in larger media markets such as Brazil, Mexico, and Argentina, major telecom companies, such as Claro Video, Cablevisión Flow from the Clarín Group, and even Movistar from Spain, have the economic, technological, material, and symbolic capital to introduce local VOD services with the real possibility of competing against the global players and the region's own technology companies.

Conclusion

Changes and opportunities in today's digital media ecology have been driven by new possibilities for distribution, introducing additional windows for the delivery of television programming and enabling users to access that content on multiple devices, with a consequential impact on the time and space dynamics of consumption. As a result, the modalities of digital distribution are reshaping production strategies. This chapter has offered insights into how digital distribution is changing the national and regional television industries of Latin America, shaking up long-standing industrial practices and disrupting the position of Latin American television corporations as indisputable hegemonic forces. Among the most visible transformations are innovations in programming and production strategies, the reconfiguring of the corporate landscape as the major and minor players in VOD emerge and new alliances are formed, and changes to ways of knowing and engaging with audience demographics. However, the possibilities for the internet to operate as a potentially democratizing space, promoting a horizontal model of communication and interaction, are shaped by the same forces that rule the broader media landscape in contemporary capitalistic societies. Thus, internet-distributed television is a media space of profound differences. In digital markets, traditional debates relating to media concentration acquire additional complexity as the internet allows an exponential capacity for delivery while at the same time creating profound asymmetries with the emergence of corporations holding hegemonic influence at regional and global levels.

A key element in the SVOD business model is the quality of the interface, showcasing the availability of content from any device and customizing what is offered through recommendation systems. Companies from the computing technology sector, working as digital intermediaries, have become key participants in the internet television distributed infrastructure, successfully positioning video streaming corporations in dominant positions. For instance, through their use of data, systems of recommendation, geofencing, and geotargeting, U.S. SVOD providers gain a disproportionate advantage in national, regional, and global markets. The imbalance of human, financial, and technological resources, with which corporations from developing countries and emerging markets need to contend, set the conditions for unequal competition due to the high cost of the required infrastructure in internet-distributed television.

In terms of the marketplace of traditional television regional flows, TV Globo and Televisa are the commanding networks, but there is also a robust presence of many other players: Caracol TV and RCN from Colombia, Telefe and El Trece from Argentina, TVN and Mega from Chile, Venevision from Venezuela, Rede Record from Brazil, TV Azteca and Argos from Mexico, and Telemundo from the U.S. Hispanic market. Ironically, internet-distributed television has mostly erased the presence of these corporations at regional levels, while opening the door to the dominant telecom companies, Claro (América Móvil) and Movistar (Telefónica).

In the past few years, media content providers, pay TV operators, and telecom companies, including mobile device makers and computing corporations, have entered this digital market, expanding the content on offer. As we have seen in this chapter, however, they were basically corporations already consolidated in their original domestic markets, with economic, technological, cultural, and symbolic capital allowing them to reproduce the strategies of their previous dominance.

Telecommunications carriers, such as América Móvil, Telefónica, and Vrio, whose operations demand strong infrastructure and large financial investment, have a significant presence in the markets researched here. When we look at national markets, the landscape of participation by mass media corporations shows more diversity but is still characterized by a few dominant television corporations: Clarín in Argentina, Globo in Brazil, Caracol TV in Colombia, Mega in Chile, Televisa in Mexico, and América TV in Peru. Weak or absent antimonopoly regulation has allowed national dominant players to strengthen their positions, in many cases becoming part of larger corporate holdings that can resist the advance of global and multinational corporations into their domestic markets. In this sense, the legal framework and market structure across the region for internet distributed television seem to reinforce concentration as the only way to succeed in the regional marketplace for SVOD services.

NOTES

1 For information on the main television markets in the region—Argentina, Brazil, Chile, Colombia, Mexico, and Peru—we have the collaboration of a team of researchers, represented by Luis Fernando da Silva University of Minho, Brazil; Pablo Julio, Francisco Fernández, Constanza Mujica, Pontifical Catholic University of Chile; Omar Rincón, University of the Andes; Gabriela Gómez, Guillermo Orozco, and Darwin Franco, University of Guadalajara, Mexico; James Dettleff, Giuliana Cassano, and Guillermo Vázquez, Pontifical Catholic University of Peru.

2 A television player that also has an increasing influence in the Spanish-language circuit of content circulation is the U.S. Hispanic television network Telemundo.

BIBLIOGRAPHY

Baladron, Mariela, and Ezequiel Rivero. 2019. "Video-On-Demand Services in Latin America: Trends and Challenges towards Access, Concentration and Regulation." *Journal of Digital Media & Policy* 10 (1): 109–26.

Becerra, Martín, and Guillermo Mastrini. 2017. *La concentración infocomunicacional en América Latina (2000–2015). Nuevos medios y tecnologías, menos actores.* Bernal: Universidad Nacional de Quilmes-Observacom.

Birkinbine, Benjamin, Ródrigo Gómez, and Janet Wasko, eds. 2016. *Global Media Giants.* New York: Routledge.

Blanco, Carlos, and Alejandro Couce. 2016. "SVOD and TVOD OTTs in Latin America." *Vindicia*, August 11. www.vindicia.com.

Braun, Joshua. 2014. "Transparent Intermediaries: Building the Infrastructures of Connected Viewing." In *Connected Viewing: Selling Streaming, and Sharing Media in the Digital Era*, edited by Jennifer Holt and Kevin Sanson, 125–38. New York: Routledge.

Burnay, Catarina, Pedro Lopes, and Marta Neves de Sousa. 2018. "Comparative Synthesis of Obitel Countries in 2017." In *Ibero-American TV Fiction on Video on Demand*

Platforms, edited by Maria Immacolata Vassallo de Lopes and Guillermo Orozco Gómez, 25–67. Porto Alegre: Sulina. www.obitel.net.

Ceurvels, Matteo. 2019. "Latin America Digital Video 2019: What's Driving Digital Video Viewership in Argentina, Brazil, Mexico and Other Markets." *eMarketer*, September 19. www.emarketer.com.

Digital TV Research. 2019. "LatAm to Add 24 Million SVOD Subscriptions." *Digital TV Research*, April. www.digitaltvresearch.com.

Franklin, Johnathan. 2019. "The Insidious Device Revolutionizing Piracy in Latin America." *Americas Quarterly*, January 23. www.americasquarterly.org.

Intricately.com. n.d. https://my.intricately.com/home.

ITU. 2018a. "Fixed Broadband Subscriptions." International Telecommunications Union. www.itu.int.

———. 2018b. "Mobile Cellular Subscriptions." International Telecommunications Union. www.itu.int.

Lotz, Amanda, Ramon Lobato, and Julian Thomas. 2018. "Internet-Distributed Television Research: A Provocation." *Media Industries Journal* 5 (20): 35–47.

Martín-Barbero, Jesus. 2004. "Memory and Form in the Latin American Soap Opera." In *The Television Studies Reader*, edited by Robert C. Allen and Annette Hill, 276–84. London: Routledge.

McDonald, Andrew. 2018. "Latin America Pay TV 'Set to Stagnate.'" *Television Business International TBI*, March 6. https://tbivision.com.

Miller, Toby, Nitin Govil, John McMurria, Richard Maxwell, and Ting Wang. 2004. *Global Hollywood 2*. London: British Film Institute.

OVUM. 2018. "OTT Video Subscription Service Provider Forecast: Americas, 2018–23." London: OVUM.

Perren, Alisa. 2013. "Rethinking Distribution for the Future of Media Industry Studies." *Cinema Journal* 52 (3): 165–71.

PRODU. 2019. "Estudio de investigación." In *Guía OTT 2019: Servicios y proveedores*, 31–40. Doral: PRODU. https://issuu.com.

Punt, Daniel, and Phillip Schuman. 2019. "Is Latin America Ready to Binge?" *FTI Journal*, August. www.ftijournal.com.

Sandvig, Christian. 2015. "The Internet as the Anti-Television: Distribution Infrastructure as Culture and Power." In *Signal Traffic: Critical Studies of Media Infrastructures*, edited by Lisa Parks and Nicole Starosielski, 225–45. Champaign: University of Illinois Press.

Straubhaar, Joseph. 1991. "Beyond Media Imperialism: Asymmetrical Interdependence and Cultural Proximity." *Critical Studies in Mass Communication* 8 (1): 39–59.

———. 2012. "Telenovelas in Brazil: From Traveling Script to a Genre and Proto-Format Both National and Transnational." In *Global Television Formats: Understanding TV across Borders*, edited by Tasha Oren and Sharon Shahaf, 148–77. New York: New York University Press.

Team Intricately. 2018. "Latino America Cloud Market Report (H1 2018)." *Intricately*, July 30. www.intricately.com.

13

VOD

Formal Challengers for Nollywood's Informal Domestic Market

JADE L. MILLER

The screens of sub-Saharan Africa and the African diaspora are domi-nated by local content. The most popular screen industry in this context is Nollywood, the Nigerian movie industry, and this chapter examines the parameters of digital distribution of this content within Nigeria, including the industry's intersection with global digital distribution and global technology investment. The industry has been characterized by its prolific production, its largely straight-to-video (STV) distribu-tion, and its televisual style (Adejunmobi 2015; Jedlowski 2012), mostly eschewing the style, venue, and business model of traditional cinema. While Nollywood movies are popular around the world, sales of physi-cal copies to domestic (Nigerian) audiences remain the lifeblood of the industry, with online consumption reaching only a very limited segment of domestic audiences. This physical distribution flows through the net-works of Nigeria's open-air marketplaces, both financed and distributed by a large opaque cartel of traders known as marketers who are the exec-utive producers of this content.

Domestic audience preference for physical copies of movies over online delivery has many drivers. The largest disincentive for online streaming audiovisual consumption within Nigeria is widely considered to be the exorbitant rates charged for frequently interrupted low-speed delivery of data by Nigerian service providers. Such challenges have not stopped speculators, however. Keen to be among the first to seize market share in an anticipated digital entertainment future, a number of key players have pursued becoming Nollywood's "Netflix of Africa." These well-funded companies include existent satellite television behemoths (led by South African conglomerate Naspers) and well-funded start-ups, most prominently iROKOtv, a company that used Silicon Valley venture capital to transform into the industry's leading global online subscription-based distributor.

This chapter explores the high-powered, heavily promoted, yet still poorly subscribed efforts of these video-on-demand (VOD) aspirants in Nigeria, with a focus on a few case studies: Netflix, iROKOtv, Africa Magic, and Canal+. The persistence of physical distribution, driven by the continued power of the marketers to shape the industry, combined with the high cost and low speed of data delivery in Nigeria, renders these investments extremely long term at best. Corporate and venture-capital-funded endeavors promise investors a formal arm of the industry in which to invest. Yet if Nigerian data prices were to drop, there would be no surety that digital distribution of Nollywood content in Nigeria would run through these formal companies, particularly given the breadth and popularity of informal digital distribution alternatives. This chapter explores the tensions between the intentionally informal hard copy distribution that still dominates in Nigeria and the formality of the industry's official formal online distribution endeavors. This formal online distribution of course also competes with informal (unauthorized) digital distribution, giving formal online distribution efforts informal challenges on multiple fronts.

Production and Distribution in Nigeria

Distribution tends to be the locus of power across media industries (Jedlowski 2017; Cubitt 2005), and Nollywood is no different. Marketers, the industry's key distributors of physical sales (primarily video compact discs, or VCDs) are also the industry's key funders and executive producers, and they wield immense power (Jedlowski 2017; Miller 2016a). The marketers are a loose collective of many small entrepreneurs, with roots in selling gray-market electronics in Nigeria's open-air markets. The networks built over many years as electronics traders have formed the backbone of their distribution. They keep their distribution figures as opaque as possible, making it nearly impossible for profit sharing or formal investment in the industry: if no one but the marketers know how many titles have been sold, no one else can partake in the profits or predict what would be a reasonable amount to invest in an upcoming movie (Miller 2016a). The bulk of titles produced per year in Nigeria have been and continue to be low-budget STV titles produced by this network of marketers. Given the geographical concentration of this production in southeastern Nigeria, these movies have lately been termed Asaba movies, after the city in and around which many are filmed.

At the same time, higher profile directors and producers have, in the past decade, begun to make higher end, larger budget movies (low to mid-six figures U.S. dollars as opposed to the mid-five figures of Asaba movies) (Ryan 2015), often aspiring to at least a brief cinematic run. These directors generally piece together funding from a variety of investors and, while still pursuing physical home video distribution, attempt to diversify the distribution outlets (such as theatrical release and sales of multiple distribution rights to online and satellite television distributors) and therefore income sources of their films. This end of the industry is known as New Nollywood and features titles with higher production values, often glossier urban settings, and themes that lionize upscale consumerist lifestyles as opposed to viewing them with a suspicious eye (Haynes 2014; Ryan 2015). These films are often considered to be more palatable to foreign and expatriate audiences. A small subset of the most high-profile of these titles might get picked up by international film festivals and global online distributors like Netflix.[1] While New Nollywood achieves a high profile with its glossier, more expensive productions, Asaba movies still make up the bulk of titles produced per year and populate the endless circle of Nollywood movies screened in a row on many of Nigeria's smaller screens. The term New Nollywood has also come to be used to describe glossy straight-to-online (or, in some cases, straight-to-television) content populating YouTube and various streaming sites to be discussed later in this chapter, ranging from shorts to television-style serials to full-length movies (Haynes 2018b). These are often episodic and made by corporations promoting themselves or streaming sites attempting to populate the content provider's channel with more self-produced content.

Endless attempts have been made to usurp the marketers' power, from government-led attempts to license distributors (see Bud 2014) to creative-led attempts to set up alternative distribution networks (see Miller 2016a). But while individual films have done well without the marketers' cooperation, all large-scale efforts have failed as the marketers' collective power does not allow room for such incursions for a wide breadth of titles. Structured by a dense network of interlocking ethnic and kinship ties, with none large enough to be targeted directly, the marketers have been effectively able to shut down any incursions on their territory: they can cut movies offered by other interlopers out of their collectively dominant physical distribution networks and can afford to flood the government's attempt at a distribution registration system to the extent it became meaningless (see Bud 2014).

While they must cooperate with one another, the marketers associated mostly with Asaba movies are often at odds with the industry's independent producers, who would like more power and bigger budgets under the New Nollywood moniker. Independent producers, including the New Nollywood contingent, still must maintain business relationships with Asaba marketers in order to be viable. These producers make agreements on who can sell their productions in which markets and even at which stalls with the marketers (Witt 2017). Agreements are almost always flat rate, not involving any percentage of the final sales: once rights to a movie are sold, there is no further need for interactions regarding the afterlives of the movie with the original directors or independent producers. While New Nollywood movies often cost more for consumers in the marketplace, Asaba movies still constitute the bulk of sales and the majority of films watched and known by the viewing public (Witt 2017). Even with flat-rate agreements between marketers and independent producers, accusations of piracy still run rampant; producers take issue, for instance, with schemes in which titles are sold ten-in-one—marketers sell older popular titles along with less popular titles to make money off of both (Jedlowski 2017). Though producers may protest, the agreements leave little room for them to have a voice in what happens to their movies once the rights are ascribed to particular marketers.

As digital distribution appears on the horizon, it would appear that nonphysical distribution is one of the few opportunities to challenge the marketers—or perhaps their weakest spot ripe for attack. Their collective power lasts only as long as their control over the physical distribution marketplaces, for this is the key to financial success in the industry. If viewers can obtain content digitally, the window is open for new players to obtain market dominance in digital distribution. This has not escaped the notice of Afro-optimists looking to invest in the continent. Media conglomerates like French Canal+ or South African MultiChoice, and online streaming companies like Nollywood giant iROKOtv have looked to this opportunity as their entrée into what would otherwise appear to be a closed market.

Digital Distribution in Nigeria

The huge amount of attention that digital distribution has gotten from investors in Nigeria stands in the face of the weak domestic consumption of digitally distributed content. Though members of the diaspora are healthy consumers of Nollywood's official online distribution, the bread and butter of Nollywood's market is physical domestic sales in Nigeria, the main source of profits.[2] The exorbitant costs Nigerian ISPs and telecoms charge for data downloads make the advent of digital streaming content particularly challenging for potential contenders. Streaming a single movie can easily cost five dollars in data charges alone, even at its most compressed packaging, and this is in addition to subscription or other access fees that would be necessary to even access the movie in the first place. This is approximately the cost of a discounted ticket to the cinema and well beyond the budget of casual consumers who may prefer to watch many Nollywood movies in a row, often in the background throughout the course of the day. And this figure is for viewers accessing movies via sites aimed at the Nigerian market, sites that optimize the size of movies for maximum compression and minimal data usage. Downloading a full movie from iTunes or streaming from uncompressed Netflix would cost much more. There are other challenges as well, such as intermittent electricity and lack of established online payment systems, but data download prices remain the biggest issue (Njoku 2015). Dovey points out the myopia in much theorizing and prognosticating about SVOD, based on an assumption of universal access to affordable, uninterrupted internet connections (2018) as well as seamless mobile payment systems. Most of those living in sub-Saharan Africa do not have this access.

While the online path is not the most popular distribution arm of the industry for viewers or marketers, it *is* seen as the main potential investment vehicle for those looking to sink formal money into Nollywood's future. Journalist Emily Witt interviewed Chike Maduegbuna, the head of Afrinolly, a start-up mobile app that distributes Nollywood content as well as information about Nigerian movies. Maduegbuna's plans for expansion and corporatization included formalizing accounting and increasing product placement and advertising deals with corporate clients, but his main focus was on "capitalizing on the potential of the vast mobile phone market of Nigeria and beyond" (Witt 2017, 91). Mobile phones have indeed been predicted as the most likely access point for Africa's digital entertainment future (particularly if a technology like Chromecast could commonly be used to stream from a mobile phone to a television), but even then the price of unlimited data is similar to an average person's annual salary (Dovey 2018, 97). That said, mobile phone penetration has far outpaced that of any other technology including television itself (Dzimwasha 2017) and is the most likely access point of a digital future, shifting entertainment perhaps to what Dovey deems the "supersmall screen" of the smartphone (2018, 98), a trend echoed by a smaller subset of users in nearly every entertainment market globally.

Digital distribution in Nigeria has thus far involved a number of creative workarounds to connectivity and data cost issues. Internet access is often acquired with dongles connecting to satellite service instead of directly wired broadband, and these dongles are sometimes shared among friends (Witt 2017). Witt (2017) reports that, for the subset of the population working in office settings, a popular practice is to download movies on an office Wi-Fi connection for later viewing. Once one person has successfully done so, they can then exchange movies with friends and associates through Bluetooth and other peer-to-peer connections including USB sticks (Witt 2017).

The scenario is the same in settings far removed from urban offices. Haynes reports recent trends in villages without electricity to have a market stall where users power their phones and then purchase extremely inexpensive pirated versions of movies via phone-to-phone connections such as Bluetooth and FlashShare at less than ten cents per transferred title, allowing (unauthorized) digital distribution with no data connection and limited access to electricity (Haynes 2018b).

Attempted authorized digital distribution services have tried to address these issues: the unpopularity of credit card and other online payment services has birthed partnerships with mobile phone service providers, in which airtime (pay as you go) can be used to pay for streaming content on one's phone. Afrinolly, for instance, lets users spend a hundred naira (less than a dollar) worth of airtime to rent a movie. iROKOtv, the most popular online distributor, opened kiosks in 2016 in which subscribers could pay for their subscriptions in cash or airtime, obviating the need for credit cards; these same kiosks allowed subscribers to download rented movies, also obviating the need for expensive airtime in the first place (Witt 2017). They later added Nigeria's Abuja and Port Harcourt as well as Ghana's Accra to this program to modest success, though the company later scrapped their kiosks in favor of devoting resources to telemarketing for new subscribers, hoping to quickly reach one million subscribers, which would then trigger an IPO and exit for all initial investors within their internal goal of a full exit ten years from inception (Njoku 2019). Another effort to avoid what founder Jason Njoku refers to as "the data burden" (2017) was retooling their digital rights management (DRM) to allow in-person, person-to-person file sharing, which still requires a subscription to their service while using nearly zero data.[3] The abandoned kiosk model, avoiding internet connectivity and just transferring titles via USB or Bluetooth, and the DRM-enabled person-to-person file transfer model also constitute digital distribution. While these practices are quite different from what is generally considered to be digital distribution globally, we can consider these efforts as a part of the story of global digital distribution of entertainment media, optimized for a landscape of expensive spotty data and electricity, in a country with a tendency toward black- and gray-market transactions in nearly all sectors.

Despite these creative workarounds, formal investor efforts remain focused on the long term and on a style that mimics formal commercial digital distributors in more formal markets, using credit card payments, and online streaming or download services using internet data. These efforts do best among the diaspora, while physical copies still dominate Nigeria's domestic marketplace. Regardless of their current profitability, we still see significant investments in digital distribution: investment levels reach millions of U.S. dollars for an industry marked by budgets in the five figures for Asaba movies, the majority of movies made in the industry. This is because global investors—both entertainment investment and tech venture capital—are compelled to invest in what they call "emerging markets" to extend the breadth of their investment (see Brannon Donoghue 2017). For tech investors, sub-Saharan Africa seems particularly rife for investment, as an anticipated (though by no means assured) digital future sits on the horizon. The goal of getting in be-fore anyone else does has led investors to look for so-called white spaces (Njoku 2019) of the market, places where services extant elsewhere in the world have yet to take hold but could exist there in the future if data, payment, or other online support infrastructures begin to look more in line with those in Europe and North America.[4] In this quest to in-vest in backing the future "[insert popular tech company] of Africa," the tech company in entertainment here is most obviously Netflix: can some company be the so-called Netflix of Africa, driven by the most popular movie industry on the continent, coming out of Africa's most populous domestic market? In other words, can a company become the Netflix of Africa by dominating the authorized online distribution of Nigerian Nollywood content in sub-Saharan Africa and within Nigeria itself? In-vestors have repeatedly returned to this question.

Formal Investment in Nigeria's Movie Industry

We can see physical distribution as the nexus of informal distribution in Nigeria. With untraceable sales by opaque parties, movies are bought and sold with little evidence visible to outside observers. While Nolly-wood mainly remains an informal industry, a formal sector has emerged alongside the existent informal networks that structure the industry. Haynes (2018b) concretizes this formal business turn into six constit-uent parts. First is multinational corporations (MNCs), particularly satellite television channels, that dominate international distribution of Nollywood content and have also produced their own content. Second is a shift toward increased nonphysical distribution and consump-tion, particularly centered around satellite television (dominated by South African MNC Naspers and their bouquet of Africa Magic chan-nels showing Nollywood and Nollywood-adjacent content) and online distribution (dominated by iROKOtv). Third is the proliferation of MNC-produced serials aimed at online or televised distribution. Fourth is the limited scale of cinematic distribution involving a small number of multiplexes generally owned by Nigerian corporations (Nwachukwu 2018 notes just seven high-end multiplexes in Lagos, Abuja, and Port Harcourt, the country's three wealthiest cities, while others [e.g., Agina 2020] cite thirty formal cinemas across the entire country). Fifth is the increasing prominence of smartphones as viewing platforms. And sixth is the ways in which online distribution has catered to diasporic tastes and consumption patterns (Haynes 2018b).

As Haynes describes it, Nollywood emerged in the early 1990s in an age (the mid-1980s to about 2006) he refers to as "Afro-pessimism" in which investing in Africa was deemed to be a pointless endeavor, full of risk for little future reward (2018a, 256). In the past decade, this pessimism has turned to a new narrative, which Haynes characterizes as "Africa rising" (2018a, 256), in which the continent is painted as a rich long-term investment opportunity, particularly in terms of digital technologies. While Haynes points to an overall era of optimism regarding investing in Africa, Jedlowski (2017) specifically highlights volatility in the prices of resources like oil and copper to explain increased attention to media investment on the continent, in efforts to diversify investments across platforms.

As technology firms continue to introduce new services in saturated markets, the sense has spread that one has the potential to garner significant returns on investment by introducing "the [extant tech company] of Africa." As broadband and connectivity continue to have high costs and low availability for the average Nigerian, a popular logic has emerged among investors that there may be money to be made by conquering the African market before the anticipated day in which online services and apps become more pervasive. I review here some of the suitors for the hand of Nigeria's digital future to give a sense of the varied strategies and positions from which this future is being courted.

Global Streaming Platforms: Netflix

Though one of the least successful contenders for streaming subscribers in Nigeria, Netflix itself is indeed one of the many companies that have attempted to become the "Netflix of Africa" and is worth mention here for that point alone. But the strategy they have implemented in other so-called emerging markets—acquiring and creating local content and adding it to their library of shiny global offerings (Brannon Donoghue 2017)—has not worked here. In their attempts to broach a market with an audience addicted to local Nigerian content, Netflix has allowed their library of Nigerian content to remain minimal, without significant attempts to buy rights to large numbers of movies en masse. While

Netflix does carry a small number of Nollywood's most well-known glossier titles, the flashy global content they do carry has been less of a draw except to the cosmopolitan elite of Nigeria: upper-middle-class and upper-class Nigerians familiar with living or traveling abroad in places like Europe and North America. These viewers mirror the viewing preferences of the diaspora because they or their family members are or have been members of the diaspora at times themselves. Netflix hasn't shown itself to have the stomach to adjust their whole platform to challenges like data costs and payment issues and has delivered content in Nigeria in much the same way as it has been delivered elsewhere in the world, via credit card payments and streaming movies in sizes that consume considerable data. This also means offering a content library that leans toward the international, with little focus on Nigerian content. Few believe Netflix's foray into sub-Saharan Africa poses much of a threat to existing services that specialize in Nigerian content like iROKOtv and iBAKATV. After all, those services have been accumulating subscribers in locations where Netflix is already available (Europe and North America), as they offer a completely different library. At best, Adejunmobi (2018) suggests that Netflix could compete by licensing Nollywood's highest profile content at high prices and offering it to viewers for relatively high subscription fees; this content is currently largely unavailable on services like iBAKATV or iROKOtv, profiled next.

Nigerian Streaming Platforms: iROKOtv

While there is a plethora of streaming services that offer at least some Nollywood content, there is one front-runner: iROKOtv. The next runner-up would be iBAKATV. iROKOtv offers a much wider library of Nigerian content than any of the other services. iROKOtv and iBAKATV feature not only popular Nigerian STV content but also their own productions, web and broadcast TV series, and films originally shown in cinemas. However, iROKOtv is known for having more high-profile content, while iBAKATV sometimes goes so far as to advertise trailers for cinema-released movies without having the actual title itself available on their service (Adejunmobi 2018).

By far, iROKOtv is the global front-runner subscription streaming service for Nollywood content. Throughout the diaspora, iROKOtv is the go-to service for those wishing to stream Nigerian film and television. iROKOtv began as a London-based aggregator of rights to Nollywood content for streaming on their YouTube channel, named Nollywood-Love, watched primarily by diaspora audiences. Advertising revenues and usage data garnered from their relationship with YouTube allowed iROKOtv to acquire significant investment from tech-oriented venture capitalists looking to invest in the African digital mediascape in one of the few avenues available at the time. Within eight months of launching the Nollywood Love channel, the company had acquired three million dollars in start-up funds and seven times that in investments within the next three years from a combination of European and American tech investment firms. They used these funds to leave YouTube to become a standalone platform and began to focus on conquering the Nigerian as opposed to the diaspora market.

In iROKOtv's quest to attract more paying viewers within Nigeria, they simultaneously compete with streaming services like iBAKATV and satellite services like Africa Magic, both on prices and on quality of content (Adejunmobi 2018). iROKOtv has been at the forefront of creative solutions for delivering digital content in Nigeria's unwelcoming environment. In 2016, after ending its streaming to desktop services in Nigeria, iROKOtv shifted to a model in which highly compressed movies can be downloaded directly to mobile phones, in an attempt to reach viewers where they are with as little data usage as possible. All signs indicate that the content viewers stream over their phones in Nigeria is short-form—clips or short web series found on YouTube (Dovey 2018). In response, iROKOtv offers highly condensed full-length movie downloads (50–100 MB), keeping data costs as low as possible, instead of streaming their content, which can be interrupted (Dovey 2018).

Given the scarcity of Nigerian subscribers, however, iROKOtv continues to attempt to diversify its strategies for generating income. They have increasingly focused on branding their offerings, introducing, for example, iROKOtv-branded channels on Chinese satellite provider Star-Times (IrokoPlay and IrokoPlus) and British satellite provider Sky TV, recognizing the difficulty in reaching audiences with an internet-only platform. iROKOtv also sold Rok Studio (their in-house production studio) content to Sky TV for the United Kingdom and to M-Net for Africa and the Middle East (Adejunmobi 2018; Haynes 2018b). iROKOtv also developed a partnership with Canal+, the primary francophone satellite pay TV provider in sub-Saharan Africa, to deliver iROKOtv-branded dubbed Nollywood content to Francophone African users via a mobile Android app. In 2019, iROKOtv achieved its biggest financial success to date in a deal to sell Rok Studio outright to Canal+, maintaining Nollywood producer Mary Njoku (wife of iROKOtv CEO Jason Njoku) as the head of the content production arm. Rok Studio, now owned by Canal+, will continue to offer content to other satellite and online channels, including iROKOtv itself (Bright 2019). These are more ways in which the digital mediascape offers opportunities for content to circumvent the existing STV producers known as the marketers.

Anglophone Satellite TV: Africa Magic

Through its subsidiary MultiChoice, South African MNC Naspers operates the dominant Anglophone satellite television network for sub-Saharan Africa, DStv. Spun off as its own standalone listing on the Johannesburg Stock Exchange in 2019, MultiChoice owns, programs, and screens a suite of Nollywood-themed channels grouped under the Africa Magic brand airing on DStv. Popular not just in Nigeria but among viewers across the continent, Africa Magic has become standard and familiar fare in homes and businesses across Africa, often playing in the background as viewers go about other household activities, helping DStv become synonymous with African programming among viewers. There are currently seven different branded Africa Magic channels airing twenty-four hours a day on the satellite service, ranging from Africa Magic Epic (generally Asaba movies) to Africa Magic Urban (usually New Nollywood content) and Africa Magic Hausa (Hausa-language movies) (Haynes 2018b).

While the Africa Magic brand is associated with content delivered via satellite television, Africa Magic is also a player in the digital spectrum. They attempted digital distribution direct to viewers with their own global streaming channel, Africamagicgogo, but this lasted just one year (Adejunmobi 2018). MultiChoice began an online streaming service, Showmax, in 2015, but, like BoxOffice, their pay-per-view service, the content is focused more on foreign imports than on exploiting the Africa Magic library they own rights to (Shapshak 2015; Adejunmobi 2018). As these forays into digital distribution have largely not worked out, Africa Magic remains successful primarily as a satellite television service.

However, the presence of Africa Magic intersects with digital distribution in three major ways. First, they produce their own original content, which they then sell to digital distributors (and other distributors), primarily in the African market. Second, when they acquire rights to content made by others (in many instances, the informally operating marketers) for channels like Africa Magic Epic, they also acquire other ancillary rights in that contract. As a result, Africa Magic has become a formal contact for distribution of that content to other outlets (and some have suggested that they become such a formal contact even for content for which ancillary rights were never included in their initial agreements). Last, they acquire rights to content made initially for digital distribution to play on their satellite channels.

Francophone Satellite TV: Canal+

Just as MultiChoice exploited the popularity of Nollywood content in branding itself as a provider of authentic African programming to subscribers across Anglophone Africa, Nollywood content has become a key strength of French multimedia conglomerate Canal+ in its forays into dominating the mediascapes of Francophone Africa (Jedlowski 2017). In interviews with the main distributors of Nollywood programming in Abidjan, Ivory Coast, Jedlowski indicates that, until 2012, the market for movies there was primarily for physical VCDs of Asaba-style content imported from Nigeria. That year, physical copies were overtaken on a mass scale by Nollywood.tv, a pay-per-view satellite channel available via Canalsat, a French satellite operator, which licensed its content from French platform THEMA's online channel (Jedlowski 2017). Jedlowski (2017) notes that by 2014 Nollywood TV was the second most popular television channel in the Ivory Coast, duplicating content that was available online under the same branding. Reliable electricity in the Ivory Coast has meant that satellite television, and particularly this satellite channel featuring content originating in an online platform, has almost completely overtaken physical copies as the dominant mode of Nollywood consumption and distribution. The tension between physical and digital or satellite distribution is not just a matter of media but also related to strain between small informal distributors (physical) and international, formal, and corporate distributors (satellite and online) (Jedlowski 2017). The constant and instant availability of Nollywood. tv satellite content severely cut into the physical distribution market in Francophone Africa, and Jedlowski suggests the same would happen in Nigeria if electricity, data, and payment services were reliable enough for satellite and internet distribution to overtake physical sales.

Each marketer had historically sold rights for all distribution in Francophone Africa to one party, an independent distributor with whom each had established a direct personal business relationship for hard copy sales. Jedlowski notes these deals between individual Nigerian and Francophone distributors were agreed upon, only to have Africa Magic sell dubbed content directly to CanalTV, using "the argument of informality as an excuse to bypass the marketers and to acquire content directly from other international corporations" (2017, 684). In other words, he accuses Canal+ of dealing with AfricaMagic instead of the actual Francophone copyright assignees due to the lack of documentation and formalization in the agreements between the marketers and their Francophone analogues. Jedlowski posits that Nollywood's self-made successes in production and distribution are now being overwritten as Nollywood content itself is used as a tool for strengthening formal entities like French media corporations and French cultural diplomacy in Africa. Their recent acquisition of Rok Studio from iROKOtv cements Canal+'s branding as purveyors of dubbed Nigerian content acquired via formal business deals with partners committed to transparent financial disclosures and the language of formal international business.

In October 2014, Canal+ opened a Francophone Africa headquarters in Abidjan and created the Nollywood-only channel A+, partnering with iROKOtv in order to do so, both licensing titles from iROKOtv and coproducing with them, opening another chapter in the interplay between Nollywood's digital pioneers and the corporations that have been courting African screens for decades. In this way, we can see any move toward virtual distribution as a move toward centralized and often foreign corporate control over this popular content. Yet Jedlowski points out that the tension between formal and informal business practices is certainly not a tension between capitalism and any alternative; it is instead, he posits, a "battle of scale" in capitalist efforts (2017, 688).

Conclusion

As Wasserman (2014) notes, trends and themes that are taken for granted as a baseline in the Global North can be neither assumed nor expected in the Global South. Digital distribution, streaming video, and online consumption may be following a common trendline in North America and Europe, for instance, but are by no means the status quo in even the most populous countries of the Global South, including South Africa and Nigeria.

By investing directly in distribution outlets that circumvent Nigeria's open-air marketplaces, the potential for online distribution to produce concrete distribution figures has galvanized global investors, from South African media corporations, such as satellite TV giant MultiChoice, to major venture-capital-funded start-ups such as iROKOtv, which have raised millions in remarkably short periods of time.

One day, it is assumed, Nigeria will be a country boasting widespread reliable data coverage, at reasonable prices and speeds. This is what global capital is betting on: the future. Once this happens, could this upend the power dynamics in the industry and open doors further to formal global capital? The answer, too, is confined to the future. Trajectories of technological adoption can foresee a future where these digital distribution services are pervasive and widespread, with fully connected smart televisions in many homes and/or 5G-enabled streaming throughout the country. If that happens, these global investors may very well be poised to take the crown. Residents of Nigeria can testify that the current state of the electricity distribution system in a major oil-producing country leaves little faith in any government-associated initiative in such a direction. Private investment is more likely—particularly in any mobile data development—but this too seems to be a distant future. Online distribution initiatives are extremely long term at best and will serve the diaspora first and foremost, before Nigerian audiences, the core of Nollywood's audience. At the same time, the unauthorized transfer of movies via Bluetooth and other phone-to-phone technologies in rural areas provides a very different model of digital distribution that requires minimal infrastructure (Haynes 2018b).

Nollywood is an industry largely structured by the marketers: the executive producers of the majority of the industry's movies with control over the physical distribution networks making up the industry. The outsiders with whom this network of individual entrepreneurs has traditionally intersected have been the few points of contact made with government agencies and initiatives at the national level (particularly the censorship board), and the informal relationships that govern the industry's labor agreements (Miller 2016b). Yet they also intersect with the global corporations vying for power in digital distribution. This includes the regional, national, continental, and global corporations offering sponsorships and product placement deals, the continental satellite television endeavors delivering content to audiences across Africa (with South Africa's MultiChoice at the forefront), and cinema chains willing to show some Nollywood movies alongside foreign fare (with Nigeria's Silverbird Cinemas running the most prominent multiplexes in Nigeria's wealthiest enclaves). Both MultiChoice and Silverbird have become part of the playing field in Nigeria's film sector, but the power they wield is limited. Big-budget movies will want to play at Silverbird to increase their clout, but they are unlikely to make much money through this route, and the bulk of the income from such movies will still come from physical sales. For some, the exchange of money runs in one direction only, with Silverbird reaping returns from producers paying to run movies on their screens and no revenue from ticket sales going toward the original producers. MultiChoice offers an option for smaller producers to sell ancillary rights on their own, but again these movies must also do well in physical sales to garner any significant payment from the satellite provider. MultiChoice can also commission entire movies on their own, but these films are not particularly popular, nor are they considered to be "regular" Nollywood fare.

Digital distribution opens opportunities for new players to gain ground in Nollywood and opens the doors for global venture capital and global entertainment investors to stake a claim. Currently, the track record of iROKOtv, the most popular distributor, has been to transform the industry in a number of ways by exponentially raising prices for ancillary rights. Global capital is trying to invest in the industry's future in many ways relating to distribution, from satellite television to digital distribution efforts. Individual producers in the industry—marketers and New Nollywood alike—are marked by their navigation of which of these to align with. They choose which they bet upon, and how they can leverage interactions with all of these at the same time to make up their budgets and profits, as power may shift to favor some of these over others over time. The opportunities offered by interaction with formalized digital distribution open the door for corporate and other formal entities to gain a foothold and perhaps eventually dominate in the industry. At the same time, Bluetooth and other phone-to-phone transfers of movies, or the unauthorized online distribution that remains popular in the diaspora, speak to the informality that is pervasive both within Nollywood distribution and in media distribution more generally.

NOTES

1 The 2018 release *Lionheart*, directed and starred in by Genevieve Nnaji, one of Nollywood's biggest stars, is an example.

2 At the same time, even glossy New Nollywood movies that are popular with the streaming public in the diaspora will need to secure physical distribution within Nigeria to ensure the domestic profits that make their production budgets possible. This broad distribution within Nigeria is also necessary to cement their status as authentic Nollywood productions, in comparison with productions made in the diaspora, movies that are generally considered to be inauthentic and less popular even among diaspora viewers (Miller 2016a). These physical distribution deals must be struck with marketers as they are the only viable network through which to reach viewers across Nigeria.

3 "We are utilising the Wifi Direct technology widely available in any and all file sharing services (xender/fileshare/flashshare et al) to firstly move files from agents to customers. Once it's battle tested, we open up and allow person-to-person movie file sharing under the .iroko drm file storage framework. In order to watch the files you will 1.need the irokotv app installed, 2.need a valid subscription. That's it. To check for a valid subscription requires <2mb in data (we're trying to find a way around this). Yet for moving files? Zero" (Njoku 2017).

4 iROKOtv founder Jason Njoku notes in an online article, "No one (Netflix included) has more than 250k+ subscribers in RoA [Rest of Africa, meaning sub-Saharan Africa outside of South Africa] as of now. It is probably one of the only white spaces left globally" (Njoku 2019).

BIBLIOGRAPHY

Adejunmobi, Moradewun. 2015. "African Film's Televisual Turn." *Black Camera* 54 (2): 120–25.

———. 2018. "Streaming Quality, Streaming Cinema." In *A Companion to African Cinema*, edited by Kenneth Harrow and Carmela Garritano, 219–43. London: John Wiley.

Agina, Añulika. 2020. "Cinema-going in Lagos: Three Locations, One Film, One Weekend." *Journal of African Cultural Studies* 32 (2): 131–45.

Brannon Donoghue, Courtney. 2017. *Localising Hollywood*. London: British Film Institute.

Bright, Jake. 2019. "Canal+ Acquires Nollywood Studio ROK from iROKOtv to Grow African Film." *TechCrunch*, July 15. https://techcrunch.com.

Bud, Alexander. 2014. "The End of Nollywood's Guilded Age? Marketers, the State, and the Struggle for Distribution." *Critical African Studies* 6 (1): 91–121.

Cubitt, Sean. 2005. "Distribution and Media Flows." *Cultural Politics* 1 (2): 192–213.

Dovey, Lindiwe. 2018. "Entertaining Africans: Creative Innovation in the (Internet) Television Space." *Media Industries* 5 (2): 93–110.

Dzimwasha, Taku. 2017. "Media Special Report: How Media in Africa Is Adapting to the Online Age." *African Business*, November 20. https://africanbusinessmagazine.com.

Haynes, Jonathan. 2014. "Kunle Afolayan: New Nollywood." *Black Camera* 5 (2): 53–73.

———. 2018a. "Between the Informal Sector and Transnational Capitalism: Transformations of Nollywood." In *A Companion to African Cinema*, edited by Kenneth Harrow and Carmela Garritano, 244–68. London: John Wiley.

———. 2018b. "Keeping Up: The Corporatization of Nollywood's Economy and Paradigms for Studying African Screen Media." *Africa Today* 64 (4): 3–29.

Jedlowski, Alessandro. 2012. "Small Screen Cinema: Informality and Remediation in Nollywood." *Television & New Media* 13 (5): 431–46.

———. 2017. "African Media and the Corporate Takeover: Videofilm Circulation in the Age of Neoliberal Transformations." *African Affairs* 116 (465): 671–91.

Miller, Jade. 2016a. *Nollywood Central*. London: British Film Institute.

———. 2016b. "Labor in Lagos: Alternative Global Networks." In *Precarious Creativity: Global Media, Local Labor*, edited by Michael Curtin and Kevin Sanson, 146–58. Berkeley: University of California Press.

Njoku, Jason. 2015. Personal communication with the author, May 26.

———. 2017. "Beyond Data." *Medium*, January 9. https://jason.com.ng.

———. 2019. "Exited ROK. What Now for iROKOtv?" *Medium*, July 23. https://medium.com.

Nwachukwu, Charles. 2018. "Multiplexes and the Cinematic Experience in Nigeria." *Global Media Journal* 16 (31): 1–7.

Ryan, Connor. 2015. "New Nollywood: A Sketch of Nollywood's Metropolitan New Style." *African Studies Review* 58 (3): 55–76.

Shapshak, Toby. 2015. "Why Netflix Should Be Afraid of Its New Competitor, Which You've Probably Never Heard Of." *Forbes*, August 19. www.forbes.com.

Wasserman, Herman. 2014. "The Ramifications of Media Globalization in the Global South for the Study of Media Industries." *Media Industries* 1 (2): 54–58.

Witt, Emily. 2017. *Nollywood: The Making of a Film Empire*. New York: Columbia Global Reports.

14

The King Is Dead, Long Live the Algorithm

MindGeek and the Digital Distribution of Adult Film

PETER ALILUNAS

Every era gets the porn it deserves.
—Katrina Forrester, "Making Sense of Modern Pornography"

In March 2005, *Forbes* magazine published a profile of Vivid Video cofounder Steven Hirsch, calling him the Porn King (Pulley 2005). It was not hyperbole: Vivid, an adult film company then generating roughly a hundred million dollars per year, had been at the forefront of the home video revolution in the 1980s, using a new technology to disrupt conventional business practices—and it succeeded to an unprecedented degree. As *Forbes* was crowning Hirsch, Vivid was responsible for a third of all adult videos in the United States (Pulley 2005). Howard Levine, Vivid's sales manager, later described just how widely that success could be measured: "When people think of porno, they think of Vivid" (Rutter 2009, 113). The company's identity had transcended pornography, as both product and industry.

The reinvention of the adult film industry in the home video era, as exemplified by Vivid Video, turned sexually explicit material into an increasingly accepted commercial good, replete with an efficient and organized recognizable supply chain stretching from producer to consumer and marketed through conventional channels and mechanisms (Alilunas 2016, 119–31). Vivid's products were available for rent or purchase and distributed to consumers on videotape through either mail order or brick-and-mortar stores. That basic system continued through the DVD era, and Vivid negotiated video-on-demand licensing deals with cable providers, hotels, and other distributors, and eventually through online, subscription-based spaces, growing the web-based share of its overall revenue from 5 percent in 1998 to 30 percent in 2009 (*Economist* 1998; Rutter 2009, 113). This business model, predicated on the production, ownership, and control of feature-length content, defined the adult film industry following the home video revolution. Prior to that, a similar (if less organized) model governed the theatrical exhibition era of adult film in the 1970s (Heffernan 2015, 46–51).

For all his creative instincts, however, Hirsch did not foresee the biggest technological change that would happen to the adult industry since home video had given him the tools to build his empire—a change that was already well under way even as *Forbes* was calling him the Porn King. That change was the technology to stream sexually explicit video online on what are known as tube sites, which are aggregators of free, user-uploaded, unlicensed material. As with home video, this new technology has once again forced the adult industry to undergo sweeping reinvention. The result is a new landscape in which data-driven decision making, advertising, and ancillary income have replaced the conventional business model that long defined the adult industry. While many companies have been part of these changes, it is now a single, vertically integrated corporate entity called MindGeek that dominates the adult industry. In the first part of this essay, I briefly trace the historical evolution of sexually explicit online content as a means of understanding MindGeek's rise; in the second part, I analyze how MindGeek's practices—and, specifically, its use of data—have radically and permanently altered the industry.

Origins: From BBS to PornoTube

These changes did not arise without warning, or in a vacuum. The online-based economy had already upended adult film distribution practices long before the arrival of the tube sites (Coopersmith 2006). Beginning in the late 1970s, consumers had been sharing images from *Playboy* and other magazines on bulletin board systems (BBS), which utilized dial-up modem technology to exchange files. Similar material was later traded with File Transfer Protocol (FTP) software and Usenet newsgroups. After web technology evolved, directory sites such as PersianKitty.com emerged. In the pre–search engine era, these sites provided text links to subscription-based pay sites, which dominated online distribution; in exchange, the directories received a small referral per "converting" subscriber. Eventually, thumbnail gallery post (TGP) sites linked free sample images to pay sites; later, they evolved into movie gallery posts (MGPs), with video samples. All of this formed into a web-ring ecosystem in which affiliates (directories, TGPs, and MGPs) earned referral payouts from pay sites (Paasonen 2019, 557–58; Wallace 2011). Streaming video and live webcam pioneers such as Private Media Group, Internet Entertainment Group Pioneers, and Danni Ashe, creator of Danni's Hard Drive, made fortunes further monetizing the affiliate ecosystem (*Guardian* 1999; Rose 1997). The tube sites dissolved the relative stability of this model and sent the industry into a tailspin of plummeting profits as consumers no longer needed to pay for sexually explicit content. Previously, those consumers might have rented or purchased an adult tape; now, they could instantly access millions of free videos.

The origin of the tube sites can be traced to the creation of YouTube in early 2005 by Chad Hurley, Steve Chen, and Jawed Karim (Graham 2005). They made an early decision to ban nudity on the site—opening the door for other engineers to replicate the technology, for the purpose of enabling customers to upload, access, and share sexually explicit content (Zeller 2006). That is precisely what happened in July 2006, when the creators of the Adult Entertainment Broadcasting Network (AEBN), a pioneer in subscription-based adult video streaming, noticed the popularity of a video sharing tool on xPeeps.com, an AEBN site modeled on the social media aspects of Myspace, and spun the tool off into PornoTube.com, the first tube site (McAnally 2016; *Sydney Morning Herald* 2007). Within months, YouPorn.com, YuVuTu.com, Redtube.com, and XTube.com went online, and soon millions of unlicensed adult videos were circulating (Blue 2006; Hoffman 2007). In mid-2007, Hirsch was approached by Stephen Paul Jones, the creator of YouPorn, who was looking to sell, but Hirsch declined—instead focusing on video-on-demand (Hoffman 2007). It was only months later that Hirsch turned to litigation to stop what was becoming a flood of online adult video: in December 2007, Hirsch sued PornoTube for $4.5 million in damages for copyright infringement, misappropriation of the rights of publicity, and unfair business practices (Vivid Entertainment, LLC v. Data Conversions, Inc. 2007).

The lawsuit against PornoTube echoed a similar action earlier that year by Viacom against YouTube, in which the same complaint of copyright infringement was alleged, albeit on a much larger scale, with Viacom asking for a billion dollars (Viacom International, Inc. v. YouTube, Inc. 2010; Belloni 2008). These lawsuits were doomed by the 1998 Digital Millennium Copyright Act (DMCA), a provision of which created a "safe harbor" for online service providers from any potential copyright infringement liability that might arise from user behavior (DMCA 1998). While the DMCA also required that website owners remove material when notified by copyright owners of infringing violations, that ended up as a farcical game of whack-a-mole on the tube sites, as users uploaded unlicensed content far faster than copyright owners could issue takedown notices (*ABC News* 2010). Ultimately, while it took seven years for YouTube (then owned by Google) to settle the case with Viacom, with no substantial penalty other than a bolstering of YouTube's content filtering system to prevent copyright infringement, Hirsch dropped Vivid's suit within a year, without a settlement, recognizing that there was simply no legal case (Roettgers 2008). With protection from the DMCA, the tube sites were firmly in control of the industry's future.

Mansef: 2003–9

It was in Montreal in 2003 that Ouissam Youssef, Stephane Manos, and Matt Keezer started a group of MGP affiliate sites, including JuggWorld.com, AssListing.com, KeezMovies.com, and XXXRatedChicks.com; after some initial success, they built their own pay sites, Brazzers.com and Mofos.com, for which they contracted with outside producers for original content, and created an accompanying affiliate network, Jugg Cash (Wallace 2011). A holding company, Mansef, covered the growing empire. Initially, it seemed that Mansef shared the industry anxiety about the tube sites; in 2007, Youssef posted messages of support on industry forum GoFuckYourself.com (Cox 2017). The tube site operators, he wrote, could not "get away with" piracy, and "their days are counted!" (Wallace 2011).

Already by that point, however, many in the industry suspected the Mansef group of some deeper involvement with the tube sites (Glass 2010). Their suspicions proved correct: Keez launched Pornhub.com in May 2007; later, Mansef added Tube8.com, ExtremeTube.com, and

KeezMovies.com—all tube sites, and all operated by Interhub, a new entity in Mansef's corporate portfolio (Wallace 2011). At once duplicitous and economically experimental, Mansef's decision illustrates the instability of the adult industry at the onset of the tube site era.

The growing Mansef empire came to an abrupt end. In October 2009, the Organized Fraud Task Force of the U.S. Secret Service seized $6.4 million from the company's bank accounts; the money had been wired from Israel and other countries on the financial fraud watch list. Mansef claimed the funds were to "ease payment processing" and eventually had some of the money returned, but the company's founders seized the opportunity to cash out (Auerbach 2014). For a buyer, they turned to German entrepreneur Fabian Thylmann, who had tried unsuccessfully earlier that year to take over their holdings (Flade and Nagel 2012). It was Thylmann who would push the tube site revolution into an unprecedented position of industry power.

Manwin: 2009–12

Thylmann's purchase of Mansef's holdings was part of a long-term plan rooted in his interest in web optimization. He had been a part of owner by 1998 of Porntrac.com, a web statistics service, and by 2001 had created a tool for tracking adult affiliate sites that had become the industry standard (Hymes 2012). Using his profits from those ventures, Thylmann purchased three affiliate sites and, using his optimization experience, increased traffic by 50 percent within three months (Buse 2012). Thylmann's initial attempt to acquire the Mansef holdings fell apart in 2009, but a successful deal was reached in March 2010 giving Thylmann all of Mansef's assets in exchange for $140 million (Buse 2012). Thylmann combined all of his operations into a company called Manwin—a name chosen because the Mansef group had struggled to get approval to put a large "M" sign on their Montreal-based headquarters; Thylmann simply chose a name that was available and would work (Hymes 2012). That logic illustrates how Thylmann was initially interested primarily in strategies around statistics, optimization, and traffic maximization rather than corporate identities, though that would change.

Later, acknowledging the inherent gamble of Thylmann's strategy during a period of industry upheaval, *AVN* reporter Tom Hymes wrote,

"Manwin is the result of not just risk, but a deep understanding of the direction the industry was taking . . . and the sorts of companies that could—if properly managed—take advantage of the changing marketplace" (Hymes 2012). Thylmann continued his aggressive acquisition strategy, buying Webcams.com and the EuroRevenue network of adult websites (Flade and Nagel 2012; Pardon 2010). In December 2010, Manwin took over the pay site operations of Wicked Pictures, one of the most successful production companies of the video era and a competitor to Vivid (*AVN* 2010). This was a clear warning sign to the industry that the tube sites were gaining power.

These early moves were parlayed by Thylmann into an unprecedented financial deal. In April 2011, Manwin secured a $362 million loan from Colbeck Capital, founded by two former Goldman Sachs employees (Flade and Nagel 2013). This investment allowed the company to expand, establishing Manwin as a global juggernaut, with offices in Luxembourg, Hamburg, Ireland, Los Angeles, Montreal, and Cyprus, and spurring more purchases. Manwin acquired heavyweight competitor YouPorn in May 2011, and in June all the assets of Carsed Marketing Incorporated, which included Twistys.com, GayTube.com, SexTube.com, and Tranny-Tube.com, along with the Twistys Cash Affiliate Program (*AVN* 2011a; *AVN* 2011b). At the end of 2011 came the announcement that Manwin would take over Playboy's television and online business operations, with Playboy staying in charge of brand management (*PR Newswire* 2011). It was a startling development, given Playboy's global brand status—but also because the tube sites were decimating the adult pay-per-view cable model, which had been extremely successful (Alilunas 2018, 369; Briel 2011). While the deal gave Manwin entry into the profitable (and respectable) world of cable television, it also brought added public exposure, given Playboy's public presence and reach. Manwin was cautious about how and when to associate publicly with pornography; the company's employees, for example, were, when asked about the company, instructed in writing to respond, "Manwin is a technically oriented service company. With specialization in design and maintenance of websites as well as the development and implementation of marketing strategies in online trading" (Flade and Nagel 2012). It was all technically true.

Public exposure reached a new level for Manwin in January 2012 at the AVN Internext Expo, an adult industry trade show in Las Vegas.

Thylmann agreed to a keynote in which he would talk about Manwin's history and future (Hymes 2012). Speaking extemporaneously in front of a crowd of eight hundred industry members, Thylmann's remarks had two primary objectives: to assert that he was not a front for anyone else (a persistent question due to Manwin's rapid growth) and to claim that Manwin's tube sites were working to be DMCA compliant in terms of takedown notifications, a clear olive branch to those in the room incensed at the rampant piracy on the tube sites. The event positioned Thylmann as a tech guru akin to Steve Jobs or Bill Gates, and it marked a turning point in which the tube sites—and especially Manwin—were literally at the front of the room leading the conversation.

That same day, Manwin announced that it had taken over all the assets of Digital Playground, another major video player, further marking the changing of the industry guard (Pardon 2012). The following day, a CNBC reporter described Thylmann as the "New King of Porn," and even Hirsch, the one being dethroned, seemed to acknowledge the obvious reality. "There's no question those Manwin guys are smart," he said. "They know what they're doing" (Morris 2012). It was becoming apparent that Manwin was taking over the industry, piece by piece.

While the industry watched Manwin's takeover, the German newspaper *Die Welt* was examining Thylmann's empire. The resulting article, published in September 2012, outlined a global empire of dozens of interlocking companies designed to optimize and monetize traffic to its many websites while simultaneously evading regulation of all kinds. The analysis was revealing: Manwin's websites totaled 1.3 billion clicks *every day*, putting the company on par with Amazon and Wikipedia. Most importantly, the article traced Manwin's efforts to evade taxes in Germany by using holding accounts in Cyprus and elsewhere (Flade and Nagel 2012). The bombshell report exposed Manwin's inner workings for the first time on a global scale.

The combination of rapid growth and public exposure caught the attention of German authorities: Brussels police arrested Thylmann in December 2012 for tax evasion and extradited him back to Germany, while more than one hundred investigators searched Manwin's Hamburg office (Reynolds 2012). Thylmann opted to leave the adult industry in October 2013, selling Manwin for one hundred million dollars to senior management members Feras Antoon (brother-in-law of original founder Ouissam Youssef) and David Tasillo (Pardon 2013). Thylmann was indicted in 2015 and in 2016 reached an agreement to pay back German taxes, effectively ending the case against him; he went on to invest in start-ups outside of adult film (Pardon 2015; *JUVE* 2016; Ohr 2016).

After the sale, without any public announcement, Antoon and Tasillo quickly changed the company name from Manwin to MindGeek. While they were clearly trying to disassociate from Thylmann's legal troubles, Antoon and Tasillo kept most of the corporate mechanisms intact, including the deliberately convoluted internal structures, layers of international offices, and obtuse financial structures designed to maximize tax optimization—practices that were becoming standard in the tube site landscape beyond their own company (*AVN* 2013; Bergeron 2016; *Next Web* 2016). Going forward, the new owners' strategy was twofold and, in some ways, paradoxical: rigid privacy for themselves and MindGeek's corporate activities, and a significant (and carefully controlled) branding initiative for Pornhub, the company's most visible core asset. The goal was for Pornhub to transcend adult film entirely, much as Vivid before it.

MindGeek: 2013–Present

The efforts to make MindGeek's brand more visible predate Thylmann's sale of the company. In October 2010, Manwin, using its Brazzers subbrand, launched a "Get Rubber!" safe-sex campaign with a billboard near Times Square (Javors 2010). Positioned as part of a commitment to "social responsibility," it was precisely the sort of strategy that could lead to greater visibility while simultaneously avoiding criticism—a lesson that the company might have learned from Hirsch, who had once said that "accessibility leads to acceptability" (O'Connor 2004). This is the eternal goal of the adult film industry, to unlock greater profits by decreasing the toxicity of its products. A key component of such a strategy is normalization, as Jonathan Coopersmith argues: "As the purveyors of pornography have shifted from the black (illegal) to grey (legal and low profile) to white (legal and 'normal' profile) markets, its profits and prominence have increased" (2006, 1). Indeed, Vivid, beginning in the 1990s, engaged in an ambitious branding effort to move out of the pornography shadows and into public awareness, beginning with a billboard in Los Angeles in 1996 (Rutter 2009, 84). After FreshJive clothing used Vivid performers in an advertisement in *Spy Magazine* in July 1997, Hirsch hired PR firm Resource Media Group to escalate the strategy (*Spy Magazine* 1997; Rutter 2009, 90). Numerous licensing deals followed, including Pony shoes, SIMS snowboards, and Control skateboards, along with a glut of Vivid-branded products running the gamut from condoms to car wheels (Brodesser 2003; *AVN* 2003; X 2008; Sword 2003; *Adult Industry News* 2005). There were also highly coveted mainstream profiles of the performers, most notably in a 2003 *Vanity Fair* issue about Hollywood, the ultimate coup for an adult film company seeking respectability (*Vanity Fair* 2003). Another billboard, this time with performer Jenna Jameson, was installed in Times Square in 2004 (Pardon 2004). Finally, and the most high profile of all, reality television series about Hirsch and Vivid were aired on Showtime in 2004 (*Porno Valley*), 2007 (*Deeper Throat*), and 2009 (*Debbie Does Dallas Again*). Such visibility—more than the actual content of Vivid's films—was how Hirsch achieved "Porn King" status.

MindGeek has followed a similar path toward branding visibility. Along with the Times Square billboard in 2010, Thylmann paid for a promotional partnership with Relativity Media in May 2012 for Joseph Gordon-Levitt's film *Don Jon*, about a young man more interested in watching sexually explicit videos online than in having a relationship. The Pornhub brand and interface made prominent appearances in the film, and the company assisted in curating the content that the character watches (Whitaker 2013). After Thylmann's sale, branding efforts were significantly expanded and turned toward other creative industries, including art and music. Most prominent among many other efforts were promotional partnerships with upscale fashion brands Diesel, Hood By Air, Richardson, and Moose Knuckles in 2016 and 2017 (Monllos 2016; Breslin 2016; Yenisey 2017; Chu 2017). These were mutually beneficial, inverse relationships: MindGeek wanted the sort of respectability created when associations with pornography are removed, thus transforming sex into art; for the fashion companies, proximity to pornography could bring in some danger and rebellion (Alilunas 2016, 16–20).

Just as Vivid sought outside experience, MindGeek hired advertising agency Officer & Gentleman in 2014, along with Vendetta Studios, a viral video production company, to create advertising and marketing strategies to reach wider audiences. Humorous, safe-for-work commercials designed for online sharing, wearable technologies (like the "wank-band," which recharges a phone during masturbation), a Bitcoin-like currency called Titcoin, and other stunts and promotions quickly followed, keeping Pornhub in the public eye while also maintaining a sense of humor (Sherwood 2015; Tiffany 2018). The overall tone to all of this was one of hip, free-spirited fun, positioning sexually explicit film as just one component of a lifestyle represented by the MindGeek brand—an updated version of the "Playboy Philosophy" that Hugh Hefner had cultivated in earlier decades, which had explicitly linked middle-class consumption and cultural capital (Fraterrigo 2009). It was also, as Kaitlyn Tiffany argues, MindGeek "buying their way to coolness" (Tiffany 2018). The strategies worked to create more traffic: in 2017, the company claimed that it transmitted more data every five minutes on Pornhub alone than the entire contents of all the books in the New York Public Library (Pornhub 2018).

MindGeek's branding efforts go beyond providing ancillary income and marketing visibility; they also distract the public from the data-driven decision making that has become the biggest and most important change to the adult industry. That process is far more advanced than simply guiding consumers through tube sites with content tags and categorization. As Patrick Keilty describes, it begins with web design itself, which accounts for the constant input of new data by browsing consumers. Keilty argues that this creates "a capacity for suggestion," which engineers can then exploit to "softly persuade viewers to continue searching for an imagined perfect image and to enable repetitive and recursive browsing, encouraging viewers to forego the pleasures of the known for the pleasures of the unknown." Ultimately, this isn't about providing potential pleasures, or creating structures to facilitate exploration—it's, as Keilty notes, because "the longer viewers browse the site, the more data viewers produce" (2018).

That data then become the fuel for an engine moving in multiple directions. The first is the most conventional in terms of online spaces: advertising. The tube sites compile and analyze consumer data to tailor and deliver advertising, but since much of that advertising emanates from within the adult industry ecosystem, it performs a double function. As Gustavo Turner argues, "The fact that the same companies [creating the advertising] also own many of the big studios means that they can use the data they collect not only to sell ads, but to make their videos even more engaging so that users spend ever more time watching them, thus generating even more data. They are creating a vertically integrated porn empire" (2019). MindGeek can then collect more data at every point along the way.

Nearly every bit of moving image content on the tube sites, whether overtly a commercial or simply a "free" video found either by engineered suggestion or through literal search, is now an advertisement. That is, a company such as MindGeek fills its tube sites with "free" samples from its pay sites, which are thus actually advertisements. Even though the tube site landscape, with its many millions of videos and visitors, appears to be a self-contained, closed loop, it continues to operate in the affiliate / pay site ecosystem of the earlier era. Of the millions of consumers who watch these clips, only a fraction might convert into paying customers—but even a fraction of millions is highly lucrative when global fees are calculated. Turner describes the data-driven results of this structure: "Porn companies, when trying to figure out what people want, focus on customers who convert. It's their tastes that set the tone for professionally produced content and the industry as a whole" (2019). Thus an ecosystem that appears to be full of endless choice is actually carefully constructed to guide consumers toward the most statistically fruitful possibilities.

That cycle carries over into the production of content. MindGeek has seized on what Kal Raustiala and Christopher Jon Sprigman call "data-driven authorship" (2018, 6). That process, in which producers create new content based on what drives traffic, has come increasingly to determine what fills the tube sites—and what, in turn, drives users to become customers. Raustiala and Sprigman trace a typical MindGeek production—one of many hundreds made every month—and show how production is algorithmically determined, down to wardrobe choices, dialogue, and background furniture, along with more predictable characteristics such as specific sex acts. All of this can change quickly because, as they note, "MindGeek can rapidly adapt new content to meet . . . emerging preferences" (2018, 43). The result is an engineered ecosystem in which what appears to be an endless, open landscape of possibilities is actually made up of tailored advertising masquerading as content leading to pay site pathways, all in order to extract data in order to keep the loop continually flowing.

MindGeek has fine-tuned data-driven decision making, advertising, and ancillary income streams into a massively profitable machine. That machine has stayed in the shadows even as the company has grown explosively and achieved unprecedented public visibility, partly because of the cultural stigma around pornography (rendering it simultaneously invisible and highly visible), and partly because the company has been so successful at writing its own narrative. One important piece of that narrative has been the Pornhub "Insights" blog, where MindGeek disseminates carefully curated narratives about its own data. This usually occurs in the context of a public event that might create more online traffic and trigger larger media outlets to write stories about the statistics. For example, a February 2019 entry titled "Polar VorteXXX" detailed traffic numbers in January 2019 as temperatures dropped to record lows in the Midwest United States (Pornhub 2019). *Newsweek* followed, noting the rise in Pornhub's traffic during the storms, citing MindGeek's statistics as evidence (Moritz-Rabson 2019). Such stories tend to have a sensationalistic and titillating tone, but also lend a mystical patina to Pornhub's self-proclaimed "statisticians," who become keepers of secret knowledge about human sexual behavior rather than employees doing public relations work. As Gustavo Turner argues, this clickbait-focused cycle has resulted in a symbiotic relationship to the mutual benefit of MindGeek and larger media outlets (2019).

The Insights blog, in addition to creating self-perpetuating news stories, also serves the more important function of rewriting the ways in which MindGeek collects, stores, and uses the data of its millions of users. The data become part of harmless and humorous anecdotes rather than described and analyzed as the primary engine of the company's profits. Just as there has been a surge in criticism of the tech industry at large for the way it has ignored privacy concerns, manipulated and mislead consumers, and altered the way societies function (Taplin 2017), there has also been a shift in attention within pornography studies to the ways in which the tube sites and tech companies have engaged in questionable and problematic practices (Jacobs 2012; Keenan 2014). With the tube sites, however, these questions extend into the areas of sexual representation and desire. MindGeek's staggering dominance of the online ecosystem—from production to consumption—means its algorithms and engineers are now organizing something far more consequential than just data. As Keilty argues, they are "responsible for . . . curating, distributing, and regulating our experience of sexual desire today" (2018). Or, to put it another way, as Kwasu Tembo notes, "our desire does not create the database, the database creates our desire" (2018).

In the end, MindGeek's rise to dominance in the industry is really two stories. The first is the one on the surface, and the company's preferred narrative: Pornhub and the other tube sites are part of a lifestyle brand, of which one component is an easy-to-use interface technology giving consumers access to what appears to be free, on-demand, sexually explicit video. The other story is more mundane. As with MindGeek's contemporaries (Facebook, Amazon, Google, etc.), it is about a machine built to harvest personal data disguised as a free product. How the data are collected, used, and saved has been shielded from public view even more than with other tech companies due to the social stigma around pornography and pleasure, a paradigm that MindGeek has capitalized on even as the company claims to be inclusive, progressive, and supportive of stigma-free pleasure.

Conclusion: The King Is Dead, Long Live the Algorithm

As the smoke begins to clear from the chaos of the tube site takeover of the industry, as well as the fallout from the Mansef and Manwin transitions, it now seems clear that much of MindGeek's strategy echoes what Playboy and Vivid successfully did before them: create a brand identity that can inoculate the sexually explicit core product from criticism, thereby stabilizing and keeping hidden the underlying economic machine. While there is no question that MindGeek's model has upended production, distribution, and reception practices, and particularly some of the conventional ways in which consumers exchanged money for adult films, new paradigms and practices are emerging—including the surge in feminist pornography that is decidedly different from MindGeek in both industrial and narrative contexts (Raustiala and Sprigman 2018, 26).

Ultimately, the new "King of Porn" is not a person, like Steve Hirsch could claim in 2005 or Fabian Thylmann in 2012. The throne is now occupied by silent, endlessly churning algorithms, collecting and analyzing the mountain of data being collected continuously around the globe, with every click saved in endlessly growing databases and efficiently utilized to create more content, act as part of an aggregate toward garnering advertising, and reside in a collection of data about individual users. Among other things, MindGeek serves as a significant component in what Evangelos Tziallas calls the "Pornopticon," a system "in which porn . . . is coded into surveillance" (2018). For MindGeek's massive network of websites, every click represents multiple profit entry points, more data for more algorithms. While it may have seemed unclear at first in 2007 how a tube site would make money, there's no confusion anymore. MindGeek harvests data about hundreds of millions of people, given without hesitation in exchange for "free" sexually explicit content. This transaction is rarely, if ever, questioned. MindGeek channels that data back into even more algorithmically generated content, advertising revenue, pay site conversions, and other mechanisms, but it also now uses that data as a product itself, and as a means to build Pornhub in particular as a brand identity that has increasingly transcended sexually explicit content entirely, the same way Vivid did at its height but with staggering increases in global scale.

The biggest change to the industry, in the end, might be what the "industry" even means in the tube site era. As Susanna Paasonen writes, "When applied to online pornography, the notion of the 'porn industry' is by necessity a rather elastic marker of individual and collective agents, some of which have no direct part in the production of porn and which merely facilitate its distribution and consumption, as though hosting services" (2015, 218). The intertwinement of technology, content, and data has created a new ecosystem in which the sexually explicit content ostensibly driving the engine might, remarkably, be the least important component even as consumers believe it to be the only one. As Raustiala and Sprigman argue, "Digital distribution is not merely a means of distributing content; *it is fundamentally a communications channel for data about content preferences and consumption*" (2018). MindGeek and the other behemoths of the adult industry are now unequivocally data companies whose platforms primarily feature sexually explicit moving images—the content of which is itself increasingly determined not by traditional creative practices and production cultures, but rather by algorithms with a primary function of facilitating more data production and collection. The consequences of these industrial practices are significant and will have long-lasting ramifications. As Mark Hay argues, "The content pushed upon us will likely reflect what is most profitable, not what is mostly widely desirable. It could well become narrowing, or at least channeling, rather than broadening" (2019). The greatest (and most predictable) risk of such a system is that marginalized sexualities, desires, and behaviors that are not profitable will be further marginalized and stigmatized.

The adult industry now increasingly resembles other big tech ecosystems, with MindGeek standing alongside Twitter, Facebook, Amazon, and Google as the giant in its sector. It will also, I believe, increasingly be faced with similar concerns about privacy and security that have come to define those companies and the entire tech landscape. It is unclear to what degree data privacy will play a role in the future of sexually explicit content and its distribution, but there can be no question people will increasingly, if slowly, begin to understand how their privacy has been systematically eroded through the adult tech industry's insatiable appetite for data collection. Of course, as the tech landscape continues to evolve, in part because of these questions, MindGeek will have to evolve as well, which will eventually and inevitably become increasingly challenging. Hirsch himself, during the onset of Vivid's tumble from the throne, intrinsically understood this even as he couldn't stop the inevitable. "It's difficult to continue to invent yourself over and over again," he noted, predicting the fall that happens to all technology-based companies, including his own (Rutter 2009, 113). Eventually, MindGeek, too, will watch as the cycle continues, most likely as another new company takes its place with a technology that better respects consumers—or better hides the ways in which it harms them.

BIBLIOGRAPHY

ABC News. 2010. "Porn Industry Struggles Against Free Content, Piracy." February 11. https://abcnews.go.com.

Adult Industry News. 2005. "Vivid Signs Deal for High End Vivid Wheels." June 8, www.ainews.com.

Alilunas, Peter. 2016. *Smutty Little Movies: The Creation and Regulation of Adult Video*. Berkeley: University of California Press.

———. 2018. "Playboy TV: Contradictions, Confusion, and Post-Network Pornography." In *From Networks to Netflix: A Guide to Changing Channels*, edited by Derek Johnson, 365–74. New York: Routledge.

Auerbach, David. 2014. "Vampire Porn." *Slate*, October 23. https://slate.com.

AVN. 2003. "Vivid and Sexy Snowboards." January 20. https://avn.com.

———. 2010. "Manwin to Manage Wicked Pictures' Online Properties." December 28. https://avn.com.

———. 2011a. "Manwin Acquires YouPorn.Com." May 10. https://avn.com.

———. 2011b. "Manwin Acquires Twistys and Sister Sites." June 2. https://avn.com.

———. 2013. "Manwin Becomes MindGeek." October 28. https://avn.com.

Belloni, Matthew. 2008. "Same Complaints, Sexier Tube in One Vivid Copyright Case." *Hollywood Reporter*, January 11. www.hollywoodreporter.com.

Bergeron, Maxime. 2016. "The MindGeek Enigma, from Luxembourg to Montreal." *La Presse*, October 10. http://plus.lapresse.ca.

Blue, Violet. 2006. "GooTube's Porn Opportunists: The Expanding World of Upload-It-Yourself Smut." *SFGate*, November 2. www.sfgate.com.

Breslin, Susannah. 2016. "How a Porn Company and a Fashion Brand Shocked New York Fashion Week." *Forbes*, September 27. www.forbes.com.

Briel, Robert. 2011. "Manwin Takes Over Playboy TV Operations." *Broadband TV News*, October 31. www.broadbandtvnews.com.

Brodesser, Claude. 2003. "Firm Boots Majority Stake in Pony Shoes." *Variety*, March 2. https://variety.com.

Buse, Uwe. 2012. "Harnessing the Internet: The German Porn King's Revolutionary Model." *Spiegel Online*, December 20. https://web.archive.org.

Chu, Michael. 2017. "Moose Knuckles Shuns IPO as It Teams Up with Pornhub." *Bloomberg*, November 3. www.bnnbloomberg.ca.

Coopersmith, Jonathan. 2006. "Does Your Mother Know What You Really Do? The Changing Nature and Image of Computer-Based Pornography." *History and Technology* 22 (1): 1–25.

Cox, Taylor. 2017. "10 Years of Pornhub." *Benzinga*, March 25. www.benzinga.com.

Digital Millennium Copyright Act. 1998. Pub. L. No. 105–304.

Economist. 1998. "Vivid Imagination." November 19. www.economist.com.

Flade, Florian, and Lars-Marten Nagel. 2012. "The Porn Empire." *De Welt*, September 16. www.welt.de.

———. 2013. "Wall Street Millions Built the YouPorn Empire." *De Welt*, March 23. www.welt.de.

Forrester, Katrina. 2016. "Making Sense of Modern Pornography." *New Yorker*, September 19. www.newyorker.com.

Fraterrigo, Elizabeth. 2009. *Playboy and the Making of the Good Life in Modern America.* New York: Oxford University Press.

Glass, Nate. 2010. "Connecting the Dots: Brazzers and the Tube Sites." *Takedown Piracy*, January 16. http://takedownpiracy.com.

Graham, Jefferson. 2005. "Video Websites Pop Up, Invite Postings." *USA Today*, November 21. https://usatoday30.usatoday.com.

Guardian. 1999. "The Porn Pioneers." September 30. www.theguardian.com.

Hay, Mark. 2019. "Micro-Targeted Digital Porn Is Changing Human Sexuality." *Aeon*, January 17. https://medium.com.

Heffernan, Kevin. 2015. "Seen as a Business: Adult Film's Historical Framework and Foundations." In *New Views on Pornography: Sexuality, Politics, and the Law*, edited by Lynn Comella and Shira Tirrant, 37–56. New York: Praeger.

Hoffman, Claire. 2007. "Obscene Losses." *Portfolio*, November. www.portfolio.com.

Hymes, Tom. 2012. "Manwin's Fabian Thylmann Gives Keynote to Record Crowd." *AVN*, January 18. https://avn.com.

Jacobs, Katrien. 2012. *People's Pornography: Sex and Surveillance on the Chinese Internet*. Los Angeles: Intellect.

Javors, Steve. 2010. "Brazzers Unveils Massive New York City Billboard." *AVN*, October 14. https://avn.com.

JUVE. 2016. "Tax Proceedings Against Porn Entrepreneur Set." November 18. www.juve.de.

Keenan, Thomas P. 2014. *Technocreep: The Surrender of Privacy and the Capitalization of Intimacy*. Vancouver: Greystone Books.

Keilty, Patrick. 2018. "Desire by Design: Pornography as Technology Industry." *Porn Studies* 5 (3): 338–42.

McAnally, Jim. 2016. "Is the Free Porn Era Starting to Fade Away?" *Xbiz*, October 17. www.xbiz.com.

Monllos, Kristina. 2016. "Why a Mainstream Fashion Advertiser Like Diesel Decided to Go Big on Pornhub." *Adweek*, February 19. www.adweek.com.

Moritz-Rabson, Daniel. 2019. "Pornhub Traffic Rose in Midwest as Temperatures Plunged during Polar Vortex." *Newsweek*, February 5. www.newsweek.com.

Morris, Chris. 2012. "Meet the New King of Porn." *CNBC*, January 18. www.cnbc.com.

Next Web. 2016. "The (Almost) Invisible Men and Women Behind the World's Largest Porn Sites." March 3. https://thenextweb.com.

O'Connor, Clint. 2004. "Cleveland's X-Rated Connection Adult-Movie Mogul Has Wealth, but Wants Respect." *Plain Dealer*, January 4.

Ohr, Thomas. 2016. "Interview with Fabian Thylmann." *EU-Startups*, September 15. www.eu-startups.com.

Paasonen, Susanna. 2015. "Online Pornography." In *International Encyclopedia of the Social & Behavioral Sciences*, 2nd ed., edited by Neil J. Smelser and Paul B. Baltes, 217–22. Oxford: Elsevier.

———. 2019. "Online Pornography." In *The SAGE Handbook of Web History*, edited by Niels Brügger and Ian Milligan, 551–63. Thousand Oaks, CA: Sage.

Pardon, Rhett. 2004. "Jenna Jameson Billboard Goes Up in Times Square." *Xbiz*, May 19. www.xbiz.com.

———. 2010. "Manwin Takes Over EuroRevenue." *Xbiz*, September 13. www.xbiz.com.

———. 2012. "Manwin Acquires Digital Playground." *Xbiz*, January 17. www.xbiz.com.

———. 2013. "Fabian Thylmann Sells Stake in Manwin to Company Management." October 18. www.xbiz.com.

———. 2015. "Fabian Thylmann Reportedly Indicted on Tax Evasion Charges." *Xbiz*, April 20. www.xbiz.com.

Pornhub. 2018. "2017 Year in Review." January 9. www.pornhub.com.

———. 2019. "Polar VorteXXX." February 5. www.pornhub.com.

PR Newswire. 2011. "Playboy Enterprises, Inc. and Manwin Close Deal." November 1. www.prnewswire.com.

Pulley, Brett. 2005. "The Porn King." *Forbes*, March 7.

Raustiala, Kal, and Christopher Jon Sprigman. 2018. "The Second Digital Disruption: Data, Algorithms & Authorship in the 21st Century." UCLA School of Law, Public Law Research Paper No. 18-28; NYU Law and Economics Research Paper No. 18-30; NYU School of Law, Public Law Research Paper No. 18-41. https://ssrn.com.

Reynolds, Emma. 2012. "'King of Porn' Arrested on Charges of Avoiding Paying Tax." *Daily Mail*, December 17. www.dailymail.co.uk.

Roettgers, Janko. 2008. "Copyright Lawsuit Against PornoTube Withdrawn." *Gigaom*, October 24. https://gigaom.com.

Rose, Frank. 1997. "Sex Sells." *Wired*, December 1.

Rutter, Jared. 2009. "The Man Who Changed Adult." *AVN*, September.

Sherwood, I-Hsien. 2015. "Pornhub Holiday Ad Is Part of a Larger, Longer Strategy." *Campaign US*, December 21. www.campaignlive.com.

Spy Magazine. 1997. FreshJive advertisement. June.

Sword, Penn. 2003. "Herbal-O, Paradise to Distribute Vivid-Brand Products." *AVN*, September 5. https://avn.com.

Sydney Morning Herald. 2007. "Porn Makers Tap into Internet Social Networking Trend." January 12. www.smh.com.au.

Taplin, Jonathan. 2017. *Move Fast and Break Things: How Facebook, Google, and Amazon Cornered Culture and Undermined Democracy*. New York: Little, Brown.

Tembo, Kwasu D. 2018. "An Engine of Confession: Pornhub, Valentine's Day, and the Lure of Free Usage." *Porn Studies* 5 (3): 343–50.

Tiffany, Kaitlyn. 2018. "Pornhub Wants to Be a Lifestyle Brand." *Vox*, September 14. www.vox.com.

Turner, Gustavo. 2019. "My Stepdad's Huge Data Set." *Logic* 6. https://logicmag.io.

Tziallas, Evangelos. 2018. "The Pornopticon." *Porn Studies* 5 (3): 333–37.

Vanity Fair. 2003. "The Actresses." April.

Viacom International, Inc. v. YouTube, Inc. 2010. U.S. District Court for the Southern District of New York.

Vivid Entertainment, LLC v. Data Conversions, Inc. 2007. U.S. District Court for the Central District of California.

Wallace, Benjamin. 2011. "The Geek-Kings of Smut." *New York*, January 28. http://nymag.com.

Whitaker, Richard. 2013. "Joseph Gordon-Levitt and the Naked Truth." *Austin Chronicle*, September 27. https://web.archive.org.

X, Nelson. 2008. "Control MFG to Introduce Vivid Girl Skateboards." *AVN*, October 14. https://avn.com.

Yenisey, Zeynep. 2017. "Pornhub Just Launched a Hipster Clothing Line, and It's Actually Not That Bad." *Maxim*, September 15. www.maxim.com.

Zeller, Tom, Jr. 2006. "A Slippery Slope of Censorship at YouTube." *New York Times*, October 9.

15

Amazon and Automated Recommendations

Distribution and Discovery in the Book Trade

JULIAN THOMAS

The "digital age" in books once offered a familiar promise, a future where the restrictions of commerce on the circulation of books would evaporate. The first public "digital library" may have been Project Gutenberg, created in 1971 at the University of Illinois by the futurist technologist Michael Hart, also an early pioneer of electronic books. Hart believed in the "unlimited distribution" of books (*Economist* 2011). On his death in 2011, his friend Gregory Newby observed that the "invention of e-books was not simply a technological innovation or precursor to the modern information environment. A more correct understanding is that e-books are an efficient and effective way of unlimited free distribution of literature" (Newby 2011). That promise remains utopian in the present world of books, where dramatic and unexpected change occurs alongside surprising continuities.

The successes and failures of the e-book over several decades exemplify the complexities of current book distribution. Digital book formats have found new markets, but rather than enabling unlimited distribution, many of them have been designed to make sharing or reselling more difficult than for print formats. At the same time, there is now reason to question the assumption that the e-book represents the book's inevitable digital future. In the United States, industry statistics based on publishers' sales report that e-book revenues fell by 3.8 percent in the year to August 2019, as revenue for paper formats increased by 2.5 percent (Association of American Publishers [AAP] 2019b). (These figures do not include sales of self-published works on Amazon and other sites.) In the United Kingdom, Publishers Association figures for 2014–18 suggest several significant trends: slowly declining e-book sales, growing physical book sales over four years before a decline in 2018, and the emergence of audiobooks as a new and unexpected source of growth, with sales increasing especially strongly since 2017 (Sweney 2019).

The complexity of the contemporary book industry is the result of not only an increasing variety of physical and digital formats but also the co-existence of multiple distribution channels, both old and new. Tracking industry trends in this environment is itself challenging. There are no longer any generally accepted metrics of book sales, and no longer any industry-wide identifiers for individual books. Readers acquire books in many ways: through online and physical retail stores, secondary-market sellers, subscription services, and the parallel system of public lending libraries. Among these diverse channels we also find apparently con-tradictory trends, divergent rates of change, and flourishing alternative models. Alongside powerful online retailers—none more prominent than Amazon—small, independent retailers are reported to be making a comeback (Edgecliffe-Johnson 2019). Commercial subscription ser-vices, such as Audible, Kindle Unlimited, Kobo, and Scribd, have proved especially popular for audiobooks. In the United States, the Institute of Museum and Library Services (IMLS) reports intensive and growing public use of libraries, with 1.3 billion physical visits in 2017 (Pelczar et al. 2019). While e-book sales may be flat or in decline, e-book lending through libraries appears to be increasing strongly, according to figures released by a leading e-lending platform (Rakuten OverDrive 2019).

In this chapter, I show how books have helped constitute the digital media present, despite the difficulties in plotting a clear course of digital transformation in this volatile sector. Books illuminate the wider sphere of digital media not only on account of their partial reconstitution into new digital formats such as e-books or audio streams, but also through important changes in their means of distribution and sale. This chap-ter considers automation in terms of two broadly framed "distribution problems" for media studies, both broadly about resource discovery in large-scale digital systems: the question of how audiences find physical or media objects, in our case books, and the question of accessibility, of which books are made available for whom. The emergence of Amazon as a rule-setting platform across all stages of the publishing value chain has had far-reaching consequences for these questions.

While it may seem unusual to focus on Amazon—known best as a retailer—in a book about media distribution, it is important to recognize that as both a marketplace for third-party sellers and a vertically integrated platform working across the entire value chain, Amazon's activities have for some time extended substantially beyond retailing into the traditionally separate realms of distribution. Amazon illuminates in particular the processes of automation at work in the book industry and in digital media more generally. This form of digital transformation is not dependent on the success of any particular digital format—it is significant for both physical and digital books. I take Amazon's recommendation system as a key example of a process of automation extending beyond digitization—a technology for the discovery of resources, designed to match, as efficiently as possible, Amazon's vast database of books with the interests of readers. Although the recommendation system is built for engagement with retail customers, it has powerful implications for actors at all points in the distribution system more generally. This approach enables us to register not only the striking technical and commercial capabilities of the contemporary global book industry, but also those cultural-political and economic aspects of distribution that remain troublesome—for industry participants, readers, regulators, policy makers, and researchers.

Books and Two "Distribution Problems"

The first distribution problem concerns the question of how books reach their readers. Here, books have much to tell us about contemporary media industries, for several reasons. First, the movement of books involves long, connected histories of regulated trade, informal circulation, taxation, and public and private institutional innovation. That history helps explain current trajectories and provides useful points for comparison, while also suggesting alternative pasts and futures for media distribution, all valuable in the current moment. Second, despite the longevity of the trade, book distribution, both physical and electronic, has also proved to be fertile ground for the more recent creation of new technologies and business models that are now vital elements in digital media distribution systems more generally. Recommender systems exemplify such an influential technology. Third, when we focus on distribution, dramatic recent changes in the business of books and in power relations across the industry come into clearer view. These changes are only partly about the appearance of digital formats such as e-books or audiobooks; in fact, they help explain the persistence of physical books. They include, for example, the transformation in the material logistics of the industry, made possible by large-scale distribution centers combining human labor and robotics, as well as the effects of new print-on-demand and short-run digital printing technologies on the economics of material book production. Digital printing has returned formerly out of print or otherwise hard to obtain books to the market and extended the commercial lives of slow-to-sell works, for example in academic and professional fields. Print-on-demand, as John B. Thompson explains, upends the conventional publishing business model of first printing books and then selling them. Instead the sales come first, then the printing (2012, 331). Automated systems raise an important further question about what is involved when a book reaches its readers, if distribution requires a two-way flow of valuable data as well as a monetary transaction.

The second "distribution problem" concerns access to cultural resources. Who has access to books, which books are accessible, and where and when is access possible? In which forms are books accessible, at what price, and on what terms? Answering these questions involves drawing on a range of fields outside media and cultural studies. We need to know more about the technologies of distribution and electronic commerce, the cultural and political economy of the book industry, the national and international legal, public policy, and regulatory frameworks that shape access, and the variable geography of book cultures. A large and growing body of research has shown how digital businesses have reduced costs and prices, opened up self-publishing, created new formats, and made a wider catalogue of books visible and readily available to book readers. The internet has also engendered new kinds of libraries and book lending practices. For booksellers and readers in countries outside the world's cultural metropolises, the global internet has made books published in different places and languages cheaper and much easier to access. In some cases, global retailers have enabled users to bypass traditional country-based distribution systems, undermining commercial and cultural policy prohibitions on "parallel importation" (Vinelli 2009).

While digital technologies have expanded book distribution, they have not produced liberalized markets. In fact, they have introduced contentious new controls on distribution, embodied for readers—as for users of other digital media—in complex end-user license agreements that often fail to capture the full legal rights of users. The effect of these has been to create new non-price measures restricting the circulation of books, in addition to the legal and commercial restrictions on distribution inherited from the analogue era. Geoblocking, the practice of restricting customer or retailer access to regionally defined markets, is one such measure, enabling online retailers and distributors to vary prices and availability across geographic borders. Geoblocking both sustains in digital form older market boundaries and creates new ones (Lobato and Meese 2016). Digital rights management (DRM) tools are another new form of control over circulation, curtailing the scope for informal and secondary market activity. Justified as antipiracy measures, such tools are widely integrated into popular distribution formats, such as PDF and EPUB document files. DRM systems for book services such as Adobe's Digital Editions, Apple's iBooks, and Amazon's Kindle all attach a specific e-book file to a particular user's account or device, so that a Kindle book, for example, purchased on Amazon's platform, will be readable only through a Kindle reader or application registered to the purchaser. The capacity of a user to share or copy material can then be "managed," whether through restrictions on the number of devices that may be used or through the identity of the users associated with those devices.

Taken together, these two problems enable us to see book distribution in terms of both its deeper pasts and its contemporary contexts. Books and their institutions are, at the same time, recognizable outcomes of the long history of print culture and instances of the expansive digital media present. Further, they direct our attention to the *social* distribution of books as well as the technology and business dimensions of distribution. We have already touched on the role of public libraries as a parallel distribution system operating alongside and in tension with retail and subscription channels. Consistent with their history and mission, public libraries have played a central role in digital literacy education and the provision of public access to the internet for people who cannot afford to connect at home (Palfrey 2015). Further, large-scale book digitization and indexing projects such as Google's famous book-scanning project venture have made the contents of libraries' physical collections far more readily accessible and searchable outside libraries. In the past decade, e-book and audiobook lending has become increasingly important for libraries. We have noted the growing volume of e-book loans through library systems worldwide. The largest platform operating in the digital library space, Rakuten OverDrive, claims that readers borrowed 185 million e-books from over 43,000 libraries and schools worldwide in 2018, up 19 percent from 2017, and a further 88 million audiobooks, up 29 percent (Rakuten OverDrive 2019). Digital collections in these libraries, including e-books and audiobooks, continue to expand. In 2017 U.S. public libraries offered users over 463 million e-books, 72 million more than the 391 million offered in 2016 (IMLS 2019; Pelczar et al. 2019).

However, e-book lending falls outside long-standing arrangements for physical books and is now a zone of intense conflict. Libraries must license e-books for lending from the publishers; terms vary, but recent research points to wide disparities in availability, cost, and licensing terms, both across and within legal jurisdictions (Giblin et al. 2019). In the United States, an e-book made available for licensing to libraries through an aggregator such as Rakuten OverDrive may be licensed for "one copy, one user" over the duration of the library's subscription to the platform (an arrangement somewhat analogous to the library's purchase of a traditional book, aside from the annual platform fee). In another jurisdiction, it may be unavailable or available only through a "metered license," restricting the number of loans and sometimes also the duration of the license.

E-lending exemplifies both the new efficiencies and global capabilities of digital book distribution and the persistence of old inequalities in market access, pricing, licensing, revenue sharing, and availability. Other informal aspects of the industry such as piracy have also taken new forms. Counterfeit and plagiarized books, both physical and digital, are now reported to be so widespread on Amazon's platform that the company signaled the risk for the first time in its January 2019 annual report, noting that it may not be able to prevent merchants "from selling unlawful, counterfeit, pirated or stolen goods" or "selling goods in an unlawful or unethical manner" (Amazon 2019a, 14; Streitfeld 2019). At the same time, Amazon charges authors and publishers additional fees for participation in programs aimed at removing or preventing the appearance of infringing or unlicensed content on the platform. These programs rely heavily on machine learning, self-service tools, and other automated systems (Amazon 2019b).

Amazon as Platform, Infrastructure, and Competitor

A wider set of issues arises from the new disposition of power across the field of distribution. Amazon's startling capabilities beyond conventional retailing were demonstrated by the 2007 arrival of the highly successful Kindle e-book distribution system, which offers fast, wireless, direct-to-the-device, and free delivery of an extensive range of titles. However, as some readers discovered in 2009, Amazon had also reserved the extraordinary ability to *undistribute* books to Kindles, as it did when remotely erasing what it took to be unlicensed copies of George Orwell's *1984* and *Animal Farm* installed by users on Kindle devices. *1984* proved a poor choice for the demonstration of these new abilities, and Amazon undertook not to repeat that dramatic intervention.

More intractable problems are likely to flow from Amazon's collection and use of the personal information of its users, especially as the company extends its presence from its original web-based store to new automated services that are increasingly embedded in everyday life, from smart speakers to cashless supermarkets. We return to these below. In terms of the larger book market, digital distribution has enabled structural changes that are now familiar in other media sectors: the major technology firms, notably Amazon, and to a lesser degree Google and Apple, have not only taken substantial market shares in the book industry but also evolved into a new generation of dominant platforms, that is, rule-setting and market-making institutions. Their capabilities encompass all aspects of distribution. Further, they provide critical digital and physical infrastructure, from logistics to business information systems, for the industry as a whole. These manifold activities have strengthened the commercial positions of these firms immeasurably, involved them in bitter conflicts with competing industry players, invited official inquiries and interventions, and—despite their great successes—raised serious policy questions as to the economic and social value of these companies in their current form.

Amazon is a critical location for the further examination of these issues. It is now the world's dominant book retailer: the *New York Times* reported in June 2019 that Amazon sells more than half of all books sold in the United States (Streitfeld 2019). This figure includes both new and secondhand physical books, audiobooks, and e-books. Most of Amazon's products are sold by third-party sellers (52 percent in February 2019), not by Amazon itself, and the trend is increasing in that direction (Kim 2019). But if Amazon were once just a bookseller, as Streitfeld observes, it is now many other things in the world of books: a publisher, a printer, an advertising medium, a subscription library, a finance provider, a logistics hub, a search engine, a market for crowdsourcing authors, and a business analytics provider. The company is a powerful force in new digital services, producing, publishing, and selling audiobooks and e-books, and making market-leading e-book readers, smart speakers, and home assistants. It controls its own proprietary Kindle file format for e-books, operates markets for other booksellers, and through its ABE Books subsidiary provides the dominant aggregation and business platform for the global secondary book market. It is a forum for book reviews, a business software platform for booksellers, authors, and publishers, and a powerful advertising service, and it runs a chain of brick-and-mortar bookstores. The extraordinary proliferation and intensification of its activities—even when we confine our attention to its activities in the book trade alone—exemplify the complexity, diversity, and dynamism of contemporary digital media distribution.

From its early days as an online bookshop on the web, Amazon has played a large part in the evolution of digital media distribution. Books are now only a small fraction of Amazon's remarkably strong business in online retailing, media, and web services; but in books alone, Amazon is a powerful instance of the forces of concentration, globalization, and mobilization observed in other strategic zones of the digital media economy. The company spans the classical book industry value chain, while dominating new digital products and services in adjacent fields. It has expanded its geographic reach, working both within and across national market boundaries, challenging economic and cultural policy regimes that are defined by state borders. Its logistical systems encompass vast warehouses and data centers. It delivers packages and transmits e-books directly to devices. It collects and deploys large pools of industry and consumer data in the development of predictive automated systems. Amazon now enjoys a degree of market power that challenges the largest corporate conglomerates in trade publishing and retail, as it does in many other markets. The scope of Amazon's activities is such that it has become a focal point for policy arguments over the technology sector, from its labor practices to taxation and market concentration. Khan (2016) has influentially argued that Amazon's market practices should stimulate a wholesale revision of U.S. antitrust doctrine.

We can describe Amazon as a platform in this context because it does not act as a simple retailer: it provides markets (competitive or not) for interactions between diverse actors, including authors, publishers, sellers, and readers. It sets rules for those players in relation to matters including royalty rates, the pricing of e-books, delivery fees, and lending restrictions. Amazon's activities exemplify both the rule-setting features of platforms often emphasized in social media studies (see, for example, Gillespie 2017) and the coordination of multisided markets, a particular focus of the economic literature (Jullien 2012). Much of Amazon's business is now as a web-based marketplace and logistics and infrastructure provider for external e-commerce. It benefits enormously from these arrangements, charging fees for its services and offering customers a vastly wider range of items than it would otherwise. However, Amazon also acts in a more conventional corporate mode, running a vertically integrated business dealing with all aspects of publishing, distribution, logistics, advertising, and sales. The Kindle Direct self-publishing service is the clearest instance of this process, revealing how Amazon's deployment of market power to disadvantage competitors (Semuels 2018).

These new commercial platforms and infrastructures are not entirely grasped in terms of "digital transformation," especially because physical infrastructures and physical objects remain central to the business. We can better understand Amazon's distribution model as the outcome of a larger and longer term process of automation, where new information technologies in combination with cyber-physical systems are reconfiguring not only the role and nature of human labor but also the decision-making processes formerly undertaken by humans (Andrejevic 2019).

Amazon and Automated Recommendations

In the next part of this chapter, I take one aspect of Amazon's complex distribution model—its recommendation system—in order to show how this particular example of media automation has enabled the development of large-scale, vertically integrated, automated platforms. I then consider the successes and failures of this system in addressing the distribution problems we have sketched, both in practice and as a matter of potential.

Digital media services typically deploy large databases of content, from which users must select. In this respect an online video service hosting licensed content such as Netflix has more in common with an online bookstore like Amazon than it does with a traditional linear broadcaster. Search engines, together with advertising in all its forms, are essential tools for discovery in systems such as these, but automated recommender systems may be equally or even more important for making valuable content findable and accessible in the digital media economy. A large number of books on Amazon reach readers because a machine has recommended them. The company's importance in the history of digital media distribution rests in part on its leading role, from the 1990s onward, in the development of this form of automation. Recommenders are now ubiquitous across the digital economy, from navigation systems to online job markets. For media platforms such as YouTube, Netflix, and Spotify, they are a vital part of the service architecture. The larger the catalogue—and Amazon lists tens of millions of books—the more important recommendations are in making attractive content visible. The success or otherwise of these systems is critical for the distribution infrastructures built by companies such as Amazon. They enable transactions across a huge and diverse physical and digital catalogue, generate important market knowledge from users, and bolster the market-making capabilities of platforms. In relation to the value of recommendation systems, Smith and Linden (2017) note that 30 percent of Amazon's page views derived from recommendations (Sharma, Hofman, and Watts 2015) and that 80 percent of movies watched on Netflix were chosen through recommendations valued at one billion dollars per year (Gomez-Uribe and Hunt 2016).

The technical challenges involved in recommenders are complex: they need to be good at predicting the tastes, moods, and interests of individual users, recognizing that these may quickly change; they need to generate results rapidly as users make selections and navigate across a platform; they need to make a small number of recommendations from a large pool; and they need to do all these things for an even larger pool of users. Because these systems are technically complex, commercially critical, and constantly evolving, recommender systems are an area of considerable ongoing investment for digital media companies, which often extol the "personalized" aspects of their platforms. A substantial technical literature has developed on recommender systems. In digital media studies much less has been published, although the importance of recommenders is now well understood (e.g., Havens 2014; Lobato 2019). Alexander (2016) points to the opaque nature of such systems, highlighting their capacity for the commercial manipulation of taste. Of course, digital media platforms do hold out the promise of expansive choice, but recommender systems play a different role. Selecting a book or a movie from a vast range of options can be a time-consuming task. Recommenders may be better understood as devices for *restricting* choice, narrowing the field for users who may be overwhelmed by too many options. In general terms, the technical research on recommender systems has been about dealing with two challenges: the *scale* of the datasets involved (the speed of the system is related to this issue) and the *quality*, or predictive accuracy, of the recommendations generated. There are established techniques to improve outcomes in each of these areas, but these often involve trade-offs (see Jarrett 2017; Bellogín and Said 2018). While a large dataset can be sampled to speed up processing, the resulting predictions may be less accurate. Amazon's distinctive contribution in the 1990s was to work out how it was possible to improve both scalability and quality at the same time.

It is not hard to see why in its early phase Amazon was interested in improving recommendations in its online bookstore. The business was already generating large datasets related to customers and the books they bought, while competing strongly with brick-and-mortar firms. Of course, recommendations in different forms have always been a large part of the culture of the book trade, whether from expert advice in book shops or book review media or, more mysteriously, through informal sources of influence, such as word of mouth. Automated recommendations, provided they were accurate, were then a distinctive and novel feature of the online experience. By 2014, Amazon had accumulated considerably greater market power, and the *New York Times* published reports that, in negotiations with the French publisher Hachette, Amazon sought payment for the appearance of Hachette titles in Amazon's recommendations service as well as for the use of Amazon's "pre-order" button (Stewart 2014).

In the 1990s, according to former Amazon engineers Brent Smith and Greg Linden, automated recommender systems generally used a technique known as user-based filtering, meaning that the systems recommended items purchased by similar users (for example, users with a similar purchasing history). The Amazon system's point of difference was that it began by looking for "related items" (not "similar users") for every item in the catalogue. As Smith and Linden (2017) describe it, the substance of the relation between two items could be complex but could be simply described as an unusually high likelihood of being purchased by someone who also purchased the other item. The result of the analysis was a large table of related items in the catalogue. In Smith and Linden's account (2017, 12–13), the Amazon recommender system then took the user's current activity on the site—what they were looking at or purchasing at any given moment—together with their history of purchases, looked up all the related items from the table, combined these, and removed items previously purchased to produce a list of recommendations.

The advantages of item-based collaborative filtering algorithms include simplicity, at least in terms of the basic principles, and explainability (in the sense that it should be possible to explain, if need be, how a particular recommendation has been generated). Scalability and speed are gained because the time-consuming computation of the related items can be done offline, so all that needs to happen in real time are the table lookups. The system's results have improved as more complex understandings of the nature of the relations between "related items" have developed, although the system has also had to accommodate rapid growth in the complexity and number of items sold by Amazon. For example, one particularly important way to judge relativities between items, in Smith and Linden's account, is across the dimension of time. Books purchased by someone in quick succession may be more closely related than those purchased many months apart; for other items, more complex relations appear. Temporal precedence might be a factor if someone is buying a series of books or viewing sequential episodes or seasons of a television show; it will certainly be important if a person is buying a camera and a memory card: one will be purchased before the other, meaning the card may be a recommended "related item" for the camera, but not the other way around.

The Amazon algorithm, developed in 1998 and patented in 2001, has been used and adapted extensively as the company's operations have expanded. Machine learning now plays a key role in building and testing models, and recommendations permeate the Amazon website, appearing on the home page, in emails, in detailed product description pages, in the shopping cart, and at the checkout. The item-based filtering approach forms the basis of systems used by Netflix and YouTube, among many other media firms. As the technology has evolved and spread through the digital economy, the costs of such systems have fallen dramatically. Several developments are changing the landscape of recommendations remarkably quickly. The recent appearance of a wide range of tools for building artificial intelligence applications, such as Google's open-source TensorFlow library (an end-to-end open-source platform for machine learning first released in November 2015), is making the development of sophisticated recommender systems far more accessible for small and medium-sized businesses, along with much else.

Perhaps even more significant is the parallel emergence of low-cost, highly configurable cloud-based systems suitable for medium-sized businesses. Amazon has itself transformed recommendations from a back-end system into a commercial service in its own right, offering Personalize, an Amazon cloud computing application that promises personalization "within a few clicks." Personalise is designed to work with websites, mobile apps, email marketing, and content management systems. Amazon's website gives the example of a media company to explain the pricing: if the company uploads 200 GB of content every month, uses that data once a day to refine and develop the decision-making system, and then uses the system to make ten real-time recommendations per second for 720 hours in a month, the total cost will be $1,552 per month. Media companies reported to be using Personalise include Spuul, a small Indian movie and television streaming business, Sony's PlayStation Network, Dutch video-on-demand provider Pathé Thuis, and RB Media, a leading global publisher and distributor of audiobooks. Personalise now competes for the media market with other cloud-based recommenders, including Google Cloud's Recommendations AI and Microsoft Azure's Decide. A notable feature of these off-the-shelf services is their capacity for flexible reconfiguration, so that a business can use them for different purposes (e.g., maximizing revenue or clicks); apply different business rules (e.g., rules for dealing with out of stock books); draw upon different kinds of data (about users of the site, or the content available); select different kinds of recommendations (such as "books you may like" or "recommended for you"); and deliver the recommendations into diverse user-facing systems, from mobile apps to call centers.

Recommenders such as these are often seen, by both their supporters and detractors, as purely commercial tools. They have an extraordinary record of success in increasing sales and user engagement. The field is characterized by constant experimentation, evaluation, and incremental improvement. According to Brent Smith and Greg Linden, "An experience for every customer is a vision that none have fully realized." They conclude, "Every interaction should be a recommendation" (Smith and Linden 2017, 18). The aim may be to personalize, but "the personal" has recently become treacherous ground for digital media companies that are facing increasing scrutiny over the uses of customer information. The further implications of such imagined systems for media distribution are worth considering. To work well, recommendation systems depend on high-quality data, particularly relating to the transactions of users, even in item-based filtering systems, which do not begin with customer profiles. Data quality may also be highly variable across different media and formats. However, further development of these systems will need to be undertaken with additional care. Amazon and Google both claim that their recommenders are compliant with the European Union's (2016) General Data Protection Regulation (GDPR), which sets out a wide range of new obligations for automated systems, with particular implications for those that use personal data. GDPR includes many provisions that may have a significant bearing on how recommender systems work in digital media industries, especially if "every interaction" does indeed become a recommendation.

Conclusion

The European Union's turn to regulation signals an array of new challenges for the vision of a personalized media experience. However, there is an alternative way of reading Smith and Linden. We can agree with their suggestion that recommendation systems are at an early stage of development and that they represent a very powerful model for the ordering and automated discovery of content in digital media systems. We can agree that in principle these systems may be simple, and, in terms of some of their operations at least, they have the potential to be explainable to users. We can also see from the diversity of recommenders already available, and the capacity to build them around the specific needs of particular businesses, that these systems need not evolve along a fixed line of development: they may have quite different futures, and they may be able to usefully address additional problems.

One reason why recommender systems may be reasonably simple is because they are designed to maximize the benefits of a transaction for two parties. The first of these is the user of a website or an app who is looking for something—a good but inexpensive book. The second party is the online service, which benefits from a successful sale. A good recommender finds the right book and makes possible a sale that would not otherwise have happened. These systems are purpose built for large, online, catalogue-based services, especially those where content is either licensed or provided by a third party, such as a publisher or author. Item-based filtering works well where huge volumes of such material are available and recommendations must be generated in real time. But it would be a mistake to see such systems as purely reactive technical developments: they preceded and then enabled the expansion of vast digital media services such as Amazon, Netflix, and YouTube. They do so by reordering the entire corpus of works available through such systems ("filtering"), defining a new set of relations between books that may come from different publishers, different authors, and different genres. Automated recommendations are by no means the only key condition of possibility for Amazon's platform and infrastructure-based distribution model, but they have proved vital to its success.

However, if "every interaction" is to become a recommendation, then it may also be that our standards for evaluating such systems should change. We could say a commercially successful recommendation system might fail if we found additional interests at stake, such as a public interest in ensuring the visibility of a diverse range of cultural works, or the absence of crudely counterfeited medical handbooks. Outside commerce, predictive algorithms are already widely used to improve public services and safety. To return to the media distribution problems with which we began, recommenders may fail by not enabling highly valued books to find their readers or by failing to ensure that audiences have the opportunity to read work produced in their own region or country.

There is now considerable private and public interest in the rapid development of artificial intelligence—an area where much is at stake for digital media distribution. Anxieties abound over the degree to which powerful, nonhuman intelligent actors of the future may be subjected to ethical control. Recommenders, such as those discussed in this chapter, often incorporate techniques such as machine learning. They are integral to the operation of a new generation of household media devices, such as the assistants built into smart speakers. They, and the media systems they have made possible, are machines that humans have designed as part of the automated media present. As Mark Andrejevic (2019) reminds us, these machines embody choices, which have significant cultural and social consequences. They render some books visible and others not, with implications for the whole of the book value chain. This means that—despite the opacity of the reasoning processes they may deploy—these machines are also open to human processes of redesign, if we want them to do their jobs differently. Instead of applying the business rules of the house, would it be possible for a recommender system to take into account public interest considerations, cultural concerns, or environmental factors, when it placed books before their potential buyers and readers? As we have seen, considerations of this kind have long shaped the distribution of books through mechanisms such as copyright law, and through institutions such as public and educational libraries. Such a machine would need to be designed and evaluated in a different way from those we have discussed so far. It would need to be built around a richer understanding of the book market and of the social, political, and cultural work of books. But such systems are conceivable as modifications of our automated media present. Just as they were unthinkable in our earlier utopia of free books and freely shared knowledge, better recommendations need not rely on an imagined future where computers will be more intelligent than humans.

BIBLIOGRAPHY

Alexander, Neta. 2016. "Catered to Your Future Self: Netflix's 'Predictive Personalization' and the Mathematization of Taste." In *The Netflix Effect: Technology and Enter-*

tainment in the 21st Century, edited by Kevin McDonald and Daniel Smith-Rowsey, 83–97. New York: Bloomsbury Academic.

Amazon. 2019a. "Annual Report 2019." US Securities and Exchange Commission.

———. 2019b. "Our Response to the New York Times' Story on Book Counterfeiting." June 23. https://blog.aboutamazon.com.

Andrejevic, Mark. 2019. *Automated Media*. London: Routledge.

Association of American Publishers. 2019a. "AAP StatShot: Trade Book Publisher Revenue Increased by 4.6% in 2018." February 12. https://newsroom.publishers.org.

———. 2019b. "AAP StatShot: Publisher Revenue at $6 Billion for First Six Months of 2019." August 28. https://newsroom.publishers.org.

Bellogín, Alejandro, and Alan Said. 2018. "Recommender Systems Evaluation." In *Encyclopedia of Social Network Analysis and Mining*, edited by Reda Alhajj and Jon Rokne. Springer: New York. https://doi.org/10.1007/978-1-4939-7131-2_110162.

Cadzow, Jane. 2019. "One for the Books: The Unlikely Renaissance of Libraries in the Digital Age." *Sydney Morning Herald*, September 28. www.smh.com.au.

Catalano, Frank. 2018. "Traditional Publishers' ebook Sales Drop as Indie Authors and Amazon Take Off." *Geek Wire*, May 19. www.geekwire.com.

Economist. 2011. "Michael Hart." September 24, www.economist.com.

Edgecliffe-Johnson, Andrew. 2019. "Audio Gives New Voice to Books in the Digital Age." *Financial Times*, December 18. www.ft.com.

European Union. 2016. "Regulation (EU) 2016/679 of the European Parliament and of the Council." http://eur-lex.europa.eu.

Federation of European Publishers. 2017. "The Book Sector in Europe: Facts and Figures." http://fep-fee.us11.list-manage2.com.

———. 2018. "European Book Publishing Statistics." December 20. https://fep-fee.eu.

Giblin, Rebecca, Jenny Kennedy, Kimberlee G. Weatherall, Daniel Ian Gilbert, Julian Thomas, and Francois Petitjean. 2019. "Available—But Not Accessible? Investigating Publisher e-lending Licensing Practices." *Information Research* 24 (3). www.informationr.net.

Gillespie, Tarleton. 2017. "Regulation of and by Platforms." In *Sage Handbook of Social Media*, edited by Jean Burgess, Thomas Poell, and Alice Marwick, 254–78. Thousand Oaks, CA: Sage.

Gomez-Uribe, Carlos A., and Neil Hunt. 2016. "The Netflix Recommender System: Algorithms, Business Value, and Innovation." *ACM Transactions: Management Information Systems* 6 (4): 1–19. https://doi.org/10.1145/2843948.

Havens, Timothy. 2014. "Media Programming in an Era of Big Data." *Media Industries* 1 (2): 5–9. https://doi.org/10.3998/mij.15031809.0001.202.

IMLS. 2019. "Public Libraries in the United States: Fiscal Year 2016." Washington, DC: Institute of Museum and Library Services. www.imls.gov.

International Federation of Library Associations and Institutions. 2019. "Library Map of the World." https://librarymap.ifla.org.

Jarrett, Julian. 2017. "A Present-Day Perspective on Recommendation and Collaborative Filtering." *IEEE Internet Computing* 21 (3): 14. https://doi.org/10.1109/MIC.2017.72.

Jullien, Bruno. 2012. "Two-Sided B to B Platforms." In *The Oxford Handbook of the Digital Economy*, edited by Martin Peitz and Joel Waldfogel, 161–85. Oxford: Oxford University Press.

Khan, Lina M. 2016. "Amazon's Antitrust Paradox." *Yale Law Journal* 126 (3): 710–805.

Kim, Eugene. 2019. "Amazon Added a First-Ever Warning about Counterfeit Products to Its Earnings Report." *CNBC*, February 4. www.cnbc.com.

Larson, Christine. 2019. "Open Networks, Open Books: Gender, Precarity and Solidarity in Digital Publishing." *Information, Communication & Society*. https://doi.org/10.1080/1369118X.2019.1621922.

Lecher, Colin. 2019. "GDPR Complaints Say Amazon, Spotify, and Other Streaming Companies are Breaking EU Law." *The Verge*, January 18. www.theverge.com.

Lobato, Ramon. 2019. *Netflix Nations: The Geography of Digital Distribution*. New York: New York University Press.

Lobato, Ramon, and James Meese, eds. 2016. *Geoblocking and Global Video Culture*. Amsterdam: Institute for Network Cultures.

Milliot, Jim. 2018. "E-book Sales Fell 10% in 2017." *Publishers Weekly*, April 25. www.publishersweekly.com.

Newby, Gregory B. 2011. "Obituary for Michael Stern Hart." Project Gutenberg. www.gutenberg.org.

Palfrey, John G. 2015. *BiblioTech: Why Libraries Matter More Than Ever in the Age of Google*. New York: Basic Books.

Pelczar, Marisa, Lisa M. Frehill, Kim Williams, and Evan Nielsen. 2019. "Public Libraries Survey—Fiscal Year 2017: Supplementary Tables." Washington, DC: Institute of Museum and Library Services. www.imls.gov.

Public Libraries 2030. 2019. "EU Library Factsheets." https://publiclibraries2030.eu.

Rakuten OverDrive. 2019. "Public Libraries Achieve Record-Breaking Ebook and Audiobook Usage in 2018." January 8. https://company.overdrive.com.

Semuels, Alana. 2018. "The Authors Who Love Amazon." *Atlantic*, July 20. www.theatlantic.com.

Sharma, Amit, Jake M. Hofman, and Duncan J. Watts. 2015. "Estimating the Causal Impact of Recommendation Systems from Observational Data." In *EC '15: Proceedings of the Sixteenth ACM Conference on Economics and Computation*, 453–70. https://doi.org/10.1145/2764468.2764488.

Smith, Brent, and Greg Linden. 2017. "Two Decades of Recommender Systems at Amazon.com." *IEEE Internet Computing* 21 (3): 12–18. https://doi.org/10.1109/MIC.2017.72.

State Library of Queensland. 2019. "Australian Public Libraries Statistical Report 2016–2017." www.nsla.org.au.

Stewart, James B. 2014. "Booksellers Score Some Points in Amazon's Spat with Hachette." *New York Times*, June 20. www.nytimes.com.

Streitfeld, David. 2019. "What Happens after Amazon's Domination Is Complete? Its Bookstore Offers Clues." *New York Times*, June 23. www.nytimes.com.

Sweney, Paul. 2019. "New Chapter? UK Print Book Sales Fall While Audiobooks Surge 43%." *Guardian*, June 26. www.theguardian.com.

Thompson, John B. 2012. *Merchants of Culture: The Publishing Business in the Twenty-First Century*. 2nd ed. Cambridge: Polity.

Vinelli, Ryan L. 2009. "Bringing Down the Walls: How Technology Is Being Used to Thwart Parallel Importers amid the International Confusion Concerning Exhaustion of Rights." *Cardozo Journal of International and Comparative Law* 17 (1): 135–74.

Wischenbart, Rüdiger. 2018. "European E-Book Barometer: A Report on Digital Consumer Publishing in Germany, Italy, the Netherlands and Spain." www.wischenbart.com.

16

Free, Bundled, or Personalized?

Rethinking Price and Value in Digital Distribution

RAMON LOBATO

The digital media economy is home to an unprecedented variety of pricing models, each of which invites us to value media commodities differently. From "free," freemium, and subscription-based services through to personalized and auction-based pricing, digital media have become a crucible in which new ways of valuing culture are invented, adapted, and normalized.

The purpose of this chapter is to provide a conceptual framework for understanding recent price transformations in digital media. Along the way, I also propose some analytical connections between professional and policy debates about digital media pricing and critical concerns raised by media distribution studies. I am thinking here especially of the work of Nicholas Garnham, who, in his important book *Capitalism and Communication* (1990), placed distribution at the very center of communication scholarship. For Garnham, the central issue in distribution was "the function not just of creating a cultural repertoire matched to a given audience or audiences but at the same time of matching the cost of production of that repertoire to the spending powers of that audience" (162). The present chapter builds on this provocative but largely underdeveloped line of inquiry into pricing as a central plank of distribution research, asking the following questions: How do we as media scholars make sense of the proliferation and coexistence of diverse price points for the same goods? How are long-standing pricing techniques (such as subscription) and institutions (such as the lending library) being repackaged for the digital age? How should we evaluate current claims about the digital "devaluation" of cultural production?

The guiding premise of this essay is that price—a fundamental yet obscure topic within media and communication studies—has both critical and practical value for current debates about digital distribution. First, price is integral to questions of media access and availability. Audiences are differentially included and excluded from accessing content based on their ability and willingness to pay. This has a clear policy implication because the cost of media is a vital element in debates about media affordability, expenditure, participation, and piracy (McCombs 1972; Karaganis 2011; Park 2017; Thomas et al. 2018). Second, analysis of pricing also has a practical value for media professionals seeking to assess the value and set the price of their product in particular markets. At a time of profound transformation of many media industries, it is important to reflect on the wider social and cultural consequences of the many different ways of pricing media—and what this means for how we as consumers understand the value of media in the marketplace and in our everyday lives.

Before we begin, a point of clarification regarding the term "media." This article makes a distinction between the pricing of *media content goods* and the pricing techniques enabled by digital *media systems*. The first half of the article is concerned primarily with media content goods, specifically certain classical commodity forms associated with publishing, cinema, and recorded music: books, movies, tracks, and albums. My focus in this part of the chapter is on price as defined at the point of consumption in business-to-consumer transactions. In the second half of the chapter I expand the scope of the argument to include digital *media systems*, including pricing optimization software and distributed ledger technologies that enable novel, automated ways of pricing goods. The chapter concludes with a case study of a controversial pricing practice: algorithmically personalized pricing.

The Specificity of Media Pricing

Price and pricing are foundational concepts within economic thought. Marxist economic theory has long been concerned with commodity pricing and exchange value, while neoclassical economics has focused on the role of price in coordinating production and consumption (Hayek 1945; Friedman 1962). Price is also central to subfields such as information economics, media economics, and media management (Shapiro and Varian 1999; Reca 2006). A rich literature can also be found in economic sociology and anthropology, where scholars have focused on the social and cultural contexts of price setting and price awareness among consumers (Velthuis 2005; Guyer 2009; Beckert and Aspers 2011). However, less attention has been paid to the topic within media studies, including media industry studies. Consequently, price is often dismissed as something purely instrumental, of concern only to industry and media business scholars, rather than a larger socioeconomic topic with implications for media production, distribution, and consumption.

One possible reason for this is the fixed-price character of many media goods, specifically the professionally produced content that is our focus in this section of the article. The structure of publishing, cinema, and recorded music, in particular, is unusual from an economic perspective because there is so little price differentiation between titles or artists. At the cinema one generally pays the same amount to see a blockbuster or a low-budget indie film, although ticket pricing may vary by time of day (matinee or evening screening) and theater type (first-run versus second-run theaters). Similarly, prices of new-release paperback books are broadly comparable regardless of whether you are buying a Booker Prize–winning novel or an obscure novel by a first-time author. As these examples suggest, competition in consumer markets between media goods is not often waged on the basis of price (Ballon 2014). Instead, historical and institutional factors are generally more important in determining prices, which vary between categories of media goods rather than individual titles.

The topic becomes more complex when we take into account the plethora of formats in which media goods are distributed, along with the complex release sequencing strategies used in many media industries. For example, book pricing follows a versioning model in which hardbacks are expensive, paperbacks and e-books are affordable, and remaindered books are very cheap. This is, in effect, temporally differentiated pricing, where newer content attracts a price premium. Similarly, the well-established windowing model of film distribution means that the price of a movie will vary significantly depending on when and where you see it, whether on opening night at the multiplex or years later on DVD or via a streaming or download service. Even within the home entertainment window for movies, multiple versions of the same film are often available at different price points, from standard-definition DVDs or streaming movies through to premium Blu-ray versions. In other words, while price differences between texts are generally insignificant, prices for the *same* text may vary considerably depending on the distribution channel, the age of the work, and the specific affordances of the format or version, such as picture or audio quality. As Jeff Ulin (2009, 252) observes, "Managing price is an art, not a science, and is influenced by factors such as the nature of the title, the competitive environment, retail pressures, inventory in the market, seasonality, life-cycle promotional opportunities, and rebate programs."

To add further complexity, media goods are often available within both formal and informal markets. For example, a Beyoncé album can be purchased from Walmart or streamed via Spotify or Apple Music, but its tracks can also be illegally downloaded via BitTorrent or ripped from YouTube. In many countries, the album will also be available at street markets and informal stores as a pirated CD or collection of MP3 files transferred to the consumer's mobile phone via Bluetooth. For a holistic understanding of the media economy, we need to consider price differences *across* these formal and informal markets, as well as within them (Karaganis 2011; Lobato and Thomas 2015).

Price in Time and over Time

Media pricing can be approached from both synchronic and diachronic perspectives. In other words, we can study prices at particular *moments* in time or over a *period* of time. The synchronic perspective typically reveals a diverse ecology of coexisting price points for the same goods, usually determined according to format and version differences. In contrast, a diachronic perspective reveals how pricing structures wax and wane over time, as different ways of distributing, valuing, and packaging media go in and out of fashion.

Consider the current prices for back-catalogue movies within the U.S. home video market. Table 16.1 shows pricing as of early 2019 for Quentin Tarantino's *Kill Bill: Vol. 1* (2003). As the table shows, *Kill Bill* is presently available to U.S.-based consumers in a wide array of digital formats, each underpinned by a different business model such as transactional purchase, transactional rental, subscription bundles, and piracy. This pricing structure allows for diverse entry points based on consumers' willingness and ability to pay. While newer releases are priced differently, the pattern below is typical of older back-catalogue movies. Consumers in the United States can digitally rent *Kill Bill* for a few dollars; they can purchase it as a digital download, DVD, or Blu-ray disc for a few dollars more; or they can download it for free via BitTorrent. They can also, at the time of writing, stream it from Netflix for monthly subscription payments of between $7.99 and $14.99, bundled with thousands of other titles. Across these various distribution channels, the price of *Kill Bill* ranges anywhere from $0 up to $14.99. In other words, price in this instance is determined less by the qualities of the text and more by the affordances of the distribution channel, including picture and sound quality, scarcity and novelty of format, and resale potential.

TABLE 16.1. The Variable Price Points of *Kill Bill: Vol. 1* (February 2019)

Price	Distribution channel
Free	Pirate torrents and streaming sites
$2.99	Digital rental (SD) via PlayStation, Microsoft Movies
$3.99	Digital rental (HD) via Amazon, Google Play
$4.00+	Secondhand DVD purchased through eBay
$7.99	Digital download (SD) via Vudu
$12.99	Digital download (HD), purchased through iTunes
$14.99	Blu-ray disc purchased at retail store

Prices for media content goods typically vary between and even within countries. Geographic price differences are a contentious issue, especially for consumers outside the major media markets. In low-income countries especially, formal media goods are often pegged to first world prices and may be quite expensive for locals (Karaganis 2011). The monthly subscription prices of global video-on-demand and music streaming services are likewise often calibrated to rich nations (Lobato 2019; Lobato and Meese 2016). This geographic dimension of media pricing is not the main focus in the present article, yet it remains a contentious issue for consumers and policy makers in many countries. For our purposes it is enough to simply observe that the price for *Kill*

Bill, as described above, seems to be anchored not primarily in a fundamental argument about the "value" of Tarantino's film, but rather by the film's movement through a temporal sequence of release windows and formats. In other words, the price of *Kill Bill* is elastic: it expands and contracts depending on distribution channel. This is one of the characteristics of media distribution generally, but it is especially characteristic of digital distribution, which tends to highlight this fundamentally uncertain relationship between price and value.

A diachronic perspective reveals how pricing structures change over time in response to evolving social mores, technologies, and regulation. To understand why new-release movies all cost the same, for example, one must consider the historical evolution of mass-entertainment markets since the turn of the twentieth century, including the relationship between cinema and fixed-price leisure attractions such as nickelodeons. Similarly, one must take into account wider societal norms regarding acceptable and unacceptable pricing practices. For example, while most consumers today think of fixed, open pricing—the same price for every customer—as a basic norm of market exchange, this practice became widespread only in the late nineteenth century following the expansion of organized retailing and department stores (Turow 2017). Prior to this, prices were generally improvised, opaque, and contestable. Traders would size up a customer and set the price accordingly, perhaps using a code noted on the product to remind them of the wholesale price. These traditions of flexible pricing persist in many bazaar and informal economies today. A diachronic perspective thus reveals the historical contingency of established practices, allowing us to see changes over time in the pricing of individual commodities as well as long-term, systemic changes to entire media markets.

The recent history of recorded music distribution offers a unique case study in price transformation. During the 1990s, music was bundled into albums, sold on CDs, and available for free through ad-supported radio and public broadcasting. The advent of Napster and other file sharing services significantly increased the informality of music distribution: peer-to-peer exchange and paid consumption visibly coexisted. In 2003, Apple attempted to re-commodify digital music by offering fixed-price paid downloads of individual tracks. Then, in the 2010s, the price point of music shifted again as monthly subscriptions to streaming services became the new normal for many consumers. In other words, the dominant pricing logic shifted over the course of a generation from bundled, to free, to unbundled, to re-bundled—while coexisting with an array of residual pricing models that often clashed in their different propositions about what music was worth. It is no wonder, then, that consumers are confused about the value of music and whether or not this is a "good" that should be paid for or can be consumed at no charge. This price volatility is especially stark given that pricing for live music concerts follows a different logic, with variable ticket prices according to the status of the artist and the quality of the seat or location (front row, back row, or standing room).

Jeremy Morris, in *Selling Digital Music, Formatting Culture* (2015), offers a powerful analysis of music's pricing crisis at the end of the past century. As Morris argues, Apple's intervention into the digital music market helped to stabilize the price—and therefore the perceived value—of music during a period of great turbulence. iTunes' signature innovation was to sell song downloads at a flat rate of $0.99, which was seen by Apple as a price point "high enough to start generating revenue for digital music yet low enough to appeal to customers who were getting accustomed to 'free' music" (Morris 2015, 151). Apple later introduced two additional price points for digital song downloads ($0.69 and $1.29), to allow labels some room to differentiate their product. However, it was the $0.99 price point that instituted a new cultural norm.

As Morris (2015, 134) observes, Apple's strategy aimed to "rebuild some of the value that drifted during the migration from music on CDs." It also had the effect of reinforcing the fixed-price character of recorded music markets, so that every song cost the same: "Bob Dylan, Luciano Pavarotti, Celine Dion, the Born Ruffians, and my friend David Myles: all $. 99. These artists may be 'worth' different things to different customers, but the lack of price fluctuation, at least initially, suggested they were all equal economically. The fact that an unknown independent thrash metal band could sell its song for the same price as a Rolling Stones classic was, in many senses, egalitarian" (Morris 2015, 152). The complex history recounted by Morris in his book has many national and regional variations (Straw 2000a, 2000b). The Japanese still buy CDs, for example, while India's music economy is known for its low-cost, mobile-phone-based distribution model. However, the basic point is worth emphasizing. In many nations, the dominant pricing logic of recorded music has changed *three times within a generation*. These price transformations are commonly glossed over when we talk about digital disruption, but they are fundamental to how consumers experience and value music.

Pricing change is never teleological, but rather the end result of disruption, experimentation, and eventual alignment of pricing practices. Nor are the dominant logics described above all-exclusive. At any point in time, a variety of different pricing models exist behind the one that rises to dominance. Even today when streaming is dominant, the other models remain. For example, recent industry research (IFPI 2017, 4) suggests that "on average, consumers [globally] listen to music in four different licensed ways," drawing from a wide range of options including radio, paid streaming, free ad-supported streaming, and paid downloads. Hence, we must be careful not to envision change as a linear evolution from A to B to C (or from analog to digital) when in fact it is a more gradual and uneven process of reconfiguration.

Every pricing practice has its own history. The free exchange model of Napster evoked a longer tradition of tape-swapping. Subscription streaming services take their cues from older subscription models such as lending libraries and video rental stores. Spotify, with its free and premium tiers, has two different pricing models built into the same platform, evoking radio and library traditions simultaneously. Individual song downloads also have an earlier precedent in vinyl singles and cassette singles. Around the edges there are pricing experiments, such as Radiohead's pay-what-you-want release of *In Rainbows* in 2007, bundling of music with products and services (preinstalling U2 albums on Apple devices), and secondhand MP3 marketplaces (ReDigi). Hence it is important to account for the coexistence and interdependence of pricing models while noting the points of obvious rupture. Television is another interesting case. The advent of subscription video-on-demand services such as Netflix, whose users pay a fixed monthly price for unlimited streaming, has changed the value regime around television. The effects of this change vary according to the prior pricing norms that applied in particular countries. For consumers in countries where pay television (cable/satellite service) is the norm, as in the United States, Netflix's price point is likely to appear tantalizingly cheap in comparison to a monthly pay TV package. In these contexts "cable-cutting" or "cable-shaving" is therefore an attractive proposition. However, consumers in countries with strong free-to-air and public-service broadcast traditions, such as the United Kingdom and Japan, where the expectation is that television is a *free* medium, are often less comfortable with paying for television services because this departs from a long-standing historical norm about what television is and how it should be consumed and financed.

TABLE 16.2. Coexisting Consumption Models for Music and Their Corresponding Pricing Structures

Radio	Free	Formal
MP3 sharing	Free	Informal
Pirate streaming / stream ripping	Free	Informal
Video sharing (YouTube)	Free	Formal and informal
Physical (CDs, vinyl)	Paid—transactional	Formal and informal
Download services	Paid—transactional	Formal
Streaming services	Paid—subscription	Formal

In other words, the overall effect of subscription streaming services on how consumers value television can be read in at least two ways: as a devaluation or as an upward ratchet to television's price point. On the one hand, subscription streaming services like Netflix may appear very cheap when compared to the premium prices historically charged for cable and satellite pay TV. On the other hand, they appear expensive when compared to free public service and commercial broadcast television. The reaction of consumers to new digital services will therefore always be conditioned by local historical norms of television pricing and availability.

Experimental Pricing Models in Digital Media

So far, we have considered prices for professionally produced media content distributed through digital channels. Yet "media" can also be defined in a more expansive sense to include all the digital, logistical systems that facilitate distribution (Parks and Starosielski 2015). In this more expansive definition, an analysis of the relationship between media and price must also take into consideration how prices are determined, measured, and communicated using digital technologies. This section of the chapter therefore shifts our focus away from digital media *goods* toward digital media *systems*.

In a provocative essay, sociologists Liz Moor and Celia Lury (2018) analyze some emergent pricing technologies and their applications. As Moor and Lury note, "Systems of 'personalized' pricing, 'fluctuating' pricing, 'dynamic,' or 'surge' pricing are on the increase," and some retailers now change the prices of many goods on a near-constant basis, with the effect that the price of certain goods might rise or fall several times in a day. Moor and Lury also note the appearance of pricing based on automated analytics of user behavior data, loyalty card schemes, membership-based pricing, pricing techniques informed by behavioral economics, and "experiments with 'live' and fluctuating prices for energy" (Moor and Lury 2018, 506).

Digital platforms have been integral to this normalization of price experimentation. Transport and e-commerce platforms have familiarized consumers with auction pricing (for example, bidding on an eBay auction) and dynamic surge pricing (where prices are automatically adjusted in real time according to supply and demand, as with Uber rides). The massive expansion of web advertising since the 1990s has also introduced another, highly complex pricing mechanism—real-time bidding on ad insertions. Real-time bidding is an automated auction system where advertisers bid on the opportunity to place web and app advertisements in front of particular users. The whole process is complete within milliseconds and has traditionally been based on a "second-price" auction model, similar to an eBay auction, where the final cost of the ad is equivalent to the second-highest bid. This pricing system was famously developed by DoubleClick (owned by Google since 2008) and has been integral to the standardization and automation of internet advertising over the past decade.

Other digital media platforms and services have breathed new life into older models. Facebook and Google have embraced the "free" price point historically associated with ad-funded broadcast media: they do not charge consumers directly for their search and social network services and run ads instead. In so doing, these platforms have triggered a far-reaching conversation about transparency and consumer consent when using ostensibly "free" services. (Of course, services like Gmail and Facebook are not really free but are offered in exchange for user data and attention.) A different example is the crowd-funding platform Kickstarter, which allows fans to contribute to various projects at fixed or variable price points (e.g., ten dollars for an entry-level donation, fifty for a "superfan" package), thus recasting price as benevolent patronage. Meanwhile, Patreon invites consumers to see payments to artists as a form of tipping.

Around the edges of the digital media industries one can also find other experiments and innovations. Some of these may become normalized over time, while others are likely to prove more ephemeral. For example, there is now significant investment in micropayment and subscription technologies that can efficiently bundle digital news content in new ways, with the implication that news could be priced per article. The New York–based company Sourcepoint, among others, is developing a "content compensation platform" that allows users to take out bundled subscriptions across various news sources (e.g., major Australian or West Coast U.S. newspapers) and then redistributes those revenues to the participating publications. The idea behind subscription "super-bundles" such as this is to more accurately allocate subscription revenue based on what the user has spent most time with, while also offering an alternative to individual title subscriptions. These super-bundles are the latest twist in the pricing crisis that has gripped the newspaper business over the past two decades. The end result of this crisis has been a bifurcation in business models whereby newspapers transform into either freely accessible ad-supported online mastheads or paywalled premium titles, such as the *New York Times*, which may offer a small number of article views before imposing a paywall. The super-bundle model is an attempt to resolve this pricing crisis through a micropayments model, as an alternative to the existing subscription-and-paywall or free-with-ads models.

Video game distributors have been especially inventive with their approaches to pricing. For example, the platform Humble Bundle offers curated collections of games and associated content such as artwork, stories, and merchandise on a pay-what-you-want basis. Users set their own prices, with tiered levels of access (although higher payments are needed to unload the full bundle). Users also decide how much of the price to allocate to authors/developers, to the platform, and to charity.

E-book platform Story Bundle provides a similar service for independent genre fiction.

Another recent development in pricing is the emergence of business
software packages that automatically calculate and set prices without direct human intervention (Gal 2019). The software package Inoptimizer,
for example, offers "end-to-end pricing automation" designed to "optimize . . . pricing and assortment across categories in real time," using
artificial intelligence to analyze competitors' prices, historical pricing
datasets, and Inoptimizer's own market research, so that vendors can
adjust their prices automatically to increase yields or stand out in the
marketplace. Another example is Feedvisor, a "repricing" product designed specifically for third-party vendors using the Amazon marketplace. Feedvisor allows its users to automatically monitor competitor
vendors' pricing and adjust their own prices in real time. Services such
as these can be purchased off the shelf, allowing businesses of all sizes to
access the kind of advanced digital pricing capability that would previously have been restricted to very large enterprises. The availability of
these software packages is likely to contribute to a general shift toward
more dynamic pricing of goods, so that prices may fluctuate as needed
over time, rather than remaining fixed at a familiar price point.

The emergence of distributed ledger technology has also enabled new
pricing experiments. The most well-known ledger technology is blockchain, which allows advanced and automated allocation of revenues according to "smart contracts" (i.e., self-executing contracts that can be
programmed to distribute payments without the need for manual processing). Blockchains are now being used to support a wide variety of
digital distribution start-ups, including video platforms such as DLive
that encourage donation-like micropayments to video creators. A different example of a blockchain-based media service is the Brave open-
source browser and associated currency (the Basic Attention Token,
based on the Ethereum blockchain), which seek to efficiently price consumer attention to advertising. Brave users pay with their attention and
receive blockchain-based tokens in return, which can be donated back
to the users' favorite publishers. The Brave browser, which also includes
an advanced ad blocker, promises to inaugurate a new kind of pricing
norm for user attention, designed to be more transparent and equitable
than the current alternatives found in the digital advertising market-

place (such as the opaque trade in consumer data that underpins real-time bidding on web advertisements). In this sense, services like Brave can be seen as experimental attempts to resolve some of the inequities of pricing and value that underwrite existing media business models.

Experimentation and innovation in pricing also occur in the informal media markets. While "free" remains the dominant price point of digital piracy, there are actually many different pricing models within informal media distribution. Ad-funded free services (e.g., pirate video streaming sites and apps) are distinct from commons-based free systems such as BitTorrent. Within the internet pirate economy one can also see transactional pricing experiments (e.g., allofMP3.ru, the famous low-priced pirate MP3 store) and low-priced subscription models (e.g., cyberlocker cloud storage platforms, where a cheap monthly subscription gives access to unlimited user-uploaded content).

As these examples suggest, digital media have enabled very diverse pricing models, reflecting the wider price experimentation diagnosed by Moor and Lury. Digital funding platforms such as Kickstarter also offer new opportunities for consumers to buy (or buy into) a media good at different points in its production chain: as investor, user, or supporter. Often, these new practices arrive in a blaze of hype accompanied by claims of revolutionizing certain industries or overthrowing long-established industrial practices. But the sophistication of the pricing system is only one factor among many others. The most cutting-edge pricing system is not necessarily the same one that users will trust, institutions will adopt, or producers will consider optimal for monetizing their goods. Media industries are more complex than this and are subject to the same kind of long-term lock-in effects that characterize most industries.

Algorithmic Price Personalization: Digital Discrimination or Supreme Efficiency?

A final consideration is the potential of digital media to enable new forms of price discrimination among consumers. In online commerce, the automated modification of prices based on information about individual customers is becoming increasingly widespread, with the effect that different customers may be offered different prices for the same good. Prices can be adjusted in real time based on a range of variables, including IP address; the customer's purchasing history; third-party data profiles (typically assembled by online data brokers); online search and browsing history; device type; operating system, language, and region settings; and behavioral attributes such as responsiveness to ads and click-through speed. Digital pricing personalization is still a nascent practice and is not yet widely used in media content goods retailing. However, the technologies enabling price personalization are increasingly pervasive and affordable for small businesses as well as large corporations. Price personalization is therefore an issue that may increasingly impact all industries, including media industries, in coming years.

The OECD (2018, 5) defines price personalization as "a form of price discrimination in which individual consumers are charged different prices based on their personal characteristics and conduct." Discrimination is used here in the economic sense to refer to price variation (although these practices are also linked in complex ways to social processes of discrimination, as we shall see below). Price personalization is attractive to theoretical economists because it enables maximization of revenues from customers with different willingness to pay. For example, personal data about past shopping behavior can be used to gauge a prospective buyer's reservation price: "Just as someone's clothing can provide pricing clues, so can the manner in which a customer accesses an online store. Is a shopper using a laptop, app, desktop, or internet on their smartphone? What operating system are they using? Where are they located? A customer's actions also provide pricing clues: What other products are they looking at? How many times have they visited the site? Much like car salespeople, web retailers can electronically evaluate the characteristics and actions of each shopper to create a profile that generates a personalized price" (Mohammed 2017).

Personalized pricing has been used within the airline industry for many years, and the practice also has a long history in insurance. Its adoption in consumer retail markets has been more limited (European Commission 2018), despite some well-known cases that have attracted media attention. Amazon, a company known for its adoption of advanced data analytics, experimented with personalized pricing in the early 2000s but stopped after a backlash from customers. Uber has been known to charge different customers different prices for the same route, based on perceived willingness to pay (OECD 2018, 17). AirAsia likewise has experimented with personalized excess baggage prices, "using data and machine-learning to better understand what passengers were prepared to pay for" (Freed 2017). In addition, it is very common for retailers to arrange and promote products differently on the home screen, based on the consumer's data profile and online behavior. Research by the European Commission (2018, 1) has shown that 61 percent of retailers practice "personalized ranking of offers, either based on information about the shoppers' access route to the website . . . or past online behaviour." The commission concluded that this kind of personalization can harm consumers "if it is used to steer them towards the most expensive products that they are willing to pay for" (6).

Another form of price personalization involves adjusting prices downward for price-sensitive customers, for example, by offering a small discount to new customers ("10% off your first order"). In such cases, browser cookies and mobile IDs are used to establish whether the user is a first-time visitor or a regular shopper, and prices are adjusted accordingly. This kind of personalization is generally considered benign, but the practice becomes highly controversial when prices *increase* as a result of personalization. A related risk is that price personalization can be used to "identify 'high value' and 'low value' consumers," thus presenting risks for disadvantaged consumers who may effectively be charged higher prices because they are not considered worthy of discounts (Nguyen and Solomon 2018, 24).

The major factor inhibiting the further spread of algorithmic price personalization is consumer distrust of this practice. In contrast to fixed pricing—with its connotations of equality, fairness, and transparency— personalized pricing is associated with opacity and deception. While many consumers are blissfully unaware of the behind-the-scenes calculations described earlier, few things are more upsetting to a consumer than being charged a higher price than the next person, especially when this process is based on analysis of personal data. Personalized pricing thus raises the ugly specter of discrimination.

A significant body of research exists to show socially disadvantaged groups are often disproportionately affected by opaque and negotiated prices. For example, a major study by Ayres and Siegelman (1995) showed that black and female customers in Chicago's used car market were offered significantly higher final prices than white men. While used cars and media commodities are inherently different, the principle of vendors asking for "as much as they can get away with" still applies and remains a basic feature of capitalist exchange whether in a face-to-face or digital setting. Price personalization is therefore contentious because it appears to extend the long-standing tradition of salespeople sizing up a potential customer—but using big data instead of visual and social cues.

The implications of personalized pricing are significant and could potentially flow through into many different media industries. The more complex effects relate not only to consumer welfare but also to the competitive advantages arising from the use of big data. Antitrust regulators, civil society groups, and legal scholars have been paying close attention to algorithmic pricing, including price personalization, in recent years (OECD 2018; Ezrachi and Stucke 2016; Nguyen and Solomon 2018). Pricing is central to several areas of antitrust law, including cartels and price fixing, so there is now increasing concern among regulators that algorithmic pricing technologies may enable novel forms of price coordination that extend older forms of anticompetitive or collusive conduct between firms.

A key issue here is access to customer data. Major online retailers such as Amazon and multifaceted digital service providers such as Google are in a unique position to use price discrimination to their advantage because of the rich data they hold regarding their users' online purchases, interests, or behaviors. Such data allow intimate knowledge of users' consumption habits and, by extension, their likely willingness to pay. Access to these data gives firms a competitive advantage in the sense that they can calibrate prices with a level of sophistication that other online retailers cannot rival.

In summary, algorithmic price personalization presents many risks and unknowns that are rightfully attracting scrutiny from consumers, civil society groups, and regulators. Certainly, the efficiency benefits of personalized pricing should not automatically be discounted. Many economists would argue that calibrating prices to willingness to pay allows poor consumers to be offered lower prices than would otherwise be possible in a fixed-price system. Proponents of the practice also point to the many free technologies available online that allow consumers to shop around and compare prices (for example, price comparison web-sites like camelcamelcamel.com that provide historical price data and price-comparator browser extensions like Honey). At a minimum, policy reform in this area could focus on increasing the transparency and accountability of personalization by requiring retailers to explain how they set their prices and what kinds of data they use to do so. In the absence of such transparency, it is likely that price personalization will remain somewhat disreputable among consumers. While the im-pact of these price personalization techniques and the digital media sys-tems supporting them has not been felt widely across markets for media goods, media goods markets have the potential to be affected alongside other areas of the economy. This would pose new and difficult questions for foundational concepts in media economics and policy, by radically complicating assumptions about the relationship between media price, access, and affordability.

Conclusion

This chapter has taken a selective tour through some of the issues that the topic of pricing raises for media industry research. As we have seen, prices are among the most familiar and mundane attributes of media goods; yet pricing, as a socioeconomic process, has obscure and fasci-nating dimensions that relate directly to many long-standing concerns of media scholarship. Prices for everyday media goods are *historical* because they build on long-established norms of distribution and retail practice; they are *cultural* in the sense that they embody, extend, or con-test assumptions about the value of media; and they are *governmental* in the sense that they do certain kinds of work and are subject to direct and indirect regulation, while acting as a form of control in their own right. Prices are never simply plucked out of thin air, in other words. As Pierre Bourdieu (2005, 197) observes, "It is not prices that determine everything, but everything that determines prices."

This chapter has provided some analytical entry points into the topic of pricing for media industry scholars. I have made a distinction throughout between the pricing of *media goods* (books, music, movies) and the pricing techniques enabled by digital *media systems*. Both di-mensions of the issue are relevant to media studies, but in different ways.

On the one hand, questions of media affordability, access, and inclusion remain evergreen concerns for scholars, as well as for regulators and policy makers. On the other hand, media studies must also attend to the more diffuse ramifications of digital media systems on diverse areas of the economy and social life. Phenomena such as personalized pricing, auction-based pricing, price comparison websites, and blockchain-based pricing experiments provide suggestive examples of what is enabled by "media," defined in the logistical sense (Rossiter 2016).

With all this in mind, we can now ask, what might a future media studies research agenda into pricing look like? What avenues of inquiry are most productive for understanding pricing as a cultural and historical (as well as professional) practice? Let me conclude with a few rough thoughts, expressed in the form of four potential research questions that can be usefully asked of any particular case study.

The first question—*how much does it cost?*—appears straightforward but is in fact fiendishly complicated. Questions to ask here include the following: Is the price fixed or variable—and according to what principle (geography, demography, distribution window, format, version)? Can the good be found at a lower price point in secondhand markets, informal markets, remainder markets, and parallel-import markets? If so, what does this co-existence of price points reveal about the way that good is valued by industry and by consumers? Questions such as these draw attention to the synchronic plurality of the price, if it exists, or alternatively to the work involved in stabilizing a particular price.

What is the history of the price? The second step is to consider the diachronic plurality of the price. How has the price changed over time? How stable or volatile has that price point proven to be? Does it build on, reformulate, or challenge longer traditions of pricing, and their underlying business models? What prior traditions and practices have contributed to how this price point is understood by consumers? Asking these questions allows us to see prices as artifacts carrying historical connotations and associations. It also opens up possibilities for historical research into media pricing, using archival sources to understand the diachronic variability of prices for particular media goods and wider media markets.

What are the social consequences of this price point? The third step is to ask what the price means for consumers. This is where questions of equity and access come in. Who is included and excluded when media are priced in a certain way? How does the price point position the good as a mass, niche, or premium product? What are the implications of this wide or restricted availability, in terms of media access and diversity? How do these distribution conditions shape any possible civic or political claims made by producers of those media goods? What commercial or social trade-offs and positioning lie behind the chosen price point?

What is the infrastructural context? Finally, research can investigate the various systems involved in creating a price, changing it over time, and communicating it to potential buyers. In other words, scholars may consider the infrastructural and logistical role of digital media (including platforms, software, spreadsheets, and auction systems) within these various processes through which price is materially produced. What technologies are involved in the calculation, display, or dissemination of the price? What combination of human and algorithmic knowledge lies behind the price? How transparent or (in)accessible are these knowledges, and what are the competition implications? Who creates pricing systems and under what conditions? Questions such as these draw our attention to the politics of what might otherwise appear to be neutral technologies and remind us that price is always more than just a number.

BIBLIOGRAPHY

Ayres, Ian, and Peter Siegelman. 1995. "Race and Gender Discrimination in Bargaining for a New Car." *American Economic Review* 85 (3): 304–21.

Ballon, Pieter. 2014. "Old and New Issues in Media Economics." In *The Palgrave Handbook of European Media Policy*, edited by Karen Donders, Caroline Pauwels, and Jan Loisen, 70–95. Basingstoke: Palgrave.

Beckert, Jens. 2011. "Where Do Prices Come From? Sociological Approaches to Price Formation." *Socio-Economic Review* 9 (4): 757–86.

Beckert, Jens, and Patrik Aspers, eds. 2011. *The Worth of Goods: Valuation and Pricing in the Economy*. Oxford: Oxford University Press.

Bourdieu, Pierre. 2005. *The Social Structures of the Economy*. Cambridge: Polity.

Edwards, Paul N. 2003. "Infrastructure and Modernity: Force, Time, and Social Organization in the History of Sociotechnical Systems." In *Modernity and Technology*, edited by Thomas J. Misa, Philip Brey, and Andrew Feenberg, 185–225. Cambridge, MA: MIT Press.

European Commission. 2018. "Consumer Market Study on Online Market Segmentation through Personalised Pricing/Offers in the European Union: Executive Summary." https://ec.europa.eu.

Ezrachi, Ariel, and Maurice Stucke. 2016. *Virtual Competition: The Promise and Perils of the Algorithm-Driven Economy*. Cambridge, MA: Harvard University Press.

Freed, Jamie. 2017. "AirAsia Testing Personalised Baggage Pricing, Eyes More Add-On Revenues." Reuters, November 16. www.reuters.com.

Friedman, Milton. 1962. *Price Theory*. New Brunswick, NJ: Aldine Transaction.

Gal, Michal. 2019. "Algorithms as Illegal Agreements." *Berkeley Technology Law Journal* 34 (1): 67–118.

Garnham, Nicholas. 1990. *Capitalism and Communication: Global Culture and the Economics of Information*. London: Sage.

Guyer, Jane. 2009. "Composites, Fictions, and Risk: Toward an Ethnography of Price." In *Market and Society: The Great Transformation Today*, edited by Chris Hann and Keith Hart, 203–20. Cambridge: Cambridge University Press.

Hayek, Friedrich A. 1945. "The Use of Knowledge in Society." *American Economic Review* 35 (4): 519–30.

IFPI. 2017. *Connecting with Music: Music Consumer Insight Report*. London: International Federation of the Phonographic Industry.

Karaganis, Joe, ed. 2011. *Media Piracy in Emerging Economies*. New York: Social Science Research Council.

Khan, Lina M. 2017. "Amazon's Antitrust Paradox." *Yale Law Journal* 126 (3): 710–805.

Lobato, Ramon. 2019. *Netflix Nations: The Geography of Digital Distribution*. New York: New York University Press.

Lobato, Ramon, and James Meese, eds. 2016. *Geoblocking and Global Video Culture*. Amsterdam: Institute of Network Cultures.

Lobato, Ramon, and Julian Thomas. 2015. *The Informal Media Economy*. Cambridge: Polity Press.

McCombs, Maxwell. 1972. "Mass Media in the Marketplace." *Journalism Monographs* 24:1–104.

Mohammed, Rafi. 2017. "How Retailers Use Personalized Prices to Test What You're Willing to Pay." *Harvard Business Review*, October 20. https://hbr.org.

Moor, Liz, and Celia Lury. 2018. "Price and the Person: Markets, Discrimination, and Personhood." *Journal of Cultural Economy* 11 (6): 501–13.

Morris, Jeremy Wade. 2015. *Selling Digital Music, Formatting Culture*. Berkeley: University of California Press.

Nguyen, Phuong, and Lauren Solomon. 2018. *Consumer Data and the Digital Economy*. Melbourne: Consumer Policy Research Centre.

OECD. 2018. "Personalised Pricing in the Digital Era: Background Note by the Secretariat." Paris: Organisation for Economic Co-operation and Development. https://one.oecd.org.

Park, Sora. 2017. *Digital Capital*. London: Palgrave.

Parks, Lisa, and Nicole Starosielski. 2015. *Signal Traffic: Critical Studies of Media Infrastructures*. Champaign: University of Illinois Press.

Reca, Ángel Arrese. 2006. "Issues in Media Product Management." In *Handbook of Media Management and Economics*, edited by Alan B. Albarran, Sylvia M. Chan-Olmsted, and Michael O. Wirth, 181–202. Mahwah, NJ: Lawrence Erlbaum.

Rossiter, Ned. 2016. *Software, Infrastructure, Labor: A Media Theory of Logistical Nightmares*. London: Routledge.

Shapiro, Carl, and Hal Varian. 1999. *Information Rules: A Strategic Guide to the Network Economy*. Boston: Harvard Business School Press.

Straw, Will. 2000a. "Exhausted Commodities: The Material Culture of Music." *Canadian Journal of Communication* 25 (1): 175–85.

———. 2000b. "Music as Commodity and Material Culture." *Repercussions* 7–8: 147–72.

Thomas, Julian, Jo Barraket, Chris K. Wilson, and Ellie Rennie. 2018. *Measuring Australia's Digital Divide: The Australian Digital Inclusion Index*. Melbourne: RMIT University/Telstra.

Turow, Joseph. 2017. *The Aisles Have Eyes: How Retailers Track Your Shopping, Strip Your Privacy, and Define Your Power*. New Haven, CT: Yale University Press.

Ulin, Jeff. 2009. *The Business of Media Distribution: Monetizing Film, TV, and Video Content*. London: Focal Press.

Velthuis, Olav. 2005. *Talking Prices: Symbolic Meanings of Prices on the Market for Contemporary Art*. Princeton, NJ: Princeton University Press.

"Every Day Should Be a Holiday"

Black Friday and the Importance of Retail in the Circulation of Media

DANIEL HERBERT AND DEREK JOHNSON

Whatever changes the holiday has undergone over the last several centuries, we can agree that Christmas represents a moment of profound "conspicuous consumption" where many people demonstrate their status by purchasing inessential commodities (or at least try to, as their credit cards allow) (Veblen 1899/2007). And with the commercialization of Christmas in the U.S. context has come the commercialization of the entire "holiday season," running from Halloween (when we rev children up with spectacular amounts of candy), through Thanksgiving (when many Americans gorge themselves on food), all the way to New Year's Eve (when alcohol becomes the commodity of choice).

New shopping holidays have appeared in this sequence, including Black Friday, Cyber Monday, and now even Small Business Saturday, growing like fungi in the fertilizer of the national economy and facilitating the commercial function of the entire season. Since the 1950s and 1960s, the phrase "Black Friday" has been used to designate the Friday following Thanksgiving, a day that many nonretail workers in the United States do not work and that is also often the busiest shopping day of the year (Pruitt 2015). By the 1980s, retailers commonly used the phrase in their consumer-facing pre-Christmas promotions.[1] Since that time, retailers have made the day a true shopping event by opening earlier, some even at midnight the night before, and by offering significant discounts. Black Friday has also expanded beyond the borders of the United States. Its migration to England (Embly 2013; London 2019), for example, signals the event's full detachment from the U.S. national holiday of Thanksgiving in an ironic twist; the Pilgrims may have left, but retail pervades.[2]

In the wake of Amazon.com's rapid growth and of online retailing more generally, Cyber Monday appeared in 2005 (King 2018). On a day when many Americans return to work after the four-day holiday weekend, online shopping and sales noticeably spike, perhaps as people avoid their work and surf online for items that they did not get on Black Friday. These two days, Black Friday and Cyber Monday, now generate an enormous amount of economic activity and play a crucial role in the nation's retail sector. More than one hundred million people went shopping in stores in 2017 (National Retail Federation 2017), and consumers spent nearly eight billion dollars online on Cyber Monday 2018 (Thomas 2018). Differentiating themselves from national retailers but embracing the logic of the retail holiday nevertheless, local businesses began promoting Small Business Saturday in 2010, while nonprofit groups have harnessed this logic to support Giving Tuesday—a holiday meant to serve as a break from the nonstop commercialism of these successive retail holidays.

Just as the media industries make up a significant part of the U.S. economy, so too does the retailing of media and media-branded commodities constitute an important aspect of the retail economy more generally. Even as sales of physical media continued to decline, consumers spent more than twenty-three billion dollars on home entertainment in 2018, which included ten billion in packaged media and electronic sell-through (Digital Entertainment Group 2019). Accordingly, media hardware and software products appear conspicuous amid the many commodities and services sold during Black Friday and these other retail holidays. Mirroring the globalized day-and-date release of films and television programs, the reach of holidays like Black Friday well beyond the United States in fact suggests the emergence of globalized media-rich retail events. This essay thus reveals how retail holidays operate as media holidays, organized by and through the texts, practices, rituals, and above all commodified transactions and interactions of media culture. We argue that media commodities play a crucial role in these retail events for both retailers and shoppers, helping to infuse these days with much of the sense of celebration, fun, and entertainment that makes them "holidays" in the first place.

This essay was researched and written before the COVID-19 pandemic created new and significant problems for the already challenged brick-and-mortar retailing sector and pushed many American consumers to engage in increasing amounts of online shopping. Clearly, Black Friday and Cyber Monday in 2020 occurred differently than as described and analyzed in this chapter. Nevertheless, retailers worked hard to maintain the senses of time sensitivity and celebration that made the weeks surrounding Thanksgiving 2020 a prolonged retail holiday. One financial commentator went so far as to assert that "Black Friday has turned into Cyber Month" (Dickler 2020). Although the pandemic's long-term impact upon retailing economies and practices is unclear, it seems likely to us that media commodities will remain centrally important to retail holidays for some time to come.

Beyond the status of media as a meaningful cultural object, however, we also highlight their power to animate retail economies while also recognizing in turn the centrality of retail to the circulation of media entertainment commodities. As we have written elsewhere, retail companies serve "as the last-mile interface between distributors' products and consumers" (Johnson and Herbert 2019, 3). If distribution moves commodities toward consumers, then it is in retail where consumers and commodities come face to face. Attention to retail helps us see distribution as part of a broader process of media circulation. Just as media commodities are crucial to retail contexts, retail is integral to any consideration of media circulation in contemporary capitalist societies. Retail is a site of meaning making at which both consumers and industries encounter media texts—and, just as importantly, one another.

Corporately constructed holidays like Black Friday highlight this dynamic especially well, calling attention to the ways in which the meanings and values of media products shape and are shaped by the transactions and interactions of the retail environment. Black Friday often depends on media products as ritualized sources of meaning, value, and navigation. While media entertainment commodities are always sold in retail, on Black Friday they spill out of their usual spaces in a "media overflow" to disrupt the everyday shopping experience and its usual boundaries. Retail thus contributes to the ritualized meanings of media products, while that media entertainment helps to make Black Friday more than any other shopping day, but a holiday.

In order to make these interrelated arguments, we draw upon a range of research materials gathered in November 2018. We looked at Black

Friday print advertisements released nationally by major U.S. discount retailers, including Target and Walmart, as well as email advertisements and screenshots of websites for these and similar retailers, including electronics store Best Buy. Additionally, we conducted on-site observation (went shopping) at several major retailers in two midwestern cities. In Ann Arbor, Michigan, this fieldwork included visits to Walmart, Target, and Meijer (a regional discount retailer) on Wednesday, November 21, to get a sense of these spaces as retailers prepared for the big event, and then again on Black Friday, November 23. In Madison, Wisconsin, visits to Target, Walmart, and Best Buy on Black Friday were matched with a follow-up visit to Target three days later on November 26 (which happened to be Cyber Monday) to see what had changed during this fast-moving retail cycle. Although the materials gathered during these shopping activities might constitute a somewhat unusual "archive," they provide a strong empirical basis for making claims about the importance of media retailing within American popular culture.

Centering Retail in the Circulation of Media

This chapter grows out of our desire to highlight the crucial role that retailing plays in the circulation of media—and in media culture more generally (Herbert and Johnson 2019). Considerable research has been conducted about media texts and audiences, and more recent media industries scholarship has helpfully called attention to the importance of media production and distribution. Yet despite being the context in which media industries present their commodities to consumers who negotiate the meaning and value of those media in sales spaces, retail has been largely neglected in film, media, and cultural studies scholarship.[3] Whether conventional, brick-and-mortar retailers like Target and Walmart, specialty locations like record stores or comic shops, e-retailers like Amazon, or even platform-based storefronts like the iTunes Store or Steam, retail occupies a major, pervasive component of the media industries and of contemporary cultural life.

As we have argued elsewhere, the particularities and complexities of media retailing require appropriately nuanced research and analytical methods in studying the topic (Johnson and Herbert 2019). Specifically, we propose that media retail must be understood as both *transactional* and *interactional*, and that research should contend with both of these aspects (Johnson and Herbert 2019). By transactional, we mean to indicate the importance of retail as a site of economic *transactions* between retailers and customers, making retail a significant locus of economic activity for the media industries. This perspective can attend significantly to the function, power, practices, and hopes of those firms that sell media. At the same time, media retail is interactional, as it involves the active engagement of shoppers and salespeople, who *interact* with retail spaces, promotions, and commodities in visceral and subjective ways as part of their everyday lives. Retail is the locus of the market, where both economic and cultural values get announced and evaluated by buyers and sellers. As the point of sale, retail is where the market actually materializes and can be experienced by the media consumer in the course of transactions and interactions in that arena. Without those retail transactions and interactions, the process of circulation would not be able to continue beyond distribution.

We contend that the utility of the transactional/interactional model is made particularly clear through study of Black Friday. As a once-a-year "retail holiday," this day takes on extraordinary pressure for retailers and shoppers alike. Indeed, as Black Friday and related retail holidays like Cyber Monday stand out as exceptional moments of otherwise habitual practices of selling and shopping, they function much like "media rituals," as theorized by Nick Couldry (2003). Broadly defined, "'media rituals' are any actions organized around key media-related categories and boundaries, whose performance reinforces, indeed helps legitimate, the underlying 'value' expressed in the idea that the media is our access point to our social centre" (2). From this perspective, retail holidays like Black Friday do much to position shopping at the center of Americans' social life and further position the selling of media as part of the celebration that makes these days special "holidays." Shopping holidays and media rituals perform strong work in normalizing the conspicuous consumption of media commodities, including hardware such as televisions and tablets as well as software like DVDs and video games, as a form of ritualized celebration. This process of connecting media with ritualized social value emerges both in the transactions imagined in Black Friday advertisements and through shoppers' interactions with those commodities in retail space. At the same time as we consider the media rituals in which consumers participate during these shopping holidays, we also analyze the specific function of media in the retail industries' ritualized construction of these holiday shopping experiences. First, attention to Black Friday advertisements reveals how media products are foregrounded as a meaningful and highly valuable kind of transaction within the holiday shopping ritual. Then, consideration of the in-store Black Friday experience demonstrates how media commodities serve as the overall interface for interactions with retail space, overflowing from their usual spaces to serve as a means of navigation and as markers of those ritualized journeys.

Black Friday Advertisements: The Magic of the Transaction

The Black Friday advertisement booklets distributed by many retailers, either as newspaper inserts or at store entrances, are media texts themselves, constructed to position commodities in meaningful ways. Yet these advertising media also place other forms of media entertainment front and center.[4] The cover for the Target flier features a large-screen television in the middle of the page, with a girl appearing to cheerfully shout out from the screen; red text next to her reads: "Ready. Set. Save! 100s of doorbusters, 1000s of deals." The promotional term "doorbuster" imagines the television as a commodity so valuable yet so significantly discounted that, hypothetically, shoppers might break down store doors to get them. Although the cover also displays an Instant Pot pressure cooker, all the other items are media products, including a Nintendo Switch and a Google Home Mini. Similarly, the cover of the Walmart ad features an iPhone, a Google Home Hub, a PlayStation 4 bundled with a *Spider-Man* video game, and two televisions, one with Vudu, Netflix, and YouTube installed; the only nonmedia item here is a hoverboard.

From page 1, then, these retailers define Black Friday in relation to media commodities. The advertisements also appeal to customers' desire for good prices, to be sure, as the phrases like "save," "deal," "special buy," and "value" appear consistently. Noticeably, too, the covers announce the specific prices of all these items, from $25 for the Google Home Mini at Target to $398 for a 4K television at Walmart, and sometimes indicate what the "normal" price of the item is so that shoppers can grasp the "savings" offered. By giving the exact dollar figures, the ads attempt to create senses of value, possibility, and excitement in customers. But more directly, these dollar figures lay bare the financial activity upon which Black Friday rests. These may be exciting deals, and the savings may be substantial, but these savings for the *customer* work to motivate transactions that will profit the *retailer*.

The advertisements also make explicit the time-sensitive nature of these potential transactions, with the Target ad announcing, "Doors open 5pm Thursday! Doors close 1am Friday; Doors reopen 7am Friday," while the Walmart flier reads, "Light up Black Friday. Begins Thursday 11/22 6pm IN STORES." Black Friday now truly begins on Thanksgiving itself, but the ads noticeably do *not* refer to Thursday as Thanksgiving, as though this new holiday consumed the older holiday. By referring to Thursday as Thursday and by concentrating on the moment that Black Friday begins (even if this moment varies from store to store), the ads collectively disavow the traditional American holiday in lieu of this new shopping festival. In these ways, these documents conflate (1) generalized appeals to "smart" consumerism and economic transactions, (2) time sensitivity, and (3) media. This articulation defines Black Friday not just as a one-day shopping holiday but also as a longer period in which retailers hope that customers will purchase an unusual amount of media products.

Looking past the covers, media commodities dominate throughout these fliers. The Target ad first displays a range of televisions and speakers, then moves to smartphones and watches, then tablets, computers, cameras, and smart speakers, and then video games. A two-page spread of DVDs, CDs, and books appears on pages 10 and 11. Finally, page 12 reveals games and children's toys, and it isn't until page 22 that we see clothing advertised. The last several pages feature household appliances, like vacuums and toasters, but again on the back cover we see a television, an Xbox, and video games featured prominently alongside a few other nonmedia commodities. The Walmart advertisement maintains nearly the exact same sequence of goods, moving from televisions to computers and tablets, through cameras and other gadgets, to smartphones, movies, video games, and game systems, and then on to toys.

These advertisements appear to privilege high-cost items and then move to cheaper items. This makes sense insofar as retailers want to entice customers to buy those items that will be the most lucrative. It also makes a certain sense for Black Friday shoppers, who might use this holiday to make unusual purchases at lower-than-usual prices. It wouldn't really be a "special" occasion, after all, unless marked by a truly remarkable transaction. Yet the logic of decreasing prices does not hold across the entire booklet; instead focus shifts from media of variable prices toward nonmedia commodities. Flipping through the flier, one encounters $6 movies like *Wonder Woman* (2017) and *Blade Runner 2049* (2017) and $5 children's books long before one sees a $75 toothbrush or a $250 robotic vacuum. Media entertainment is foregrounded, while all other types of goods are relegated to the second half of the flier. This sequence of items in the flier suggests that retailers see media transactions as central to their Black Friday activities and thus to their industrial ambitions more generally.

The flow of different goods signals retailers' hope to instill particular fantasies of consumption on Black Friday. Retailers hope to entice large, once-a-year purchases of not just anything but specifically new, expensive media technologies such as televisions, iPhones, and so on—devices aimed at providing pleasure through media entertainment. And while media hardware gets more emphasis, software too plays a key role. Customers will likely buy books, games, and movies from these retailers more regularly than they buy televisions or PlayStations. Yet Black Friday retailers will highlight these smaller, less expensive media products so as to affirm the ritual value of the related hardware. After all, if one is contemplating buying a new television or gaming system, what better way to feed the consumer fantasy than to imagine precise ways in which it will be used. Through the combined promotion of hardware and software, Target and Walmart situate Black Friday as a crucial occasion for accessing media and, as a result, as sources of unrealized leisure and gratification. The "Magic System" of advertising creates the magic of the holidays (Williams 2000).

Notably, Black Friday prices for DVDs and Blu-ray discs at both Target and Walmart appeared, to our eyes, remarkably low compared to everyday retail prices. DVDs were advertised for as little as four dollars at Target, including such titles as *Dunkirk* (2017) and *Ocean's 8* (2017), while Walmart offered a number of movies at two dollars, including *The Secret Life of Pets* (2016) and *Jurassic World* (2015). Some Blu-ray and even 4K discs could be found at either store for nine dollars. On the one hand, this low pricing echoes the way these retailers have treated "packaged media" for some time, namely, as low-priced bulk "loss leaders" that drive traffic into and through the store. On the other hand, these prices support retailers' effort to communicate Black Friday's particular significance; if movies are always cheap, then Black Friday movies must be *really* cheap. This presents an odd situation, where media occupy a place of importance in the retailers' presentation of Black Friday, and yet individual movies are priced so low that their value might be questioned.

In their totality, then, advertisement fliers from Target and Walmart define Black Friday as a temporally unique shopping experience strongly associated with the sale of media entertainment. On the covers and throughout, the clear marking of prices firmly links all the other "meanings" of the holiday with the retailer's ultimate goal—purchases. Along with whatever other work they do, these fliers uphold the retailers' basic economic needs and the transactional aspect of retailing more generally. Imagined as the kind of transaction that will motivate shoppers to participate in meaningful ways, the media commodity creates social and ritual value for the retail holiday.

Spilling into the Aisles—Interactions in Media Overflow

While these advertisement booklets foreground potential transactions, a small supplementary flier offered at Walmart in Ann Arbor gestured toward the interactional experience shoppers would have when actually entering stores on Black Friday. This "Insider's Guide to Black Friday Deals" featured a color-coded map of a store interior, with areas labeled "General," "Apparel," "Home," "Toys," and, of course, "Entertainment." With the imperative "Map your Black Friday game plan," it urged customers to download the Walmart app on their phones to access even more detailed maps with item locations clearly marked. As an attempt to combine smart technologies with shopping experiences (Turow 2017), this flier and mapping app point toward the potential problems associated with brick-and-mortar shopping, especially on Black Friday: getting turned around, not finding what you want, and so forth. Additionally, the flier states that shoppers should arrive early on Black Friday for "treats," including coffee, cocoa, and cookies.

Thus this flier points toward aspects of Black Friday that, for customers, go beyond the transaction itself to encompass the very physical and mental activities involved in the interactional process of *shopping*. The experience of Black Friday shopping can be an intense process because of the number of fellow shoppers one finds in stores that day. And just as media commodities defined Black Friday in the advertisements, so too did media play a striking role in our Black Friday shopping experiences.

In fact, in our Black Friday visits to Target, Walmart, and Best Buy, we found that media products had expanded beyond the usual boundaries of the electronics department and other designated areas for shelving books, movies, and software, proliferating throughout almost every part of the store. Of course, the imperative to sell as much merchandise as possible on this retail holiday typically leads stores to jam as much product as they can into already crowded aisles and flex normal store layouts and shelf planograms as much as possible. The presence of media hardware and software outside normally designated environments on Black Friday is no more surprising than the presence of kitchen appliances or sporting goods in special displays or end caps elsewhere in the store. However, our observation of media commodities and their placement throughout Black Friday store displays suggests that they perform specific roles for retailers not just as a potential focus of consumer attention but also as a means of turning the aisles between departments into a shopping space of their own. Media commodities frequently served as a medium through which the aisles of Black Friday would be navigated.

At both the Ann Arbor and Madison Hilldale Target stores, for example, Black Friday shoppers immediately encountered media products on entry. Faced prominently at the edge of the women's clothing department that all shoppers must pass on initial entry to the Madison Hilldale Target (whether heading left to the back of the store or right onward toward the checkout lines and health and beauty department beyond), a special display of retro media objects featured vinyl Bob Marley and Guns N' Roses records, games based on the television series *MacGyver* (1985–92), DVDs of catalogue films like *Grease* (1978), *The Sandlot* (1993), *Dirty Dancing* (1987), and *Footloose* (1984), as well as the more recent 1980s-themed television series *Stranger Things* (2016–), and T-shirts packaged in boxes meant to look like VHS cassettes for *Robocop* (1987), *Fast Times at Ridgemont High* (1982), and *Bloodsport* (1988).

On Black Friday, shopping for women's clothing meant also engaging in nostalgia for popular media entertainment of the 1980s and 1990s, not just at the level of the content but also in the materiality of the audio and video formats through which those media commodities would have been sold. The display asked the Black Friday shopper to reminisce about the media retail cultures of the past—and hopefully engage in new transactions through that nostalgic interaction.

Even though this display was so prominently placed, shoppers un-interested in browsing the women's clothing department could have missed it. Yet the Target shopper would find it much harder to miss the additional media displays installed on a temporary basis just a few meters down the aisle that separated the checkouts from the women's clothing department. Resembling a series of islands or pillars placed ap-proximately six to ten feet apart, each cardboard display stood about four feet high and presented an assortment of media commodities for shoppers to browse as they stood in line. These displays contained many of the film, television, and music titles advertised as doorbusters in the Black Friday advertisement. Some of them also included headphones and other small media devices consumers might need to engage with media content. Similarly, Walmart stores in both Ann Arbor and Madi-son had several bins of DVDs placed in the middle of the main aisle both near the checkout registers as well as in select spots around the store.

Such displays served several key functions. First and most basically, they created a dividing line to ease traffic as new shoppers moving deeper into the store tried to get past those waiting in extended checkout lines. Better than a simple barrier of stanchions, however, these displays bordered the longer checkout lines snaking beyond their usual confines to create opportunity for more point-of-sale purchases. The aisle became a space not just for walking or waiting but for captive consumer interac-tion with product displays. In the same way that small media commodi-ties figure prominently in advertising as "doorbuster" lures to attract shoppers to Black Friday events, here they represented the retailer's last best bid to convince customers to part with a little more cash before heading back out the door.

In both Ann Arbor and Madison, these pop-up media displays con-tinued beyond the checkouts throughout the aisles that followed the

Target store perimeter. Although not as concentrated as the checkout displays, more temporary media displays could be found in the main aisle deepest in the Madison store that ran from the seasonal/holiday department to sporting goods, toys, movies and music, electronics/tech, baby supplies, and men's clothing. These larger cardboard displays contained children's books, board games, console video games, doorbuster DVDs and Blu-rays, as well as headphones and other media accessories. In this way, store navigation was mediated by the experience of browsing media commodities. Similarly, the Ann Arbor Target featured a massive display of DVDs occupying most of the main aisle near the checkout lanes. These main walkways were also notably occupied by numerous television boxes. Stretching to the back of the store, these clusters of televisions served as their own in-aisle display, with little cardboard end caps declaring "Sale!" Here, large media hardware commodities created aisles within aisles, shaping the flow of shoppers' movement through the store. These televisions were actually *unavoidable*, demanding constant attention to prevent tripping or cart collisions.

In these store displays, media commodities were not just objects of desire to which interested consumers must navigate themselves but also a medium of retail navigation in their own right. That is to say that the experience of shopping on Black Friday required the Target and Walmart shopper to pass through media software and hardware in the course of any and all shopping they might wish to perform. The experience of shopping at these stores and navigating their aisles more generally turned on consumers' interactions with media specifically.

This navigational dynamic was even more pronounced on Black Friday at the Madison West Best Buy, where the displays of media hardware and software functioned like an extended cattle run that the shopper had to follow. Like those visiting the Ann Arbor Walmart, shoppers arriving at this store were similarly handed on entry a store map that laid out the subdivision of departments around which the space was organized: a perimeter around the store that connected the big-ticket areas devoted to appliances, car audio, home theater, and computers, which surrounded a core of smaller departments like movies, gaming, portable audio, cameras, mobile phones, and connected home devices. However, this map failed to capture the true navigational dynamics of Best Buy on the Black Friday holiday. Although the map represented the aisles between departments as empty white space, in reality these spaces were a site of media overflow in which the major displays and interactions of Black Friday shopping were most located. Furthermore, the experience of being in the store was not one of free exploration of these departments but one of following a current or flow through the aisles that privileged certain paths through the store—paths that prompted confrontations with media products. In this sense, the aisles between departments became, on Black Friday, spaces of media interaction.

Immediately on entering this Best Buy, the Black Friday shopper encountered a stack of televisions to the right—seemingly paid for and marked for later pickup by previous shoppers. These big-ticket media commodities stood as testaments to an idealized Black Friday experience, role-modeling the potential results of the experience for later arrivals. As shoppers tried to move around the long checkout lines at the front of the store, the easiest path seemed to be a narrow aisle bounded by displays of small media commodities. Although similar to those at Target and Walmart, the Black Friday media displays in the aisles of Best Buy presented a longer unbroken barrier to divide incoming and outgoing traffic. These included a large cardboard display of "TV and Movie Favorites Collection" DVDs, a smaller Disney DVD display, wireless audio accessories, several bins of discount DVDs (one marked as "$5.99 and up"), two more large cardboard DVD displays including holiday films, and several smaller video-game-related displays. When turning the corner from this checkout waiting area to the appliance department, however, this encounter with media continued. In the aisles between the appliance department and the movies and gaming departments, no fewer than seven large blue displays marked "Movies Black Friday Deals" (as well as smaller green displays for "Great Games $19.99 each") exploded the boundaries of the latter areas on the map as they bled into the aisles and neighboring departments. Although displays for KitchenAid mixers and Garmin GPS devices got mixed in to these media offerings, the sense of the aisle as a space for consumer interaction on Black Friday depended significantly on the continuity of entertainment media commodities. They served as the primary product category through which shoppers navigated and interacted with this expanded retail holiday space.

Thus, when shoppers following this traffic flow turned right once again upon reaching the back perimeter of the store, entertainment media remained a constant touchstone for navigating the space between departments. As traffic moved between home theater and audio on the back perimeter and cameras and connected home devices at store center, the aisles simply shifted to media hardware including TVs, soundbars, and other playback equipment. Even as media hardware dominated these particular lanes of traffic flow, DVD displays at the specialized checkout aisle for televisions and other large electronics reminded consumers of the need for content to support their new hardware purchases. It may be somewhat unsurprising to hear that Best Buy—a retailer that specializes in the software and hardware commodities related to media entertainment—relies heavily upon media commodities in constructing experiences for consumers on Black Friday. Nevertheless, what is significant here is not media entertainment as retail commodity but its function as the interface through which once more spacious and relatively empty aisles become highly constructed, codified, and ritualized spaces for the special consumer interactions of Black Friday. Indeed while Best Buy presented a more intensified and unbroken form of media navigation, the Black Friday shopper at Target and Walmart too experienced the retail holiday as one of intensified crowdedness, clutter, and even chaos, where the continuity of media displays balanced the disruption of everyday retail boundaries. Media spilled into the aisles in meaningful ways to grant value to the holiday shopping experience for the stores and shoppers alike.

Media scholars have long depended on concepts like flow and overflow to theorize the relationship between media texts, the capacity for assemblage, and the experience of media consumption across those boundaries. In Black Friday, we see another kind of media overflow—at the level of retail, not textuality—in which boundaries that normally define shopping experiences get disrupted and media commodities serve as a point of convergence between consumers' interactions across once subdivided spaces and product categories. In that sense, media commodities present a means of constructing navigable shopping experiences but also evidence persistent industrial challenges in managing the boundaries upon which those experiences are built. Frequently, while the display cases remained to control traffic at these stores, Black Friday shoppers often found them empty when arriving later in the day. By midafternoon, many of these displays spoke to media transactions that were no longer possible when doorbuster DVDs, Blu-rays, and games had long ago sold out. Yet while consumers in this situation could not engage in transactions, their interaction with the space of the stores continued to be structured by this absence and the trace reminders of media's value as an object of desire to those who had arrived earlier.

Meanwhile, the predominance of media commodities as ritualized objects of Black Friday desires gives way to what we might call abandoned media. Consumers may consider purchases from these special displays, but think better of it before leaving, picking up Black Friday media items and then discarding them in random locations throughout the store. At the Madison Target, for example, doorbuster DVDs could be found scattered everywhere—from a *Home Alone* (1990) disc chucked onto the floor under a loungewear display to an *Infinity War* (2018) disc unceremoniously discarded on an island of vinyl records. In their displaced ubiquity, media commodities signaled as much what consumers did not choose to buy as what was most in demand.

This sense of media commodities as retail holiday detritus was perhaps most keenly felt at the large DVD displays occupying Walmart's central axis. Although surely the large displays had once been subject to some organization, hours of browsing by consumers had caused the DVDs to overflow beyond the neat, cardboard-divided rows and shelves of each display. Instead, discs sprawled out randomly across the tops of the displays, while those still on the cardboard shelves sat at odd angles or dangled precariously over the edge. TV box sets comingled with new-release movies, with no pricing consistency shared across adjacent titles. So while media overflow animated Black Friday aisles, it did not always do so neatly, and consumers' interactions with media entertainment often related more to transactions that did not happen on this holiday than to those that did. The ritualized value of media commodities, in other words, depended as much upon absences in the context of this retail holiday as presence.

Conclusion

Across Target, Walmart, and Best Buy, media commodities literally spilled into the aisles of Black Friday 2018. By exceeding the boundaries of their normal display areas (although they could be found there too) to occupy the aisles through which shoppers maneuvered, media commodities became a defining feature of the holiday retail space. If Black Friday is defined, at least in part, by the supposedly unruly crowds of shoppers moving through retail stores, then it is notable that these retailers crowded their aisles further with media. Simply put, one could not shop at these stores on Black Friday without encountering media commodities. The products of media entertainment became the physical medium through which consumers navigated intensified retail environments; the circulation of the media shaped the circulation of consumers in a rather direct way. The unusual placement of media within the store furthermore marked the day itself as unusual and special, reinforcing the sense of exceptionality upon which holidays are made meaningful. At the same time, the rituals of this retail holiday worked to reshape the meanings and values of media commodities. Not only did media entertainment products get centered within the consumerist shopping rituals of the holiday season, but they also accrued new value as objects of desire (and by that same token, abandonment and disinterest) within the retail context.

Of course, Black Friday is only one of many retail holidays through which we might better understand meaning, value, and ritual in media circulation. Given the growth of online retailing, Cyber Monday deserves equal if not greater attention as a retail holiday shaping and shaped by media circulation. Notably, by our return to the Madison Target store three days later on Cyber Monday, all the special displays and dynamics explored in this chapter had vanished. The swift retail holiday season had moved on, with promotions in the physical store yielding to those in the digital realm. Yet while much seemed "back to normal" at the brick-and-mortar Target, a closer study of the media rituals of Cyber Monday would likely reveal a new matrix of transactions and interactions in which media and retail cultures interoperate. Rather than isolated exceptions, retail holidays operate as part of an interrelated set of media rituals. As such, studies of media and retail holidays might look productively beyond the end-of-year "holiday" season alone to consider the larger variety of rituals and events, like Record Store Day or International Independent Video Store Day, that articulate the meaning and value of media commodities to the retail institutions that help circulate them. Occasions like Free Comic Book Day and San Diego Comic-Con have already supported significant study (Hanna 2019; Johnson 2019), and more research in that vein can help move media, retail, and ritual into closer relation. The COVID-19 pandemic calls further attention to the need to attend to the virtual contexts in which media retail unfolds—not just as shopping continues migrating to online environments, but also as retailers devise new strategies for making media central to those remote transactions and interactions.

In doing so, media scholars can speak to fundamental questions about popular culture and the role of media commodities as they circulate in everyday consumer capitalism. What do retail practices reveal about the role of media and its circulation in consumer cultures? How and why do media commodities accrue new value and meaning when circulating in different retail contexts? How and why has media become a crucial element in the linkage between shopping and celebration in these contemporary cultures? The study of media circulation through its retail contexts holds great promise as a means of understanding the social, economic, and political value of entertainment commodities. Further, it sets into relief the boundaries of "distribution" as an industrial and cultural aspect of the media, as in fact most consumers never encounter or interact with distributors in financial transactions or personal interactions. At the same time, the diversity of retail contexts—as only partially evidenced by the vast number of retail holidays in which media circulate—demands close attention to the different retail transactions and interactions in which media circulate. This means thinking about special holidays, but also the everyday contexts in which meaning and value are generated in the retail circulation of media culture.

NOTES

1 The contemporary understanding of Black Friday appears as a redemption of some earlier "Black" days in the United States, which notably were moments of financial crisis: the gold crash on Friday, September 24, 1869, and the stock market crash during the "Black" week at the end of October 1929, which inaugurated the Great Depression. The Black Friday of today thus recuperates these earlier moments of crisis and, more importantly, serves to mitigate the possibility of another national economic crisis (Pruitt 2015).

2 London (2019) suggests that Amazon brought Black Friday to England, linking transnationalization of this retail holiday to the transnationalization of online retailing.

3 There are notable exceptions. For instance, Ellen Seiter (1993) examines toy retailing and retailers in her consideration of children and media culture, and Avi Santo (2019) similarly calls for media scholars to study retail.

4 The Meijer advertisement flier deviated from this rule, with televisions, DVDs, and video games not appearing until more than halfway through the document. However, Meijer stores offered a separate, two-page "Tech Guide," which exclusively displayed tablets, smartphones, televisions, speakers, and other media hardware and smart devices.

BIBLIOGRAPHY

Couldry, Nick. 2003. *Media Rituals: A Critical Approach*. New York: Routledge.

Dickler, Jessica. 2020. "'Black Friday Has Turned into Cyber Month'—Here Are the Best Deals." *CNBC*, November 24. http://cnbc.com.

Digital Entertainment Group. 2019. "Year-End 2018 Home Entertainment Report." January 8. www.degonline.org.

Embly, Jochan. 2013. "Black Friday Hits the UK, But What Is It?" *Independent*, November 28. www.independent.co.uk.

Hanna, Erin. 2019. *Only at Comic-Con: Hollywood, Fans, and the Limits of Exclusivity*. New Brunswick, NJ: Rutgers University Press.

Herbert, Daniel, and Derek Johnson, eds. 2019. *Point of Sale: Analyzing Media Retail*. New Brunswick, NJ: Rutgers University Press.

Johnson, Derek. 2019. *Transgenerational Media Industries: Adults, Children, and the Reproduction of Culture*. Ann Arbor: University of Michigan Press.

Johnson, Derek, and Daniel Herbert. 2019. "Introduction: Media Studies in the Retail Apocalypse." In *Point of Sale: Analyzing Media Retail*, edited by Daniel Herbert and Derek Johnson, 1–20. New Brunswick, NJ: Rutgers University Press.

King, Pat. 2018. "A Brief History of Cyber Monday." *Metro USA*, November 21. www.metro.us.

London, Lela. 2019. "Where to Find the Best Black Friday Deals for 2019—Our Predictions for the UK Sale." *Telegraph*, September 24. www.telegraph.co.uk.

National Retail Federation. 2017. "Consumers and Retailers Win Big over Thanksgiving Holiday." November 28. https://nrf.com.

Pruitt, Sarah. 2015. "What's the Real History of Black Friday?" History.com, November 23. www.history.com.

Santo, Avi. 2019. "Retail Tales and Tribulations: Transmedia Brands, Consumer Products, and the Significance of Shop Talk." *Journal of Cinema and Media Studies* 58 (2): 115–41.

Seiter, Ellen. 1993. *Sold Separately: Children and Parents in Consumer Culture*. New Brunswick, NJ: Rutgers University Press.

Thomas, Lauren. 2018. "Cyber Monday Sales Break a Record." *CNBC*, November 27. www.cnbc.com.

Turow, Joseph. 2017. *The Aisles Have Eyes: How Retailers Track Your Shopping, Strip Your Privacy, and Define Your Power*. New Haven, CT: Yale University Press.

Veblen, Thorstein. 1899/2007. *The Theory of the Leisure Class*. Oxford: Oxford University Press.

Williams, Raymond. 2000. "Advertising: The Magic System." *Advertising & Society Review* 1 (1). https://doi.org/10.1353/asr.2000.0016.

ACKNOWLEDGMENTS

The editors would like to thank the contributors for generously sharing their commitment, expertise, energy, and thought-provoking research in the growing area of media distribution studies. We are honored to have worked with such an outstanding group of international scholars as our collaborators on this collection. The initial idea for this collection emerged from conversations and brainstorming at the Society for Cinema and Media Studies and continued to take shape over a few years of workshops and panels with a number of our contributors.

A huge thank-you to the Critical Cultural Communication series editors Jonathan Gray, Aswin Punathambekar, and Adrienne Shaw as champions of this project. We truly appreciate your investment and enthusiasm as we developed and shaped this book. The collection would not be possible without the support of New York University Press. Thank you to Eric Zinner, Dolma Ombadykow, and Furqan Sayeed for your patience and guidance throughout the entire process.

We are thankful for the support and encouragement of our colleagues and departments at the University of Iowa, King's College London, and the University of North Texas.

Finally, we would like to thank our loved ones for their endless support and inspiration throughout the journey of this collection: Courtney thanks Brian; Paul thanks Tamar; and Tim would like to acknowledge Rita, Robi, and Reni.

ABOUT THE CONTRIBUTORS

PETER ALILUNAS is Associate Professor of Cinema Studies at the University of Oregon. He is the author of *Smutty Little Movies: The Creation and Regulation of Adult Video* (2016).

COURTNEY BRANNON DONOGHUE is Assistant Professor in the Department of Media Arts at the University of North Texas. Her research areas include conglomerate Hollywood and international operations, local-language productions, Brazilian media, distribution studies, gender equity and female-driven films, and blockbusters and franchising. She is working on a book about industrywide barriers impacting female-driven films and filmmakers in Hollywood and the global film industry. Her first book, *Localising Hollywood* (2017), explores the localization of Hollywood operations across Europe and Latin America since the 1990s based on industry interviews and international fieldwork in eight countries. Her publications have also appeared in *Cinema Journal, Feminist Media Studies, Media, Culture & Society*, and various edited collections.

JOSHUA A. BRAUN is Associate Professor of Journalism at the University of Massachusetts Amherst and an affiliated fellow of the Information Society Project at Yale Law School. His work examines sociological questions surrounding media distribution. His book, *This Program Is Brought to You By . . . : Distributing Television News Online* was published in 2015, and his papers have appeared in *Communication Theory, Communication, Culture & Critique, Journalism, Journalism Practice*, and *Digital Journalism*.

JOONSEOK CHOI holds a PhD from the University of Iowa, and works as an independent scholar in Korea. His research interests include the distribution of global TV formats, global media industries, and global television marketplaces.

DAVID CRAIG is Clinical Associate Professor at the University of Southern California in the Annenberg School for Communication and Journalism and Director of the Master of Global Communication program with the London School of Economics, and he is Visiting Professor at Shanghai Jiao Tong University. He is a Hollywood producer and television executive, and his projects have garnered over 75 Emmy, Golden Globe, and Peabody nominations. Along with his co-authors, he has published books, articles, and chapters about the emerging social media entertainment and wanghong industries.

VIRGINIA CRISP is Senior Lecturer in Culture, Media and Creative Industries at King's College London. Her most recent work is the co-edited collection *Practices of Projection: Histories and Technologies* (2020). She is the author of *Film Distribution in the Digital Age: Pirates and Professionals* (2015) as well as numerous articles and book chapters on formal and informal media circulation. She is also the co-founder and director (with Gabriel Menotti Gonring) of the *Besides the Screen Network* (www.besidesthescreen.com) and the co-editor of *Besides the Screen: Moving Images through Promotion, Distribution and Curation* (2015).

STUART CUNNINGHAM is Distinguished Professor of Media and Communications, Queensland University of Technology. He is a Fellow of the U.K. Academy of Social Sciences and the Australian Academy of the Humanities, and a Member of the Order of Australia, and his most recent books are *Social Media Entertainment: The New Intersection of Hollywood and Silicon Valley* (2019, with David Craig), *Media Economics* (2015, with Terry Flew and Adam Swift), *The Media and Communications in Australia* (2014, edited with Sue Turnbull), *Hidden Innovation: Policy, Industry and the Creative Sector* (2014), and *Screen Distribution and the New King Kongs of the Online World* (2013, with Jon Silver). Forthcoming is *Creator Culture: Studying the Social Media Entertainment Industry* (edited with David Craig).

EVAN ELKINS is Assistant Professor of Film and Media Studies in the Department of Communication Studies at Colorado State University, where he writes and teaches about media industries, digital culture, and globalization. He is the author of *Locked Out: Regional Restrictions in Digital Entertainment Culture* (2019), and his writing has appeared elsewhere in *Media, Culture & Society, Critical Studies in Media Communication, Television & New Media*, and several other journals and edited collections. He is currently researching the relationship between the internet and the U.S. American West.

TIMOTHY HAVENS is Professor in the Communication Studies Department at the University of Iowa and holds affiliated appointments in African American Studies and International Studies. He is the author of *Black Television Travels: African American Media Around the Globe* (2013) and *Global Television Marketplace* (2006); the co-author with Amanda D. Lotz of *Understanding Media Industries* (2011, 2016); and co-editor with Aniko Imre and Katalin Lustyik of *Popular Television in Eastern Europe Before and Since Socialism* (2012). He is a former Fulbright Scholar to Hungary.

DANIEL HERBERT is Associate Professor in the Department of Film, Television, and Media at the University of Michigan. He is the author of *Videoland: Movie Culture at the American Video Store* (2014) and *Film Remakes and Franchises* (2017) and the co-author of *Media Industry Studies* (2020). He is the co-editor of *Point of Sale: Analyzing Media Retail* (2020) and *Film Reboots* (2020).

DEREK JOHNSON is Professor of Media and Cultural Studies in the Department of Communication Arts at the University of Wisconsin–Madison. He is the author of *Transgenerational Media Industries: Adults, Children, and the Reproduction of Culture* (2019) and *Media Franchising: Creative License and Collaboration in the Culture Industries* (2013). As editor or co-editor, he has published several additional books, including most recently *Point of Sale: Analyzing Media Retail* (2019) and *From Networks to Netflix: A Guide to Changing Channels* (2018).

APHRA KERR is Professor in the Department of Sociology at Maynooth University in Ireland, Chair of the MA in Sociology (Internet and Society), and a collaborator with the ADAPT Centre for Digital Content Technology. Her books include *Global Games: Production, Circulation and Policy in the Networked Era* (2017) and *The Business and Culture of Digital Games: gamework/gameplay* (2006), and she was associate editor of *The International Encyclopedia of Digital Communication and Society* (2015). She was chair of the Communication Policy and Technology section of the International Association for Media and Communications Research (IAMCR) 2016–19.

RAMON LOBATO is Associate Professor in the School of Media and Communication at RMIT University, Melbourne. His research focuses on the international dynamics of media distribution, copyright, and piracy. His books include *Shadow Economies of Cinema: Mapping Informal Film Distribution* (2012), *The Informal Media Economy* (2015, with Julian Thomas), and *Netflix Nations: The Geography of Digital Distribution* (2019).

AMANDA D. LOTZ is Professor at the Queensland University of Technology, where she also leads the Transforming Media Industries research project in the Digital Media Research Centre. She is the author of five books, including *We Now Disrupt This Broadcast: How Cable Transformed Television and the Internet Revolutionized It All* (2018), *Portals: A Treatise on Internet-Distributed Television* (2017), and *The Television Will Be Revolutionized* (2nd ed., 2014), and co-author of *Understanding Media Industries* (2011, 2016, with Timothy Havens) and *Television Studies* (2011, with Jonathan Gray). Her newest book, co-authored with Daniel Herbert and Aswin Punathambekar, is *Media Industry Studies* (2020).

PAUL MCDONALD is Professor of Media Industries at King's College London. His books include *Hollywood Stardom* (2013), *Video and DVD Industries* (2007), *Hollywood and the Law* (2015, co-edited with Emily Carman, Eric Hoyt, and Philip Drake), and *The Contemporary Hollywood Film Industry* (2008, co-edited with Janet Wasko). Since 2002, he has co-edited (with Michael Curtin) the International Screen Industries series from the British Film Institute. He is a member of the founding Editorial Collective for the online journal *Media Industries* and founder of the Media Industries Scholarly Interest Group of the Society for Cinema and Media Studies (SCMS) and the *Media Industries* conference.

JADE L. MILLER is Associate Professor of Communication Studies at Wilfrid Laurier University in Waterloo, Ontario, Canada. She works on media industries from a global networked and geographic perspective. Her first book, *Nollywood Central*, on the industrial structure and global connections of the southern Nigerian video industry, was published in 2016. Her research has been published in academic journals including *Global Media and Communication*, *Journal of Popular Culture*, and the *International Journal of Communication*.

SRIRAM MOHAN is a doctoral candidate in the Department of Communication and Media at the University of Michigan, Ann Arbor. His research examines digital media cultures, political expression, and state-citizen relationships in South Asian contexts. His work has appeared in journals like *Television & New Media*, *International Journal of Communication*, and *International Journal of Cultural Studies*. He is also the co-editor of *Global Digital Cultures: Perspectives from South Asia* (2019).

ALISA PERREN is Associate Professor in the Department of Radio-TV-Film and Co-Director of the Center for Entertainment and Media Industries at the University of Texas at Austin. She is co-editor of *Media Industries: History, Theory, and Method* (2009), author of *Indie, Inc.: Miramax and the Transformation of Hollywood in the 1990s* (2012), and co-founder and editorial collective member of the journal *Media Industries*. She recently published *The American Comic Book Industry and Hollywood* (2021), co-authored with Gregory Steirer.

JUAN PIÑÓN is Associate Professor in the Media, Culture and Communication Department at New York University. He has a PhD in media studies from the University of Texas at Austin. He is interested in the intersection of Latin American transnational media corporate dynamics with the established mode of production of U.S. Latino media. He is the U.S. coordinator of the Ibero-American Television Fiction Observatory (OBITEL), an international research project on television fiction. His work has been published in *Television & New Media*, *Global Media and Communication*, *International Journal of Cultural Studies*, and *Communication Theory*, among others.

ASWIN PUNATHAMBEKAR is Associate Professor in the Department of Media Studies at the University of Virginia. His research and teaching focus on the impact that globalization and technological change have on the workings of media industries, formations of audiences and publics, and cultural identity and politics. He is the author of *From Bombay to Bollywood: The Making of a Global Media Industry* (2013), co-author of *Media Industry Studies* (2020), and co-editor of *Global Bollywood* (2008), *Television at Large in South Asia* (2013), and, most recently, *Global Digital Cultures: Perspectives from South Asia* (2019). He is currently working on a co-authored book, provisionally titled *The Digital Popular: Media, Culture, and Politics in Networked India*. He currently co-edits the Critical Cultural Communication book series for New York University Press, and serves as an editor of the peer-reviewed journal *Media, Culture & Society*.

EZEQUIEL RIVERO has a PhD in social sciences from the University of Buenos Aires and is a National Scientific and Technical Research Council grant holder (2021–23) and Professor of Public Communications Management at the University of Business and Social Sciences (UCES in Spanish). He has co-edited *Cooperative and Community Television: Analysis, Diagnosis and Strategies for the Convergence* (2018) and has contributed several book chapters and articles in Spanish, Portuguese, and English in peer-reviewed journals. He was a co–principal investigator on an Argentine Ministry of Education project founded on the theme of proximity television in the digital age.

NAOMI SAKR is Professor of Media Policy at the Communication and Media Research Institute (CAMRI), University of Westminster, and former Director of the CAMRI Arab Media Centre. She is co-author, with Jeanette Steemers, of *Screen Media for Arab and European Children: Policy and Production Encounters in the Multiplatform Era* (2019) and author of *Transformations in Egyptian Journalism* (2013), *Arab Television Today* (2007), and *Satellite Realms: Transnational Television, Globalization and the Middle East* (2001). She has edited the collections *Women and Media in the Middle East: Power through Self-Expression* (2004) and *Arab Media and Political Renewal: Community, Legitimacy and Public Life* (2007), and co-edited *Arab Media Moguls* (2015, with

Jakob Skovgaard-Petersen and Donatella della Ratta) and *Children's TV and Digital Media in the Arab World* (2017, with Jeanette Steemers). Her research focuses on the political economy of Arab-owned media, with particular reference to law, regulation, human rights, journalism, and cultural production.

JEANETTE STEEMERS is Professor of Culture, Media and Creative Industries at the Department of Culture, Media and Creative Industries at King's College, London. She gained a PhD from the University of Bath in 1990 and has worked as an industry analyst (CIT Research) and Research Manager (HIT Entertainment). She is the author of *Creating Preschool Television* (2010) and *Selling Television: British Television in the Global Marketplace* (2004), co-author of *European Television Industries* (2005, with Petros Iosifidis and Mark Wheeler) and *Screen Media for Arab and European Children* (2019, with Naomi Sakr), and co-editor of *European Media in Crisis: Values, Risks and Policies* (2015, with Josef Trappel and Barbara Thomass), *Global Media and National Policies: The Return of the State* (2016, with Terry Flew and Petros Iosifidis), and *Children's TV and Digital Media in the Arab World* (2017, with Naomi Sakr). She has written numerous articles about the children's TV industry.

JULIAN THOMAS works on social and regulatory aspects of new communications technologies at RMIT University in Melbourne. He is Director of the Australian Research Council Centre of Excellence for Automated-Decision Making and Society.

PATRICK VONDERAU is Professor of Media and Communication Studies at the University of Halle, Germany. His recent book publications include the co-authored *Advertising and the Transformation of Screen Cultures* (forthcoming) and *Spotify Teardown: Inside the Black Box of Streaming Music* (2019). He currently holds a three-year grant for the project "Shadow Economies of the Internet: An Ethnography of Click Farming" (Swedish Research Council). He is a co-founder of NECS, the European Network for Cinema and Media Studies.

INDEX

Pages numbers in *italic* indicate illustrations; those in **bold** indicate tables.